Praise for Ted Conover's

THE ROUTES OF MAN

"This always compelling book serves as both a philosophical narrative and an adventure tale." —*The Dallas Morning News*

"Conover is a master of first-person immersion journalism; his road trips are both entertaining and poignant." —*The Boston Globe*

"Ambitious.... [A] vivid, smart, an evenhanded book.... Ted Conover may be one of America's toughest nonfiction writers." —*Salon*

"Smart and lively.... The byways of human travel afford a sharp observer like Conover a platform to observe how societies grapple with changing economies, politics and lifestyles." —*Bloomberg*

"Above the ranks of travel-as-usual literature.... [The book's] polyglot sections are individual gems of journalistic work." —*Chicago Tribune*

"Vivid.... In striking detail, Conover thoughtfully explores how roads, especially in rapidly changing countries, are contested boundary lines where the demands of the environment, traditional cultures, educational opportunity, and industrial progress collide." —*Fresh Air*

"Graceful and evocative.... Mr. Conover here has taken an unpromising subject and turned it into a book that is about far more than just the strips of tarmac that criss-cross the world." —*The Economist*

"An armchair traveler's dream.... Conover, a superbly talented writer with a keen eye for detail, has produced an evenhanded look at what, precisely, the road brings, for better or worse."
—*Richmond Times-Dispatch*

TED CONOVER

THE ROUTES OF MAN

Ted Conover is the author of several books, including *Newjack: Guarding Sing Sing* (winner of the National Book Critics Circle Award and a finalist for the Pulitzer Prize) and *Rolling Nowhere: Riding the Rails with America's Hoboes*. His writing has appeared in *The New York Times Magazine*, *The Atlantic Monthly*, *The New Yorker*, and *National Geographic*. The recipient of a Guggenheim Fellowship, he is a distinguished writer-in-residence at the Arthur L. Carter Journalism Institute at New York University. He lives in New York City.

THE ROUTES OF MAN

THE ROUTES OF MAN

Travels in the Paved World

TED CONOVER

Vintage Books
A Division of Random House, Inc.
New York

TO JAY LEIBOLD

I began to see how the road altered
not only the way people travelled,
but how they perceived the world.

—J. B. Jackson,
The Necessity for Ruins

CONTENTS

THE ROUTES OF MAN

INTRODUCTION

He used often to say there was only one Road; that it was like a great river: its springs were at every doorstep and every path was its tributary. "It's a dangerous business, Frodo, going out of your door," he used to say. "You step into the Road, and if you don't keep your feet, there is no telling where you might be swept off to."

—Frodo Baggins of his uncle, Bilbo,
in J. R. R. Tolkien's *The Fellowship of the Ring*
(*The Lord of the Rings*, Book One)

EVERY ROAD IS A STORY OF STRIVING: for profit, for victory in battle, for discovery and adventure, for survival and growth, or simply for livability. Each path reflects our desire to move and connect. Anyone who has benefited from a better road—a shorter route, a smoother and safer drive—can testify to the importance of good roads. But when humans strive, we also err, and it is hard to build without destroying. Robert Moses, the controversial creator of highways around New York City in the middle of the twentieth century, wiped out numerous neighborhoods with his projects, turning vibrant communities (notably the South Bronx) into wastelands that have yet to recover. Of his actions he famously said, "In order to make an omelet, you've got to break a few eggs." In a related way, the same roads that carry medicine also hasten the spread of deadly disease; the same roads that bring outside connection and knowledge to people starving for them sometimes spell the end of indigenous cultures; the same roads that help develop the human economy open the way for destruction of the non-human environment; the same roads that carry cars symbolizing personal freedom are the setting for the deaths of more people than die in wars, and of untold numbers of animals; and the same roads that introduce us to friends also provide access to enemies.

In this book I present six of these roads that are reshaping the world. I do it by joining up with people on them—travelers to whom they matter in an immediate and practical way. The roads are presented roughly in order of increasing complexity, which is also the intentional order in which I traveled them over the past several years. Each has a theme: development vs. the environment, isolation vs. progress, military occupation, transmission of disease, social transformation, and the future of the city. Not each of the chapters is about a single road, precisely; one tells about a trip on a series of roads in China, and another about roads and streets in Lagos, Nigeria. Each is a story and a meditation.

We in the twenty-first century are more numerous and better connected than people at any previous time in history. Networks are a principal theme of our age, and as the networks we are a part of continue to grow, we struggle to understand what that connectedness means. Not all connections are good. We save hours or days when we fly; yet it was the globe-hopping of a single promiscuous flight attendant that got the AIDS epidemic off to a fast start. We are threatened by terrorist networks such as Al Qaeda. The complex integration of the electric power grid, in North America as well as other parts of the world, means that a failure in suburban Ohio can black out large sections of the Northeast, the Midwest, and Canada, as happened in 2003. Politics and financial markets in one corner of the globe can affect financial markets everywhere. On a small scale, this means that a rebel attack on a Nigerian oil pipeline can cause a spike in world prices that will be reflected at the pump within days. Writ large, this means that a mortgage crisis in the United States can devastate financial markets around the world. Connection means vulnerability.

But most of our networks, most of the time, appear to advance human progress, leading to greater efficiencies and broader knowledge. We realize, for example, that we are part of social networks that extend far beyond our immediate circle of friends. (John Guare's play *Six Degrees of Separation* popularized the notion that everybody on the planet is connected to everyone else through a maximum of six intermediaries.) The extension of social worlds beyond a network of local friends is greatly abetted by electronic communications networks—wired and, increasingly, mobile telephones and text messages, and, most transformative of all, the internet with its e-mail, instant messaging, and World Wide Web. E-mail, instantaneous and practically free, seems overnight to have supplanted first-class mail, a staple of the postal network that only two or three generations ago was itself a transformative network.*

Have electronic communications rendered road networks less important? Hardly. Our inner circle of friends, our home communities, are still connected by roads. Everything real, by which I mean everything non-virtual—food, furniture, goods of every description (including computers, I should add)—might be ordered online but they actually arrive overland, by train or plane, perhaps, for some of their journey, but always substantially by road. (The bumper sticker you see on trucks reminds us: "If you've got it, a trucker brought it.") Roads remain the essential network of the non-virtual world. They are the infrastructure upon which almost all other infrastructure depends. They are the paths of human endeavor.

Roads have probably always played a role in the shaping of human settlement, but it was the Romans who first demonstrated what a large network of roads could do. The Appian Way was only the most famous road leading out of Rome; eighteen others did as well, part of a system that, at its peak, extended 53,000 miles. The Roman roads—and the empire—extended as far as the British Isles, over the Alps to Spain and central and eastern Europe, east to present-day Greece and Turkey, and through the Holy Land, all the way around the Mediterranean, including North Africa.

Constructed over eight hundred years, they allowed for the movement of armies and the expansion of empire. Roman roads were nonpareil. Soldiers—roads were built by the military—dug a deep bed and then filled it with layers of gravel or other rocks, depending on the location. Principal routes were paved with cut stones that fit together with mosaic tightness; their bottom surfaces, sunk into the substrate, were diamond-

*I was four degrees of relationship away from Zhao Xiangjie, the owner of the Chinese auto club I joined in chapter 5; between us were my friend Cathi Hanauer, a writer; her mother in New Jersey, who had taken a trip through China; and Zhao Jing, who had shown the mother around Xi'an in northwest China. And much of my trip to China was organized via instant messages, of which the Chinese are very fond. Ten years earlier the trip would have been put together over the phone, at significantly greater expense, with voice calls or faxes.

shaped. The road was cambered—higher in the middle and gently sloping to the sides—to allow for drainage, and drainage ditches along the
side were a common feature. So well were Roman roads made that many
still exist. The empire's most enduring monuments, some rutted with the
tracks of hundreds of years of wagon wheels, these remnants run alongside ruins of inns or barracks, and parallel or undergird modern roads.

As the Roman Empire grew weak, the Janus-headed nature of the
network became clear. The advantage of the road could be a drawback:
"barbarian" tribes began making use of Rome's own roads to attack the
empire. Armies of Ostrogoths, Visigoths, and Vandals, Germanic tribes
once in the Roman service, rebelled. Alaric, the Visigoth king, first
attacked Constantinople and next Italy, around A.D. 400; Rome finally
capitulated after a blockade of roads around it in 408 threatened citizens
with mass starvation. The fine roads were instrumental in effectively
ending the Western Roman Empire.

It would be more than fifteen hundred years before nations again took
up road-building on such a grand scale. Among the things lost, in the
centuries that followed, was Roman road-building know-how. Not until
long after the Middle Ages, in fact, did any civilization approach the
engineering artistry of the Roman road. Even if the legions of skilled
stonemasons and other workers had been available in the eighteenth
century, the narrow, metal-rimmed wheels of fast carriages would have
rendered the Roman method impractical.

Evenly cut stone blocks were still commonly used as a "course" underneath a gravel running surface when John Loudon McAdam, a Scottish
roads official, thought that a superior pavement would be based on angular chunks of broken stone held together by natural interlock between
the pieces, and then covered with a layer of even smaller stones, "small
enough to fit in the stonebreaker's mouth." The grinding action of passing wheels would compress the two into a durable surface. In McAdam's
view, no rock bottom layer was needed—a huge breakthrough. The prin-
ciples of macadam are still used today in highway construction.

The other transformative technology, of course, was the internal
combustion engine. High-speed vehicles required roads with different
pavements and gradings. The era of prosperity that followed World
War II, along with new mass manufacturing of cars and trucks, prompted
unprecedented booms of road construction in the United States (notably
the interstate highway system) and in Europe. As cars became available

for purchase by millions of people, their use promoted the growth of suburbs, their demand for petroleum changed the geopolitical arrangement
of the world, and their exhaust—and that from other machines—began a
warming of the planet's atmosphere whose ramifications become better
understood, and more feared, every day.

Being on the road is one of the ways I have always felt most alive in the
world. Road travel has been a main story of my life, beginning with bicycle tours in the years before I could drive, intense pleasure in getting my
driver's license, and road trips and hitchhiking after I had, mainly during a
college career that involved a few detours. One of these was a few months'
living with railroad hoboes—professional itinerants, essentially—in an
experience that I turned into my first book, *Rolling Nowhere*. After graduate school it was back on the road for a year, in Mexico and the United
States, with Mexican undocumented migrants, travels that became the
basis of my next book, *Coyotes*. Higher education; road trip; higher education; road trip—the alternation was not coincidental. While I have
benefited enormously from formal education, it has never seemed to me
sufficient; it has repeatedly sparked in me a visceral longing for the lessons of life outside.

What's that all about? College to me, particularly at the beginning
before I figured out how to use it, was about imposed learning. Travel, on
the other hand, was an expression of personal curiosity, of a broader education less mediated by received thought. It was also a test of personal
resources beyond essay-writing cleverness and the capacity to handle
course-induced stress.

And travel on roads seemed especially the right kind. Growing up in
the American West, I had the idea that coming of age meant leaving the
city, being tested in a place that was a little bit wild. Roads *were* the West
in certain ways—civilized and yet often remote and unsupervised. Without question I was influenced by the ethic of the Beat and hippie generations that came before me, which saw travel as a masculine prerogative, if
not duty. Kerouac's *On the Road*, with its celebration of movement and its
equation of travel with poetry, got under my skin; the day I left my aunt
Janet's house near Morristown, New Jersey, to begin hitchhiking west on
my hoboing trip (Kerouac and I had New Jersey aunts in common), I
remember Jan happened to be playing on her eight-track Glen Camp-

bell's "Gentle on My Mind" ("It's knowing that your door is always
open / And your path is free to walk"). Like so many songs of the day—
the Allman Brothers' "Ramblin' Man," the Temptations' "Papa Was a
Rollin' Stone," and the Grateful Dead's "Truckin' "—it extolled the spirit
of the travelin' man, of unfettered life on the road.

Of course it goes back at least to Walt Whitman, the great American
poet of the road. When I first read "Song of the Open Road," I knew that
we were from the same place. The speaker of this poem is happy to be
going, glad to meet those he encounters (he lists them at length), raptur-
ous at the journey and its possibilities, his travel a celebration of pop-
ulism and democracy.

> From this hour I ordain myself loos'd of limits and imaginary lines,
> Going where I list, my own master total and absolute,
> Listening to others, and considering well what they say,
> Pausing, searching, receiving, contemplating,
> Gently, but with undeniable will, divesting myself of the holds that
>   would hold me.
>
> I inhale great draughts of space;
> The east and the west are mine, and the north and the south are mine.

My last book, *Newjack,* was about working as a guard at Sing Sing
prison. One night I was part of a transportation detail, relocating to a different prison upstate a gang member who'd been involved in a brawl. For
me, it was a rare opportunity to work outside of prison walls. For him, it
was a rare opportunity to see the outside world. Our van pulled over for
dinner at a service area on the New York State Thruway. I brought some
fast food to the prisoner in the van and we talked while we ate. He kept
looking over my shoulder to the big trucks he could see parked outside,
the semi rigs, and as one pulled out, he told me, "That's what I want to do
when my bid's done. Drive one of those things."

His wish made all the sense in the world. Roads are in so many ways
the opposite of prison. Once I was finished wearing that uniform, I
wanted to get back on them, too.

One way to understand roads is to look at a map. I love doing this—
following routes, tracing them with my fingertip, choosing turns, seeing

a squiggly line and trying to picture the road it represents. Augustus Caesar put his son-in-law Marcus Agrippa (63?–12 B.C.) in charge of mapping the known world, a project that took twenty years to complete. Agrippa's map was engraved in marble on a colonnade near the Roman forum. It not only located roads and towns but "illustrated the breadth of empire" and became, as John Noble Wilford writes, "an object of Roman pride. Maps have served this dual function in all subsequent empires."

Most recently, this pride can be felt in Asian countries, notably China and India, which are expanding their road networks at a rapid pace. China has announced a target of 53,000 miles of highway by 2020—a figure somewhat longer than the present-day length of the United States Interstate Highway System. (They are on course to equal us in cars just a few years later.) As I write, India is at the beginning of a fifteen-year project to widen and pave some 40,000 miles of narrow, decrepit national highways. Smaller nations are also rapidly paving—Vietnam's new Ho Chi Minh Highway is just one of many new regional roads in Southeast Asia sometimes referred to in aggregate as the Asian Highway. Kazakhstan's plan to rebuild its highway linking China to the east and Russia to the west is being billed as "the new Silk Road"; that would strengthen a weak link in the giant road network known as the Trans-Siberian Highway. In the developed countries of the West, formerly dirt roads continue to be covered with asphalt as traffic grows. We've reached the point where it seems nowadays as though we're paving the world.

In fact, almost 1.5 percent of the surface area of the continental United States—an area about the size of Ohio—is now covered with "impermeable surfacing": roads, parking lots, buildings, and houses. Roads constitute the largest human-made artifact on earth. American landscape architect J. B. Jackson concluded in 1980 that roads are "now the most powerful force for the destruction or creation of landscapes that we have." The siting of roads determines patterns of settlement, the locations of houses and businesses. The speed of cars upon them plays a role in how far from the road a structure will be: the older a dwelling in this country, it seems, the greater the likelihood that it was built near a road—sometimes right next to it, as in the case of my wife's family's farmhouse in New Hampshire. Horses and wagons were the traffic back then, and you had plenty of time to see them coming. These days the road is paved, and the cars whizzing by feel a little too close.

A road can change a shoreline, offering motorists great views but restricting access for pedestrians. A new highway can bypass a little town, killing its main street, or bisect a neighborhood, killing a sense of community. A father at my kids' school declared to me bluntly that as an ecologist he is "against roads," and I know he is not alone: for those whose focus is protecting nature, roadless areas have a status approaching sanctity.* It is not hard to enumerate the ill effects of roads. As road-building continues its global acceleration, and the car hunger of Indian and Chinese consumers pushes global car ownership into the hundreds of millions, those of us in nations whose roads are well advanced (and a few of those in nations where they're not, such as Amazon tribespeople threatened by roads) wonder whether there's a limit to how much pavement and driving the earth can stand—how long, in the words of Joni Mitchell, you can "pave paradise and put up a parking lot."

And yet, without roads and cars—or a viable alternative, which has yet to appear—all human progress, all economic activity, would stop. The kids need to get to school, Mom and Dad to work, food (and everything else) to market. Watching roads can be a way to look at history, to measure human progress and limitation. In the past century, the global road network has become a thing that might finally, truly, impress the Romans. With near unanimity, we proclaim their usefulness. They are the human world's circulatory system.

Where are they taking us?

*In an e-mail, he wrote me, "I'm a conservationist and a deep ecologist and roads to me are barriers and intrusions. They create 'edges' to ecosystems and are conduits for 'aliens' and 'exotics' which wreak havoc in ecosystems. They are precursors to development and so-called 'improvements on the land.' They promote erosion and pollution. I'm against them, big time."

ONE

FOREST PRIMEVAL TO
PARK AVENUE

MY STORY BEGINS where another one ends, on a corner of Park
Avenue on Manhattan's Upper East Side. It is one of the most expensive
neighborhoods in the United States, and home to some of its wealthiest
residents. It is an area of liveried doormen, polished brass railings, tiny
dogs, and elevators that lead to only one or two grand apartments, frequently encompassing more than one floor. One rough visitor was nevertheless warmly received here at the end of a long journey, due to his
celebrated beauty: a big shipment of wood—mahogany—from South
America.

As the limited global supply of it dwindles, mahogany has become
extremely valuable. Like other scarce natural resources—diamonds, gold,
and oil come to mind—it is pulled, as though by magnetic force, from
sparsely populated parts of the world where there are few roads, if any, to
densely populated parts that are heavily paved, and where wealth is concentrated.

The apartment that was this wood's destination was notable for two
reasons. First, the wife of the middle-aged and childless couple who
owned it was descended from a famous American dynasty and heir to a
significant portion of its wealth. (A condition of my access to the apartment was that I not name her.) The apartment is in a building known as
high WASP, the kind that doesn't take celebrities. Even with their pedi-
gree, I was told, the couple weren't approved as tenants by the building's
board until a senior member of the family interceded.

The second interesting thing about the apartment—where the new
mahogany would be used in moldings, paneling, doors, cabinets, and
bookshelves—was the company it would keep. The two-floor maisonette
was conceived by the wife partly as a home for her extensive collection
of eighteenth-century English furniture, itself mostly made of mahogany.

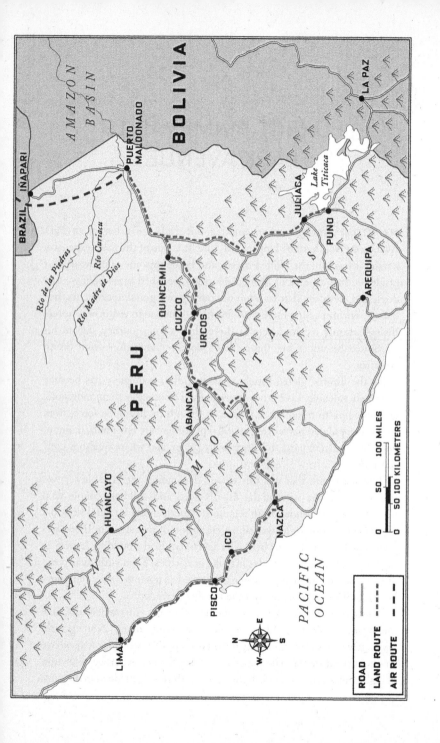

So the new wood, harvested mainly in Brazil and Peru, would be complementing old wood that probably made its way to England from Central America or Caribbean islands such as Cuba and Jamaica—places where harvesting in the 250-year interim has left mahogany "commercially extinct." The furniture collection includes Georgian sideboards, secretaries, breakfronts, commodes, side chairs, and armchairs, each exquisitely detailed and worth, in aggregate, many millions of dollars. But the pieces of which the owner is most proud are a set of doors designed by Robert Adam, the Scottish architect whose neoclassical interior designs came to characterize the entire period. The doors, with book-matched panels of thick mahogany veneer on solid walnut, each edged with ornately hand-carved molding, hang at the entrance to studies on either side of the entry hall, and fairly glow.

I learned about this apartment when my friend Peter was hired to work there. A Yale-educated sculptor, Peter earned a living at the time making high-end custom cabinetry as well as architectural models. He would remark constantly on the number of tradesmen at the job site (up to twenty-eight at once, not including "armies" of men and women who would come in to laboriously French-polish the wood once a room was finished), the high cost of the materials, and the exacting standards of the owner. When slight cracks were detected in a new marble countertop, he told me, yards of it were torn out; when a new oak floor was deemed imperfect, it was replaced entirely—6,500 square feet of it.

At the same time, the situation was an artisan's dream, approaching something out of medieval or Renaissance times, where the patron's resources seemed endless and nothing mattered so much as doing it right. Peter loved working with mahogany, as had generations of his predecessors going back as far as the carpenter on Sir Walter Raleigh's 1595 voyage to the West Indies, who used the wood to repair the ship. (It would be another century before craftsmen in England began to use it alongside walnut in furniture and fine cabinetry.) Mahogany was beautiful to look at and nice to hold, strong but easy to work, not as hard as maple and "doesn't beat the shit out of tools like teak does," according to Peter's boss, David Morton, sixty-one, of Big Tree Woodworks, Inc. Its figure, or grain, came in an array of patterns that vary according to the tree and how it was milled (plain-sawn, quarter-sawn, or rift-sawn)—David showed me a bubbly pattern he called quilted, another known as plum pudding ("like quilted that didn't quite get there"), bird's eye, tiger stripe, and curly. And there wasn't the time pressure of a typical job and the stress that comes with it—the couple had gotten off to a bad start with a different contractor, according to David, and "came around to the view that decisions were best made based on quality." Waiting was made easier by another apartment they had in Manhattan, the house in Westchester County, the property or two in California.

And so the work went on and on—three years for Peter and six years for David Morton. During this time, David bought some 30,000 board feet of mahogany, the rough equivalent of between seven and ten of the giant trees. He designed, fabricated, and hung fifty-six solid mahogany doors. He designed and built a massive yet delicate mahogany media center (the owner's key instruction, in so many words: *Don't embarrass my antiques collection*). He installed fifteen and a half miles of trim moldings—baseboard, chair rail, picture rail, and crown. From the beginning of the job to the end, he watched the price of mahogany nearly quadruple, as Brazil ceased exporting the wood, at least temporarily, due to concerns about the environment and the corruption of officials who were supposed to protect it. And he watched the mahogany available to him drop from boards twenty feet long, four inches thick, and thirty inches wide, to smaller pieces that reflected a diminished supply.

When all the work was done, the furniture in place, and the couple moved in, David drove down from his workshop in the faded Hudson River town of Kingston, New York, to meet with me and Peter and tour the place. It was April 2007. He left his aging Toyota Matrix hatchback in a garage off Park that was filled with much fancier cars. His former patroness showed us around, but David already knew every inch of the apartment. He showed me closets with paneling *inside,* drew a sketch to show the method he'd devised to embed electrical wire in the picture molding, demonstrated how many of the door and window frames were held together by nothing more than a perfect fit. He moved with respect around the antiques, which mostly had arrived after he left but which he had studied, in books and dealers' shops and museums, to improve his design work for the client.

Afterward we walked to another apartment nearby, where David had recently delivered a graceful $80,000 mahogany credenza his craftsmen had labored on for months; I had seen the piece on its side in the workshop in Kingston. The apartment also contained a sculpture by Giacometti and an oil by Diego Rivera. David felt that his piece fit right in.

Back on the street, he pointed out some of his personal landmarks: the building on Park designed by the father of Jacqueline Kennedy Onassis, the co-op with the apartment full of antique firearms, the place across from the church where the doorman wouldn't let him in but the guy who controlled the service elevator would, any day. Though he lived and worked outside the city, approximately 70 percent of his customers were here in Manhattan's Gold Coast, 20 percent lived on the Upper West Side ("much time in the Dakota"), and maybe 10 percent were in Brooklyn Heights. His work in the neighborhood was finished for the moment, but he'd be back.

"You know," he said, as we walked down Park, "my first ten or twelve years in the city, I never got off of 72nd Street. Because so much money lives here."

Trees, however, live mainly elsewhere. The world's remaining stands of *Swietenia macrophylla,* big-leaf mahogany—genuine mahogany, not the cheaper substitutes known as African mahogany or Philippine mahogany—are mostly in the rain forests of South America. Brazil has the lion's share, but since its 2001 ban on exports, Peru is the leading exporter. The United States is the world's largest importer of mahogany, and most of the wood, as of this writing, comes from the portion of the vast Amazon rain forest that lies in Peru.

The trip can be traced backwards. To get to Manhattan, the wood used in the apartment came in trucks from a "concentration yard" (a place where wood is gathered before being distributed) in Hanover, Pennsylvania, run by one of the two largest firms that import the wood from Peru, TBM Hardwoods. (The other is Bozovich Timber Products, of Evergreen, Alabama, and Lima, Peru.) The boards, rough-cut by makeshift mills in the rain forest, arrive in a wide assortment of shapes and sizes. First they are placed in the company's kilns to dry out. (Time spent in the kiln depends on the thickness of the wood—boards one inch thick take a week, and those four inches thick take three months.) Next they are sawn—not to make them all the same, but to make them square. (Mahogany boards, unlike the pine you'll find at a Home Depot, are not often sold with standard dimensions: cutting them to standard size would waste too much wood.) Then they are graded according to quality. David Morton was buying so much mahogany for the apartment, and of such a high grade, that TBM Hardwoods agreed to do a special "sort" for him so that he could find just the boards he wanted.

But having a contractor buy for an individual job is unusual, said Hugh Reitz, the president for imports at the company; most of the buyers are distributors. More than half of the mahogany Reitz buys goes to architectural millwork shops, he says—ten- to twenty-employee outfits doing "extremely high-end work" fabricating things like doors, chair rails, and moldings for wealthy individuals or university or corporate settings. Makers of electric and acoustic guitars are another important clientele. Surprisingly, furniture production is now less than 10 percent of the market for *Swietenia macrophylla*; in recent years, furniture and casket makers have shifted to the cheaper, African mahogany (*Khaya spp.*).

Wood moves easily on American highways—Reitz can receive his from Baltimore hours after it clears Customs, and delivery in the eastern United States rarely takes more than a day or two. The wood also moves fairly quickly across the sea, taking two weeks, in a container ship, from the Peruvian port of Callao, an industrial suburb of Lima, to most American ports, even less if it's headed up the West Coast and doesn't need to pass through the Panama Canal.

The going gets far tougher inside Peru. The problem is roads, in the mountains and in the jungle. It's easy to drive north–south along the Pacific coast of South America—the Pan-American Highway has been in place for years. East–west, however, is another matter. Like Colombia, Ecuador, Bolivia, Chile, and Argentina, Peru has the Andes Mountains running through it, north to south. Significantly higher, in many places, than the Rocky Mountains, the Andes pose a daunting obstacle for transportation. The mahogany, and the jungle, are on the east side of the mountains, making them remote by definition. While Brazil is developing its Amazon at a rapid pace, turning rain forest into fields for soybeans and pasture for cattle, Peru has done fairly little on its side. In fact, in much of its corner of the basin, it has turned swaths of rain forest into nominally protected areas, trying to safeguard indigenous peoples as well as stunning biodiversity. Unfortunately for that admirable goal, these forests also contain the last significant supplies of big-leaf mahogany.

There are plans afoot to change the east–west transportation situation—and there have been for years. Peruvians understand the economic benefits of regional integration, and the idea of a road link to Brazil, the regional economic powerhouse, is a longtime dream. So long has a prospective "interoceanic" highway, linking the Pacific to the Atlantic, been on the drawing board that the project has acquired a not-likely-in-my-lifetime, Holy Grail status.

Just as there is more than one route designated the Pan-American Highway, several east–west "interoceanic" highway routes are being developed simultaneously, and not just in Peru. Peru has at least three or four, Bolivia about three, Ecuador at least two. What they have in common is the idea of connection to a Brazilian highway (and thus a path to the Atlantic) that already exists. Brazil is well along on road infrastructure, and in fact is eager for a route across the Andes: it would save Brazilian exporters from having to ship Asia-bound soybeans, beef, and other products around the Cape of Good Hope or through the Panama Canal, and it would open up markets for Brazilian goods along the west coast of South America. The most likely route connects Lima/Callao up to Cuzco in the Andes and then down to Puerto Maldonado in the rain forest, and from there to the Brazilian border town of Assis in Acre state. Puerto Maldonado also happens to be the capital of Peru's mahogany-producing zone, where loggers drive the drumbeat for road construction. To retrace the wood home to its source would be to see a road's promise in the economy of a poor country, and its threat to pristine wilderness. It would also be a good way to see Peru.

Sometimes it's easy to find a truck, and sometimes it's not. I learned that most Peruvian trucking is based in Lima, and faxed several companies cold from New York to see about a ride. Only one responded—the executive, Antonio Ponce, didn't send trucks over the mountains, he mainly stuck to the coast, but he liked my idea and said his friend's company would take me.

He turned out to be a generous man, Señor Ponce, who not only took me to dinner near my hotel in Lima, but supplied me with a road guide for tourists. He apologized, from his dingy office in an ugly neighborhood, for the uglier neighborhood the truck would leave from, and declined to send me in a taxi, because it wasn't safe.

But it's always easier to leave an ugly place, and I was not upset. The La Victoria district of Callao, where he took me, had no green plants. Dirt streets. A large pile of trash not far from a garbage truck that had apparently disgorged it on the street, and many people digging through, skinny dogs getting as close as they could. A naked toddler; some older kids walking by in school uniforms, looking out of place. Some prostitutes in the shade provided by low concrete buildings. Fences and sheet metal, too much light. And plenty of trucks.

Ponce brought me to a tandem rig parked outside the office of his friend's small company. The firm mainly worked the route up to Cuzco, carrying industrial supplies over—and wood back. Outside the truck was Sebastián Cisneros, forty-four, the driver of a tandem semi rig, and inside Edgardo Rojas, twenty-five, his assistant. Edgardo had been asleep on a narrow bunk behind the front seats, but sat up when his boss shouted, then nudged him. "He is fat and lazy," bearded Sebastián said with a smile. In fact, Edgardo was neither—though he was a bit round. He sat up, found his rubber sandals, and walked around the open-topped, wooden-sided trailers to make sure the tires were full and the tarps securely tied down.

Our cargo was some large commercial scales, barrels of paint, and chemicals for making asphalt. Our estimated travel time was two days. We would not drive at night, Sebastián said; it was too dangerous due to banditry. My goal was Puerto Maldonado, but they could take me only halfway—up the Andes to Cuzco. There I'd have to switch to a smaller truck for the ride down into the rain forest. Big rigs like Sebastián's couldn't make it down the other side; the turns were too tight. Our route would take us along the coastal highway south of Lima to Pisco; inland across the desert to Ica, Palpa, and Nazca; and then, leaving the route of the Pan-American Highway, up into the mountains through Puquio, Chalhuanca, and Abancay to Cuzco.

It took a couple of hours to get free of Lima. No sooner were its low buildings behind us than we came to the peripheral slums, seeming miles of *pueblos jóvenes* where the walls of people's homes consisted of cardboard, sheet metal scraps, and woven cane mats. We saw a small Indian family—mom, dad, kids—sitting by the side of the road with no clear purpose, as if waiting for fortune to swoop them up. We passed billboards for junk food and one advertising a new subdivision: it said, cruelly, *Live like an American,* and showed a light-skinned family on bicycles on the grass in front of their new house.

One other billboard was notable: it had a picture of a truck on a mountain road, and the words "*324 puentes a lo larga de la vía*" ("324 bridges over the length of the road"). The advertisement was part of a series of government-sponsored signs for the *carretera interoceánica,* or Interoceanic Highway, a big project of nationalistic importance. At the bottom, this billboard, like others, had the slogan *"Perú—Sí Podemos"* ("Peru—Yes We Can"). Tellingly, the sign didn't specify which route would boast those 324 bridges—not surprising, since this question was the subject of intense regional rivalry, and planning announcements over the years that seemed to favor one area over another had prompted riots and work stoppages. But Sebastián and Edgardo thought it would probably be the route we were on: Lima to Cuzco, Cuzco to Puerto Maldonado in the rain forest, and Puerto Maldonado to Brazil.

For an hour or two, the divided highway was swift and modern. To the right, occasionally, you could see the Pacific, and some sea lions on dark, wave-splashed rocks. To the left were dunes—and an evidently disturbed man making his way across one expanse of them, jerking through the hot sand barefoot and half-clothed.

The sere coastal desert yielded to greener climes and a narrower road. We braked and stopped to buy a burlap bag of *cayotes,* a root vegetable popular along the coast but sometimes hard to find in the mountains. ("We will give them away as presents in Cuzco," Sebastián explained.) And then near Cañete, as it got dark, we pulled over again, abruptly, after passing two women standing near piles of boxes. The boxes contained green grapes, it turned out, and after a brief discussion, Edgardo began loading them into one of the rig's two trailers. Then one of the women came into the cab with us, and we were back on the road.

Her name was Lyda, she was about thirty-five, and she and the grapes were bound for Abancay. Her family had a fruit stand there, and every week, she said, she hitched a ride down here to the coast, bought grapes, and then found a ride back home for her and her grapes. It was usually a three-day trip. (Sebastián would be paid a nominal amount for his help; he could use the money—and truckers always appreciated female companionship.) "Is that ever hard to do?" I asked, thinking that to be female, in the dark, by the side of the road with a ton of grapes and your thumb out was not the best situation to be in. She shrugged and said no, it almost never was.

We ate chicken and potatoes at a down-at-the-heels diner outside Pisco, a town that was home to a grape liqueur used in the famous Peruvian cocktail with frothed egg white, the Pisco Sour. Lyda had short hair and pearl earrings; she was chatty and seemed perfectly comfortable eating with three strange men. Around midnight, Sebastián pulled into a gas station with a large guarded truck park and turned off the engine. He lowered a narrow upper bunk to horizontal position and sent me up there. Edgardo retired to the roof, to protect our load from thieves. As Lyda got settled in the lower bunk, Sebastián cranked the windows down about an inch. Then he lay on the lower bunk next to her, head-to-feet.

It was hot and stuffy and mosquitoes buzzed all around. I heard my cabinmates shifting restlessly. "Maybe we could open the windows a little more?" I suggested. "But people would be able to reach in!" Lyda objected. Then I understood: it was all about thieves.

We tossed and turned until four a.m., when some sharp raps on the door woke everybody. Management wanted the trucks out of there. Sebastián started the engine as we washed up at a tap and then, just before shifting into gear, crossed himself.

During the night, he and Lyda had been speaking in a language that was not Spanish. They confirmed to me that it was Quechua, the ancient tongue of the Andes. I knew that Lyda was from the *sierra;* Sebastián now told me that his family had moved to Lima from a little mountain town up north. In Quechua, Lyda said, the way to ask someone's name was *Imata sutiqui?* The answer was *sutiymi* and then the name: *Sutiymi Sebastián Cisneros.* "If the Spaniards hadn't come, we'd all be speaking it, all the time," Lyda said. This conversation coincided roughly with a sign announcing how many kilometers remained before we came to Nazca, of the famed desert figures. We were on a modern highway and in a modern truck, but it became clear we were passing through a place that was very old. It was not hard to get them to talk about what had been here.

Peruvians all know that the Inca empire, pre-Columbian America's largest, was not the first civilization on their soil. Somebody was constructing pyramids and raised platforms by 3000 B.C.—about the same time civilization began in Mesopotamia and Egypt. The Chavín culture, dating from 900 B.C., is the oldest one to have a name, but many came after, inhabiting coast, desert, and mountains up until the aggressive Inca state, with its center in Cuzco, arose in the early fifteenth century.

One of the earliest was the Nazca, which flourished on the coastal plain we were driving across, toward the foothills of the Andes, between the second and fifth centuries. While the Nazca left behind scraps of vividly embroidered textiles and sections of canal (they lived in a narrow valley along a seasonal river that flowed down from the Andes to the sea), what they are remembered for are the Nazca Lines. This series of geometric shapes (rectangles, trapezoids, in a straight line over five miles long) and giant drawings is etched over nearly four hundred square miles of desert. The fact that many of these drawings, seen from above, are recognizable figures (a monkey, a hummingbird, a spider, a flower) was lost to human knowledge for hundreds of years until a scientist looking for evidence of ancient canals flew over the area in 1927. Tourists—unlike the Nazca, who had to imagine it all—can now have the same aerial view for about fifty dollars. The Peruvians I was driving with, however, had never flown in a plane. Sebastián could tell I was interested and pulled over at an observation tower where we could get a better look.

It wasn't ideal: all we could see from the top, about the height of a three-story building, were short sections of figures known as The Tree and The Hand. It was actually more interesting down on the ground, where you could see for yourself how removing the top inch or so of gravelly desert surface revealed significantly lighter stones underneath.

Lines like these were etched on deserts elsewhere in South America, Central America, and North America long before Columbus came. Most were long presumed to be roads; not until the past fifty years have many been shown to have astrological significance, with lines pointing at a spot on the horizon where the sun sets at the beginning of a solstice, for example. Some of the Nazca Lines apparently were a calendar; scholars have suggested that keeping track of the seasons helped the Nazca anticipate when the streams from the Andes would begin to run in spring, for example. But it's also tempting to articulate what seems obvious, using that word scientists so avoid: that the drawings were pictures for God. Or gods.

That made it feel a bit uncomfortable to be back in the truck, driving across them. It was like stepping on a church pew, or dropping the flag. Then again, the desert has been crisscrossed for centuries by subsequent cultures, not least of them the Inca. Of the many more recent lines cut across this particular canvas, several are thought to have been Incan roads. This plain between Cuzco and the sea was traversed by, among others, runners called *chaski*, who, in a sort of Pony Express relay, could complete the 150 miles—and an elevation gain of 10,912 feet—between Cuzco and the sea in a day. Among their missions: to carry fresh fish to the rulers in Cuzco.

The difficulty of that became clear as the road began to curve and climb outside Nazca: it would be pure mountains from now on. The land was dry and the people poor. A short, round woman with a black top hat and braids seemed amazed when Sebastián asked to see the dusty music cassettes behind the counter at her roadside shop; and downright shocked when he bought two, mountain music by Peruvian groups. He popped them into the truck's deck and for a while the mood was light. Then he told me that, for a few years during the 1990s, because of guerrilla activity—the Shining Path—he'd been unable to take this relatively direct route to Cuzco, and had to drive via Arequipa instead. As the truck groaned up a canyon, we passed a pull-out on a straightaway where, he said, one day guerrillas had set up a roadblock. They took just money from him—a "revolutionary tax"—but he watched as two Frenchmen and an American were singled out from the passengers on the bus ahead of him and, by the side of the road, shot dead.

The Maoist doctrines that had taken root in large zones of the arid, impoverished mountains were now in retreat, or at least in abeyance. But radical sympathies lived on in this land of the dispossessed. From the truck window, I saw a stall in a market town that offered not only T-shirts with the visage of Che Guevara, which you might see in an American mall, but also those with that of Osama bin Laden, which you would not.

(In a different mountain village, later, I would ask a teenager wearing a bin Laden shirt why he was doing so. He looked at me quizzically and replied, as though it were obvious, "Because he's a champion of the world's poor." I thought about that for a moment. "Of the world's poor Muslims, maybe," I said. "But not of you." He just looked back at me without saying more.)

When the road started getting narrow and tortuously curvy, Sebastián would reflexively tap his horn as he swung into the opposing lane at the beginning of a turn. It was practically aerobic exercise, whirling the steering wheel back and forth, trying to keep his trailers on the pavement. The quality of the road surface varied widely, and when it got particularly bad, a common sight would be a man with a shovel standing near a pothole, purportedly chucking some dirt into it, and with his hand out—seeking a donation for this work that he may or may not have been performing. Once or twice Sebastián leaned out the window to give change to these beggars, but mostly he just kept going.

He did not have that option around noon that day, near a verdant area called Pampa Galeras. A man presented himself squarely in the middle of the road so that Sebastián had to either stop or hit him. He stopped. The fellow presented himself at Sebastián's window, and put his hand out. He had a deranged look, his clothes were tattered, and he didn't really speak. Sebastián offered him some coins but he wasn't interested; he was hungry, and pantomimed eating. But apart from the grapes in the trailers, we had no food. Sebastián had a liter bottle half full of water and passed it through the window. The man took it and shuffled away.

At this point I was feeling very odd. It was only cool in the mountains, not cold, but I had a little shake. I'd had less than four hours of sleep, and restless sleep at that, so that was a possible explanation. A small amount of exhaust from the engine seemed to make its way into the cab; it could be that. I was carrying pills for *soroche,* altitude sickness, having once suffered it after flying into Cuzco on a family trip. But I felt that gaining elevation at the sluggish speed of a loaded tandem rig wasn't likely to be an issue. Then there was the fact that we had just encountered our third wandering man with mental problems in less than twenty-four hours. The previous one I had noticed at dawn in the middle of the vast desert, maybe a hundred yards off the road, between two earthen walls of an old structure: a wild-haired guy sitting shirtless and bearded before the flames of a tiny fire. Could it be that for him the highway was a way to live on the margins, to find the peace of being alone, but also, presumably, a way not to starve? The thought of these desperate-looking wanderers was upsetting, but I didn't think it was making me feel physically ill.

We stopped for an early dinner in a town called Lucanas. The simple restaurant was, unfortunately, in the shade, and my shivering increased. Sebastián donned one of the knit alpaca caps, with pointy top and tasseled ear flaps, that tourists to Cuzco come home with. I took aspirin and I took the *soroche* pills, just in case—one was supposed to start them twenty-four hours in advance of the elevation change, but I figured it couldn't hurt. Lyda and Sebastián were discussing an upcoming festival in honor of Cuzco's patron saint, Nuestro Señor de los Temblores. "Our Lord of Tremors?" I asked, in my near-incapacitated state.

"Our Father of Earthquakes," Sebastián corrected me.

Fortified by the meal, he kept driving, and as night fell, we climbed higher and higher. I got worse and worse. Despite the pills I had taken, a wrenching headache set in. A bit longer, and I got dizzy. Then restless: I needed to sit in front, instead of on the bunk in back; then I needed to sit in back. Sebastián started looking worried. Lyda entered nurse mode, rubbing my shoulders, putting a blanket around me and then taking it off when I began to be soaked with sweat. Sebastián asked me things I could no longer make out; he declared my illness to be *soroche*. Instantly I knew he was right and also knew that meant there was a potentially steep downside for me, a chance of cerebral edema if I didn't get to a lower elevation. I told him he'd better turn around, that otherwise his gringo might die. He looked torn: we were already at our highest elevation, he said, on the *altiplano*, about 13,000 feet high. Getting down would mean two hours of backtracking, or two and a half of forging on.

Suddenly I told him to stop. I was going to throw up. I rolled down the window as Sebastián pulled the truck over. Edgardo preceded me down the passenger-side steps to make sure I wouldn't fall off. It was pitch-black and a cold gale whipped our hair; yet still I couldn't take a full breath. I walked a couple of yards away from Edgardo—he was wearing rubber flip-flops in the frigid cold, I recall—and realized that what I really needed to do, instead of vomiting, or in addition, was empty my bowels.

With tears, fever, despair, and a headache equal to that of my worst hangover ever, I weathered the next few hours. The truck's headlights probed the darkness, and hurt my eyes. No cars came the other way; we passed nothing. At eleven p.m., having descended somewhat, Sebastián pulled over to doze; I saw that we were off the plain and into mountains again, so we must have descended some, but still I wheezed, shook, and held my head.

Sebastián awoke at two a.m., eager to make it to a river crossing by six a.m., when road construction would close a part of our route near Chalhuanca. When we stopped for breakfast, at a tent by the side of the road, I was better but could not eat. My map revealed that the pass we had crossed, at the peak of my misery, was the Abra Huashhuaccasa, at 14,107 feet.

By midmorning we were in Abancay. I was no longer quaking or thinking of death; I remember the town vividly. We pulled over and, while waiting for a taxi driver friend of Lyda's to load his car with her grapes, all had tea and rolls. Lyda paid Sebastián a *flete*, or cargo fee, of 120 soles (US$35). Flirtatiously, he told her he'd pick her up anytime.

"I'll stay with you," she said, "until a better ride comes along!" He held up to the light the 100-soles bill she had given him, reflexively checking to see if it was counterfeit.

We talked about our families (all of us were fathers—I have two children, Sebastián three, Edgardo four), about Machu Picchu (neither of them had been there; I had), and about a festival near Abancay in which villagers tied a condor, representing Andean culture, to the back of a bull, representing the Spanish, and cheered while the giant bird pecked savagely at the bull and the bull, leaping in pain, tried to stop it. They couldn't recommend a hotel in Cuzco for me—that was expensive tourist stuff. They just slept in the truck.

At dusk a few hours later we had reached the bustling little city of Cuzco, onetime center of the Inca empire, and the oldest inhabited town in the Americas. It was as far as our truck could go; eastbound freight would get transferred to smaller trucks. That was true of me as well, so Sebastián and Edgardo dropped me on the edge of town, where I would get a cab. I tipped them and waited to see if they'd hold the bills up to the light (they did not). I spent the next few days in the old capital recovering from altitude sickness and preparing for the next part of my journey.

Cuzco, the gateway to Machu Picchu, is still a place where roads meet, but four hundred years ago it was a very different kind of nexus.

The Inca road system was huge, extending from Quito, Ecuador, in the north past the present location of Santiago, Chile, in the south. Cuzco sat astride the more important and mountainous of two main north–south routes, the other one coastal, and many links joined the two routes. The 14,000-mile network, if placed in Africa, would extend from Cape Town, South Africa, to the south of France.

European chroniclers of the Inca likened their road system to that of the Roman Empire. The Spanish conquistador-chronicler Cieza de León wrote of the portion that went from Cuzco up to present-day Quito:

In human memory I believe that there is no account of a road as great as this, running through deep valleys, high mountains, banks of snow, torrents of water, living rock, and wild rivers. Through some places it went flat and paved; it was excavated into precipices and cut through rock in the mountains; it passed with walls along rivers, and had steps and resting spots in the snow. In all places it was clean and swept free of refuse, with lodgings, storehouses, Sun temples, and posts along the route. Oh! Can anything similar be claimed for Alexander or any of the powerful kings who ruled the world, that they were able to build such a road or provide the supplies found on it?

Alexander von Humboldt, the Prussian historian and scientist (and a traveler not given to hyperbole), called the roads "among the most useful and stupendous works ever executed by man." Hernando Pizarro, one of the conquistador brothers, wrote, "The road through the mountains is something to see, because in truth, nothing in Christendom equals it." And indeed, it is mainly the mountain roads that have endured, because so many of them, like Roman roads, were cut from stone.

One doesn't need to venture far from Cuzco to appreciate the unique character of these roads: the Inca Trail, a high-altitude, three- to four-day walking path to Machu Picchu with hundreds of stone steps chiseled into steep valley walls, is part of the original network. Unlike other roads, earlier and later, the Inca roads were not made for wheeled vehicles, for the Inca had not discovered the wheel. The roads of other cultures might be thought of as evolving from footpaths for people, to trails for pack animals, and then finally to tracks for horse-drawn carriages and motor vehicles. As roads evolved they emphasized gentle gradients and turns, and prized straightaways: they tried to accommodate increased velocity. This was not the case with Inca roads. They were intended to accommodate people on foot and the agile Andean beast of burden, the llama.

The Spaniards' horses had considerable trouble with the mountain roads. In his classic *Conquest of Peru*, William H. Prescott recounts how on Pizarro's march to Cuzco, "the mountain was hewn into steps, but the rocky ledges cut up the hoofs of the horses; and, though the troopers dismounted and led them by the bridle, they suffered severely in their effort to keep their footing."

Other roads were vested with symbolic meanings difficult for us to understand. In parts of the Andes some stone paths are nearly one hundred feet wide. These were apparently not for common passage; they crossed lands that had been conquered by the Inca tribe and were a symbol of the Incan state, their use apparently restricted to those on state business. Commonly, local people were forced to do road work as part of the *mita* system of forced communal labor. One sixteenth-century chronicler described how Emperor Atahualpa and his retinue entered the plaza of the city of Cajamarca: "There were in front of him many Indians who cleaned the road in spite of the fact that it was rather clean and there was nothing to pick up."

Modern Andean scholar John Hyslop has described how in some "Inka centers the entry and exit roads, and other major corridors, were planned divisions that separated groups of people with different status and function"—suggesting that in the Inca empire some must have lived, as we say, on the wrong side of the tracks. Other roads were used for pilgrimages; still others apparently "marked certain astronomical and calendrical concepts," as was true elsewhere in the Americas.

The Inca even thought differently than we do about where a road should go. The contemporary British explorer Hugh Thomson recently noted how "the Quechuan guides I've worked with always travel instinctively on the high side of any given valley, while the natural tendency of European or American mountain trekkers is to keep to the bottom if they can." Having spent a lot of time retracing Inca paths and exploring old ruins, Thomson has concluded that Incan roads "are written with a different grammar to our own." He describes a trip on which

> I came across a magnificent decayed stairway high up in the Choquetecarpa valley. The stairway rose out of the grass ahead of us, seemingly out of nowhere, stone tread after stone tread, a full twelve feet wide, the width of a royal road . . . Even higher in the valley were some stone llama pens, built just below the pass at a chilling 13,700 feet: circular buildings, 13 feet in diameter, clustered tightly together to give protection against the wind. Above, a vertiginous stone stairway cut its way directly up towards the pass. No travellers now ever passed along that road—those few that came would use the modern mule track instead, which wound its course in a more sedate and European style over the other shoulder of the pass. We had found this alternate ancient way because we knew where to look.

In Cuzco today most antiquities date from Spanish colonial times—the cobblestone streets, for example, and the Plaza de Armas and the cathedral that graces it. But Inca walls and foundations abound, and walking from my hotel, on Choquechaca Street, to a pedestrian alley called Hatunrumiyoc Street, which leads to the plaza, I daily passed a celebrated wall, part of the palace of the sixth Inca, Inca Roca. Twice my height and long as a block, the smooth wall is made of large stones of irregular shape, all hewn together to fit like jigsaw pieces. The particular stone for which Hatunrumiyoc Street is named is several feet across and has twelve separate sides that mesh perfectly with the stones around it; the effort required to achieve the fit is mind-boggling.

Along the wall, leaning against it most days, were groups of Quechua-speaking women who hawked souvenirs to tourists. The juxtaposition of their trade with the ancient masonry was striking: in the thin air of Cuzco, the grandeur of a lost civilization lingers alongside the poverty of its descendants. When a vendor with beautiful waist-length braids, necklaces, and a funky velvet top hat demands payment for having her photo taken, you can understand why but are put in mind of the continuing indignity of the Indians, the evident absence of skills as sublime as those of the ancient stonemasons.

Pizarro and his conquistadors had several rationales for their horrific deeds. They were seeking to expand the dominion of King Carlos V of Spain. They were seeking converts to Christendom. And, as poor men from a dry corner of Spain called Extremadura (which means "very hard"), they were seeking wealth and power. Their looting of the Incan empire, their means of extracting its gold, is a tale widely known but one that deserves brief retelling.

Using the Inca roads leading to the mountains—these were several, and excellent—the Spaniards invaded Cuzco and later Cajamarca, where they captured the Incan emperor, Atahualpa. Instead of simply killing Atahualpa outright, they ransomed him, holding out the prospect of his eventual release as a means to summon gold and silver from all over the empire. The Incas used the metals not as currency but as decoration for shrines and public buildings. Except for a few decorative pieces to intrigue King Carlos V, Pizarro wanted it all in the form of bullion he could most efficiently export to Spain. So the same Inca craftsmen who had worked the metal into fine shapes were now compelled to melt it back down. The object, according to legend, was to fill a room in Cajamarca, where Atahualpa was being held hostage, up to the top, at which point his freedom would be won. The "ransom room" was finally filled but then the emperor, to the Spaniards' everlasting infamy, was executed by garrote—strangling a person from behind with rope or wire.

Thus, the first great export of the New World to the Old was gold—taken by force, at a cost of Incan pride and identity. As Old World culture took root in the New World, the indigenous people changed, grew, suffered, threw off the colonial yoke, matured. Peru, over the next nearly five hundred years, became a democracy with a market economy.

Now foreigners had to pay for her gold. (On a back street in Cuzco, I paid $70 for a wedding band in white gold to replace one I had lost. The gold came from Hueypetue, a mining area I would soon pass by.) But what the world really wanted from Peru at the beginning of the twenty-first century was her wood.

I carried a phone number from Antonio Ponce: another friend of his, another office on the industrial side of town, another truck idling out back.

My new driver was Braulio Quispe. He was handsome, compact, curly-haired, about thirty years old, and filled with energy. His truck was compact and energy-packed as well: like most of those that plied the east side of the *sierra*, it was a Volvo fuel tanker, loaded with diesel and emblazoned with the words INFLAMABLE and PELIGRO (DANGER!) on the sides. The big metal tank was flat on top and there was a little metal fence around it that in effect turned it into a giant pickup truck with a very high bed. On his return trip to Cuzco from the jungle, with the tank empty (its diesel transferred to tanks in Puerto Maldonado, where it would power other trucks, and electrical generators), that bed would be stacked high with mahogany boards. On the outbound trip, however, as I would soon discover, it would be filled with about two dozen human beings. Braulio, in other words, would be driving a highly explosive bus.

To fly from Cuzco east to the jungle town of Puerto Maldonado, in the Amazon basin, takes less than half an hour. But to drive the tortuous mountain route takes about twenty-four hours, if you're lucky. A normally difficult situation is made worse by the rainy season (December–April), which we were in: the route, which is mostly unpaved, turns to mud. Trickles become torrents. The month before, a mudslide had closed the route for two weeks. More than a hundred vehicles had been backed up on either side at the time, most of them trucks, which were the road's main traffic. But they weren't the only ones to suffer: within a few days of a road closure, shops in Puerto Maldonado are empty of most produce and dairy products; after a week, filling stations tend to close. The unreliable road is the jungle residents' lifeline.

There are other routes from the rain forest over the mountains to the coast, and some are shorter, but this one, through Cuzco, is the most heavily traveled; the town has the longest, tightest integration with the forest. Most of the "pioneers" working to settle the rain forest, for example, are poor Indians from the *sierra;* Quechua is commonly heard in jungle work camps. It is hard to imagine two more opposite climates more closely linked: Cuzco with its thin air and desertlike aridity, the jungle with its heat and mop-your-forehead humidity. But there they are. The road goes up and down so often that it makes sense to think of it as part elevator.

Before we could descend, we had to head sideways for a while. We pulled over at Oropesa, a humble roadside settlement a few miles out of Cuzco. A woman emerged from a low wooden house, smiling and holding out a small pile of folded clothes for Braulio: it was his wife. His kids came out, too, and I watched from the cab as he hugged a toddler but not a teenage daughter. He gave his wife some money but didn't hug her either; I could see it was not the custom. His round-trips to Puerto Maldonado and back, Braulio told me, usually took about eight days, so his family was accustomed to his absences.

The town where we stopped next, Urcos, is described by Prescott as being "about six leagues from the capital"—eighteen miles. Conquistadors sometimes were competitive with one another, and in 1537, rivalries played out here: Diego de Almagro, a challenger to the Pizarro brothers who had already claimed Chile for the crown, mustered some five hundred soldiers in Urcos and launched an attack on the Pizarro army that had taken Cuzco. He succeeded in displacing them and in capturing two of the three Pizarro brothers, Hernando and Gonzalo, but his ascendance was short-lived. The next year the Pizarros retook Cuzco. They captured Almagro and condemned him to death. Almagro begged for his life. To this Hernando Pizarro coldly replied that "he was surprised to see Almagro demean himself in a manner so unbecoming a brave cavalier; that his fate was no worse than had befallen many a soldier before him." Almagro was garroted in prison, then publicly decapitated.

The plaza in front of the Urcos cathedral was crowded on the afternoon we arrived; there was a funeral procession, and pallbearers of a simple casket made their way up the church steps, tears streaming down their faces. As Braulio's truck pulled up near them, however, a significant number of people I had mistaken for mourners began to swarm up its sides: Braulio and most other truckers made significant extra money by carrying passengers.

Once the space on top of the fuel tank had filled with riders, Braulio told those hanging on the sides to get off—he was full. A dozen people reluctantly climbed down. That still left about twenty more people on the fuel truck than when we started; Braulio seemed content. Still, it didn't take a worrywart to look up past the giant letters warning INFLA-MABLE to all those dark heads, some with alpaca-fur knit hats on (it was getting cold) to think that, hmm, maybe this wasn't the perfect marriage of automotive technology and function.

We lumbered out of Urcos, soon left behind the pavement—and encountered the police. It was drizzling now in the twilight, and two police officers got up from under a plastic sheet to demand Braulio's papers.

"What's up?" I asked him from the cab, where I had continued to sit—gratefully, for the people in back were about to get soaked.

"It's illegal to have those passengers," he noted, pulling out one of the banknotes secured over his visor with a rubber band. He tucked the money into his documents folder. When he returned to his seat, the money was gone, and we were off. Braulio wasn't angry; this was just a cost of doing business. I have seen the scene repeated scores of times: the poorly paid policeman, the relatively prosperous trucker, the safety violation that should not be allowed to stand, and yet . . . how else were all these people going to get over the mountains? In the absence of public transportation and living wages for police officers, this kind of transaction constitutes traffic law enforcement in much of the world.

As the rain picked up, the road quickly turned bad. Ten minutes past the police stop, where the route crossed a small gulch, part of the road had washed out in a torrent of water and we had to wait behind three other trucks. Deliberately, if not hastily, various people were dragging

*Passengers climb onto the top of Braulio's fully loaded fuel truck, outside Cuzco,
for a ride down into the rain forest.*

assorted tree trunks, limbs, and rocks to the site, first aid for the road.
Braulio took the opportunity to unfurl a tarpaulin his passengers could
pull over the back of the truck, to keep themselves dry. He also invited a
young mother, Natali, and her toddler son, Carlos, to move into the cab
with us.

To the clicking of windshield wipers, Braulio interviewed his pretty
passenger. She was from Puerto Maldonado, she said, but only going as
far as a high mountain town en route "to attend to my business." Braulio,
flirtatious, worked hard to find out what that business was, but the young
woman was reticent. It dawned on me that bringing her into the cabin
might not have been a purely altruistic move on his part.

I noticed that the first truck on the far side of the washout was loaded
with thick boards, and asked Braulio why a couple of them couldn't be
thrown across the breach. He looked at me as though I were as naïve as
little Carlos, and explained why that would never happen: *"Es caoba."* It's
mahogany. I crossed over and took a closer look: the boards were dark
brown, thick, coarsely sawn, no two the same shape. Most had a number

Braulio guides his fuel truck down the Andes and into the Amazon basin while passenger Natali and her son, Carlos, take a nap.

or letter—it was hard to tell what it was—sketched on the end in pink or yellow chalk. The wood was headed from the jungle up to Cuzco, and from there to, well, maybe Park Avenue. *So we meet again,* I thought.

Finally the road was shored up enough for a single vehicle to pass. Accelerating slowly while shifting through several gears, Braulio crossed the breach. Given the bumpy dirt road and its numerous curves, almost the entire trip down into the Amazon basin would be driven at under twenty-five miles per hour. The atmosphere was misty, mysterious; the landscape varied from a few humid valleys with pasture, fruit trees, and boulders to the more usual dry mountainsides interrupted by the occasional rushing stream. In the fading light we saw stone terraces planted with potatoes, farmers eking a living out of terrain that seemed hostile to the idea.

Only when it became truly impossible to drive without the headlights did Braulio turn them on. More than three-quarters of the vehicles we passed were trucks similar to his—*cisternas,* as the flat-topped tankers were called. The rest were an assortment of four-by-fours, a motorcycle or two, and the occasional donkey-drawn cart. As we rounded one

treacherous curve, the headlights lit up a bus that had slid halfway onto
the shoulder; its many passengers were outside, busy coaxing it back onto
the road. This, explained Braulio, not slowing to see whether he could
help, was the weekly bus from Puerto Maldonado to Cuzco. One could
understand why trucks were more popular, and useful, among travelers.

We pulled into a village called Ccatca for dinner. There was one place
to eat on the town square, and one thing to order: chicken broth, with
bread. It took the restaurant a while to serve the passengers, and while we
waited I wandered around town a bit. Two blocks off the square was a
tiny shop with a high ceiling, and hanging from it one dim bulb; toward
the back was a small display of candy and chips, maybe five different
items for sale. At first I didn't notice the old Indian woman seated at the
counter, some four feet away—she was so still. Then, out of the corner of
my eye, I saw some motion: she was gnawing on something, like a bone.
I said good evening to her, paid for a candy bar and bag of chips, turned
to go, then paused. The bone had a strange shape.

"Excuse me," I said. "But what were you eating?"

She opened her hand a bit sheepishly to reveal the small skull—it was
leftovers. *"Cuy,"* she said. Guinea pig.

The rain picked up. Outside of town, Braulio paused, and at first I
couldn't see why. Then I noticed that the road ahead of us was now part
of a stream. Braulio turned off the engine. There was no apparent
washout, no missing bridge; it was simply too deep. We would wait.

We dozed. Around two a.m., a Range Rover came up even with us,
paused, and then successfully forded the stream, which was lower now.
Another truck followed, and Braulio got us back under way. We continued on through the night, pausing occasionally to remove the odd boulder or branch that had fallen in our way. I could feel us getting higher but
by now my body had acclimated; I did not feel ill. I was a bit concerned,
however, when dawn saw us at a summit of 15,000 feet, with snow all
around, on a road so narrow that if two trucks met the lower one would
have to back up to a wide spot and let the higher one pass. The idea of
backing up on what amounted to a curvy, narrow ledge, particularly now
that I could see the huge drops below, was nerve-racking. Along with
these breathtaking landscapes of sheer-drop terror, we passed through

occasional woods, and even pasture with alpacas grazing. On a second barren summit, at 15,585 feet, Braulio parked the truck and added two big candles to the four already burning in the tiny roadside chapel to Nuestro Señor de Huanca. He knelt, said a prayer, and got back on the road.*

From then on, it was all downhill, with every turn seeming to bring a little more warmth, a little more humidity, plants and trees we hadn't seen before. The view was still limited until one particular turn revealed the sudden vista, one of those spectacular places through which you come to understand the shape of the planet: the wrinkled green mountainsides spread out before us, dissolving suddenly in the vast, smooth green sameness of the Amazon basin, a flatness that stretches two thousand miles to the sea. Interrupting the mountainside below were little brown threads, glimpses of the same road we were on, a thread that writhed back and forth like an earthworm held by the tail.

Into the spectacle we descended. We stopped for a breakfast in Echapampa, at a small, smoky place filled with rough wooden tables and benches and run by four women with long, black, braided pigtails. A fireplace flickered in the back of the room. They were serving lamb broth with *chuño*, a kind of potato. I saw a movement at my feet and recoiled, but it was just a guinea pig. In fact, they were everywhere, nibbling up the table scraps that one day they would become. Little Carlos, delighted, set off after them.

Lunch was five hours and scores of switchbacks further down, in a large, airy hall in the town of Quincemil ("Fifteen Thousand"). Braulio informed me that the generously proportioned, stately woman who served our chicken stew and potatoes was his mother: this was the town where he had been born. He was the fifth of eight children. He'd been driving the road over the mountains and back since he was fourteen, hundreds of times, "even a thousand"; he didn't know. It didn't get boring because the road was always different, he said—one or another bridge out or a new bridge built, some kind of holdup, an accident, passengers to meet. The world of the drivers, though, he acknowledged, was fairly lim-

---

*The chapel celebrates a visitation by Christ to a cave on nearby Huanca Mountain during Spanish colonial times. An Indian laborer, Diego Quispe (the surname, common in the Andes, was the same as Braulio's), singled out unfairly for a whipping at the silver mine where he was forced to work, had escaped and sought shelter in the cave.

ited: "everybody on this road knows each other," he said, and indeed I'd seen him gesture with more or less enthusiasm at many, many passing trucks.

We'd passed through a town where every shop had a new metal address plate, giving a number and the street name, Avenida Transoceánica. It was a political stunt, said Braulio. "They think if they say it enough times, maybe it will happen. I don't know. I don't think so. They've been talking about it too many years."

But what if it did? I asked. What did he think would change? Well, you'd be able to make the trip quicker if the road were paved, he replied—maybe in just a day, instead of the two or three or more it took now. But that could mean the road could get more crowded—more vehicles, which would mean more competition, and less of the community of drivers that existed now (which I knew functioned as a lifeline, of sorts, if there was trouble).

Braulio slept a bit longer that night, though he still woke before dawn, perhaps not by choice—a passenger had decided to take his leave, and wanted to pay him. At three a.m., or whatever it was, he started banging on the door of the cab. Soon after, we were driving again. Once it was light, Natali and little Carlos got off as well. Braulio eyed her hungrily as she paid him and walked away. I took the occasion to climb up onto the back—not perfect timing since, as the morning went by, the road became both straighter and much more dusty. Like the others on top, I learned how to hold my breath for a while when we passed another vehicle and had to eat its dust.

Mostly, the passengers were young men, heading down to the jungle to work in wood. Two brothers from the mountains, Efraim and Raúl Andrade, and their cousin, Nico, got off at Laberinto, a settlement on the Los Amigos River. From there, Efraim explained, they would take a boat upstream to a lumber camp where Nico had worked previously. Such camps on the Los Amigos, I knew, were illegal—the area was protected, a park. But they abounded anyway, and were almost always involved in cutting mahogany, the region's number-one moneymaker. It would take a week or two of travel—no mahogany was left near the road—but they assured me that, in short measure, if things worked out, they'd be hard at work with chain saws. Two other men were headed for a sawmill.

One passenger uninterested in wood was another single mother with her son. Mary Luz Guerra was a nursery school teacher in Puerto Maldonado, and her son, Alex, was fourteen. Alex had a plastic camera and seemed to be enjoying himself. But his mother was not. Alone among the passengers, she was trying to keep clean. Uncomfortable, now, in a white cowl-neck sweater (the day was growing very warm), she explained that she had never planned to come home on a truck. She and Alex had taken the plane to Cuzco to visit relatives at the beginning of a school break. But when it came time to leave, the fare for the thirty-seven-minute flight had gone up and she discovered she could not afford two seats. They'd been reduced to taking a truck back, essentially coming home through the service entrance.

With a gasp of brakes, Braulio slowed to navigate over another one-lane bridge. On top, we held our collective breath as the wave of dust that had been following the truck slowly caught up and washed over us. To everyone's surprise, Braulio did not accelerate after crossing the bridge but pulled over, into a small roadside settlement called Libertad. It had the distinction of offering not only a swimming hole that extended into the shade under the bridge, but a small restaurant next door.

Many passengers swam—the water felt fantastic, and some washed out their clothes on the rocks at water's edge. But few went into the restaurant: these people were poor, and even the ramshackle place, which today was serving fried bush meat (a large jungle rodent called *picuro*, like an agouti), was too great a luxury. I invited Mary Luz and Alex to be my guests. She hadn't swum—too modest—but I had and, free of dust at last, I felt sorry for her in that sweater. We sipped cold sodas as we waited for our meals. Beyond the swimming hole, a toucan flew low across a small field, bobbing up and down with each stroke of its little wings—a thrilling sight. I thought about how a better road—especially a through road, spanning the continent—would lead to bigger fields, more room for soybeans and cattle. And less room for toucans.

A beer truck pulled up to the restaurant. The name of the distributor on the door logo was Transoceánica, a variant of Interoceánica, and I pointed it out to the others.

Mary Luz, cooled only slightly by the shade and the soda, dabbed at her moist forehead with a tiny, thin napkin that was not nearly up to the job.

"I can't *wait* till they build that highway!" she said.

On the evening of the third day we pulled up to the fuel depot on the outskirts of Puerto Maldonado, and everybody climbed down from the truck. We all settled up with Braulio and went our separate ways. Mary Luz and Alex transferred to another unusual form of public transportation, a three-wheeled motorcycle taxi with a fabric roof, known locally as a *motocar*. It looked like fun so I flagged one down, too, and was soon putt-putting through the frontier jungle town en route to a hotel, grateful for the moving air.

Puerto Maldonado was pretty much the end of the road. With giant rivers lining it on two sides (and joining at one corner of town), the only way to keep driving was to put your vehicle—and it would have to be a small one—on the ferry. Looking overwhelmed by the task ahead of it, the rickety vessel chugged upstream across the mighty Madre de Dios River, inching crablike toward the far shore. On that other side was a dirt road that led to another ferry over another river, many hours away, this one at the border with Brazil. During the rainy season, the road was often impassable.

Puerto Maldonado itself had only four paved streets, and a distinctly frontier feel. The main streets were crowded with motorcycles, many of them taxis; if the passenger was female, she sat sideways, knees together. A helmet law had recently gone into effect, but many drivers ignored it. Others wore a construction hat or a bicycle helmet. Most side streets were empty. The buildings were low. Many were made of wood. Concrete, though, was the favored material for things monumental, including the town plaza and the clock tower at its center, a Catholic church across the street, and many of the gravestones in the "pioneers' cemetery," an overgrown place that few seemed to visit. The only other place I could remember a cemetery with a name like that was in Alaska.

You could understand the widespread use of concrete, in a place where organic things, like wood, tended to rot. But it had been used to fabricate even a giant obelisk in an intersection a couple of miles from the main plaza: the Monument to Biodiversity, of all things. According to a Peruvian government study, cloud forests in the mountainous western edge of Madre de Dios, the state we were in, have the greatest biodiversity of any place on Earth. The seven- or eight-story tower, with green glass sides and an elevator to the top (nonfunctional, alas, during all three of my visits), had concrete "fins" extending out from the base at four corners, to suggest a rain-forest tree, and on each of the four sides was a scene from the region's history, set in concrete. One side showed indigenous peoples in the jungle; another showed rubber tappers (it was ironic that such a transportation-challenged part of the world had helped to usher in the automotive revolution, by providing the rubber for tires); another portrayed Brazil nut harvesters; another, gold miners; and the last, woodcutters.

In a way, the shiny glass sides mirrored Puerto Maldonado's contradictions. It was a jungle town full of mountain people. It touted the forest's biodiversity while inevitably, through human incursions and extractive industries, reducing it. It was the capital of a department, or state, 65 percent of whose territory had been declared parkland, and yet it wasn't easy to find local people in favor of those protections. Its airport brought in scores of tourists every week en route to eco-lodges; but they almost all skipped the town itself, which didn't have much "eco" to offer.

What little it had, I think I found: my hotel, the Wasai, was a thatched-roof place overlooking the huge Madre de Dios River. The open-air reception area had a jungle lodge ambience, and adjoined a breakfast platform on the river's steep bank. Elevated walkways connected restaurant and reception area to the hotel's dozen or so bungalows, most of them small, dark rooms on stilts. There were plenty of colorful lizards around, an abundance of birds attracted to fruit set out for them on the breakfast platform, and moths, butterflies, and frogs. (Later I returned to the Wasai with my family. We were to go from there to a jungle lodge down the Tambopata River, but my ten-year-old son, enamored of all the life around him, thought we were already there.) At breakfast one day, as I drank strong coffee and some fresh-squeezed orange juice, I noticed something large up in the tree canopy, maybe fifty or sixty feet above.

"*Es un perezoso,*" the waitress explained—a sloth. They occasionally passed through, she said, very slowly. I checked for the sloth every morning; it was never more than one tree away from the last place I'd seen it, always hanging upside down. The animals' main predators, I learned, were eagles. Their main defense was the camouflage of their fur, which even had algae growing on it, and their incredibly subtle movement, also unlikely to attract notice.

Then one morning the sloth was gone. The hotel staff shrugged: sometimes they just go, but they always come back. As it happened, I was just returning to the Wasai two afternoons later when this one came back. I didn't recognize it at first: the hotel's porter and another man were walking across the street, each holding one end of a broom from which something heavy hung. It was the sloth. They were returning it to the sanctuary of the hotel. They paused so I could get a better look at its coat (which, unlike every other mammal's, started on its stomach and went to its back, so the rain would run off properly) and then, miraculously, its face. For some reason I'd thought a sloth would look like a bear, but the face reminded me more of a human child, a little bit like one with Down syndrome—gentle, vulnerable, a being that deserved some extra consideration.

While there were few tourists, there were many non-governmental organizations (NGOs) from various countries committed to helping preserve the environment. Conservation International, World Wildlife Fund, ProNaturaleza, the Frankfurt Zoological Society, and the Amazon Conservation Association all had offices here, and others were arriving: so many were there, said a young couple (she from California, he from France) who had recently arrived to establish a new NGO, the Giant Otter Conservation Project, that it was hard to find a place to live. In terms of First World comfort, Puerto Maldonado was maxed out.

All of them were worried about the mahogany business, which did not respect park boundaries and brought woodcutters into conflict with indigenous peoples: the densest concentrations of the wood were far upriver, where the "uncontacted" live. Before there was something so valuable in their midst, the distances had protected the indigenous. But now, infection by a disease carried by a woodcutter—one of the last reverberations of the plagues visited on the New World by the conquistadors—could wipe out a tribe. The few people authorized by the Peruvian government to visit remote tribes had to follow a strict protocol that entailed wearing latex gloves, using breathing filters, and keeping a distance of several yards at all times.

On a more practical level, explained Antonio Iviche, the leader of a group called FENAMAD, which advocated for the indigenous, the woodcutters stole their food. In FENAMAD's raggedy offices Iviche, whose parents were indigenous, complained bitterly about the incursions. "When the invaders arrive in these lands to harvest wood, they also hunt, because they need to eat, and they fish." The reduction in available bush meat could be huge: a study had shown that loggers could deplete an area of edible animals in a few short weeks. The infections, encroachments, and competition for food forced tribes to move to less hospitable areas and were linked to increased mortality. The opening of a regular highway to Brazil, he added, would encourage more workers to come to the area—even Brazilians—and make matters worse.

As I sat on a small, sagging couch in FENAMAD's tiny waiting room, I was approached by the group's accountant. We got to chatting. He wanted me to understand that the indigenous were not going to go quietly. He told me that the day before, a woodcutter had arrived in town on a boat and been rushed to the hospital.

"Yes . . . ," I said.

"Oh," he continued, realizing that I didn't get the point. "He had an arrow lodged in his ankle bone!"

He watched as it dawned on me what this meant—the Indians are fighting back.

Another friend of the indigenous was Alfredo García Altamirano, a Peruvian anthropologist. He had partnered with an English biologist to start a small NGO called TReeS Perú, which they ran out of a small house. There was a red motorcycle in the front yard, and García wasn't wearing shoes. There was a lot the state could do to protect the tribes, he said. It could give them title to specific parcels of land. It could provide for better enforcement of the law. It could better regulate logging companies.

But as far as working against an interoceanic highway, well, that was a non-starter. "You can't have an anti-highway discussion here," he said. Too many people, practically everybody local, supported it, and you would be marginalizing yourself to do it, writing "kook" on your shirt. "All you can do is to plan for its bad effects, and try to find ways to avoid them."

Just what were the bad effects? García referred me to a paper delivered the year before at a major conference in Arequipa called Regional Integration Between Bolivia, Brazil, and Peru. A forestry professor who advised the Inter-American Development Bank reviewed a long list of the drawbacks a new road would bring to the area. In fact, two lists—one of the environmental ill effects and the other of the social. On the first list, he included

- deforestation of lands ill suited to agriculture
- degradation of the forest from logging
- increased risk of forest fires
- illegal hunting, and increased traffic in live animals
- abusive fishing, using dynamite and chemicals
- loss of species
- reduction of landscape and touristic values.

Socially, the region would suffer from

- invasion of indigenous lands by farmers, woodcutters, and miners, and eventual massacre of Indians by disease or in skirmishes
- displacement of tribal peoples, leading to conflict between them as they invade each other's land
- illegal expropriation of tribal lands
- proliferation of illegal crops such as *coca*
- stimulation of migration to urban areas, and the decline of social services and quality of life in towns and villages
- growth of slums
- growth of labor exploitation and prostitution
- loss of traditional cultural values.

A scientist from the Woods Hole Research Center who was at the talk told me it was sparsely attended, in stark contrast to lectures on the business opportunities regional integration would bring, which were packed.

The five-hundred-pound gorilla in all of these scenarios, of course, was Brazil. Relative to Peru, Brazil is a highly advanced country with a powerhouse economy. And in exploiting its rain forest, Brazil is far ahead, a major global producer of soybeans and beef, most of it raised on lands from which the rain forest has been burned off. The road, of course, was the necessary precursor to such burning: until there was a road, what was the point of having a farm or ranch of any kind? You had to have a market, and to have a market, you had to have a road.

The starkest way to see this power of a road was from the air, and on my first visit to Puerto Maldonado, Maria Stenzel, a photographer from *National Geographic* magazine, and I hired a plane to do just that. It was not easy to do in Peru: planes were so associated with cocaine traffickers that the government had put a stop to nearly all civil aviation. And even when a pilot had permission to fly, it was dangerous: the year before, the Peruvian air force had mistakenly shot down a Cessna carrying a family of missionaries out of the rain forest. When our pilot had to put down on a semi-abandoned strip near the border with Brazil due to a sudden lowering of the visibility ceiling, the plane was quickly surrounded by soldiers, and we were given permission to take off only after considerable showing of documents and radio calls to army and aviation authorities.

But renting the plane was worthwhile. The road to Iñapari, on the border with Brazil, was a muddy strip through dense jungle that took hours to traverse in a passenger car, if you were lucky. And the bridge over the border stream was a rickety affair that could never hold a heavy truck. As we entered Brazilian airspace, the picture changed entirely. Suddenly there were fields full of crops, with shiny farm machines in them, and pastures full of cattle, who stampeded in alarm under our low-flying plane. The highway beneath us was largely paved, and on either side of the pavement the forest was cut back for hundreds of yards, even miles. In the distance were other fields, as well as the smoke from newer fields being created. It was as though the development clock had been turned ahead a generation; this was a country on the move, and the road's role as precondition was clearly evident.

Brazil was so eager for Peru to have the same kinds of roads that by late 2004 it had completely paved its road to the border, spent $7 million to upgrade that rickety bridge over the border river, and had even offered to help finance work on the Peruvian side.

Alfredo García felt that just having a road wouldn't bring the same kind of prosperity to Peru; it would bring a different kind of prosperity, a lesser one. Perhaps more than anything else, Peru would profit by playing host to Brazilian trucks and providing highway services to Brazilian vehicles. Peruvian gas stations are known as *grifos;* and in García's words, "I'm afraid we're going to become Brazil's *grifo.*"

There were many fates worse than that, of course, from the perspective of the poor people who streamed down from the Andes to try to make a future in Peru's jungle. To them, the restrictions on use of the nation's jungles—the rules keeping them out—were outrageous, and the foreign NGOs were meddlers, pure and simple. The Peruvian government's own control apparatus, however, seemed to attract most of their wrath. Not that it was tremendously effective in preventing illegal logging—its inspectors were notoriously corrupt, perhaps unsurprising given the high stakes of mahogany cutting—but INRENA, the federal natural resource agency, was perhaps the most visible symbol of this hated authority. In 2002, a mob in Puerto Maldonado burned down the INRENA headquarters there, and set fire to an impound lot that held confiscated wood. Another mob destroyed the Department of Agriculture offices. Another firebombed a car in front of ProNaturaleza, a Peruvian NGO. Hundreds of soldiers and police were sent in from across the mountains to restore order. Not long after, the apparent leader of these insurrections, Rafael Ríos López, by then a fugitive facing federal charges, was elected governor of the state.

After turning himself in and spending six days in jail, Ríos took office at the end of 2002. But a few months later he went back underground due to the charges pending against him; eventually he was sentenced to three months in prison and removed from office. I had the good fortune to be in Puerto Maldonado during the brief window between his incarcerations, and I stopped in to see him.

Andean *huayno* music was playing softly from a boom box when I walked into the governor's office. He was not the firebrand revolutionary I had pictured but a small, balding, nondescript man of about forty. He explained to me that his popular nickname, *el loro pihuicho,* was the name of a small parrot that was often heard but seldom seen. That described him, he admitted, during his three months on the run from the authorities. It was illegal for an elected official in Peru to advocate disobedience of the law, and he was charged with, among other things, promulgating violence during the recent demonstrations and encouraging woodcutters to ignore park rules that kept them away from mahogany. He also maintained that there was no longer any such thing as uncontacted peoples.

Ríos played for me a video taken on the day of his most recent release from prison, just to demonstrate his popular support. It was impressive: as he emerged from the prison gates into a crowd of scores of cheering people, he was hoisted onto the shoulders of some supporters; flower petals filled the air. His backers, he said, were poor people just like him who lived in new communities on the edges of town. He himself, he claimed, had not worn a pair of shoes until age thirteen. "I came from slavery, and it has to change."

But Ríos's idealism had been compromised by alliances he made along the way. The scuttlebutt around town was that his agitation against the government was largely financed by local power brokers who stood to gain if more wood was harvested; most prominent among these was a young Peruvian named Alan Schipper Guerovitch, whose family owned one of two large lumber mills in town. Ríos did not deny the association. "I've had many friends over time," he told me.

Maria Stenzel, the *National Geographic* photographer, had already had an encounter with Schipper. Spotting large pieces of a mahogany tree that were about to be transported across the river to Puerto Maldonado, she followed them as they were loaded onto a truck, snapping pictures of it as it made its way around town. When the truck stopped in front of a small office building, according to Maria, a man ran out of it, screaming at her that she had no right to take photos of his wood. "Do you know who I am?" he asked heatedly. It was Schipper.

Perhaps to bring closure to that incident, Schipper agreed to see me when I called. Every taxi driver knew the location of his lumber mill, and indeed, the outside of the compound was impressive: an imposing wall of wood, like a stockade, with a guard tower on the second floor, and gates sealed shut. I passed a business card to a guard behind a little window, and like the drivers of the several trucks lined up and idling outside the gates, awaiting loads, I waited. Presently the guard unchained the gate and let me pass.

Down a slope to my left was a large, open-air mill, where a dozen workers sent pieces of tree through a large, noisy blade. Straight ahead was a river: that was how much of the wood arrived. To my right, some distance away, sat a house on a hill, and that's where I met Schipper.

The blond, slender, clean-shaven thirty-one-year-old wore blue jeans and a polo shirt. His gold watch looked expensive and his leather boots were nicer than mine. He showed me to his office, leading me through a room where three secretaries worked. The doors were all made of mahogany, he acknowledged, and yes, his large, beautiful desk was solid mahogany, as well. And yes, he did business with Bozovich, one of Peru's largest companies and one of two principal suppliers of mahogany to the United States. But he did not, he repeated several times, mill mahogany himself—that was too controversial, too much of a headache. Rather, the mill processed mainly other red hardwoods, like cedar, and a local tree called *shihuahuaco*.

Schipper put his boots on his desk. His ancestors were Eastern Euro-

pean, he explained to me in Spanish, and had immigrated to Peru generations before. He had no quarrel with *National Geographic,* he wanted to
make clear; he himself had stacks of the magazine at home. He himself
had a degree in forestry engineering from a university in Lima. But, he
said, his business, the timber business—"the *only* business in Madre de
Dios"—was under siege, trying to survive "a wave of environmentalism."

In recent years, he explained, nearly three-quarters of the state had
been made officially off-limits to loggers, placed in sanctuaries for nature
(65 percent) or native peoples (10 percent). "We are the least developed
department in Peru, and the most isolated," he said, and saddled with
policies that left it "no way to develop, no possibility to grow.

"I ask you: what nation in the world can sustain its people on only
25 percent of its available resources?

"To be named the world capital of biodiversity—is that a blessing, or a
curse?"

As Schipper saw it, developed countries—as represented by the World
Bank and the NGOs—wanted to put Peru's forests in preserves, effec-
tively freezing the country's resources, "because the United States and
Europe have no forests of their own left!"

The *interoceánica,* Schipper asserted, could only be good for development. It would, among other things, lower shipping costs, and mean the
wood could be brought to market much sooner, and in better shape. He
talked about the government's new plan for logging concessions, which
was meant to apportion the legal mahogany among players big and small.
If the system worked, he asserted, and smaller, illegal players (he called
them "ants") could be kept out of the woods, why, there was even a
chance that the mahogany could be harvested sustainably.

Schipper talked about mahogany a lot. "In a less developed country,
you need to produce something the world really wants, and what the
world really wants now is mahogany." Its price on world markets now
was two dollars a board foot, several times that of other woods. The law
limiting the harvest of mahogany was misguided because "we have all climax forests. There are really old trees dying in them, and we can't get at
them." But, he repeated, "we do not cut mahogany here." The reason he
kept saying that, I guessed, was that a big problem in Madre de Dios was
that freelance loggers were going deep into forbidden forest, cutting
mahogany, and floating it downriver, then selling it surreptitiously to a

mill, which sold it on the black market. Several people had told me Schipper participated in this market.

We left the office so he could show me the mill. It was getting dark, quitting time. A worker with a submissive demeanor approached Schipper. "Please, sir, would you mind if I took some of those mahogany scraps?"

"Excuse me?"

"Some of that extra mahogany, that's by the gate."

"What mahogany?" Schipper said sternly.

"The mahogany we cut that's by the gate."

"There *is no* mahogany by the gate!" his boss replied, glaring at him.

The man paused for a moment, apparently not comprehending. "Yes, you know. That mahogany we cut."

"There is no mahogany. You can have some of that *tornillo* that's by the gate, if that's what you're thinking of."

"The *tornillo*?"

"Yes. That is all that's by the gate."

The man looked confused, didn't seem to get the message. I could see he was not bound for a management position.

"Thank you, sir."

In an e-mail Schipper sent me some weeks after our interview, he revised his position. He did mill mahogany, he said, sometimes. I was glad to hear him recant, because in denying it he had seemed buffoonish.

It had also made him seem as though he was doing something wrong. And maybe he was—buying wood that had been cut illegally and working to subvert national laws were bad things. But his argument about developing the country by exploiting natural resources deserved a serious hearing. It wasn't merely the self-serving credo of a rapacious businessman; on a larger scale, it was the dilemma faced by practically any country that was trying to feed its people while saving its nature at the same time—which is to say, practically every nation on earth. Peru's great novelist, Mario Vargas Llosa, has grappled with the question at various times, but nowhere more directly than in his 1989 novel, *The Storyteller.*

The book's narrator is a college student in Lima. His classmate, a student of anthropology, takes his championing of Peru's indigenous people to an extreme, eventually going to live among them permanently. But before he leaves, the narrator questions his friend, nicknamed Mascarita:

> Occasionally, to see how far his obsession might lead him, I would provoke him. What did he suggest, when all was said and done? That, in order not to change the way of life and the beliefs of a handful of tribes still living, many of them, in the Stone Age, the rest of Peru abstain from developing the Amazon region? Should sixteen million Peruvians renounce the natural resources of three-quarters of their national territory so that seventy or eighty thousand Indians could quietly go on shooting at each other with bows and arrows, shrinking heads and worshipping boa constrictors? Should we forgo the agricultural, cattle-raising, and commercial potential of the region so that the world's ethnologists could enjoy studying at first hand kinship ties, potlatches, the rites of puberty, marriage, and death that these human oddities had been practicing, virtually unchanged, for hundreds of years? No, Mascarita, the country had to move forward. Hadn't Marx said that progress would come dripping blood? Sad though it was, it had to be accepted. We had no alternative. If the price to be paid for development and industrialization for the sixteen million Peruvians meant that those few thousand naked Indians would have to cut their hair, wash off their tattoos, and become mestizos—or, to use the ethnologists' most detested word, become acculturated—well, there was no way round it.

I'd begun Vargas Llosa's book on a flight to Lima. I finished it in my room at the Hotel Wasai. My country's native peoples were descendants of those who had survived the shock of contact with the European, the genocides of disease and war. Now they, though still marginalized, were part of the body politic. That made it easier to understand the vulnerability of the uncontacted indigenous peoples in Peru, whose concerns could not be considered separately from those of the natural environment. Here, the endangered species included human beings. That made the decisions—and the things that happened without decisions—all the more agonizing.

The rainy season was coming into its own. Almost every December afternoon there were torrential downpours, which emptied the streets of traffic as they filled them with water. The Madre de Dios River, out my window and down the hill, was brown and swollen, touching the trunks of trees along the riverbank. It may have occasionally risen higher than it was right now, but not often. The American forester and environmentalist Aldo Leopold, who never saw the Amazon, was nonetheless fixated by the Madre de Dios River as seen on a map. Ever since the conquistadors, he wrote in 1924,

> some maps of South America have shown a short heavy line running eastward beyond the Andes, a river without a beginning and without an end, and labeled it the River of the Mother of God. That short heavy line . . . has always seemed the perfect symbol of the Unknown Places of the earth.

My room had mildew, yes, and fleas, but I loved being so close to the River of the Mother of God. It was a giant, wild thing. Boats struggled noisily to cross it; I watched them from up on the breakfast floor, satisfied with their difficulty, for I knew this was the last big obstacle to a highway across South America, and I didn't want it to fall quickly.

Back when the River of the Mother of God got its Spanish name, there were no roads through the jungle, only the paths of animals and the paths of the first human beings to live in this place. The only way to get anywhere with any speed—and then only in one direction—was the river itself, one of the traditional roads of the region.

To see where mahogany came from, I had to go up this road. That was the only place mahogany remained. Because a lot of the people up this road were doing something illegal, I thought it best to have a companion. I invited a young Canadian who had spent years in Peru to travel with me. Tim Currie, bespectacled, thinner and taller than I, had a good sense of humor and an easy way with people. Instead of finishing high school, he had come to the Andes to climb mountains, first in Ecuador, then in Peru. In Lima, he had run the South American Explorers Club for five years, so he knew the country well. Now he was living in Portland, Oregon, and preparing to go to college and study geography.

Tim already knew a good boatman, Gilberto Cárdenas. His wooden craft, *El Caballero del Río* (The Gentleman of the River), was typical of the better riverboats of the region: long (41 feet) and narrow, with wooden benches along each side and a roof over the center section, to ward off rain and sun. Power came from a 55-horsepower Marina outboard at the stern. Like me, Gilberto had hired an assistant, a young man named Edilberto, who would work as driver, because running the rivers during rainy season was clearly a two-man job.

Gilberto was known in Puerto Maldonado, as was Tim, and knowing people was the way you got things done here, such as arranging to visit a mahogany camp. Gilberto made inquiries. A friend of his, or maybe it was a relative, had an operation about five days up the river, off the Río Curiacu, which was a tributary of the Río de las Piedras, itself a principal branch of the Río Madre de Dios and nearly as big. Part of the Curiacu could be logged legally, if you had a permit. More of it could not. Where was this camp, exactly? It would be better not to ask, Tim suggested, after I kept asking. We shopped for food, bought rubber boots, and staked Gilberto the cost of a couple of barrels of fuel.

I have floated wild rivers in several countries, but for wildness none come close to an Amazonian river in rainy season. The town docks consisted not of fixed jetties but of small floating platforms that could move up or down the banks depending on how high the river was running. And on the day of our departure, it was running very high, indeed—the highest all season, said Gilberto. There was no bank to speak of, no dirt visible: the water ended in some grass. Our food and fuel packed, Gilberto pulled in the plank that connected us to neighboring boats, took a seat on the bow, dipped his hand in the muddy water, and closed his eyes and crossed himself. Then he caught the eye of Edilberto in the back, and gestured to him to head out.

Within a couple of minutes we were at the confluence of the Madre de Dios and the Río de los Amigos, which defined the other limit of Puerto Maldonado. The murky water roiled and chopped—but it was nothing like the week before, Gilberto said, when boatmen near shore had waved him away from the spot midriver where he was headed. There, he said, waves nearly the height of his boat marked the collision of the two rivers; you never knew how the river would be at any particular moment.

On the other hand, you could sometimes predict. Where the river was wide the horizon was low, and on it you could see a concentration of dark clouds and know that somewhere, miles ahead, rain was falling. If it was a lot of rain, it would translate, three or four or six hours hence, into a higher river.

Volume and waves weren't the only challenges to navigating these rivers. The things they carried were another. Big rainstorms flushed the gullies and gulches of the giant basins that fed the rivers, clearing out months' accumulation of forest flotsam, including branches and sometimes entire trees. Some of these would float. Others would drift just under the surface, with only a small branch visible. So, when the river rose (as it did several times during our journey), the swell was often accompanied by a lot of detritus. Gilberto would then move to the front and hand-signal Edilberto in the back, usually to steer port or starboard, often to slow down.

It took me a while to realize that, in addition to watching out for dangerous wood, Gilberto was also scoping pieces that were valuable: mahogany planks. Mahogany could float, and it was brought to market as rafts—scores of thick, long boards lashed together by rope, typically with a handful of woodcutters seated near the middle with their blankets and belongings, and a single one standing toward the back, wielding a pole for steering. Or there might be a cheaper version of Gilberto's boat in the middle, with boards tied to either side, and sometimes a motor. Occasionally, in rapids or a collision, these rafts would break apart. This was calamitous for the woodcutters, who might see months of labor disappear before their eyes (not to mention that many of them couldn't swim). But to boatmen like Gilberto, who might snag a random board hours or days later, it was like free money: Gilberto had sold a small board for $85 the month before. (*"El dinero hace bailar el mono,"* he liked to say—money makes the monkey dance.)

We passed one mahogany raft our first afternoon; the next day we passed three. The first of these had six young men relaxing on top, dozing on rolled-up blankets. They looked friendly enough; we pulled alongside, and they said I could come on board.

The first plank, dark chocolate in hue, submerged only slightly into the *café con leche*-colored river when I stepped on it, easily holding my weight. I was curious how something so dense and heavy could float. The workers were glad to be coming out, they said; they'd been working in the *monte,* or jungle, for three months. Though this load of wood could be expected to fetch about $16,000, the profit would not accrue to them, but to the boss who sent them. They'd made only about $16 each per day, or $450 apiece total—less charges for food and supplies. From the description of how long they'd been floating, we later concluded that, without a doubt, the wood had been harvested illegally. They even told us they'd had to pay $500 at the "line of control" three days upstream, which they

*Though famously hard and dense, mahogany floats. These woodcutters are guiding
two rafts of boards to market in Puerto Maldonado, Peru.*

should not have had to do if the wood were legal. Nevertheless, they happily showed us the paperwork, or *guía*, that was required to make the
wood appear legal, and thus fetch a premium price. The document said
they had 302 boards, more than 8,000 board feet. That would be just over
a quarter of what was used in the apartment I had seen on Park Avenue,
if the document was accurate (often they were not) and if the wood was
properly sawn (it was still quite rough).

Encounters with human beings became less frequent the further we
got from a real road. We passed a few farms the first day but none after
that. Being near the water and in motion made the air seem cooler,
though it was hot when we stopped. Once, we saw a family of capybaras,
the hog-sized rodents, crossing a sandbar as we came around a bend.
Often we caught flashes of macaws, usually scarlet and usually flying in
pairs. One night we slept on a sandy bank, and in the morning our hands
and legs were covered with bites: sandy places were often infested with
fleas. We all knew to be wary of the swarms of white flies occasionally
visible near the sand at water's edge: these carried leishmaniasis, the

hard-to-treat tropical skin disease that can cause disfiguring lesions and sores, among other maladies.

Still, the river and its surrounds were mysterious and magical, and not only for me. Gilberto told us there was a tree called a *sangapilla* that smelled wonderfully fragrant, but only from a distance—get closer and you couldn't smell it. Then there was the *zorrino*, or *ituto* in native parlance, a long-snouted fox whose meat was bitter unless, according to Gilberto, you cut off its tail immediately after killing it. Another notable feature was its caustic urine, which burned the skin—the fox could flick this through the air with its tail. Oh, and the *gamungo*, a big hawk—if you shot it you had to stomp on it thoroughly, otherwise its meat was too spongy to eat.

The river itself, roiling and unpredictable, was also an object of fascination. Sometimes there were rapids where the water was wide and deep—how could that be? Other times the boat seemed to pause or stall on great upwellings, places where it seemed a giant must be about to emerge from the river bottom. Gilberto told how he had been swimming in the river one day when a whirlpool sucked him under—only to spit him back out thirty feet away. He was not cavalier about the river, didn't joke about it. As we learned on our third day out, his third son—one of five children—had drowned while learning to swim in it.

Our immediate destination was the mouth of the Curiacu River, and we arrived at dusk. The settlement on the left bank, Boca Curiacu, consisted of a sawmill, a small engine shop, and four bars, all crowded onto a narrow strip of land at river's edge. The river ran alarmingly high just a few yards from the open-air, dirt-floored, thatched-roof structures. A sign outside one said in Spanish:

WE SELL
beer
soda
cigarettes
cooking oil
I BUY GOOD WOOD
servicio chicas

Servicio chicas might best be translated "attention from girls."

On the Curiacu River edge of things, there was a stretch of riverbank where a bunch of men were assembling a raft of mahogany boards. They were in the water, on the raft, on the shore, back in the water, tying boards next to each other with rope. Like the other boards I had seen in rafts, these varied in size, but on average were perhaps six to eight feet long, a foot to eighteen inches wide, and two to six inches thick. They were rough-cut, but essentially straight. The wood had obviously been harvested over a period of time; the more freshly cut pieces had a reddish glow that made them stand out from the others.

When the raft-builders had quit for the evening, Gilberto suggested we use the raft as a swimming platform. I'd heard that bathing in the Amazon River wasn't such a good idea, but we desperately needed a clean-up. Tim thought it was probably okay, as long as none of it passed our lips.

We first let ourselves in slowly, then later we jumped—the river was deep. The water felt good. But it was utterly opaque, and disconcerting to have your hand disappear from view the instant it went under the surface. We shampooed. After my hair dried, it felt clean but nevertheless produced a small shower of brown dust on my shoulders whenever I ran my hand through it.

That evening, I had one of the worst night's sleep I'd had since my kids were small. Tim and I each had a small tent, but the recent eroding of the riverbank by high waters had left no ground on which to pitch them. A barkeeper we approached said we could put them on his terrace—it was looking to be a slow night. An hour or two after sundown, we did, and retired.

A large group of woodcutters arrived perhaps an hour after that. They were just down from camp, they had just been paid, and they had money to spend on the overpriced beers—Boca Curiacu bars charged 5 soles ($1.50) a bottle, as compared to 3 soles (90 cents) in Puerto Maldonado. The barkeep cranked up his generator and brought out a pair of giant speakers; he set them up about six feet from our tents. To his credit, he did not otherwise disturb us; and to the woodcutters' credit, none of them did anything worse than occasionally step on us. When I got up in the morning, having slept maybe two hours, I saw that if you were a woodcutter, you sometimes might not have the benefit of any sleeping quarters at all: men were splayed upon benches, on the concrete floor of the patio, on the dirt path that led to the other bars.

One fellow, though, stood clean-shaven, sipping a mug of coffee while looking over the river. He was older, maybe fifty-five, wore a clean shirt, and showed no sign of a hangover. Also, as we later learned, he would not be riding down on a raft, but in a proper boat. We introduced ourselves; he was Romualdo, he said, and he was a *rumbeador*. I was unfamiliar with this term, and he explained: bosses hired him to go into the *monte* and locate mahogany trees. Sometimes this was on land they had permission to log; sometimes it was not. On the land where harvesting was permitted, he said, there was practically no mahogany left. So he ventured further afield, camping out, whacking his way with a machete, wandering through the woods by himself. The work was hard because mahogany did not grow in stands; the trees were always found alone. He could spot one from an uncommonly great distance through the woods, he said, just by a glimpse of the trunk, or sometimes by the plants growing nearby. And how do you mark the trees, I asked him—with plastic tape? I pictured the fluorescent kind that surveyors and tree surgeons use to mark trees that are coming down.

"No, no!" he laughed, amused by my ignorance. "I use a GPS!"

This modern tool of earth awareness, beloved of hikers and geocachers and sold by REI, enlisted in the cause of cutting mahogany trees—and accurate to within a few feet! It was the perfect tool.

Gilberto, who had slept in the boat, summoned me to have a mid-morning beer with a relative who might help us get where we needed to go. This man—I will call him Paco—owned a different bar and sponsored a lumber camp or two. Our drinking began with the ritual sprinkling of the first drops of the bottle on the earthen floor: "Santa Tierra Pachamama," they intoned, the traditional offering to the Incan fertility goddess who could cause an earthquake. There were recollections of smuggling electronics over the Brazilian border in days gone by, before wood became worthwhile. There was an assurance that I would not identify anyone by name, which might get them in trouble, or give the exact location of the camp. And finally there was the appearance of a blond brother, Oreste, who would follow Gilberto's boat up the Curiacu, and take us when it could go no further.

This turned out to be not very far, we discovered, when we set off that afternoon. Though it had less free-floating wood, the Curiacu was narrow and twisting and hadn't seen as many downpours as the Las Piedras. Where it widened, a couple of hours up, Gilberto's boat had too deep a draft and started scraping on the shallow rocks. Tim and I threw our packs into Oreste's boat and, wading in water up to our thighs, helped lift and point Gilberto's boat the right way down the river. He would wait for us back at Boca Curiacu.

The new boat was a rougher, shorter version of Gilberto's. And unlike his smooth 55-horsepower motor, it used the engine typical of woodcutters: a 16-horsepower Briggs & Stratton, jury-rigged with a six-foot propeller shaft. It was loud and percussive, and we thump-thumped our way up the river for many hours before coming to a place along the riverbank that looked to us like any other. But behind foliage lay a narrow inlet. Oreste steered there, tied up, and led us on a trail into the dusky wilderness.

In places the canopy was so dense it was hard to see. Under such conditions, it was especially disconcerting to feel something about the size of a bird whoosh by my face: was it a bird? a bat? a moth? A bat, I concluded, because we saw more as we went, fluttering around just slightly higher than our heads. Other movements, we concluded, were those of monkeys—a whole band of spider monkeys swung by fifteen or twenty minutes into our hike. Then we crossed a stream over a very slippery log, and we were there.

In the clearing were two thatch-roofed structures: a cooking shack, with smoke issuing slowly from the eaves, and a dormitory of sorts, with four raised platforms for sleeping, and mosquito nets around three of them. Laundry hung from lines. There were several chairs, a table, and a stool, all crudely hewn from mahogany.

Resident here were three small children, two women, one boy of about seventeen, three young men in their twenties, and a baby monkey named Susy. We got to know them all a little bit over the next few days. They were poor people, from Puerto Maldonado, from Pucallpa, a jungle town in the north, and from the mountains.

Oreste introduced us to Miguel, whose wife was one of the women and whose toddler was one of the kids. They lived in a third structure in a nearby clearing, along with his sister-in-law, the other woman. Miguel was like the crew boss. He welcomed us and suggested a place to put our tents at the clearing's edge—the same spot where the *rumbeador* had also pitched his tent some weeks before, as it happened.

We met the crew as they returned around dusk: a tall, untamed man with an unusual full beard, named Pablo; a muscular, unassuming man,

Rolando, who looked as Inca as Pablo looked Spanish; and a slight teenager, David. Miguel explained that for the past ten days they'd been working on one tree, cutting it down and sawing it into rough boards. They had finished today. Meanwhile, he himself had felled another big tree a quarter-mile away. The next project, which would begin in the morning, would be to relocate their mini lumber mill from the old site to the new and to reestablish it: the trees had to be sawed where they lay. How else to get them out?

Miguel had shot a wild turkey that day; that would be our dinner. But it wasn't too early to start looking for tomorrow night's meal, and Rolando invited us to go with him. He borrowed the boss's shotgun for the expedition. He gave us the lay of the land as he looked for animals.

All the rain lately could get in the way of work, he acknowledged, and your clothes never really dried. But they were glad of the rain, because they needed it to fill some dry washes that led down to the Curiacu, so that they could float the boards they had cut over the past few weeks, and get them to market. He took us to one such wash, which had only a few inches of standing water in it. "Wild pigs come here at night," he said, pointing out their hoof prints, and then their droppings, floating in the pool. After a big storm, he explained, water would run through here swiftly, a foot or two deep.

Where there was no nearby stream, Rolando explained, they cut their own road. He showed us a stretch of one: it was about ten feet across, just wide enough for rolling a good-sized chunk of trunk down the hill. As we paused to take in this corridor, I noticed a stream of activity down around my boots. It was a causeway of leafcutter ants, many of them with trapezoids of green leaf held aloft in their jaws as they walked from a plant to their underground nest. Giant soldier ants guarded the perimeter, their heads as big as BBs, jaws held open—they were so big they were easy to see with the naked eye, even in low light. This stream of hundreds of thousands of ants extended several yards in either direction, as far as we could see and "much, much further than that," said Rolando. "It's their highway."

Rolando peeked under a few logs for crocodile eggs, but didn't shoot anything that evening. Later he would: on subsequent nights, we would eat monkey and a pretty bird with red plumage. Neither Tim, mainly a vegetarian, nor I was happy eating these things, but it's what we were offered, and there was not much else to eat. The monkey Susy was the

*Miguel's three-year-old daughter,
Nallely, with her pet spider monkey,
Susy. The story of Susy is,
unfortunately, less delightful than
the photo might suggest.*

dear pet of Miguel's daughter, Nallely; the two were fairly inseparable.
Tim correctly guessed that Susy was there because her mother had ended
up in the dinner pot. It's a common story around jungle camps. Back in
Puerto Maldonado, I was told, Oreste had a pet tapir. Same story with
the tapir's mother.

The men listened to a soccer match on a battery-powered AM radio
after dinner, in the dark. When it was over and the radio off, the air filled
with a loud and layered chorus of animal song. Most noticeable at first
was the little, loud-mouthed frog in the slight space between Tim's tent
and mine: it made an unpretty blast like an ambulance coming up in traffic. When it went away, we picked up on castanet frogs, clickity-clacking
rhythmically. Deep in the background came a sound like the deep,
rubber-bandy *bonk! bonk!* of North American bullfrogs, but it was easy to
lose amidst the sharper, higher peeps and tweets that, until you knew
better, sounded as though they were coming from birds but were still
other kinds of frogs. Occasionally something would crash down through
the brush, sounding awfully large—a monkey? a bird? a big bat? Moths
banged headlong into my tent whenever my headlamp was on for more
than a moment.

But the very coolest noise was the roar of the red howler monkeys.
This sounded nothing like the chimpanzee hoot of television and
movies; in fact, I didn't understand how it came from a monkey at all. It

was an extended, whooshy roar, somewhere between the wind howling through trees and a blast furnace. It made you think a twister was about to hit; it rose and fell like the background music to a thriller.

Sometimes the night grew extraordinarily still, preternaturally full—everything had stopped to listen. But never for long.

The next day began with a baby's cry, and ended with the roar of chain saws.

Rolando had been up a while, and when I explained my surprise, saying I'd expected someone who worked hard like him to sleep as late as possible, he replied, *"La cama mata al pobre"* ("Bed kills the poor man"). We accepted tea, which worried Tim because it was only lukewarm, and we had no proof that the water had actually boiled, and thus was safe to drink. (About a month later, we would wonder if that tea was what caused Tim to be hospitalized more than a week with lungworm, a jungle parasite, which I miraculously avoided.) We saw Pablo, a muscular man, scratching away at his thigh, blaming it on a fungus that he said a shot in Puerto Maldonado would clear up right away. He watched with some interest as I applied mosquito repellent, and examined the label on the bottle. "Gasoline works too," he said. We set off into the woods toward the mahogany.

Pablo explained that the *rumbeador* we met had been useful, but a really good *rumbeador* would know in advance which mahogany trees were too decayed to be worth harvesting. About a third had so much decay inside the trunk that it was a waste of time to cut them up, he said. But of course Pablo wouldn't know that until it was too late. "We have to cut them down to see if they're worth keeping" is the way he put it. It reminded me of the line from the Vietnam War, about having to destroy a village in order to save it.

The four workers set off to relocate their mill to the site of the freshly fallen mahogany tree. The old site was about half a mile's walk from camp. It was a clearing, deep in sawdust and littered with branches and fragments of stumps. As with any fresh disturbance in the rain forest, it attracted a million flies, as though the carcass of a dead animal were lying there. Miguel, the boss, confirmed my impression that a lot of the tree had not been used. "We saw it up the best we can," he said, "but there are always rotten parts, and much of it gets wasted."

A portable sawmill reduces mahogany trunks down to
boards that can be carried (or sometimes floated, on
seasonal streams) from the forest down to the river.
Note the flies on Pancho's back!

The main components of the mill were a shiny steel saw blade with carbide tips, at least a yard in diameter, and a Briggs & Stratton engine identical to those that powered the workers' boats up and down the rivers. It seemed to me these engines, as much as anything, made possible the commercial exploitation of trees from the rain forest. They were known by their onomatopoetic nickname, *peque-peque*, which describes the sound they make, at least when they're idling. Once they're gunned, their roar is hard to find a word for.

The men all had their shirts off now, and flies covered their torsos when they stood still, which was not often. Rolando used a length of rope to strap the engine directly to his back, without any pads or cushioning.

The engine appeared to be half his size. He had only rubber flip-flops on his feet. He set off down the trail, Pablo not far behind with the giant saw blade tied to *his* back—again with no cushions, the carbide blade tips just inches from his skin. Miguel carried two chain saws, one with the longest blade I'd ever seen—over a yard long. He and David, the teenager, wore an ankle-high version of the cheap rubber boots I had on. David carried jerry cans of the fuel and oil that would power this machinery.

The procession rested about twenty minutes later, next to a very large tree that had recently been felled. It rested in the middle of a long space just slightly larger than itself. The trunk was nearly five feet across at the base, and it was hard to take our eyes off the place where it had been cut through: it was bright red, the most striking thing in sight. It was almost pornographic, the way the tree's insides had been laid bare like this.

The long, straight trunk of the mahogany tree brought down all manner of smaller trees, vines, and understory plants when it fell. They were tangled up all around the periphery, in such profusion that the workers found it easier to climb up onto the trunk and walk down it to get to the

Woodcutters at the camp I visited, near Peru's Río Curiacu, pose atop their trophy.
Left to right: Rolando ("Pikachu"), Miguel (the boss), David ("Shakira"),
and Pablo ("Barbas").

other end of the clearing. I watched as they hopped aboard, treading briskly upon their trophy.

I felt less comfortable, hopping aboard. The scene looked like others I'd seen in photos: hunters standing atop their fallen walrus, or whale, triumphant after bringing down a creature much larger than themselves.

The workers decided to build the sawmill at the far end, and set about clearing a space for it with machetes. I arrived at the top of the tree. It was big-leaf mahogany, *Swietenia macrophylla*—an odd name for something that, I could now see, had tiny leaves. Furthermore, all the leaves were concentrated near the top: like other rain-forest trees, it competed for light up at the crowded canopy of the jungle. The trunk was essentially long and bare, its smoothness interrupted only by some encircling vines. Producing leaves that were confined to the shady understory would be a waste of the tree's energy.

As the workers hacked and swung their machetes, the sun bore down through the new hole in the canopy and the flies massed. Pablo's sweaty back was covered with them. I returned to the big end of the fallen tree and stood back a ways in the woods, hoping the flies wouldn't notice me. Miguel fired up the Stihl chain saw and sunk its giant blade into the flesh of the trunk at the other end.

It began to rain lightly, then heavily. Smoke and steam from the hot two-cycle engine drifted through the air. My view turned a bit more gray, but with one exception: remoistened by the rain, the trunk of the mahogany became a deeper, more brilliant red than before, almost like a switch had been turned on inside. It demonstrated how varnish, polyurethane, French polish—human contrivances—do nothing more than bring out a color of the wood that was already there. A color of life.

A neighboring camp was floating a raft of logs down the Curiacu, so Tim and I said goodbye to our camp and left to float down with them. They said I could pilot the raft, so I took off my shoes and rolled up my pants and climbed aboard. They gave me a very long pole. It was like punting in Cambridge, England, one of my favorite parts of graduate school, only this was better: the river was wild, my companions were rough, and the water felt warm and good around my bare feet.

Oreste came alongside in his motorized boat, and the workers splashed him. The mood was festive: they were headed out of the woods, and back into town. I didn't want to surrender my command, but as we approached Boca Curiacu, I thought I'd better, because joining the Río de las Piedras would be like merging onto the Cross Bronx Expressway from a dirt road, and I was a student driver.

Their plan was to dock in Boca Curiacu for the night, and I can't really explain how or why it went wrong, except that the landing required the assistance of Oreste—to keep the raft against the shore, as we rounded the corner and flowed into the powerful current of the big river—and Oreste wasn't a very competent boatman. He arrived where he needed to be a few crucial seconds late, and tried to compensate by pushing the raft too hard: his boat rode up on the boards, submerging some of them. The workers pushed him off, but the damage was done: a few boards came loose and started to float away, like money blowing down a street. When his boat veered around after them, its propeller crossed another part of the raft, freeing a couple more planks. He managed to recover all but one or two of them, then headed back to where we stood on the riverbank. The water was running exceptionally high, taking pieces of earth with it from under our feet, and exposing Boca Curiacu's archaeological past: stratum upon stratum of Cusqueña beer bottles, hundreds or thousands of them. I looked up as Oreste tossed us a rope to draw him in, then realized the other end of it wasn't tied to anything.

Back in Puerto Maldonado, the wood was unloaded and "certified," the board ends marked with colored chalk to keep count of each lot. From storage yards such as the one by the port from which we departed and to which we returned, or others such as the one at Schipper's mill, loads were dispatched to trucking companies for transit across the Andes. The wood went first to Lima and from there, in all likelihood, to the United States, perhaps New York. Some of the wood-carrying trucks took a different route over the mountains, not to Cuzco but to Puno. And of course they took passengers, atop the wood. One of them was me.

As the wood climbed out of the Amazon basin, higher and higher into the Andes, the day grew dark and the air thinner and cooler. My companions were a welder, a mom with a toddler, and two teenage sisters with matching Shakira T-shirts. We tied a tarp across the top of the truck's bed as rain began to fall again. Sometime in the middle of the night, the road became paved; the truck sped up and the breeze was cold,

The road from the rain forest up over the Andes is often abysmal,
especially in rainy season.

but I took enjoyment from the smoother ride and increased speed—to the prospect of leaving the backwoods and finding good food, a good bed, and fast internet service.

Under a blanket against the dark boards, I thought about the things I'd miss when I left Peru, like the great rivers and remote forest and, for some reason, the sloth at the Wasai hotel, the *perezoso*. I knew that land adjacent to the Wasai was being considered as the location of one end of the suspension bridge that would cross the Madre de Dios—and, as was confirmed in coming years, that's exactly where it would go. It was to be named the Puente Billinghurst, after an early president of the republic, and it would be the largest bridge in Peru. Debris from construction would fall down on the hotel.

I thought about how, over the thousands of years it took to evolve, the *perezoso* had never been at a real disadvantage for being slow. I was told that, when a *perezoso* wanted to cross a river, it simply walked in, closed its eyes, and then paddled slowly, slowly, until its feet touched the bottom again. If that bottom was on the opposite side, it was in luck; if not, no matter. It would just set off again.

But within ten years, people said—maybe sooner—the bridge would be complete and there would be a through road. And soon the road, like other new roads, would be busy. And, while the Wasai's *perezoso* might still make its way across the river, I didn't think it could ever make it across that road.

ROAD OR NOT A ROAD?

A ROAD IS A ROAD IS A ROAD. Except when it's not.

Just as a guinea pig in the Andes is less likely to be found in a terrarium in a child's room than on a platter at dinner, so there are paths that might look like roads but are not really roads as we understand them. Not roads, that is, built with purely utilitarian intent, to help move people and things from one place to another. They are roads built with other things in mind.

Some extra-wide Inca roads, as mentioned, were reserved for rulers and their emissaries. They functioned as symbols of an empire's dominion over subject tribes.

To the north, in Central America, the Maya (A.D. 200–1000) and civilizations that preceded them left behind their own special kind of road, the *sacbe*, or "white road." *Sacbes* were paved ways of stone that often used a limestone mortar. Some were also extra wide—up to fifty feet. Many connected ceremonial centers, often pyramids or burial mounds; alongside them have been found shrines, places to burn incense, and stone vessels for water storage, suggesting that they were traveled by pilgrims.

But other qualities set them apart from ordinary roads. One is that *sacbes* are perfectly straight—always. Not a single one curves. This meant a lot of extra work: in the Yucatán near Cobá, a ceremonial center and hub of *sacbes*, a pair of paths runs parallel across the land like a miniature divided highway. Then comes Lake Macanxoc. Instead of curving slightly to avoid the lake, one of the pair runs directly through it. The water is not terribly deep there, but in order for the *sacbe*'s surface to remain above water level, obviously, its foundation had to be built up from the lake bottom.

Other *sacbes* are elevated a few inches or feet for no obvious reason; sometimes they look like a very low wall running across the landscape.

The longest *sacbe* from Cobá extended sixty-two miles and was originally two to eight feet high, with sides built of blocks of cut stone. The first time I saw a photograph of a reconstructed one, traversing a field, its brightness and designed-for-walking scale reminded me of the yellow brick road—if the yellow brick road had been ramrod straight. Evidence supports the idea that *sacbes* were aligned with constellations. But it's speculation that the white color made it easier for *sacbes* to be traveled at night.

To a kid growing up in Denver, Colorado, in the 1960s and 1970s, "ancient roads" were in Europe. In fact, there were ancient roads less than five hundred miles away, in northwestern New Mexico near the Four Corners area. Some of these, probably built by Pueblo people between A.D. 900 and 1130, converge in Chaco Canyon, which was not explored by an archaeologist until 1896. It took even longer to appreciate the extent of the nearly two hundred miles of ancient road that are known to exist in the area. Unlike many of the Mayan *sacbes*, the Chacoan roads are usually very hard to see from the ground. As with the desert figures in Nazca, many weren't discovered until air travel made it possible to see them from the sky.

They had other things in common with the Nazca Lines: instead of being built up like the *sacbes*, they were scraped so that their surfaces were slightly below grade, with stones sometimes demarcating the edges. This resulted in the "roadbed" having a lighter color and different texture than the surrounding soil.

But like the Mayan roads, the Chacoan roads were perfectly straight, they were built near ceremonial centers, they sometimes came in parallel sets, and they were oriented toward the stars.

The longest and best-known is the Great North Road. From the ruins at Pueblo Alto, which was the nexus of several roads, the Great North Road extends about thirty-one miles on a path heading almost exactly true north, ending dramatically at an isolated canyon where there is evidence of wooden stairways and platforms that allowed descent straight down the canyon walls. Like most Chacoan roads, it has a width of about thirty feet—wider than many of today's two-lane highways. For one long stretch it has a parallel road a few yards away; an aerial survey in 1983 discovered a short section with *four* parallel roads.

The San Juan Basin, which these roads traverse, is an open, arid land of expansive views dotted with buttes and small hills. There is scattered sagebrush and grasses. The Puebloan peoples of the Chaco culture built many great houses of up to several hundred units, often with large ceremonial kivas. Archaeologists at first assumed the great houses were like little towns and that the roads connected them to each other, allowing for the transportation of goods for trade. But closer examination turned these assumptions on their heads. Many of the roads do not go to great houses at all; they lead to outsized features of the natural landscape such as pinnacles, springs, or now-dried-up lakes. Other roads leave the great houses but peter out only a few hundred yards away from the buildings.

And though their ruins remind us of towns, the great houses apparently were not designed for ongoing habitation at all. Evidence suggests that they were occupied only occasionally, perhaps in conjunction with seasonal visitations by large numbers of pilgrims. Exactly how the pilgrims used the roads is unknown. Archaeologists have found large quantities of pottery shards not in the great houses but along the roads; the earthenware was not made locally but carried in from the Chuska Mountains to the west, perhaps with the goal of being intentionally broken as an act of ritual.

Today's Pueblo peoples (a group that includes the Hopi, Zuñi, Keres, and Jemez) still occupy large parts of this region, and have ties to the old ways. Their traditions vary, of course, but they have in common the idea that souls live underground (as in a canyon; kivas were also sunk into the ground) and that certain sites, like Chaco Canyon, are sacred; and the solar calendar often specifies the timing of ritual journeys to certain mountains, canyons, lakes, and caves that represent *shipapu*—that is, places of emergence, portals to the spirit underworld. The road to the *shipapu*, frequently described as "straight," is depicted in a nineteenth-century ethnographer's report as "crowded with spirits returning to the lower world, and spirits of unborn infants coming from the lower world," which suggests that the roads weren't exclusively for the use of the living.

Many Pueblo communities reenact creation and emergence events around important solar times like the solstice. Phillip Tuwaletstiwa, a Hopi, attended numerous *niman* ceremonies at the end of which "the kachinas leave, they exit the village on a particular path, and they just disappear off into the countryside, it's called *they're going home*" in the Hopi language.

Now retired, Tuwaletstiwa was deputy director of the National Geodetic Survey, a branch of the National Oceanic and Atmospheric Administration. He has assisted in surveys of great houses and documented the ways in which they were laid out in alignment with cardinal directions and the stars. A common feature of a Chacoan great house, he told me, is an enclosing berm with cutouts where segments of roads come into it. These roads remind him of the paths where kachinas would exit the pueblo in Hopi ceremonies; he suspects that the way many such roads peter out not far from the great houses means that they were ceremonial, "and that the passages into and out of the Great Houses were probably covered [tunnel-like, with wood or other material] to make it seem like people were emerging [from the underworld] who came out of them" during ceremonies.

The longer roads were virtually unknown until fifty or sixty years ago, "because you just couldn't see them." Many were revealed by satellite images. From ground level, he says, the uninitiated have little chance of spotting a road unless they're with someone who can help them and "unless you've got oblique light." In other words, direct overhead light renders them practically invisible. Winter is the best time to search for east–west roads, because the sun shines from lower on the horizon. For north–south roads, sunrise and sunset are the best times, and "around the equinox is even better, because then the sun's more east or west."

Tuwaletstiwa appreciates that expectation might also play a role—and not always a helpful one. Near Kutz Canyon, where the Great North Road abruptly ends in a series of now-broken stairs and scaffolds, many maps show a short road branching off northwest ("at about a 300 degree azimuth") toward a ruin known as Salmon. He was exploring the area with a fellow enthusiast who took him "out there to see a cut through a dune," which showed the supposed path of the ancient road. But Tuwaletstiwa doubts it, as he said most experts do now. That particular road "is like an urban legend—a Chacoan legend, if you will—that got on the map maybe forty years ago when people thought these places would [naturally] be connected." But that's when they still thought these roads were like other roads. Now that we're pretty sure they're not, he wishes people would stop copying the old maps and also, really, stop calling them roads, because "roads are utilitarian, and these were not. It'd be better just to call them pathways."

The ancients could do even better than that. According to research by Anna Sofaer, an archaeoastronomer, the word "road" translates in Tewa, a Pueblo language, as "channel for the life's breath."

TWO

SLIPPING FROM SHANGRI-LA

THE LINE OF FORTY WALKERS moved quickly, which was good for keeping warm but bad for keeping my balance. Because we were walking on ice, a frozen river. The Zanskar, walled in on both sides by a towering gorge, is the closest thing Zanskaris have to a winter road—the only link, once snow begins to fall, between their Himalayan villages and the outside world. And it's only there for a little while, in deepest winter, when the river's surface freezes enough to support human footsteps.

Zanskar is part of Ladakh—the eastern, Buddhist part of the Indian state of Jammu and Kashmir. At about 11,500 feet above sea level, it has long been defined by remoteness. The valley has the feel of a cul-de-sac, because there is only one traditional road in and out—a dirt track from Kargil, an untouristed and predominantly Muslim town just a couple of miles from the disputed border (or "Line of Control") with Pakistan, to Padum, the main town of Zanskar. Summers are short here, and the Kargil road is only reliably open four or five months a year, from the end of May to early October. After that, snow makes it impassable and the valley gets very, very quiet. Another road has been promised: construction has begun on an all-weather route through the gorge. But it's a very big, very expensive project, and appears to be years away from completion. So for now, as they have for probably hundreds of years, Zanskaris rely on a traditional way in and out: an ice road, a forty-mile trail upon the frozen surface, which is called the *chaddar*.

The walkers were mostly teenagers. They had maxed out the educational opportunities in Reru, their medieval hamlet, and were taking advantage of the cold to get out of Dodge—to make their way to boarding schools in Srinagar, the summer capital of Jammu and Kashmir, and in Leh, the capital of Ladakh, not far from the end of the *chaddar* along the Indus River. They also were taking advantage of scholarships, offered

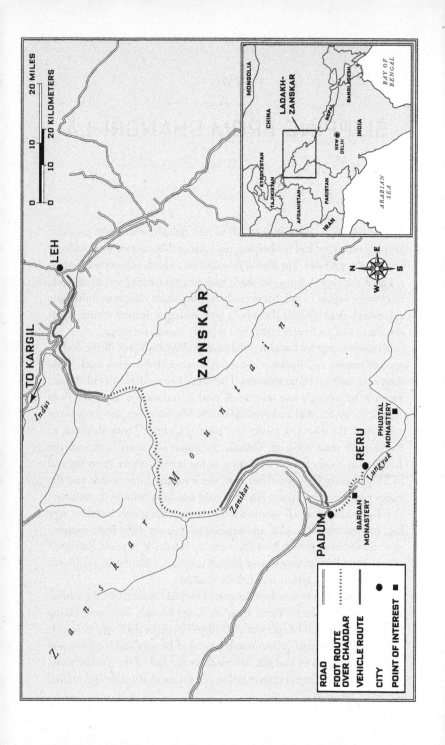

*In the coldest part of winter, Ladakhi teenagers bound for boarding school leave
their remote valley via the frozen river trail known as the* chaddar.

by Europeans sympathetic to young Tibetan Buddhists in this poor, traditional part of the world.

To claim their new lives, the teenagers of Reru had to do just two hard
things. They had to leave their ancestral home. And they had to go by
way of a frozen river. But they would not have to go alone. A number
of male relatives would accompany the group—as well as a handful of
students from even smaller, outlying villages. Last, there would be me
and my guide, Seb Mankelow (an Englishman who was first drawn to
Zanskar as a climber, then studied its agriculture as a graduate student,
and now welcomed any chance to go back), and my interpreter, Dorjey
Gyalpo (a clerk for the local government who was both a deeply religious
Buddhist and a worldly Renaissance man, fluent in Harry Potter and
eager to discuss the recent eclipse of the sun)—plus our cook and four
porters. So, in all, about forty people walking the *chaddar*'s ice. As fast as
we could.

Walking fast shortened the trip, allowing the students to carry few
clothes and little food. Raised on steep mountains at high altitude, the
Zanskaris were adept at walking fast, even on ice. I was not. The ice

could be extraordinarily slippery. Sometimes it wasn't—sometimes it was dimpled or topped with rough crystals or had dirt frozen in, so your boots could get a purchase. But most times it was the very soul of slipperiness, smooth like a mirror or, even worse, smooth like a mirror hidden under a thin layer of snow.

And here and there, there are breaches, most often toward the middle, where it is perfectly possible to step into open water. Depending on the light and the sky, the water will be pitch-black or pellucid blue, the surface rippled by crystals of ice, a giant moving Slurpee, swirling around frozen banks and then disappearing under sheets of ice. And even the frozen surface does not stay still. At night, sometimes, you hear the loud reports of the ice cracking. And, during the day, the *chaddar* can change while you are on it. You take a step and hear a deep *whump* and feel a loss of elevation of maybe an inch or so and think *uh-oh*.

Villages in the Himalayan mountains are among the most remote on earth. That isolation goes hand-in-hand with religiosity: Ladakh, in eastern Kashmir, has long been a center of Tibetan Buddhism. Stunning monasteries perch on hillsides (local families still try to send one son to become a monk, and thus earn merit), and rare is the road or trail that does not feature a *chorten*—a whitewashed shrine on the corner of which walkers place a pebble, as they walk around clockwise—or a *mani* pile: a long, thick wall of small flat stones, each engraved in Tibetan script with the mantra especially revered by devotees of the Dalai Lama, *om mani padme hum*.

The road connecting Zanskar to Kargil was not completed until 1980. Even during the short summer months when the road is open, travel in a bus or four-wheel-drive vehicle takes at least eight hours, and may take much longer. My first ride out of Zanskar one June was delayed when a dramatic slide of rocks and mud came to a stop across the road just in front of us; passengers in taxis and a bus piled out and began working as a group to clear the road. Later in the day, another slide roared through a ravine we had crossed maybe two minutes before.

This limited access to the outside world; the traditional, organic architecture of its buildings; its friendly, attractive inhabitants; its traditional social arrangements; and the frequent absence of features of modern life that people in the West take for granted (round-the-clock electricity, phone service, crime, drugs, the stresses of fast-paced living) might evoke the idea of Shangri-La, of an alpine utopia. In the novel *Lost Horizon* (1933), the basis of the movie that popularized the idea of Shangri-La, James Hilton conjured up a hidden valley run by enlightened and ageless lamas who jealously guard their isolation, knowing that paradise could be ruined by exposure to the outside world—a place that, in the wake of World War I, appeared to the lamas (and to Hilton) to be veering toward self-destruction.

This idea of alpine paradise, of innocence in a setting of natural beauty, preserved by isolation, has certainly endured in the West—and the American West. High alpine cul-de-sacs like Aspen or Telluride, Colorado, cultivated this mystique, especially in the years before they became jet-setter destinations. Even down in smoggy Denver people loved the idea of Shangri-La. A hundred yards from the semi-suburban house in which I spent my teenage years, in fact, a businessman built a replica of the gleaming white mansion/lamasery from the movie *Shangri-La.* His property was on a bit of a rise and he had a nice view of the Rocky Mountains, but, alas, he was irretrievably on the plains: an iron gate had to substitute for a blizzardy mountain pass when it came to keeping the outside world at bay.

But Zanskar—Zanskar was the real thing. I wondered: Did people there feel they lived in paradise? Were they wary of the outside world?

It seemed an especially good place to ask these questions because roads figured into the answers. High above the *chaddar,* at both ends of the gorge, cuts blasted out of the rock were the beginnings of an all-winter road the government wanted to build in order to make Zanskar accessible to the outside world year-round. Who wanted that road? Who did not? And until it was finished, who dared to walk the *chaddar*?

I took two trips to find out, the first in the summer of 2004 and the second the following winter.

In June, I traveled by bus from Leh, the pretty but touristy capital of Ladakh, to Kargil, and from there by four-wheel-drive truck to Padum. Though Leh and Padum were less than seventy miles apart as the crow flies, the trip took two full days of travel—it was less direct and had more ups and downs than even the road from Cuzco to Puerto Maldonado. The high snows were melting and the rivers were high, but the climate was arid, the slopes mostly brown. Scenery included giant glaciers and vistas across ranges much higher than the Rocky Mountains, a daunting and inhospitable landscape that, though lightly populated, was fervently disputed: Pakistani forces had infiltrated and attacked Kargil in 1999, prompting a mobilization of at least 20,000 Indian troops. In Leh I was less than one hundred miles from Tibet, and even closer to India's disputed border with China. And from Kargil it was only about three hundred miles to Afghanistan, where NATO forces battled the Taliban insurgency.

But when I crossed the Pensi La pass and entered Zanskar, it was easy to forget all that. The wide valley was sparsely settled. Near streams the land was irrigated and green with fields of barley, lentils, and potatoes. The summer was short, so everybody seemed to be outside: children clad in robes walked alongside their mothers by the roads or worked in fields; Buddhist monks in maroon robes were commonplace; a golden light of evening warmed the cool breeze. There wasn't much traffic and there was plenty of space; people seemed happy and friendly.

Accompanied by Seb and Dorjey, I talked to road crews, government officials, the titular king of Zanskar (now a schoolteacher), teenage ponymen, and many monks; and we trekked to the fabulous cliffside monastery of Phugtal, several stories tall, stopping along the way to visit with Buddhist nuns.

And then in early 2005, just when it was getting really, really cold in Zanskar, I went back to see the valley's other face—the frozen side. And that's how I found myself, on a February day as snow swirled and people huddled in their winter kitchens around stoves fired by dried animal dung, sitting in the tiny village of Reru in the house of its headman, among people preparing to do something scary and risky that on the one hand was going to make some of them very sad—and that was, on the other hand, a glorious expression of hope.

Lobzang Tashi was a fifty-year-old widower with seven children and many counselors. As headman of Reru, he had a big decision to make: when the group should head down the *chaddar*.

Lobzang took his duties seriously. The *chaddar* journey with children happened once a year, at most—and this year one of his own daughters would be part of it. By late January, reports from travelers were dribbling in. The ice was pretty good, said many; there was little open water. A little soft yet, said others. He spoke with other parents and with elders in

The village of Reru, a medieval warren of mud-brick houses in the Zanskar valley

the village of 250 people. He went down to the river himself—Reru is perched on a steep hillside about three hundred feet above the Lungnak River, a tributary of the Zanskar, which is in turn a tributary of the Indus. The Lungnak seemed pretty well frozen, but it was smaller than the Zanskar. Lobzang then did what any reasonable person would do: he consulted a monk.

The monk, thin, thirtyish, and wearing the traditional maroon *goncha*, a woolen robe tied at the waist, arrived from a village several hours' walk upstream. He sat cross-legged with a number of the men on a rug atop an earthen floor, drinking salt tea. After a while, the monk took out his packet of hand-painted prayer texts and began chanting quietly. The others continued to converse. Then he finished and arose; deciding upon a date would take him a day or two, he said, and in the meantime he'd return to the monastery. A messenger would return with the news.

While we waited, I got to know the village.

Five girls were going, and four boys, all from different families. In the entire village, perched on a mountainside, there were only twenty-five houses, so the journey was a major event for the community. A number of fathers, uncles, and brothers would accompany the group, as well as a handful of boys who wanted to take a look at Leh.

The village was an intriguing medieval warren of mud-brick houses three and four stories high, some whitewashed, uneven and irregular. Roofs were flat and often piled high with hay and the dried animal dung that fueled stoves; tattered strings of prayer flags fluttered over many. The ground level was devoted to animals: sheltered spaces where goats and oxen and dzos (a yak-cow mix) could spend the winter. Every day they were walked to water. Not all the houses were stand-alone; many adjoined others, sharing walls (and probably some heat). There was no electricity except for a few small solar-powered, fluorescent fixtures distributed by the government. Rooms on the corner of a house could be quite chilly; Seb and I shared one in Lobzang's house, and always had our parkas on. Lobzang would light a fire in its stove every morning to help us out of bed; the warmth lasted about an hour before dissipating through the barely caulked windows. When we finally left the room, several days after arriving, we noticed that the snow that had fallen off our backpacks in a corner had never melted.

We walked around the village to meet students in the days before departure. Stanzin Zoma, sixteen, was in the kitchen with her mom and dad, two younger sisters, and a grandmother. After she served tea, I asked her about the trip. It would be her first time on the *chaddar*, she said, and her first time to Leh. "I am packing wool socks, wool clothes, a sleeping bag and pad, gloves, butter, cheese, *tsampa* [roasted barley flour, a local staple, that a traveler could mix with tea], baked bread, sugar, and tea. Also, pictures of my family, my house, my aunt and uncle, my village, and my school." She would also bring a single pair of silver earrings, her only jewelry. Though a fire was burning in the small stove on the floor, it was cold inside the low-ceilinged kitchen. We sat cross-legged on rugs. Almost everyone in the room wore a hat, except for Stanzin. "I am worried about leaving my parents here and being alone. And about the *chaddar*: they say that sometimes you have to take off your shoes and walk through the water—I think that is scary. But I have my best friend, Sonam Dolma, and she will walk with me. I would like to become a doctor, because there are no doctors here." Stanzin seemed mature and responsible and probably the least worried person in the room.

Her friend, Sonam Dolma, lived in a house with a brighter, sunnier main room that had pillows on the floor. She wanted to be a doctor, too—people had only traditional medicine to treat their coughs, earaches, bad backs, and dental problems, she explained. She seemed nervous but not upset. In fact, she said, she'd been at a party the night before with other girls her age, at which lots of special food was served. Some of her formality melted away as she described in detail the dishes they'd eaten—the *momos*, or meat dumplings; the egg curry; the special *tsampa*. Like Stenzin she said she would miss her family, but she explained that leaving would be easier because her father and brother would walk on the *chaddar* with her. Sonam seemed bright-eyed and on the tips of her toes, and I got the feeling that both she and her friend were excited about the prospect of busting out of their little village, at least for a while.

That was clearly not the case, however, with Tunzin Thongdol, at fourteen the second youngest of Lobzang's seven children, and the first one to have the opportunity to leave. She didn't want to go at all. Apparently she viewed me and Seb as harbingers of departure, and tried very hard not to talk to us—we'd been living in the house for at least three days before we even knew she was there. But Lobzang coaxed/compelled her out of her room and into the winter kitchen. "I don't feel good about leaving," she said. "I've never left home before, and I don't want to leave my family." I had some more questions, but Tunzin couldn't bear them; she fled back into her room.

Also upset was the mother of Thinlay Angmo, seventeen—she broke down in tears as Thinlay listed for me the things she'd miss about home: "family, mountains, school, the land—I will miss them all." Like all the other girls, Thinlay made tea and served it to us herself. Her hands, when she passed me the steaming hot teacup, were callused and able to withstand a lot of heat: all of the girls spent hours a day around the hearth. However, said the petite young woman, "I'm not going to miss some of my chores." (Teenage girls were depended on heavily by most families to do all manner of jobs, from cooking to caring for animals and younger siblings. Two people told me, in fact, that Thinlay's mother was possibly most upset about all the additional work she would now have to do.)

The three boys professed not to be worried at all. Two had been to Leh already, one via the *chaddar;* Tenzin Namdol, fifteen, said it was "no problem. I'm a fast walker." Another, handsome Lobzang Teshi, came from a family that was noticeably poorer than the others. Their kitchen was dark and dusty; his mother and siblings wore tattered clothes. His father, he explained, had died a few years before. His mother prayed that he'd eventually be able to support the family from afar.

All three of the boys wanted to become engineers; an engineer, to each of them, was a man who supervised road construction (and got paid well for it). "Roads are very important to our lives," explained Tenzin Namdol.

Exhibit A was the dirt road that ran by the village's edge. Reru had been linked by the road to Padum, about twelve miles downriver, just a few years before. Government crews were now using the warm months to extend the road to Reru further up its valley. Their progress was slow because at many points the valley wall was pure rock.

But the road by Reru was part of a much bigger effort to connect Zanskar to the rest of India. India's objectives, like the goals behind many roads, were multiple, and they were interrelated: economic development, national integration, and national security—particularly the last. Because, though exceedingly remote, Zanskar was not far from geopolitics. During the brief Kargil War of 1999, Pakistani troops took up positions inside India; their artillery shells killed several farmers near Kargil before the troops withdrew. But what raised the stakes of territorial disputes over this and other parts of Kashmir were weapons of a different order of magnitude. The border skirmishes—some of which erupted on freezing glaciers, far from any settlement—mattered because India and Pakistan were both nuclear states, presumably with warheads aimed at each other.

A history of fractious relations with China, the other northern neighbor, complicated matters further. In 1950 the Chinese invaded Tibet, resulting in the exodus to India of thousands of refugees including, in 1959, the Dalai Lama. Monks from Zanskar and other parts of Ladakh were cut off from Tibetan monasteries to which they had been connected for centuries. In 1962 the Chinese pushed farther, occupying parts of eastern Ladakh as well as another region of northern Kashmir. One map I bought in China, published in Singapore in 2005, showed all of Kashmir within China's national boundaries, though a dotted line around it said "subject to dispute." Sensitivity over the issue led to the closure to outsiders of many beautiful valleys north and east of Leh, and the border with China, as of my visits, remained off-limits. At the same time, relations between China and India, the two developing giants, seemed to be warming; commercial ties between them were growing. The more ongoing problem was Pakistan.

In fact, several people I met in Ladakh observed that nothing would be likely to accelerate construction of the *chaddar* road more than tension with Pakistan. The reason was military and economic. Both sides of the India-Pakistan border were heavily militarized; India's had thousands of soldiers, many of them in Leh. Feeding them was expensive, because for much of the year, winter snow prevented highway access from the south. Food had to be flown in. An all-season road through Zanskar, linking Leh and the border region to Manali, in Himachal Pradesh state, and to other points south, would ultimately save the military a great deal of money.

It would also help consolidate India as a nation. Many Zanskaris barely felt part of India at all; people departing on a trip to the south would say, "I'm going to India for a while," as though they were not already in it. And indeed, the mainly Buddhist Zanskaris felt a greater kinship to the Tibetan Buddhists across the border in China than they did to local speakers of Hindi. The Indians considered the Zanskaris a "scheduled tribe," meaning a group with its own ethnic background that was poorly integrated into the nation and required special attention, such as federal grants for things like medical care and education. The classification was designed in part to quash any separatist sentiment and to encourage the building of a unified nation.

Most Zanskaris seemed to favor the road. One of the reasons was politics: at present, Zanskar's affairs were administered not by Leh, the closest city and the most Buddhist, but by Kargil. And Kargil was Muslim. As one Zanskari observed to me, in Kargil, when a soccer team from India was playing a soccer team from Pakistan, the crowd watching on television normally cheered for Pakistan. (I did not have to ask whom the Zanskaris would cheer for if Tibet fielded a team.) A direct all-season road to Leh would consolidate Buddhist political power.

Another reason was business. Locals expected growth as roads brought more visitors into Zanskar, and major players were already jostling for position. The developer of a new commercial building in "downtown" Padum was none other than Phugtal monastery. A monk was the general contractor.

But other religious people—and almost everybody I met in Zanskar seemed pretty religious—had their doubts. The aging headman of Stongde, a village between Padum and the *chaddar* that was benefiting from road construction employment, said he felt sure that the road would make people less religious. As life sped up, he said, people would have less time to pray. And strangers would arrive, people with different beliefs. Urgan Tundup, the monk who ran the Bardan monastery, was also skeptical. Bardan was directly on a dirt road to Reru, and already the blasting by road crews had shattered several of their windows, he said. The ruckus was not conducive to worship.

The price of an all-season road into Zanskar would also be high in rupees. And it would take a toll on the environment: the chosen route would lead right into the pristine Zanskar River canyon, home of the *chaddar,* a corridor people couldn't even get into most of the year. Still, local enthusiasm for the idea of a year-round connection to the outside world was overwhelming. And it felt strange to notice myself nodding in agreement with those conservative, religious few who were most worried; you didn't need to be terribly worldly to appreciate that the cost of a new road might be considerable in terms of lost serenity, lost culture, lost paradise.

A note from the monk arrived for Lobzang Tashi. It said Saturday, February 5, was auspicious. The Reru village headman immediately spread the word.

But word came back that people in the outlying villages needed one more day to get ready. So Lobzang compromised in the traditional way: on the auspicious day, he staged a mock departure.

Seven of the nine students from Reru participated, along with a small number of spectators, mostly kids. They gathered in the center of town—an open, snow-packed area with a community center on one side, a stone outcropping on another, and in the middle (nobody could tell me why) a large, unused fuel tank upon which a few children sat. Lobzang chanted from a prayer book held in one hand; with the other, he swung a censer filled with burning juniper twigs, a common element of many Buddhist *pujas,* or prayer rituals. The teenage boys, meanwhile, put out the cigarettes they had been smoking, shouldered their rucksacks—mostly empty—and, joined by the girls, walked single file through the snow away from town and down the valley, until they were out of sight. Five minutes later, they turned around and came back.

Final preparations now began in earnest. In a room on the lower level of Lobzang's house, a group of men put finishing touches on a small sled made of bent branches of wild rose with strips of black plastic tubing nailed on as runners. This Lobzang could pull with a rope that he either tugged or tied around his waist—it was an ice trailer. And when it wasn't on ice, Lobzang demonstrated, the framework could easily be fitted with straps to allow it to be carried as a backpack. In other houses, bread was baked, *tsampa* mixed, amulets wrapped, clothing mended and laid out. Siblings watched, mothers feared, and everyone was worried and excited.

Early on departure day, the whole village came out into the chilly, overcast morning. Mothers were clustered in the middle of the action, many of them sobbing; some younger sisters were among them. Lobzang stood with a tall, stiff, elderly man and tied pieces of *katak*—flowing white cloth—to the branches of a rose bush that grew from underneath the large snow-covered stone outcropping that overlooked the village "common." The rock was a village deity; though fervently Buddhist, the villagers retained animist beliefs in protective spirits that could inhabit rocks and trees. These were a feature of the Bon religion, which had preceded Buddhism by hundreds of years. By tying on the piece of *katak,* the elders were aiming to please the deity and thereby ensure a safe journey on the river. Lobzang lit more juniper twigs in his censer as the crowd grew. Now I saw his daughter and two of the other girls in the group with tears streaming down their faces.

Nobody blew a whistle, nobody shouted out that now it was time to leave . . . but suddenly departure began. Girls took the lead, the five from Reru in front. The line moved not toward the roadbed, which was deep in snow, but over a rise and then down toward the frozen river. I scrambled to get into the file close after them, and was glad I did: in that monochromatic tableau, with everything else snow or rock, the vibrantly clad teenagers were a string of bright energy. The boys wore knit hats, dungarees, and modern (if not new) parkas and fleece of dark green, red, and tan; the girls added many other colors to the picture with their more varied attire. Each wore a silk scarf that covered her hair and made its way around her neck before hanging loose in back; it could be wrapped over her face in case of extra cold or wind or desire for modesty. Under their jackets they also wore the loose-fitting, pajama-type garment called a *salwar kameez* in purple, orange, royal, and emerald green, often with bright patterns. And beneath that, there were certainly layers we couldn't see: Seb commented that, since their rucksacks were relatively small, the group was probably transporting much of their wardrobes by wearing them. The girls wore thin knit gloves; the boys did not.

Then, just as the leaders started to descend from a flat stretch—at the moment the town would disappear from sight—they all stopped, took seven steps backward, and each tossed a pebble toward home. No one could tell me what their cue had been, nor could anyone really explain what it meant. But it seemed part of the family of gestures that includes Braulio's crossing himself before beginning a truck journey and my own muttering of "Praise God, from whom all blessings flow" (sung in many churches as the doxology, and by my non-devout father as a goodnight prayer to me when I was a boy) when I'm in a plane taking off—rituals of departure, prayers that ask for safe arrival and safe return.

The girls were still at the head of the file of forty travelers, and I have never seen such a large group move so fast. We descended the steep hillside to the river on a trail with a couple of switchbacks, and paused once we got there to deal with some matters of equipment and route—the river surface wasn't completely frozen, and a couple of the grown men, seasoned *chaddar*-walkers, went first, using five-foot-long walking sticks to tap-tap-tap the ice surface before taking a step, sussing out a good route. Once the ice seemed more solid, the men carrying the homemade rosewood sleds took them off their backs and began pulling them on the slick surface, the ropes tied around their waists so their hands would be free. Most did not wear gloves.

The Zanskaris' everyday walking style seemed well suited to a trip across the ice. They tended to take short, quick steps. In part this was a function of stature—few of them were tall people—but it was also a question of method: no footfall was emphatic, each was as light as possible. For many the passage across ice became a rapid shuffle; this seemed good for not breaking through. The style seemed to me the opposite of, say, that of a Texan clomping around his ranch in boots, or a businessperson assertively crossing a bare floor in hard-soled shoes.

I am not tall, but Seb is six-foot-three and strong. Keeping up with the group on the ice was not hard for him, but after a couple of hours, as the line began to climb out of the riverbed, he had his work cut out for him. Where the snow was deep, each walker stepped in the track of the person directly in front. The problem for Seb was that these holes were very close together. "It's like walking in a really tight skirt," he said as he minced his way through the deep snow, up the steep hill.

Girls from Reru climbing out of the chaddar *on their way to Bardan monastery*

The day's objective was Padum, and to get there we'd been walking what was essentially a mini-*chaddar* on the Lungnak River. The Reru–Padum road was deep in snow, and most of the way it was easier to walk on the frozen Lungnak. But at a certain point the road represented a shortcut to Padum and so, leaving behind the mini-*chaddar,* the group broke a path up the steep, snowy hillside to the roadbed. Soon we arrived at Bardan monastery, an ancient redoubt, famous for its huge prayer wheel, that overlooked the Lungnak. A few minutes at Bardan's gate would be our only rest until Padum, where most of the travelers had friends or relatives. There, after a night's rest, a bus or truck that had yet to be arranged would take us across the wide Zanskar Valley to the head of the great gorge into which the Zanskar River flowed. Where that road ended, the real *chaddar* trek would begin.

As the sun set that day and the air became especially frigid, I thought a few months back to summer in Zanskar, that enchanted season, all the more precious for being brief. The only snow had been on mountaintops, and every day it seemed to shrink. But now the cold was ascendant, and I wondered how bad it would get. Afraid of the cold, I'd packed too many clothes and had been slowed down on the day's walk by the weight of my backpack and by all the extra layers I'd worn. The maladjusted, over-heated, out-of-my-element feeling put me in mind of a man I had met during the summer, Engineer Gupta.

Accompanied by Seb and Dorjey, I had walked to the office of Gupta, who was in charge of local road construction. The road-building head-quarters was a half-hour walk from Padum. While parts of Padum feel like a medieval village, this base of operations was up-to-date industrial barren: a large, fenced-in lot containing big trucks, metal sheds, outdoor storage of things in barrels, and piles of rock and gravel. In the middle, though, was a homely touch: a small white house with a little picket fence in front—the office and quarters of Engineer Gupta.

It was very hot inside, and this was because Engineer Gupta missed Calcutta. Like so many people who came to Zanskar from more devel-oped parts of India (including army officers, teachers, and doctors), he felt he had been shunted to one of the ends of the earth. His dark skin tagged him as an outsider from the south. Yes, he said, it was much warmer down there; keeping the heat cranked up inside made him feel more at home. He thought about home all the time—he had only five more months to endure of this two-year posting. On his desk were pho-tos of his wife and children, whom he missed a lot. No, he said, they had not visited, nor had he ever entertained the idea (he looked at me with shock when I asked about it, as though to say, *Are you kidding?*). He wore big round glasses and a loose-fitting *salwar kameez;* near his breast was a logo with flying birds and the words *Home Sweet.*

He was pushing to extend the road at both ends, one up beyond Reru and another at the head of the canyon that contained the *chaddar.* Because most Zanskaris were busy with their crops during the short har-vest season, he had imported hundreds of workers from Bihar, one of India's poorest provinces, most of whom lived in tent camps out on the plains. They had very little machinery; the road was mostly being built one rock at a time, as the Biharis, for pennies a day, broke big rocks down into smaller ones and fitted them into the roadway foundation, bridge buttresses, and drainage ditches. The road was coming together, but with the construction season nearly as brief as the growing season, it was com-ing together slowly.

We had met some Biharis one day on a summer drive up to Reru when, rounding a corner, we came upon a group of them who waved down our driver. They could get us a really good deal on cement, they said (and indeed, one of our party later took them up on the offer for a project involving a monastery). As everyone knew, the cement was stolen from the road project—road projects in India, and many, many other places, were notorious sources of graft, corruption, and contraband.

Engineer Gupta said he was too busy to join us on a visit to any of the construction sites, but what happened next suggested that some of the most interesting aspects of the road-building business took place right there in the bungalow.

Gupta's aide-de-camp arrived carrying a big stack of forms with carbon paper to be signed and initialed; Gupta begged for a moment of our forbearance. He began signing while the aide flipped the pages, but partway through he paused and angrily rejected one of them, to the aide's consternation. Grabbing a calculator, he furiously punched in some numbers and showed them to the aide: he was really steamed. The aide backed out of the room and returned with a local man, the contractor whose bill was under dispute. (I was amazed they let us see all of this.) While they argued, Dorjey explained: The contractor, bringing in twenty-five barrels of diesel fuel, each meant to be holding 200 liters, had been caught delivering several of them with only 135 liters. Gupta eventually dismissed the man, signed the paper, and turned to us. The problem, he explained, was that the bad roads leading to Padum had caused barrels to leak; some of the diesel spilled. If he didn't pay for it, the poor contractor would have to. But it was clear to us that he was only covering for a scam, which perhaps it was easier for him to go along with—or participate in—than to battle.

Engineer Gupta was only a small player. In Leh that summer, having been unable to arrange to speak with the chief engineer of the project, Seb and I talked our way onto the military base where he was quartered. After almost stumbling into his actual office, Seb and I were more properly ushered in by his secretary, and were warmly received.

Brigadier M. A. Naik was a tall and handsome man with the well-trimmed mustache that one might reasonably suspect, from its ubiquity, is required for male members of the Indian armed forces. His office was full of maps and plaques. He buzzed in an assistant baroquely uniformed in epaulets and feathered hat to take our tea orders. The specific organization of which he was a high functionary, HIMANK (formerly the

Border Roads Organisation), crowed its successes in large signs all over the border region: *HIMANK,* they said, often with a picture of a ferocious tiger, *The Mountain Tamers, the Tough and the Free.* In addition to his career as a roads engineer, Naik told us, he was an athlete and mountain climber, and was just back from a special assignment: helping train the Indian athletes who would compete in shooting later that summer at the Olympic games in Athens. (The country would bring home a silver.)

He welcomed his current posting, said Naik, even though there were extreme challenges in building a road through the gorge where the *chaddar* formed. He ticked them off for us. First was the very short season in which work could be performed: only 126 days. From October to May there could be no blasting, concrete pouring, or paving. "You cannot do concrete work in the cold—it will turn out brittle, and crumble off." The same with bituminous paving. "The water goes under, and creates cracks."

Another problem was that you could not have multiple construction sites—teams working simultaneously at different points—because in the gorge there was no place for a crew to live. Nor was there any way to drop in a bulldozer. "Often we drop dozers [with helicopters], but at this altitude the helicopter can only lift one ton, and the dozer weighs twenty-two tons. So we have only two cutting edges"—by which he meant one team at either end of the gorge.

Naik said he had studied European road-building methods in the Alps for this project, including "attaching" the roadway to the cliff face, cantilevering it out, by supporting it from beneath. But he said this would be too expensive. Instead, he anticipated more than twelve miles of "U-cut," blasting a U-shaped indent into the wall and putting the road in there—a technique used by Bolivia in some of its most challenging Andes passes. But Naik was not enthusiastic about the prospect. Though the *chaddar* canyon had a lot of hard rock, he explained, it also had a lot of "fissured or disintegrated rock—not very good rock," which was a challenge because "it keeps falling. The more you have a disruption [e.g., blasting], the more rock falls down." The likelihood of a ceiling collapse along the way, with "heavy human casualties," was therefore quite high.

The other extraordinary method that might be employed was bringing in a "jumbo drill." Normally used for tunnels, this had a single drill bit with several cutting heads for a 20- to 35-meter (65- to 115-foot) cut. But that would slow the project down a lot because the drill they had in mind was already spoken for, employed in the larger project of which the *chaddar* road was a part—the "alternate route to Ladakh," which included the 5.5-mile-long Rohtang Tunnel, under construction, as well as a new route, with tunnels, over the 16,500-foot Shingo La pass.

The construction difficulties didn't even include another set of concerns that were key to the project's success, namely maintenance, and how to keep the road clear of snow year-round. Of the 11,000 people hired for the larger project, between 2,500 and 3,000 were local. They would be useful doing maintenance near their villages once the road was finished, but what to do about the stretches between villages, Naik conceded, was "a major problem." Snowplowing would be necessary, as well as repairs after the inevitable washouts, and there just weren't enough people around to cope.

For HIMANK, he said, "it is definitely the hardest project so far, definitely the worst of all. The conditions are extreme, they are adverse climatically, geologically, and logistically. I have worked in a number of countries, and never seen conditions like this. Where a human cannot go, it is always difficult."

Of course, we reminded him, humans did go through there during the winter, on the frozen river. Yes, he said, and he wanted to try it himself. He was also interested in exploring the idea of a summer rafting trip down through the gorge. He thought that local outfitters had tried this a few times for tourists, but with the logistical support of the army, you could make a real expedition of it. Seb mentioned that he and his girlfriend had been hoping to put together just such an expedition that summer; Naik promptly invited them to join his. A road through the canyon was a prodigious undertaking that would take years and years, much longer than the twenty-two months Naik was assigned to the posting. But a float trip: that they could do.

As we woke in Padum before dawn that morning after the trek down from Reru, preparing for the first real day of our *chaddar* trek, I thought how reassuring it would be to have the Indian Army behind you on an expedition into the wilderness. (Seb said the float trip had gone well.) But, in the absence of the army, I was glad to have Seb, who had done this before.

Seb's experience and his web of local contacts made him a valuable companion. I usually preferred to travel alone because it nudged me toward more interaction with local people. But Seb made meeting local people easier. And in a situation that was possibly risky—such as the visit to the logging camp in Peru—having dependable company seemed like a good idea. Seb had advised me on gear: I wouldn't want a tent, for example, because of the huge amount of condensation that formed inside one in this climate. And instead of sleeping on an air mattress, which could be easily punctured by the rocky ground, he suggested I carry a really thick pad for use under my sleeping bag, and named the Canadian company that was the best supplier.

Seb had introduced me to Dorjey, whose services as translator and fixer were indispensable, but I had balked at his suggestion that I also hire a cook and porters. I had never liked the old model of Himalayan mountaineering, the picture of a couple of white guys leading the climb while a score of brown-skinned men shouldered their voluminous kit; a real man should be able to shoulder his own stuff. Okay, said Seb, but how do you intend to keep up with the teenagers, who carry practically nothing—and are already better at walking on the ice than you or me? Food weighs a lot, unless, like them, you're able to survive on snacks for several days. How will you collect wood in the evening, when you're exhausted, in order to have a fire?

He also helped me appreciate that porter work, rare as it is, was one of the only jobs available to Zanskari men during the long winter months, and that being a trekker who employed porters gave you a status they understood: it explained your presence in their villages, or as a guest in their kitchens. "Also, if you get hurt, it's not such a bad thing to have people along to help carry you out." And so I conceded the point.

From Padum to the head of the *chaddar* was about twenty-five miles. The Reru gang would travel in the available school bus. A highway truck had originally been sought for transporting me and my crew. I had taken a winter ride in the back of this truck before, and had possibly never been colder in my life; even the Zanskaris who'd been with me appeared nearly frozen. So I was relieved to hear that, at the last minute, another, smaller school bus had been lined up for us.

We gathered on the dark and icy street at about four a.m. There was no moon, though the huge sky over the valley was filled with thousands of stars. I'd met my crew before and greeted them anew: there was Punchok Chosphel, the cook, in his mid-twenties, who had a wide, winning smile and good fashion sense (he had hand-sewn his leather boots, wore a variety of hats and scarves, and eschewed traditional Zanskari winter wear for a parka); Tsewang Rinchen, forty-two, a workhorse of incredible muscle and endurance; Tsering Dorjey, a thirty-something plasterer inexperienced in the *chaddar* who had gotten the job through connections; and Lobzang Tashi, fifty, the Reru headman who had been my host in the village. Lobzang Tsetan lived in the village of Zangla; we would pick him up on the way. Though he had only one eye, this Lobzang was probably the best ice-walker of the group, and like Tsewang he was steady and indefatigable.

My relief at having a bus was premature. The only advantage the bus had over the highway truck, I soon discovered, was that it was mostly enclosed. But not all the windows would shut and surprisingly, like a majority of the vehicles in service in Zanskar—indeed, in greater Ladakh—it had no heater. This became a significant problem about forty-five minutes into our journey, when we stopped on the road opposite the village of Zangla to pick up Lobzang Tsetan. It was sometime before five a.m., and no amount of blasting on the bus's horn appeared sufficient to rouse him, though I imagine it woke up everyone else in the village. Finally it became too cold to simply sit in the bus; we got out and walked on the dark, icy road. The sky, with the earliest hints of dawn, was deeply, hauntingly blue, and thank God Seb took a picture because I couldn't appreciate it: I'd put on every stitch of warm clothing I'd brought (down parka with hood, insulated pants) and yet my feet, even inside my insulated boots, were on the verge of freezing. Seb and I jogged up and down the deserted road to keep warm while somebody went to drag the porter out of bed. It took a long time.

Our flock of students, meanwhile, was somewhere behind us on the road, delayed with a flat tire. They huddled three to a seat inside their bus, they told me later, and made the best of it. They were more accustomed to the cold than I; but still, it made me understand just how vulnerable one is when traveling in the Himalayan winter, outside the umbrella of officialdom.

About half an hour further along, the wide-open valley closed in, and within a couple of miles the road was no longer on the valley floor but on a hillside. The ribbon of ice-topped river ran below us now, down snowy, rocky slopes at the bottom of the deepening gorge. As we neared the peaks that ringed the valley, their summits disappeared from view (so big were they, and so close were we) even as other details became visible in the rising light of day.

I recognized the end of the road from my summer visit. It ended where there was no more soft hillside to bulldoze, only rock. On that trip, I spent time with the construction team, a group of seven or eight men who had just set a number of explosive charges into holes they'd drilled in the rock. They showed them to me about three minutes before they lit the fuses, and advised that I retreat a safe distance. Soon they came running toward me. A thunderous blast followed a few seconds later, which I could see before I heard or felt anything; we were in no danger from the rock that sprayed out, but it shook the mountains so forcefully that rocks from the hillside above our observation point came down in a light but alarming rain. Nobody was hurt. When things had settled, a bulldozer cleared debris from the blasting area—shoved it into the gorge, essentially. The road cut had just been extended another few feet.

As we pulled our packs and sleds from the bus, I could see that since our visit the previous June the blasting had progressed only another fifty yards or so. The *chaddar* gorge was so long, and so intimidating, that odds were it would remain intact for many years to come.

There was no waiting around. The porters knew that the Reru group was traveling lighter than we were, and would catch up. And that, more crucially, movement and speed were how you kept warm outside in the wintertime. We broke a trail sideways down the mountain toward the river, Seb and I carrying our own gear in backpacks, four porters carrying cooking equipment and food for the group. Each porter had on his back one of the handmade sleds that doubled as a rucksack frame, like the one I'd seen Lobzang make. Dorjey wore white, rubberized, insulated Indian Army boots, as did one porter; the other porters wore thin leather boots except for one-eyed Lobzang Tsetan, who wore cheap leather oxfords (we could see his white socks).

There is a moment of magic when your boots first touch the ice: you know you're on a special road that will extend, deities willing, uninterrupted for the next forty miles, taking you out into the larger world. It was like a train track that way—something solid that allowed for more speedy, efficient travel than caroming over the adjoining rock and dirt. Indeed, there were many points ahead where, were there no ice, there would be no human passage at all (though mountaineers might get through with concerted effort).

And yet from the first step you also appreciated that ice had unique perils. My first steps, small and tentative, reflected my twin fears of slipping or falling through, especially given the weight of my pack. My feet were cold enough already without being soaked! But here the ice looked firm, and the need to keep up with the porters overcame my caution.

One reason I wanted to keep up with them—in addition to the fear of being left behind—was to learn how they navigated the *chaddar*. Of the five, three had sticks, and tapped the ice just in front of them constantly as they moved. It made different sounds when they did, usually firmly resonant, but sometimes hollow-sounding, at which time the forward motion of our line slowed. The surface it presented changed, as well, from perfectly smooth to the texture of coarse sandpaper, with tiny crystals or windblown dirt on top, to truly rough ice that had cracked and healed. The surface was not perfectly flat, as a frozen lake might be; underneath was a huge, moving river whose flow waxed and waned, pushing the ice up or allowing it to slowly cave in. You might not notice that the pitch had changed, and that could lead to a fall.

Another thing that changed was opacity. The ice could be translucent, like cubes of architectural glass, sometimes laced with cracks and fissures; other times it was milky. But occasionally it was startlingly clear, and you could look several feet down to the pebbles at the bottom, almost as if you were walking on water.

The *chaddar* started shallow; the canyon walls were not steep here, nor were they pure rock. Trees and shrubs grew out of snow-covered gravel. Above was the short gash that the dozen-man road crew had managed to blast away in several weeks of summer work. In the sun that hit the rim of the canyon we spotted a roosting lammergeier, a huge vulture. But the view quickly changed as we walked, in the *chaddar*'s shadow, lower and lower into the channel that had been eroded into rock over centuries, back into geological time. The rock walls moved closer and closer to the river until there was no soil left, no plants within reach. The wind seemed to abate as they did, and the sense of entering a special, private world increased.

I shuffled behind the porters, tracing a meandering path down the frozen riverbed, following them toward whichever way looked firmest. An hour or two into our trek, the teenagers, delayed by the flat tire, caught up with us, and the two groups merged into one long single file. The sun rose but the gorge deepened, keeping us from its rays. When we reached a junction—another river, the Oma Chu (Milk Water), flowed in from a side canyon to merge with the Zanskar—Lobzang Tashi, the

*The frozen river briefly lets walkers deep into a zone they could
never otherwise visit: the Zanskar River gorge.*

headman, declared a meal stop. I wasn't sure I was glad, since a chilly
breeze rushed in from the side canyon and I still wasn't quite recovered
from the predawn freeze. But then someone pointed out a cave maybe
fifty feet above the ice, and not too hard to reach via a series of natural
and manmade steps. There was a series of caves, I knew, up and down the
chaddar. Most weren't very deep, but they had sheltered travelers from
wind and precipitation for generations; most even had names. This one
was known as Tsarag Do. The walls, darkened by soot from countless
campfires, attested to this history. Men gathered driftwood and brush
from the surrounding area and carried it up to the cave, and in twenty
minutes fires were burning and tea water boiling.

Seeing the older men and young people mix was intriguing, because of the stark difference in their clothing. These kids had never been to a mall, but they were already absorbing Western culture. The grown men all wore the *goncha,* a knee-length Ladakhi robe made of heavy wool dyed maroon and tied around the waist with a sash. The teenage boys, by contrast, wore a variety of fleece and nylon jackets of many colors. Little boys were still dressed by their mothers in *gonchas,* and nothing was cuter. But on the rare occasion when I saw a teenage boy in Zanskar wearing a *goncha,* I immediately thought he either was from a *really* isolated village or was a bit of a hick.

The old and the new seemed to meld more easily with the girls. Over their pajama-like *salwar kameez* most had jackets or fleece. I caught up with Stanzin Zoma and Sonam Dolma in the cave, nibbling on cold *tsampa* with some pickled cabbage and carrot while they waited on the tea. I was surprised to see that both were wearing only pink sneakers with wool socks. In the bus en route, said Stanzin Zoma, her heels had gotten really cold.

"Aren't you worried about snow getting in there?" I asked.

"If you just step in the tracks in front of you, sometimes you can keep away from snow," explained Stanzin. "What I'm really worried about is falling in water. We heard there is some open water further down."

"Won't your families buy you boots?"

They looked a little embarrassed. "It's just that we don't go out walking so often in deep snow," said Stanzin.

Most people had left their packs down on the ice; the view out from the cave was almost monochromatic except for the synthetic fabrics: the bright yellows, reds, and greens of knapsacks and jackets. Thirty years ago, I was pretty sure, you would never have seen such colors in here. In fact, thirty years earlier, much about the *chaddar* was different.

The earliest account of *chaddar* travel I could find comes from James Crowden, an English explorer and poet who, at age twenty-two, spent the winter of 1976–77 in Zanskar. He claims to have been the first Westerner to walk the *chaddar.* "After three days waiting around for the auspicious moment we finally left at three in the afternoon," he wrote. His companions were carrying tubs of yak butter to trade in Leh for cooking pots, soap, and fresh vegetables, among other things. Their shoes were handmade and of a kind hard to find in Zanskar anymore: leather and pointy-toed, with woolen uppers that extended up to a tie below the knee. Nobody wore socks; instead, the shoes were stuffed with straw for warmth. Everyone in his group wore a *goncha*.

Caves along the *chaddar* were as important when Crowden traveled as they are today, particularly for sleeping, as they help keep one out of wind and moisture. In many caves, walls of stone helped to partition the protected space into even smaller spaces. Just as they did not carry water bottles, though, the Zanskaris did not carry sleeping bags or tents. Instead, as we saw when it darkened that first night and the group stopped at another cave, they laid out a plastic groundcloth and stayed warm by lying together, and by using the *gonchas* and other clothing that had warmed them individually to warm them as a group. (When he was there, wrote Crowden, the most popular Zanskari sleeping style was kneeling, preserving heat by putting the arms around the legs.)

Seb and I, by contrast, carried big Arctic-class sleeping bags with several inches of lofted down, and laid these upon the thick foam pads to insulate us from the cold of the ground. We wore knit hats and each of us kept a specially marked pee bottle inside the bag with us, so that if the need arose we would not need to climb out into the frigid night air. I was torn between a sense of deep fondness and gratitude for my massive sleeping bag, and a nagging concern that our equipment-intensive solution was inferior to the Zanskaris' community-intensive one, and set us apart as rich. Still, I knew that it was too late for me: as a younger man, I had slept spooned with Mexicans crossing the Sonoran Desert into Arizona in January and knew that, while it had kept me fairly warm, sleep had been practically impossible. You had to grow up doing that for it to work.

The worst part of the day, of course, was dawn, and the first minutes out of the sleeping bag. I waited until the porters had brewed a pot of tea and then joined the knot of people seated around the fire. A mini-thermometer on Seb's pack said it was -12 degrees Celsius (10 degrees Fahrenheit). Lobzang Tashi withdrew from his bag a pile of block-printed pages of prayers, wrapped in cloth, and commenced quietly to chant; I noticed he did this whenever there was a chance, usually several times a day. One of the porters reached for his cap, meanwhile, and produced a needle that he stored there. He tapped gently into the surface of a block of ice he had carried up from the river and, like magic, it fractured the cube neatly into smaller pieces that would fit into a pot for melting.

It was going to be a long day, and nobody was getting any warmer by waiting around. Snow had fallen overnight, and we set new tracks alongside others that had been made while we slept: rodent prints now crisscrossed the river, along with the tracks—Dorjey claimed—of a snow leopard. "Are you sure?" I asked. They were so big and catlike they could be nothing else, but books like Peter Matthiessen's *The Snow Leopard*, about Tibetan Buddhism and a trek with a biologist in search of the endangered animals, had led me to believe there were practically none left.

"Oh, yes," Dorjey replied, and we stepped out of the single file a few moments later so that he could show me more evidence. He found it on the sides of two rocks at river's edge, where the leopard had slowed and walked in a circle. "Look," he said, urging me to get close. On the rough surface of the rocks were two or three hairs; he pinched them between his fingers and held them up for me to examine; they were three to five inches long. "It is his whiskers," explained Dorjey. "Here he scratched his face."

The passage of such a large predator just yards from where we'd slept didn't put me any more at ease on the *chaddar*, but Dorjey laughed and said the snow leopard wasn't interested in us. In their scat one found mostly the bones of small animals, he said—marmots, pikas, and wildfowl. In rare cases they might eat one of the larger animals that lived in these parts and which we could see as we walked, sometimes high up on the canyon walls: ibex, blue sheep, possibly argali. Leopards willingly came near humans only in coldest winter, and then only in hopes of finding a captive farm animal such as a dzo. He reminded me of a house we had stopped at the previous summer, in the valley above Reru as we trekked to Phugtal monastery. After dinner, the family gave Dorjey something to show me: a large piece of stiff snow leopard pelt. I was amazed to find myself suddenly holding such a mythic relic in my hands.

"Did they hunt it?" I asked.

"Actually," said Dorjey, "they found the beast in the toilet."

He explained. Like most traditional Zanskari dwellings, the house was made of mud bricks, and the ground level was devoted mainly to sheltering animals in cold weather; a small separate section of it was reserved for the household latrine. The mother had gone to squat in one of the holes in the second floor that opened onto the latrine space, when she heard a growl and peered down on the frozen stalagmite of feces below: a snow leopard showed her its fangs. Stalking the farm animals, the leopard had gotten trapped. The family promptly did what any local family would have done in such a circumstance: they stoned it to death.

Dorjey understood the irony. He was an interesting mix of older generation and younger, and a delightful guy to have around. Forty-something, he tended toward Western dress, but he was very religious; some part of him, I'm sure, would have been happy to have been a monk. He was married and had six children. This did not prevent him from taking a little time off to assist people like me and Seb, or to make a pilgrimage to a religious center such as Dharamsala, where he had followed a lama's instruction to perform ten thousand prostrations as a step to enlightenment. But religious practice had not narrowed his mind. The day I met him, he was seated on the floor of the living room in his traditional earthen house in Padum, eating lunch in the company of two maroon-clad monks; the group was watching a fuzzy Indian television broadcast about an impending eclipse of the sun. Attached to the plaster wall of his son's bedroom, I noticed, was the same magazine photo of pop singer Avril Lavigne that my daughter had on her bedroom wall in New York. Dorjey prayed and chanted several times a day, but he also loved to discuss the characters in the Harry Potter books (which English-speaking friends would send him), and some of the vocabulary he'd picked up there—*gruesome,* he liked to say, and *goblet.* His favorite character was Hagrid, though Dorjey himself resembled no Westerner more than the jolly comedian Buddy Hackett. He laughed at the sight of me imagining a snow leopard, so elusive to Matthiessen on his spiritual journey into Nepal's Dolpo region, a symbol of rarity and the beauty we can't see, meeting its end in a frozen latrine.

We stopped for mint tea on a graveled section of riverbank, in the sun. I chatted with two of the boys, Lobzang Teshi and Tenzin Namdol, who said they weren't tired at all. Tenzin, I noticed, was carrying a second rucksack; he admitted that it belonged to a girl in the group. The sky was blue, but you had to look way up to see it. And for the first time in quite a while, no part of me was cold. High, high up on the canyon wall across

The chaddar *changes constantly. Here a porter negotiates a narrow ice ledge, all that remains of the path on one side of the gorge.*

the river, someone spotted an ibex; its distance from us, and the immense scale of the rock walls, made me feel small.

Some Zanskaris came shuffling into view, walking the *chaddar* in the opposite direction. It was two groups, actually, and they stopped to chat with us and compare notes on the terrain ahead. Three of the walkers, it turned out, were mailmen, carrying bags of letters from the big post office in Leh to the tiny one in Padum—in a good year, they said, there might be three mail runs on the *chaddar*. After that, Zanskaris had to wait until the spring thaw for mail service.

With the weather a bit warmer, we started seeing more and more open water. I was intrigued by the little birds, white-throated dippers, that skipped and dashed alongside it: they could submerge in a patch of open water, disappear for several seconds, and pop up again a few yards downstream, and some of them did it again and again, searching for food in the depths. Among our group, however, the more seasoned trekkers began to worry. Our path down the *chaddar* began to meander more as the open water increased, and patches of ice began to seem suspect. More than once, loud *cracks* and *whumps*—deep movements of frozen, fractured water that I've heard nowhere else in nature—brought the group up short as everyone silently wondered: Was something cataclysmic about to happen? Would the surface hold?

Sometimes I imagined that our continued progress depended on faith, that we could walk without falling because we *believed* we could, a mass delusion. Sometimes I seemed to have better luck when I didn't look too carefully at the next step. I'd heard ski instructors say, *Don't focus on your skis,* and skating instructors say, *Look straight ahead,* and I imagined that some Zanskari *chaddar* sage had intoned that same advice. Certainly there was a lot to see. When the gorge opened up you could glimpse ragged peaks, sunny in the distance while it was shady on the ice. Once, when the surface of the ice was like a mirror, I saw such a peak while looking down. But it seemed like such bad luck, I looked away, straight ahead.

There were landmarks our guides knew to watch for along the way. One was a giant juniper tree at a spot called Shukpa Chenmo: it had fallen over but lived on, and its trunk and some branches were festooned with prayer flags. (Due to the importance of juniper in ceremonies, the trees were respected and cared for.) Others were interesting stone formations. Thermally heated water spewed out of the canyon wall at one point, creating a ring of green around rocks that vaguely resembled a nose; this was Palda Tsomo, or Nose Spring. Another formation was known as the Clitoris. "We don't tell that to the children," Dorjey assured me.

And there was one cave that, because of its history, nobody *ever* used, even in an emergency. A king of Zanskar, Gyalpo Gyazo, had stopped there with his entourage many generations before. But overnight the river rose, and they could not leave. Days later, out of food, the king ate a knapsack made of animal hide; and his men "plotted to slay the cook for food." But the cook, said Dorjey, got wind of the plan. When night fell, he joined together several walking sticks and laid them out in the water. Floating fragments of ice attached to them, making a partial bridge. He added more wood, and the bridge grew large enough that he could escape. Soon the others did, too—probably hot on his trail.*

As the day warmed, the ice became more and more questionable. Larger patches of open water appeared, and near the shores, where the ice seemed thinnest but the water was not deep, a couple of people broke through and got their shoes wet.

Dorjey's experience of the larger world, his many trips through the *chaddar,* and, probably, his status as our translator may have made him overconfident. As the leaders of the students slowed on the uncertain surface, Dorjey took the lead. For a while he followed the meandering game tracks across the thin layer of snow, on the theory that animals might possibly know something about the thickness of the ice below that we did not. But when the game trails disappeared, he marched boldly ahead anyway—and promptly fell through, up to his calf. Laughing, he pulled his leg out and forged ahead over the thin ice—and soon went through again, this time up to his thigh. Unluckily for him, the entire line of walkers had now stopped to watch. He tried to extract himself quickly, but no luck: leaning on the surrounding ice to pull himself up, he crashed through completely, this time soaking himself from the waist down. There was little danger—the day not terribly cold—but some embarrassment.

Finally heading toward shore, he soldiered on a bit farther until he came to a flat spot where we could "take tea." We made our way cautiously to the spot and then helped Dorjey collect firewood, pausing now and then to watch others negotiate the tricky stretch of ice. Two or three chivalrous young men, including Tenzin Namdol, took off their shoes and socks and ferried many of the young women over the bad spots by carrying them on their backs, so that they would not soak their sneakers. They could not have enjoyed walking barefoot over ice and snow, but there were no theatrics as the young men did it, no shows of discomfort or suffering. They, and their feet, were admirably tough. Dorjey, as the tea fire grew hot, removed his trousers, wrung them out, and placed walking

*Zanskaris were hoping to encourage adventure travelers to take a walk on the *chaddar.* In a market in Leh some time later, I came across a *chaddar* video featuring Dorjey as narrator; he had also written the script. After recounting the legend of the king's cave, he added, "To avoid this kind of episode, it is advisable to the new trekkers to take the service of well-experienced porters and guides, preferably the native of Zanskar."

*Mushy snow tests the Zanskari conviction that
there is only one thing worse than going
barefoot on snow: soaking wet shoes.*

sticks through the legs, which allowed him to spread them out for maximum exposure to the heat. "It seems the departure day was not auspicious
for me!" he joked. As the fabric dried, we talked about other falls.

They could be quite serious. A few years before, Seb had been walking
on the *chaddar* with a group of English mountaineers who wanted to try
climbing some of the frozen waterfalls; unlike the Zanskaris, they sometimes spread out as they walked, faster walkers moving ahead and some
people walking alone. Seb was ahead of his friend, and couldn't see him,
when he thought he heard something. He stopped, waited a moment,
and turning saw a head bobbing even with the ice. His friend had fallen
through in the middle of the river and, laden with backpack and heavy
clothing, had little chance of pulling himself out. When he saw him,
what Seb really feared was that the man would be swept under the ice by

the swift current: even if you were a strong swimmer, the chances of bobbing up downstream where there was a gap in the ice were extremely slim. With Seb's help, though, he was soon extricated. The shivering fellow hurriedly stripped down—to the amusement of the porters—and put on a set of dry clothes. However, he declined to backtrack to the cooking fire they had recently left in a cave, because it would mean recrossing the river. So his friends watched him carefully, and he warmed up by walking. Seb's policy ever since then was that *chaddar* walkers had to stay within each other's sight at all times.

Seb himself had taken one bad fall on this trip: his feet had simply slipped out from under him, landing him squarely on his tailbone. It hurt, but he could keep going. I myself had fallen several times, though never, yet, as badly: so far I'd been able to see it coming and put out a hand to cushion the blow. When falling, or the possibility of falling, left me particularly exhausted, I would stretch onto the soles of my boots a pair of rubbers with tiny metal studs—postal carriers and others in northern climes wear them—which provided dreamy traction. They also prevented me from shuffling along in the efficient Zanskari way and could slow me down. But where the ice was superslick and my nerves frazzled, they were a godsend.

Others fell, too—in particular, Tsering Dorjey, the novice porter who was a plasterer by profession, and a bit clumsy. His *goncha* had rips and tears caused by various encounters with rocks and timber and ice, and holes from getting too close to fires. I knew he had a fondness for drink. Unlike the other porters, who were a bit shy around me, he would occasionally walk right up and say something: "Did you see that bird?" or "The water is moving very deep beneath the ice—can you see it through there?" I found Tsering interesting, but Dorjey seemed annoyed by him and didn't like to translate what he was saying. One morning Tsering came up and happily tickled the whiskers under my chin, leaving me perplexed.

One day he tied our little kerosene stove to the top of his pack. When he bent over without thinking, the heavy metal stove bonked him on the head, resulting in a cut. A fall on the *chaddar* caused him the greatest distress; I didn't see it happen but I asked about it after he turned up at lunch with a bloody gash on the side of his nose. All the other porters were chortling as he explained it to me through Dorjey, who could barely contain his mirth.

"He says," Dorjey began, hardly able to speak, "he says the ice shifted and made him slip. As you can see, he fell through. He also has cut his leg."

Tsering, miserable, showed me the superficial gash on his shin, and then made a further, more vehement statement to Dorjey.

"He says," Dorjey began again, this time pausing to wipe away tears of laughter, "he says . . . he says . . . that when he went in the water—" Peals of laughter resounded from the other men, some of whom spoke some English and wanted to hear Dorjey say it. "He says," Dorjey began again, this time determined to finish, "that when he fell in, he saw . . . he saw . . . th-the Dark Lord!" At this, Dorjey exploded in laughter, and the others doubled over with mirth. It was hard not to laugh along with them, but I tried my best, since Tsering was looking mournfully at me, perhaps waiting to see if one person here would offer some sympathy.

"The Dark Lord," I repeated to Seb. "Does he mean, as in Lord Voldemort from *Harry Potter*? He-who-must-not-be-named?"

"I don't think so . . . ," Seb began.

"It is sort of like that," Dorjey said, regaining his composure, "but different. Really, it's the Lord of Darkness. Our version, you might say." He left it at that.

In any event, these mishaps were all part of traversing the *chaddar*. It would be a mistake to think of the river as moving and the *chaddar* as still; the *chaddar* did move and shift, sometimes dramatically, as when its surface gave way to a footstep. Other times it shifted slowly. Across the ice were always pressure fractures, looking like scars. Occasionally the pressures seemed to push on a single point near the *chaddar*'s middle, resulting in a gently raised cone with fractures all around it, like a low volcano. In some places you could see where pieces of ice had cracked and tipped or fallen into the water below; sometimes, afterward, fresh water would rush up and over the opening, creating a new, uneven surface as it froze on top of the existing ice. Seb said that sometimes this was caused by dropping temperatures: deep cold could thicken the ice and decrease the space available underneath for running water, forcing it onto the surface. Conversely, snow could function as an insulating blanket, warming the ice and encouraging breakup. Day and night we would hear groans, creaks, and harsh reports that made me want to tiptoe: the ice was just the frozen skin of a hibernating giant below.

———

As we continued it got warmer and warmer—a function of the weather, not of the change in our location—and the ice became even less predictable. I was following in the footsteps of Stanzin Zoma on the afternoon of the second day when the line of walkers slowed, then stopped. At first I felt relief. It was a chance to take off my jacket, which was too heavy for the strenuous pace and warming weather; I was wet with perspiration. But then relief turned to alarm because ahead, in place of silent ice, I saw there was open water, the dark, rushing river risen back to the surface. The only remaining ice was clinging to the edges of sheer rock walls. Everyone waited as Lobzang Tsetan, the one-eyed porter who was in the lead, tested the narrow remaining stretch of ice by tapping gingerly with his stick and then with his lead foot. He retreated to an area of loose rocks a few yards back, got two handfuls of dirt, and returned to the ledge to toss it onto the ice in front of him to give it some friction and reduce the chances of falling into the dark deep water that rushed alongside. From there he turned toward the wall and hugged it, shimmying along until he was past—and the danger confronted the next person.

The next morning, our third, was brilliantly sunny and warm, and briefly the ice disappeared altogether. But here the river was wide, slow and shallower. For twenty or thirty feet, everyone had to wade. Apart from those few girls lucky enough to be carried, everyone took off their shoes and socks. The water was very, very cold. Downstream from this spot, as feet were dried and laces tied, a group approached from the other direction: tourists. They were French, men and women, and they had good equipment, including neoprene divers' booties for situations such as the one that lay just ahead of them. And they had a small army of porters, many of whom paused to chat with people in our group.

While most of the traffic we had passed on the *chaddar* was Zanskari, Seb said that tourism, mainly European, was growing every year. Virtually all of it was centered on Leh, which not only was picturesque but was thoroughly imbued with the Tibetan Buddhist culture that so interested many in the West. Those who moved further on, to places such as Zanskar, tended to have trekking or mountaineering ambitions, as tourist infrastructure (hotels, restaurants) outside Leh was fairly nonexistent. It was good employment for Zanskaris, but the journeying was unpredictable.

The *chaddar* did not always behave in a way that meshed well with Western schedules. On the afternoon of our third day—another warm one—we passed a group of Englishmen who were being led up the *chad-dar* into Zanskar by Sonam "Jimmy" Stopgais, a friend of Seb's at whose house I'd eaten a dinner of *momos* (meat dumplings) the summer before. Jimmy, normally sunny himself, looked troubled: in the day since our group passed through, the watery area upstream had grown; the *chaddar* there was now impassable. His clients—mainly businessmen who had taken a week off from work and family—looked restive. They had reason to be concerned: two weeks later Seb and I would read in the Indian press that the *chaddar* had broken up especially early that year, stranding nearly fifty foreign tourists whom the army had had to evacuate in helicopters. Jimmy and his group were almost certainly among them. We were among the last to get through.

As we passed these tourist groups, I got the chance to see myself, as it were, from the outside. Seb and I had been exclusively among Zanskaris for many days—indeed, Seb had immersed himself in Zanskar for weeks at a time, many years in a row—but clearly we belonged to this other tribe of brightly jacketed, impressively assisted, high-tech-equipped Western-ers. Back when James Crowden had been the first Westerner on the *chad-dar,* in 1977, the sight of people like us would probably have brought most Zanskaris up short. Zanskar had never been completely isolated, how-ever: traders on the various silk routes of central Asia had passed through Leh for centuries. Zanskaris had traded directly with nomads such as the Chang-pa of Tibet, with whom they exchanged grain for salt and wool, and Gaddi shepherds from their immediate north and south, from whom they got wool. And yet, the arrival of Western culture, in the form of peo-ple like us and various academic researchers and development workers, but even more potently, I imagine, as conveyed by television, movies, and magazines, was a visitation of an entirely different order of magnitude. Silk route traders may have arrived with wonders, but it is doubtful they ever inspired a generation to abandon its ways of dressing, of trading, of religiosity (for who could worship Buddha the same way outside a land where doing so was such a part of daily life?). Those earlier trades didn't move the Zanskaris to leave home and learn things you could only learn from the outside world—among them, medicine and the technology for building roads. Western culture, personified on this trip by brightly dressed tourist trekkers, was unspeakably powerful.

A Swedish linguist, Helena Norberg-Hodge, arrived in Ladakh in 1975. Until the autumn of 1974, the entire region had been closed to foreigners for years due to Indian insecurity over the nearness to China and Pakistan, fears of infiltration and divided loyalties. A road connecting Ladakh to Kashmir had been completed in 1960, but it had only begun to usher in modernity. Over the next years, Norberg-Hodge, who quickly learned the language and became enamored of Ladakhi culture, got to watch as it began to change.

Her writings follow a narrative that will be familiar to those concerned with globalization: Ladakh was perfect, it was heaven, it was sustainable, it was humankind in harmony with the earth. Cooperation was the social model, not competition, and there was a palpable joie de vivre. But now it is being ruined, and the agent of ruination is Us, the West, consumer culture and market capitalism.

"Since Ladakh is in many ways a model society," Norberg-Hodge has written,

it is tragic to see young people starting to reject their culture as primitive and filthy . . . Because of the very distorted picture of the outside world that they are gaining through contact with tourists, young people are beginning to think of themselves as poor and deprived. Since Ladakh first opened up, there has been an annual invasion of wealthy Westerners [who] are rich, and can travel thousands of miles for pleasure. They come for a few days, and spend perhaps £100 a day. In a subsistence economy, where basic needs are met without money, this is as if Martians would come to Bristol and spend £50,000 a day. £100 is what a family in Ladakh might spend in a year. . .

The impact on the young is disastrous; they suddenly feel that their parents and grandparents must be stupid to be working and getting dirty, when everyone else is having such a good time—spending vast quantities of money travelling and not working. For Ladakhis, work means physical work; the notion of stress resulting from mental work is unknown. So they get the impression that if you are modern, you simply don't work; the machines do it for you. Understandably, the effect is that they try to prove that they are not part of this primitive bunch of farmers, but part of the new elegant modern world, with jeans, sunglasses, a radio, a motorbike. It is not that the blue-jeans (often uncomfortable) are intrinsically of interest; they are symbols of the modern world. Similarly, cinema films give the impression that racing around in sports cars shooting people—that violence—is modern and admirable.

Suddenly, being a Ladakhi is just not good enough; everything is done in order to seem modern. Tragically, this means leaving the village for the capital, where the money can be earned that will buy all the trappings of the modern world. It follows that basic needs can no longer be met locally. . . .

I was never in Ladakh at the same time as Norberg-Hodge, but I caught up with her in Manhattan in 2004, before a lecture she gave at an alternative downtown bookstore called Bluestockings, and we had a long talk. Over the years, her defense of traditional Ladakh has grown into a critique of the corporate production of food (and the centralization of any product that was once made locally) and globalization in its many aspects. I felt I could understand where she was coming from. But I wondered if she could still understand where Ladakhis were coming from, thirty years after her arrival, and asked her to put herself in the place of a young person, today, in a Zanskari village such as Reru: Wouldn't she be in favor of a road? She thought about this for a moment.

"If I lived there and I only had the information they have, I would want the road," she finally answered.

But wasn't that like telling kids they shouldn't eat too much sugar because of the likelihood (which you could appreciate only from having experience, and education) of tooth decay? You could do it if you were a parent. But tragically or not, we were not their parents. And yes, it was sad when a Zanskari replaced a beautiful thatched roof with an ugly corrugated metal one—but if it was your house, and the thatched roof leaked, might you not do the same thing?

The larger point, she responded, was that as an educated person with a broad experience of the world, you had a duty to help others find a better way, to learn from the mistakes all around you, mistakes that your culture was inflicting upon theirs.

I was familiar with these critiques of Western culture before I went to Ladakh. But their site-specificity, and Norberg-Hodge's long engagement with Ladakhi culture, gave hers some added oomph. I knew she could go overboard: at her Centre for Ecological Development in Leh, I had watched a movie she had produced in which two Ladakhi women take a trip to London, and their experience proves what you suspected it would: that urbanized Westerners are wasteful, alienated, crime-prone, ambitious, and all the rest. She had discouraged Ladakhi farmers from using imported fertilizer, and had tried to dissuade Ladakhi women from wearing jeans. Male Ladakhi teenagers, the number-one adopters of Western ways, were her number-one cultural betrayers. Still, I felt that some essence of her message—the part about being proud of local custom and how you were raised—was true and needed to be heard.

On the other hand, I had not yet been to Reru when I spoke with Norberg-Hodge. And I had not met the children's schoolteacher, Tenzin Choetop. Choetop, twenty-seven, was an interesting guy. He had been raised in a school run by the Tibetan Children's Village (TCV), a famous institution established by the Dalai Lama for Tibetan refugees, in Choglamsar, just outside Leh. After years at the boarding school, he had lived and studied in Bangladesh, Dharamsala, and, most recently, Delhi, where he had worked as a cameraman on video productions. But life in Delhi had gotten too hectic, he explained, and he had sought out this job because it offered "time to think, and to read books." He also saw rural teaching as a kind of giving back: at TCV, he said, "everybody was united, everybody was caring about one another."

There were several teachers during the rest of the year but only him during the winter, and frankly, he admitted, he was going a little stir-crazy. He seemed to turn up in every house I visited; he was thirsty for exposure to the outside world. Local protocol appeared to allow him to be a guest in anyone's house at any time, and he joined in on several of the meals we were invited to—not that he gained many pounds from it. He was rail-thin and his *goncha* was ragged, but he had bright eyes and a quick mind, and we talked about many things. We discussed his students, and in particular, we discussed the new road.

"The roads will liberate them," he declared in the kitchen of Lobzang Tashi. "They've spent a long time in a remote, secluded place. The Kargil road has improved Padum. If more roads open, with more movement of people, it will be good—everything will become cheaper, ideas will come. Right now people here are too involved in religion—they have too much culture, too much religion. They don't think enough about outside ideas and people. The road leads to education, which will lead to more doctors, more teachers."

Too much culture? There was a phrase you were unlikely to hear in a Western college or university. I asked what he meant by it.

"We need to escape from small-mindedness," he asserted in the house of Sonam Dolma. "We need to keep up with the rest of the world. We need to know languages other than our own, so people on the outside don't stare at us. Now, there's a problem with interactions with other people: when people see us, they're amazed. We don't know how to interact with people."

The shyness of the village's young people, which I had viewed neutrally, as a cultural trait, Choetop saw as their impediment.

"Right now, most of them do not think about what education they will need—they would be happy to get a job in the army. And the girls, to marry someone in the army!" This time, Choetop spoke in the tumbledown home of Stanzin Lotus, sixteen. The teenagers who were leaving now would benefit from the exposure, but might not succeed immediately; sometimes it took a generation or two for things to change. "It takes time," he said. "Their children will learn a lot."

When there is a road, Choetop believed, more links between Reru and everywhere else, then "they will know there is a big world beyond this valley, so many cultures. Right now, they don't know, and they don't care." Again, their isolation and lack of knowledge, which I had halfway taken for granted, Choetop saw as unacceptable, as a barrier to development.

"If they do not change, and keep up," he concluded, "the poor will be left behind." The poor! Until people in a barter culture start interacting in a money culture, "poor" is not a word that comes up a lot. Norberg-Hodge has worried that people in Ladakhi villages are using it more and more. A shame, yes, but the cat is now out of the bag, and will not be going back in.

On departure day, Choetop came to see everybody off. But this time, as they bid goodbye to family and other friends, he stood apart. I knew he had some misgivings: he worried that the boys in particular were a bit immature for city life, and might not be well-supervised outside of class. I imagined that, like the many tearful parents, he was sad to see the youthful vitality leaving the village. But I also believed he was glad, because he believed that connection was necessary, connection was progress.

On our last day of walking, the Reru contingent pulled ahead of the rest of us. Rather than progressively exhausted by their travail, they seemed energized, like horses approaching a stable—the difference being that in this case most of the teenagers had never seen the stable before.

The end of the *chaddar* was the hamlet of Chiling, famous as the home of four metal-working clans. The copper and brass pots for tea and *chang* (an alcoholic homebrew), often decorated with silver and gold, that are proudly displayed in the houses of comfortable Ladakhis, are generally made here. Tradition has it that Chiling's smiths are descended from four craftsmen brought from Nepal in the seventeenth century to construct the two-story-high image of the Buddha at the Shey *gompa* (monastery) south of Leh. When they were refused permission to return to Nepal with their wives, they were offered their choice of places to settle in Ladakh and chose this sun-drenched site on the side of the river, which had plenty available timber for their smelting. But Chiling was now gaining a different sort of fame, as the roadhead, so far, at this end of the Zanskar gorge. The frozen Zanskar River continued another nineteen miles, to its confluence with the Indus, but nobody walked it anymore because there was a road. The road had afforded access to a pair of small, rickety buses, into which the teenagers and their retinue promptly piled.

When we caught up in the late afternoon, they were sitting there, four to a seat, on a launch pad, as it were, to the outside world. Some of the dads and uncles were busy tying gear to the buses' roofs—including, I noticed, one of the *chaddar* sleds made of bent rosewood, with its short black plastic PVC skids. There was something poignant about the sight: a Zanskari not wanting to give up an important piece of kit that had taken hours of careful work to assemble, had served him well, but would henceforth, in the larger world, be all but useless. Maybe he would store it somewhere in Leh, in preparation for the return trip.

But surely, for many of the young people in the bus, there would be no return trip. In my travels the summer before, I had tracked down a young man from Zangla whose tuition at a TCV boarding school in Choglamsar had been sponsored by an American documentary film company that had done a film in 1995 about Zanskar. Out of four Zanskari kids sponsored, three had never been back home, and he was one of them. I talked to several people, including him, about why. First, his family was poor, and travel back and forth was expensive. Second, others told me, his family had several other children, and had felt somewhat relieved that somebody else had been able to take responsibility for this one; it wasn't like an upper-middle-class Western family sending a kid to boarding school and waiting for his holiday visits. Third, to the boy, returning home to Zanskar once he graduated was increasingly inconceivable: What would he do back there, he asked me when I visited him in his dorm—become a *farmer*?

I was not eager to see a road built through the *chaddar*. The valley was so beautiful as it was. Bad things were bound to come in; life would change, and not always for the better. But Zanskar was not a museum, and though there certainly were many Zanskaris who were satisfied with the status quo, Shangri-La was not a local idea. It was a Western idea, a symbol of what we lost when we advanced, a seductive nostalgia, a dream. Tenzin Choetop was more concerned with local reality, and with the concrete challenges faced by his students. If, of all the beautiful adolescents trekking down the dangerous ice to the unknown perils of the outside world, one—even one—came back a doctor, how beautiful would that be?

ROAD ECOLOGY

I'M MAKING A SUMMER NIGHT'S drive from city to country. Leaving my driveway, I move from local street to parkway to interstate highway (several hours on this) to state highway to county road. I have to slow down as I approach the country house, of course, be more careful: the road's shoulders are narrower, the verges less clear, the turns sharper, and there are no streetlights. Like every driver almost everywhere, I run things over—insects, mostly, but also rodents and the odd frog, snake, or bird. Unavoidable, of course; regrettable, yes; but not dangerous to me unless the thing is big. Deer and moose I very much do not wish to hit.

Maybe because I'm thinking of my five-year-old son back in the city, I notice a thing he might notice if he were here: a small shape near the shoulder, just starting across the road. I swerve to avoid it and then stop, alone on the road at this hour. I put the car in reverse and get that shape back into my headlights—it's a toad. I climb out and, approaching it from behind, grab it. Near the headlight I take a closer look. It's a pretty big American toad, *Bufo americanus,* enjoying the warm blacktop at day's end. I place it in a paper bag and tie the top shut. It's June. The toad can live with us back in the city until the fall, in a terrarium outdoors. My son will be thrilled. And I can congratulate myself on having killed one less thing on this drive.

Roads represent human progress, there's little doubt. And yet, particularly in countries that have many roads and a long history of human settlement, more attention is being paid to the ways in which roads are obviously bad for other creatures.

After all, it is usually the case that one road follows another. Roads not only connect but intersect, again and again, ultimately dividing the land into polygons. The population of human beings thrives and expands: these are paths of *human* endeavor. The population of animals, however, and the number of plant and animal species decline.

The same road that lets me drive from home to mini-mart makes it challenging for a deer to get from forage to water, or a squirrel to exploit all the trees whose fruit is available at a certain time. If chickens were smart, they probably wouldn't cross the road at all; but because living things want to move, to check things out, they do. For many animals, movement is not optional; it's what they must do to find food, to survive.

The ones who fail are squashed on the pavement; some call it roadkill, others an animal holocaust of gargantuan proportions. Most are common species, but this is also a principal way the Florida panther, down to fewer than a hundred individuals, is going extinct, one rare animal after another, on highways like Alligator Alley near the Everglades.

But roads affect nature more subtly as well. In the 1960s and 1970s, biologist Edward O. Wilson's research into the flora and fauna of islands led to recognition of what has come to be known as "edge effect." Islands are particularly vulnerable to invasive species, he observed; they can encroach from all sides. Endemic species suffer when they do, and if the island is small enough, extinction may result. Wilson and others have since applied the "edge effect" concept to the "islands" of land created by roads. Roads, they argue, reproduce the edge effect by allowing for avenues of invasion.

The edge effect is part and parcel of habitat fragmentation, a major consequence of roads. Researchers are looking closely at its implications. It turns out that the size and the shape of the piece of land partly determine what can live there: a few large parcels are better than many small ones, even if they add up to the same area. Certain species, for example, move away from the edge—they don't like the commotion. Others are attracted to it—"weedy" and non-native exotic plants, and scavengers who eat roadkill. Edge zones can also be affected by chemical runoff from the road, including nitrogen oxides, herbicides, heavy metals, and road salt.

People have thought creatively about how to mitigate some of these ill effects. In the 1960s, at the behest of hunters, some 150 "game bridges" were built in France, which animals could use to cross over highways. Florida has built twenty-four passages under highways for animals, and modified others for their use. In the 1980s, hundreds of tunnels for migrating reptiles were built in Europe.* Amherst, Massachusetts, has two, designed to avert the slaughter of the spotted salamanders that migrate every spring.

Of course, larger forces are at work here than can be countered by fences, wildlife bridges, and a few pipes under roads. The road ecology movement aims to get planners and transportation departments thinking about better ways to build roads and minimize their detrimental effects on the environment. In the preface to *Road Ecology*, a 2002 book that is the movement's manifesto, fourteen co-authors wrote, "As collaborating transportation specialists and ecological scientists, we are awed by both the present and imminent environmental challenge. With an additional 60 million North Americans anticipated in thirty years, how will society accommodate their desire for space and travel? Can society halt, or even reverse, the environmental deterioration caused by more roads and vehicles?" And that's just North America. Populations are growing faster, and roads being built more quickly, in many other parts of the world. The coming of roads seems about as easy to resist as the incoming tide. And yet, maybe matters can be improved, with raised consciousness and some concerted effort, if only a bit.

When late September came around and cooler weather seemed to be slowing our toad down somewhat—he was eating fewer of the flies we caught for him, emerging less often from his grassy hiding place to catch the sunset—we took him from his outdoor terrarium on a family trip back north. He needed to hibernate and New Hampshire is where he would naturally do it. The leaves were changing and the nights were cool, but in the daytime it still got warm enough that we could imagine the toad finding his way to a good spot for the winter.

Still, we returned him to the wild with reluctance. He'd been an easy pet. My wife had nicknamed him Mr. Toad, after the character in *The Wind in the Willows*. We'd read parts of it out loud to the kids at bedtime. My favorite was the passage where the horse-drawn cart carrying Toad,

---

*Around that time, I became a member of the British Hedgehog Preservation Society. Among its campaigns was installing little escape ramps inside cattle guards on roads, so that hedgehogs who fell in would be able to climb out. In a more recent campaign the society got McDonald's to modify the plastic lids on its McFlurry desserts: scavenging hedgehogs could get into the cups, but then couldn't escape.

Rat, and Mole was driven into a ditch by a passing "motor-car" whose horn made the sound "poop-poop." The Rat was furious, but Toad just sat in the road:

> They found him in a sort of a trance, a happy smile on his face, his eyes still fixed on the dusty wake of their destroyer. At intervals he was still heard to murmur "Poop-poop!"
>
> The Rat shook him by the shoulder. "Are you coming to help us, Toad?" he demanded sternly.
>
> "Glorious, stirring sight!" murmured Toad, never offering to move. "The poetry of motion! The real way to travel! The only way to travel! Here to-day—in next week to-morrow! Villages skipped, towns and cities jumped—always somebody else's horizon! O bliss! O poop-poop! O my! O my!"

Mr. Toad had fallen under the spell of motor vehicles, and would soon become a famously bad driver.

Having a toad around also reminded me of a couplet from a Robert Frost poem, "Ghost House," about an abandoned farm:

> On that disused and forgotten road
> That has no dust-bath now for the toad.

Anyway, he had to go back. The morning after we arrived, my son and I took the toad from his container and placed him in some grass well away from the road. He looked no worse for wear, and in the light rain that was falling, I even imagined he looked rather pleased. The next time we checked, he was gone.

That afternoon we took a walk on the road. Rain always attracted numbers of brilliant orange red-spotted newts (*N. v. viridescens*), tiny, gelatinous, slow-moving, one to two inches long. Many were already squished; we saved a handful by carrying them back into the woods. I didn't tell my son that I'd unintentionally killed hundreds or thousands or, realistically, tens of thousands of organisms in my thirty years as a driver. Some of those I mentioned a moment ago, but I could get more specific and admit they included butterflies, dragonflies, moths, grasshoppers, caterpillars, a turtle, a number of birds—including a hawk, an owl, and once, almost, a wild turkey (it bumped off the windshield and possibly lived)—chipmunks, a squirrel, a rabbit, a cat, and I'm sure others I've successfully forgotten about. Saving the newts was a little act of contrition and a symbolic offering to the animal kingdom on behalf of all drivers of my species. (We didn't mean harm—could that be taken into account on Judgment Day?) And the same was true of the return of Mr. Toad to the wild: after many wrongs, something done right.

Later the sun came out, warming and drying the pavement near the house. We walked down the dirt driveway toward town and as we approached the pavement I saw something that gave me a start. I steered my son the other way, so he wouldn't see it: right there at the bottom of the driveway, about a foot from road's edge, Mr. Toad, foolish Mr. Toad, Mr. Toad who (I should have remembered) had a thing for warm blacktop . . . flat as a pancake.

THREE

THE ROAD IS VERY UNFAIR

IN 1992, I TRAVELED TO Kenya because of something I'd read in the newspaper. A report on an international AIDS conference in Amsterdam briefly mentioned research suggesting that long-distance truck drivers might be spreading the disease, by sleeping with prostitutes along the routes they plied between central Africa and the continent's east coast, on the Indian Ocean.

At the time, most Americans knew AIDS as a disease of gay men, junkies, and Haitians. Randy Shilts's important and influential *And the Band Played On* (1987) focused on the role of a promiscuous flight attendant, Gaetan Dugas, in spreading the disease to several countries, suggesting that Dugas was the "Patient Zero" of AIDS among gay men. But AIDS was a developing story, and five years later, when I read the article on the conference, it was generally thought that the epidemic had originated among people unknown, possibly in central Africa, and that presumably it spread first not by air but by road.

My college roommate of two years, Doug Dittman, who was gay, had died of AIDS a year before I read the article. His partner, Mark, my other roommate, had become infected as well; and between Doug's death and Mark's illness, I found myself thinking about AIDS a lot. Other people seemed to be trying hard not to think about it (President Ronald Reagan resisted mentioning the epidemic for years), and that was something I wished I could change. When I read about the African truckers, a lightbulb went on: because of our own trucker culture, I thought, this story might interest American readers in AIDS in Africa (where it was expected to be much worse than in the USA). And it offered the chance to ride along on some trucks and see the life firsthand, which I always preferred.

A Kenyan doctor and immunologist who had co-authored the study

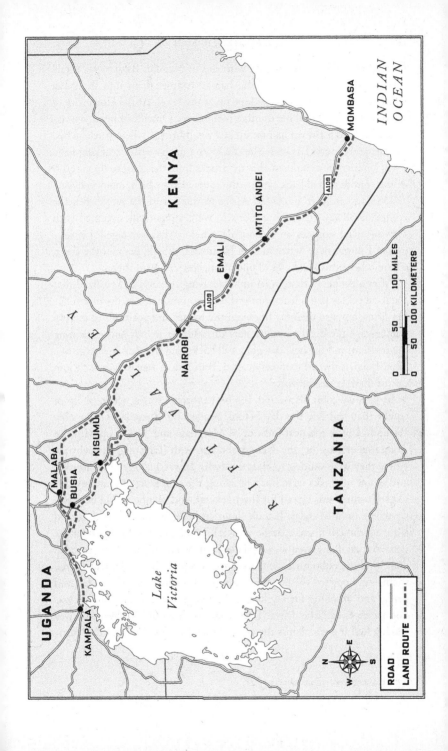

I'd read about, Job Bwayo, met with me in Nairobi. Bwayo was a tall, soft-spoken, handsome man who had to contort to fit into the small white sedan in which he picked me up at my hotel. At the University of Nairobi, he introduced me to other researchers. Outside of town, we visited a clinic that Bwayo had set up at a weighbridge, where truckers had to stop, and—a crucial piece—he tried to set me up with a trucking firm. I was looking for a company that ran trucks from the coast to the interior of the continent and back again—the route along which, many believed, AIDS had spread from central Africa to the rest of the world. But the companies Bwayo had connections to were temporarily occupied with ferrying relief supplies up to Somalia, where a civil war raged. He suggested I might have better luck in Mombasa, the big port on the coast, where other firms had bases of operation, and so I went there.

After a couple of days in Mombasa having no success, I realized that the local yellow pages listed not just the main numbers of the big trucking firms, but also their fax lines and the names and positions of the top managers. I faxed off several letters introducing myself and explaining my mission, and the next day got a call back from the man in charge of a large Belgian-owned company called Transami. I was welcome to join one of their trucks, he said.

In fact, we soon discovered, the best prospect was a whole group of trucks that had left the day before, headed for Rwanda and possibly Burundi. I took the next bus out of Mombasa and caught up with the Transami convoy on the Kenyan border with Tanzania, at Isebania, where they were waiting to clear Customs. It was a cool, rainy Saturday, and scores of trucks were lined up along the shoulders of a muddy dirt road. Customs was closed for the weekend, and no one would be going anywhere until Monday. It took about an hour to find my truck (called Fleet 19, though it was a single vehicle). Tired and wet, I banged on the door. A man in his twenties rolled down the window, peered out, realized who I was—a radio message to a company rep on the border had alerted them—and opened the door with a smile. Obadiah Okello was tall and genial and, reaching for my knapsack, invited me into the cab. He was not, he explained, the driver. That would be Bradford Mulwa, who was "taking tea" at a tent across the way.* Rather he, Obadiah, was the "turn-

---

*Obadiah and Bradford are pseudonyms.

boy," or driver's assistant, whose responsibility it was to guard the truck twenty-four hours a day.

Obadiah, Bradford, and I (along with four other semi-trailer rigs in the Transami convoy) traveled together for the next few weeks, slowly bouncing over the crumbling roads of western Tanzania, into war-torn Rwanda, and finally into Burundi, which was on the verge of its own civil war. The trucks stuck together mainly out of fear of robbery: they carried imported goods, manufactured items including roofing, chemicals, window glass, beer bottles, medicines, bicycles, tires, secondhand clothes, and electronics. Imported goods were by definition valuable, so much so that the trip had begun with a police-organized nighttime convoy of several dozen trucks. But once past Nairobi the police escort disappeared, leaving the drivers to their own devices. Adding to their vulnerability, the old British Leyland trucks (ours had served in the Falkland Islands war) were prone to breakdown, especially given their overloaded trailers.

For most of that first journey, there were twelve employees—five drivers, five turnboys, and, from the first breakdown in Tanzania, a mechanic

Obadiah, right, with fellow turnboy Stephen in Tanzania in 1992. The region, and the men's profession, were both near the center of the AIDS pandemic. Stephen has since died.

and a supervisor who followed along in their own Toyota Overland Cruiser—and me. Obadiah was my favorite, and my main link to the others.

A Luo from the region east of Lake Victoria, he was opinionated and assertive (as Luos are said to be). Much of what he said seemed to require an exclamation point after it on paper. Regarding my sunglasses, which I often loaned him, he said, "Such nice goggles! So green!"; of the awful roads of western Tanzania, "The road has much corrugation!"; on the speed of Bradford, the driver, whom he felt drove overcautiously, *"Haraka! Haraka!* (Faster! Faster!)."

Many of his exclamations involved his dissatisfaction with Bradford. The two could hardly have been more different. Bradford, in his late forties, had spent thirteen years in the Kenyan army. They must have been formative ones: he was disciplined and reserved. Every morning he shaved and put on a clean button-front shirt. Where Obadiah was expressive, Bradford was taciturn; he had, as far as I could tell, three facial expressions: impassive, frowning, and, rarely, slightly smiling. In his twenty years of driving big trucks, he claimed never to have had a single accident, and he attributed this to being careful and following all the rules.

To Obadiah, however, Bradford's caution was extreme, and maddening. "That man is slow, *sooo* slow!" he would say. "He is slow the way he drives and slow the way he talks. He is just too slow." More often, he would complain to Bradford directly. If the road had opened up, for example, and it appeared to be smooth sailing ahead but Bradford was in a low gear, Obadiah would start up with his *haraka*s, as though the driver required reminding. "Overtake that man!" he would instruct, when Fleet 19 came up behind some slower vehicle and the way was clear. Occasionally Bradford would glare at him in response, but more often he would simply ignore Obadiah, because he resisted hurry. And because he could.

Slowness was also the way Bradford handled being shaken down, whether by a Customs official or by a local policeman who had set out spikes on the road in hopes of extracting a small tip. Obadiah's approach was to banter with such extortionists, joking and pleading poverty, trying to keep everything on a genial level without acceding—or by barely acceding—to a demand. Bradford's method was simply to stare stonily back at an official as though he didn't get it. The net result was often the

*Turnmen, as they now are known,
are responsible for everything the driver
would rather not do: guard the truck
at night, cook roadside meals, and fix
the numerous* panchas *(Swahili
for "punctures") caused by rough roads
and overloaded trailers.*

same—the officials tired of attempting to communicate with a sullen dullard—but it took a lot longer.

Obadiah also complained because Bradford didn't do him many favors. Since drivers were at the top of the highway caste system and turnboys at the bottom, and since drivers could make so much more money (not only in salary, but in various contraband-carrying and fuel-selling schemes), the job entailed a bit of noblesse oblige—drivers typically bought their assistants a meal now and then, a drink, a cigarette. But unlike the other drivers he had worked for, said Obadiah, Bradford, in the three years they had worked together, had offered him nothing.

Obadiah occasionally got behind the wheel—when the truck needed to be moved in a parking area, for example. Other than that, I did not know what kind of a driver he would make. But, assuming he was a good driver, you could see how, in a different kind of business culture, he would quickly rise above a man like Bradford. He was eager, he was in a hurry, he was less interested in rules than in getting the job done most efficiently. He was certainly better educated, having completed O-levels and some post-secondary training in marketing before leaving Luo country for the coast, on a job tip from an uncle.

That said, Bradford was perfectly nice to me, and took pains to invite me to accompany him at the various places we stopped—tea stalls, restaurants, lodgings—along our journey. I bought beers for him and he bought beers for me. But when we drank, I often thought about Obadiah, stuck back at the trucks with the other turnboys.

Over the five weeks or so we were together, I found Obadiah to be friendly, energetic, good-humored, curious, and loyal. Back home, I missed his lively intelligence and vigorous, argumentative personality. I sent him some things he'd asked for—sneakers, books—and we stayed in touch. Over the years, his occasional messages always cheered me, not only because staying in touch was difficult but because his work was dangerous, in ways both expected and unusual, and each letter was evidence that he was still alive, still driving.

In some ways, an African truck driver's work was easy: there was little anxiety about timetables, since so much was out of their control. Several times a day, the convoy pulled over at a roadside settlement for chai. They never drove at night: between bandits and bad roads, it was too dangerous. But on the other hand, the job was difficult: the drivers were gone from home for weeks at a time. And, typically, the turnboys were essentially tied to the truck, to protect the load, the fuel, and the tires from getting stolen. At night, they generally slept underneath or on top of the trailer, a wrench at hand for use as a weapon.

But worst of all the risks they faced was disease. At the time of my visit, malaria was still the number-one killer in sub-Saharan Africa, and all of the men I got to know had had bouts of it. Worse, though, was the disease on the horizon: AIDS, or UKIMWI, as the Swahili acronym had it, or more commonly, "slim"—short for "the slimming disease." The drivers knew about it and worried about it, not least because research like Job Bwayo's had resulted in some negative publicity about their profession. "LORRY DRIVERS SPREAD AIDS," warned the tabloid headlines. Drivers took it as a slur, and maintained that few of them had, in fact, died of AIDS. When drivers died, they said, it was most often malaria, but sometimes also "pressure" (high blood pressure), diabetes, fever, tuberculosis, and "spells"—not to mention collisions and wrecks.

Not that anyone actually knew the cause of death much of the time. In those days, for most of those plying the truck routes, medical care was so rudimentary that not only did you have to go out of your way to get tested for AIDS, but when a person died, there was often no testing to see what he or she had died of. Still, research like Bwayo's had begun to steer a lot of foreign public health money toward Africans like them. Stores sold condoms (even if they were supposed to give them away free), and shops and lodgings had pamphlets and posters about AIDS. Many of the truck stops we passed had been visited by health workers armed with condoms and diagrams.

From what I could see, however, none of this had influenced the men's behavior much. You could have a lot of sex on the road in East Africa, and from what I could tell, the great majority of it was still unprotected. In part this was because the men were fatalistic about disease. "If I'm going to get it, I've already got it," said a driver named Sami—and it was very possibly true. Others thought they could avoid AIDS by steering away from women who looked unhealthy. And many, at least in the back of their minds, believed that if they got it, they would find a way to get rid of it—through an AIDS vaccine, which the Kenyan government was said to be working on, or (and I heard this horrific opinion several times, and rebutted it every time I did) by having sex with a virgin.

Of all the men, only Obadiah, with whom I discussed the subject at length, appeared to understand that a person with HIV was infectious even when he had no symptoms of illness.

Some of their attitude was denial, but it was more than that. In many of the men's minds, Western explanations of disease were hardly the last word; a sick driver was likelier to consult a faith healer (and believe her explanations) than a medical doctor, particularly about a condition that Western medicine could not cure. At one outdoor market where we stopped, Bradford bought a kit for snakebite from an aging healer: it was five little chips of black plastic, hand-wrapped in cellophane. Bradford related to me her instructions in careful detail: Using a knife, make three cuts near the bite. Place a piece of plastic atop each one. It will stick. When it falls off, place it in boiling water or milk. Wait until it sinks to the bottom. You're cured!

It was hard, in any event, to blame these men for preferring not to dwell on their vulnerability to a nefarious plague.

That trip was eventful. There were numerous breakdowns, a collision in Kigali, and many nights in "lodgings" where prostitution was, well, ordinary. In remote western Tanzania, we traveled with live chickens so we'd have something to eat in case we got stranded; my job was to feed and water them. Drivers had a reputation as cowboys of a sort—independent, self-sufficient wanderers. My companions were enterprising, resilient, and protective of me.

Because of AIDS, they were in a world that was changing very quickly. But not only was Obadiah still on the road in 2003—and now as a driver—he was still with Transami. And so, eleven years later, I went back to travel again with Obadiah and see what had changed since my first visit.

In some ways, Kenya felt reborn in the fall of 2003. Nine months before, leadership of the government had transferred from longtime strongman Daniel arap Moi and his KANU party to a new leader, Mwai Kibaki, in elections that were widely considered free and fair. This was a considerable achievement in sub-Saharan Africa, and in a republic so young: Kenya achieved independence from Britain in 1963. Kibaki (as yet unsullied by his election fraud of 2007, which would plunge the country into chaos) had run on a platform of fighting corruption, and there was expectancy in the air.

On the other hand, plenty had gotten worse. In 2002, surface-to-air missiles had been fired at a Boeing 757 full of tourists as it took off for Tel Aviv from Mombasa's Moi International Airport. They missed, but minutes later a suicide bomber blew himself up at an Israeli-owned hotel on a nearby beach, killing three Israelis and ten Kenyans. Four years before that, suicide bombers in trucks attacked the U.S. Embassy in Nairobi, killing over two hundred people, mostly Kenyans, and injuring four thousand others.

Statistically, of course, there was more danger elsewhere; the AIDS epidemic had swelled since my last visit, fulfilling many awful predictions. Antiretroviral drugs, which were saving the life of my friend Mark, were making their way into clinics, but for many people it was too late. And here the disease was less discriminating than at home: the presence of other sexually transmitted diseases, such as gonorrhea and chlamydia, appeared to facilitate infection by AIDS, which accounted for much of its spread among women. And though clinics were actively screening and counseling pregnant women about the transmission of HIV via breast milk, nursing infants were still getting infected. The commercial landscape around the hospital near my hotel in Mombasa had been transformed from a variety of shops to just one kind: coffin-makers. They displayed their wares outside, and what caught your eye was how many were for people who were very, very small.

Another difference about AIDS in Africa was that its victims came from all up and down the socioeconomic ladder. On my earlier visit, I'd been struck by reports that seemed to show the toll was worst among the better-off. The best explanation I heard for this was that wealthier men could afford to have more sex: they were more likely to have mistresses than working men, and more likely to travel for business and to patronize prostitutes.

It went to the very top. A few years before my first visit, the president of Zambia announced that his son had died of AIDS. In Kenya, however, officials were less forthcoming. Two weeks before my second visit, Britain's *The Economist* magazine stated outright that the recent death of Kenya's vice president, Michael Wamalwa, in a London clinic was a result of AIDS. Kenyans were told by their government that the vice president died from a heart attack related to kidney failure. Uganda's government-owned *New Vision* newspaper reported that Wamalwa had been treated for pancreatitis, and that his doctor was a leading AIDS specialist. Nairobi's *The Nation* did point out, seventeen days after the death, that "the clinic Mr. Wamalwa checked into in London is noted for outstanding work relating to HIV/Aids. It has also been established that one of the causes of pancreatitis, which the Vice-President was suffering from, is excessive use of anti-retrovirals." But they quickly added, "We are not saying Mr. Wamalwa, or other leaders who have died in the recent past, suffered from these diseases."

The hint was hard to miss. But no Kenyan I asked seemed to suspect it, and many openly doubted me when I mentioned it. (Three years later, the vice president's AIDS was still cloaked in euphemism. "Wamalwa died in London in August 2003, after a long illness," wrote *The East African Standard*, in "The Man Who Died Just as the Party Began," a remembrance published in 2006.) Because of its association with sex outside marriage, death by AIDS was still deeply stigmatized.

I was met at the Mombasa airport by Suleiman Abdallah, forty, Transami's dispatcher of twelve years ago who, despite changes in ownership and management, had retained his job. Back then, Suleiman had been the man at headquarters responsible for checking up on me; he had been genial and reliable, and I had kept up some with him, too. Medium dark, he wore glasses and had been a bit chubby back in the day. Now he was graying and skinny, which I found a bit worrying, but he said he was fine—Ramadan had started, and he was losing weight from fasting. (Islam is the dominant religion in coastal Kenya; elsewhere in the country most people are Christian.)

Suleiman was driving a Transami pickup truck. The company was now owned by the French conglomerate Bolloré, not by Belgians, but Suleiman's new supervisor, a British expat in his forties named Mike Keates, who was transport manager, was aware of my history with the company and had not objected to my hanging out again there for a while. I wanted to meet Mike, but he was busy yelling at a driver on the phone when we arrived, so Suleiman showed me around the new office and paved truck yard. The dirt yard I remembered was two locations in the past, he told me. Since then, the new owners had made many other changes. The tarmac out back was one of them; Mike had blamed puddles of standing water in the previous yard for his getting malaria. I noticed that there were many more trucks now (ninety, up from forty-seven) and they were a lot newer, and mainly made by Renault; in the old days, all the trucks appeared to be British Leylands, on their ninth lives. (Global corporate ownership was starting to shake up patterns of brand loyalty. Up to the early 1990s, trucks you saw on the road in East Africa tended to reflect countries' colonial masters: Somali truckers drove Fiats; Tanzanian truckers, Mercedes-Benz; central Africans, Renaults; and Kenyan and Ugandan truckers, Leylands.)

"Oh, a lot has changed," said Suleiman, chuckling. I might not have realized, he said, that the driver Mike had on the line was speaking to him from his cell phone, a vast improvement over the patchwork system of shortwave radios that had been in place before. When I reflexively said that was great, remembering how seldom the Transami radios had worked in the old days, Suleiman shook his head: "I'm not sure all the drivers would agree with you," he said, and there was laughter from the half-dozen men at desks nearby. Drivers could receive calls for free, and it appeared that, like it or not, many of them often did—from Mike.

In a similar vein, said Suleiman, all the trucks had been recently equipped with GPS devices. This allowed headquarters to track their every movement, part of the newly efficient regime with its higher expectations of profit. Weeks-long forays into central Africa with grossly overloaded trailers were mostly a thing of the past, as well: Transami now focused on speedy round trips to Kampala, Uganda, which normally could be accomplished in less than a week. I saw the computers where the tracking took place, and briefly met Mike's boss, a twenty-four-year-old Frenchman named Nicolas, whose large desk was piled high with computer printouts and who seemed perpetually glued to his monitor. Crunching the numbers, now, was what management was all about.*

Obadiah arrived in the afternoon. We embraced and had a public catching-up in the main room outside Mike's cubicle. Still rangy and fit at age thirty-eight, he had gone even grayer than Suleiman. Now that he was a senior driver, he was paid extra for stopping to help out other Transami drivers who encountered trouble on the road. I took out a stack of photos from our earlier journey. Suleiman and employees out of Mike's field of vision clustered around to look at the snapshots of men they had known. "There's Francis!" "There's Sami!" "Cromwel!" I wanted the news about all of them, so I made a list of each truck that had been in our convoy, along with its driver and turnboy:

Fleet 19:
Bradford (died)
—Obadiah (now senior driver)

Fleet 35:
Zuberi (died)
—Mlaghui Mwaruruma (died)

Fleet 10:
Malek (fired for stealing fuel, now driving a bus in Dar es Salaam)
—Stephen (died)

Fleet 37:
Francis (died)
—Duma (still a turnboy)

*Nicolas and Mike were the only white people in the office. They appeared to hire people from across the spectrum of Kenya's tribes and religions. When I asked if that was for reasons of equal opportunity, Mike replied, "That, and it's no good to have just one tribe. Then it's too easy for them to maneuver anything." In other words, with one tribe there would be more employee solidarity. Also, Mike explained, they could speak to each other in their mother tongue instead of Swahili or English, so "you wouldn't know what they are saying."

Fleet 31:
Sami (sick, unemployed)
—Hassan (now a Transami driver)

Toyota:
mechanic: Cromwel (died)
caravan leader: Mwalimu (retired).

Over eleven years, six of the twelve men I'd gotten to know had died, and at least one more was quite ill. I knew it would be wrong to assume all the deaths were due to AIDS; life expectancy in Kenya was low, and I had been gone a long time. Still, this seemed like a high number, particularly given that several of the dead had been young. Most jolting to me was the death of Cromwel, a jolly, robust, intelligent mechanic who spoke English well and devoured the thrillers of Nelson DeMille. "What did he die of, do you know?" I asked the gathered employees. There was some shaking of heads—people didn't know, or would not say.

I persisted in trying to establish causes of death. Somebody else had died of diabetes, they said; another had died of malaria; another had died of "heart." Mike emerged during this discussion as Suleiman was telling me that Sami, a skinny driver from the Kalenjin, one of the Nandi-speaking tribes famous for producing marathon runners, who was fond of seventies-style zip-up shirts, white patent leather shoes, white leather jacket, and big long sideburns, was quite ill from "TB."

"You know, Suley, that TB is an opportunistic infection," Mike interjected, speaking more gently now than he had on the phone. "TB doesn't get you—it's AIDS that gets you." Everyone nodded deferentially, but nobody looked at Mike and nobody wanted to take up this line of thought. Mike signaled to me to follow him back into his office, but before he could get there his cell phone rang, his desk phone rang, and he caught sight of an employee he'd been looking for. He chose to go speak to the worker, and appeared to forget about me completely. The worker looked stubborn and not too smart as Mike yelled at him. Suleiman intervened to explain a few things in Swahili, but the man didn't seem persuaded. Mike screamed, "If I gave your ass a bucket you wouldn't know how to fill it with your own shit!" to general tittering around the office. The man didn't laugh; I guessed he didn't understand enough English to know what Mike had said. Mike took a little walk around the yard to blow off some steam before returning to talk to me. Finally he came back and apologized to me for the wait.

"It's permanent crisis management here," he said, explaining his ongoing agitation. The crises, in order of occurrence, were:

1. accidents
2. thefts (mainly of cargo from containers)
3. mechanical breakdowns.

Making them all worse, he said, was the "constant bloody pressure" of having a budget with monthly targets. His job boiled down to making sure the Mombasa operation was grossing about $717,000 every month: a recurring deadline to get things delivered and receive payment. I supposed this was the way business worked in the developed world, but Mike's stress level suggested it was a new way of thinking for Kenya. "We're under intense pressure to make money," he summed up. "It's not made easier when your average African has no perception of time."

Or perhaps of *haste*, I thought later, as I weighed Mike's remarks. In any event, the pressured atmosphere around the office made me happy that I was about to get out of there and hit the road.

Two days later, we were in the cherry red cab of Obadiah's Renault semi rig. "Where's the turnboy?" I asked, climbing up into the passenger seat.

"No turnman!" Obadiah replied, using the current terminology. "They want to see if we don't need one. It's experimental." This reminded me of North American freight trains slowly shedding their cabooses, a process begun in the 1980s and mostly completed during the 1990s.

"I see. So having a *mzungu* for a turnman," I joked, using the Swahili equivalent of *gringo*, "is like having no turnman at all?"

"That is right!" Obadiah laughed.

His truck, laden with two cream-colored containers, lumbered out of the guarded gate of the Transami yard and onto the dirt road that ran between the walls of other big companies on this industrial side of Mombasa. Soon we were on a paved street lined with commercial stalls, then we passed through an intersection.

"Last week the police shot two robbers here," Obadiah said. "In their car. It was stolen. Yes, they took guns and killed them." Two intersections

*By 2003, Obadiah was a senior driver and team leader,
and drove a bright red Renault truck.*

later, pieces of sheet metal slid off a truck ahead of us, which pulled over; Obadiah swerved to avoid the obstacle. Driving here required a different set of skills.

The road took us past the port of Mombasa, with its high fences and a distant view of cranes used for unloading ships and stacks of containers. Beyond that was the Indian Ocean, where now and then you could still catch a glimpse of the trapezoidal sail of an old-fashioned boat. Old ways were fast disappearing around Mombasa, as they do in any port town that is a nation's door to the outside, and it seemed material culture was the first to go—the wooden boats, the row houses on narrow streets in the Old Town, some with narrow wooden second-floor balconies supported by wooden scrolls. But Fort Jesus, the stone garrison built by the Portuguese in the days of colonialism and the city's main tourist attraction, wasn't going anywhere; and the two huge pairs of tusks that curve over Moi Avenue like a welcome sign seem nearly as permanent.

Other durable links to the past can be found in the language. To take a colonial example: "turnboy" dates from early in the twentieth century, when the operator of a vehicle (most likely a white man) wanted somebody to turn the crank to start the engine. The grown man who performed this menial task became a turnboy, and a turnboy's job came to include many other duties related to the operation of vehicles: keeping them clean, changing tires, guarding against thieves and vandals. By the start of the twenty-first century, "turnboy" had updated itself to "turnman."

Among themselves, most drivers spoke Swahili. Like English, Swahili is a lingua franca—but one lacking the taint of colonialism, which makes it popular in East Africa (and especially in Tanzania). Associated with a coastal tribe, the Swahili, which is predominantly Muslim, the language has been influenced by Arabic over hundreds of years of trade and conquest along the coast. Swahili traders began regular expeditions into the interior of East Africa starting early in the nineteenth century, spreading their language along the way. Long before English became East Africa's language of government and education under the British administration of the first half of the twentieth century, the region's many tribes did business in Swahili. At Transami, the tradition continued.

It's fascinating how the language adopted words relating to trucks and travel. Many were simple English cognates for manufactured things that did not exist in early-twentieth-century Kenya: a mechanic's *tulboksi* contained a *tork renchi* that could be used to work on the *silinda hedi* or other parts of the *mota*. Other words revealed the pastoral origins of the speaker. The slang word for the tractor part of a semi rig was "horse" (*farasi*). A truck's wheels, *magurudumu*, were often called "legs" (*miguu*) and slang for refueling was the same as "feeding." A rig that traveled fast was said to be "running."

As Obadiah and I crossed the bridge from Mombasa Island to the mainland and headed west on the motorway, we followed a trail of trade and migration that was centuries old.

I enjoyed being back in a truck with Obadiah, and seeing him in charge. He seemed proud to have this job and I could see why: working in international trucking for a European firm had a fairly high status in East Africa. You were well paid, mainly in salary but also through the opportunity to take advantage of the difference in countries' official prices and sell fuel on the side. You were in charge of an expensive piece of manufactured equipment, which you got to operate—at high speed, if you so chose. And though management exerted control through productivity targets and supposed deadlines and GPSs and cell phones, everybody knew that once you were out there on the road, things could come up, trouble could happen, delays. The road brought unpredictability, which could mean peril, but it also meant freedom.

Though gleaming and much newer than the last truck we'd sat in together, Obadiah's Renault was also bought used. He had been given charge of it two years ago. At the time, its odometer read about 400,000 kilometers (almost 250,000 miles); now it said 682,310 kilometers (almost 425,000 miles). He was particularly proud of the driver's seat, which had bouncy air suspension; I nodded my appreciation, having already noticed that Transami had not seen fit to install the same thing on the turnman's side. The big cab had two sleeping bunks, which the Leyland had lacked; back then, management thought that giving the drivers a place to sleep would just encourage visits by prostitutes. Given the number of cheap lodgings you could find along the highways, I had always doubted that was true.

As much of an improvement as Obadiah's truck represented, though, he confessed that its suspension was better suited for European roads than African ones: the shocks and struts constantly needed replacement, he said. "Our roads are too rough and this truck is too fast."

Obadiah's trailers weren't loaded until about three p.m. so we had gotten a late start and didn't expect to get too far that first day. The most memorable sight, as we left the coast, was the primary school students heading home in groups alongside the road. All of them wore uniforms, and the colors were glorious combinations seldom seen on students in North America: orange shirts or blouses paired with gray shorts or skirts; white paired with purple; kelly green with orange or khaki; pink with blue, pink with black.

By and by, an hour or two from Mombasa, we came up behind a grown man wearing a very plain gray uniform. Obadiah pulled over to give him a lift. This was the sort of thing Bradford would never have done: a violation of company rules! But it turned out that the fellow worked at the weigh station ahead. Weigh stations were too common in East Africa, and generally ineffective: they were supposed to keep overweight trucks off the road, because, over time, overweight trucks caused considerable, expensive damage to the road surface. Often, though, the driver of an overweight truck simply bribed his way through. I didn't know whether Obadiah was overloaded or not, but any way you looked at it, doing a favor for the official made good business sense.

The man got off as we came up on the queue of thirty or forty trucks waiting to be weighed. I could tell Obadiah chafed at being last—he kept leaning out his window, watching our former passenger's progress as he walked toward the front of the queue. Once the man was out of sight, Obadiah jerked our truck out of the queue and trundled toward the front.

"There is another truck, a Transami truck, up here, and he will let us in," he assured me. That was exactly what happened. Drivers clearly could act as a team, to their mutual benefit.

Obadiah showed me his paperwork after he returned from the weighbridge office with the necessary approvals. One of our two twenty-foot containers held medicine and other medical supplies from a Catholic church in Louisiana, the other wax and solvents. When I asked whether the containers actually weighed what the bills of lading said—many firms were known to overload trucks beyond the limit, because it increased their profits—Obadiah smiled and said, "Close." Closer now, anyway, than in days of yore.

I had noticed that Transami loaded the containers in an unusual way, with their doors facing each other instead of toward the rear. Obadiah explained that this was intentional, a strategy for reducing theft: the easiest way to break into the containers was through those doors, and if neither one was exposed, they were that much more secure. "It is a very good idea," he said. I remembered how, eleven years earlier, Bradford had made him go hang off the rear of the trailer as the truck labored slowly up a particularly steep hill. He knew from experience that thieves lurked along that incline, and loaded trucks moved so slowly that the thieves had time to break in and throw cargo to the ground that would then be carted away. If the driving crew wasn't alert, they wouldn't know that they had been robbed until the next time they stopped, and found the doors swinging loose.

The sun was going down, and I knew we wouldn't drive much longer. The road was straight and only two lanes, and the angle of the light betrayed the deep grooves that westbound trucks left in the pavement; I had never noticed that before, and to me it made no sense. Was there always more traffic in one direction than in the other? "Why aren't those grooves in the oncoming lane, too?" I asked Obadiah.

"Oh, because we usually come back empty," he explained. Trucks carried goods in from the coast, but there wasn't much for them to ferry back—mainly just tea, now and then, and coffee. This road thus revealed an essential fact about the economy of East Africa: many imports, few exports; much going in, little going out.

We pulled into a broad dirt parking lot at the side of the road in a village called Mtito Andei, and Obadiah turned off the engine. I wondered now about the absence of a turnman: Who would watch the truck while we slept? Obadiah explained that this lot had an *askari* (guard) whom he could pay to watch the truck while we ate, and he could just pay the man a bit extra to watch it while we slept.

Our meal was in a large, fluorescent-lit hall, and certainly 90 percent of the other customers were drivers and assistants. It was your basic rice-and-chicken place, though you could also get fried potatoes, or goat. The men often ate in pairs, or in small groups, and those groups often looked ethnically the same: most trucking companies were small and, unlike Transami, hired men from the same tribe. No two diners looked as different from each other as Obadiah and I. I kind of enjoyed that.

Obadiah woke me while it was still dark. I'd slept—or tried to—in the tractor's narrow top bunk, where it was very stuffy, and it took me a moment to figure out where I was. We'd be on roads where there was a lot of construction today, he explained, and passing through Nairobi, as well, so we needed an early start.

The A109, the highway that connects Mombasa and Nairobi, Kenya's two principal cities, carries most of the country's traffic. The road had been a mess for years, Obadiah explained, perpetually under construction, a symptom of the corruption besetting his country. The week before, while I waited in Mombasa for Obadiah to return from a previous trip, I had read in the newspaper of a nightmare traffic jam: heavy rains had washed out a portion of the road, stopping traffic in both directions and leaving cars at a sodden, miserable standstill for eighteen hours. Obadiah showed me where the washout had been, thanking his lucky stars that he had missed it by a couple of hours. Today it was merely several hours of stop-and-go, and of dodging potholes and cracks that left me looking more and more enviously at Obadiah's bouncy shock-absorber seat.

Traffic speeded up briefly but slowed again in Nairobi. We watched planes taxi while we waited to refuel at the Transami depot next to the airport. Obadiah, the professional traveler, revealed to me that he'd never flown. "Very nice, Teddi, it must be very nice to be in that plane." Fast but dull, I said.

Nairobi had gotten rougher since my previous visit. Homeless "parking boys" lingered by the side of the road, some selling things, some begging. A group of a dozen or so lounging around a grassy patch in front of an office building, in the vicinity of a lone adult, made me think of Oliver Twist and Bill Sykes, reincarnated from Victorian England into twenty-first-century Africa. Twice, as we crept through the urban slowdown, around traffic circles with trees containing big Marabou storks and their nests, Obadiah called a boy over and sent him to buy a couple of cigarettes from a nearby kiosk. I noticed he only summoned boys who were not part of groups, and he acknowledged that the groups worried him. "They are the bad sort," he would say.

Outside Nairobi, when we headed northwest into the Kenya highlands, the roads improved. After climbing gently for a while past large farms and stands of cedar, we came to the lip of a huge escarpment that was the scenic highlight of the trip: the edge of the Great Rift Valley. Before us extended a vast bowl of haze. Obadiah wrestled his rig around turn after turn as we crested, and then, with the incipient plunge, placed it resignedly in first gear. He hated to go slowly, but this was a place where, truly, your life was in danger if you did not. The speed put him in mind of our old driver: "Brad Mulwa—he was a very slow man, very fearful, so afraid. He did not believe in himself." We passed baboons, and vendors of roasted maize on the cob who jogged alongside the truck and even climbed up it briefly to make a sale. I bought us each one, through the window. It had a good, smoky flavor but was tough.

Trucks and cars of various sizes roared slowly by us in the other direction, as they climbed out of the valley, most of them belching smoke and moving about the same speed as we.

Then a smaller truck, heavily laden and going downhill, passed us on a curve as we munched. It was a dangerous move, as the charred wreckage of totaled vehicles that shadowed us the entire way testified. Being passed always provoked Obadiah, who was convinced that, in his muscular Renault, he was always doing the maximum speed possible for a big truck under the circumstances; he was always staying just this side of the red line of safety. Anyone faster was by definition reckless. "That man does not care for his life," he said of the driver who passed us. "He does not care!

"You see, Ted, I am the best driver there is. I am very confident. If I can safely overtake, I do; if I don't then it's impossible." He claimed to have never had an accident. But later, at the bottom of the big drop, he told me a story of having come pretty close. It was somewhere in Uganda, a steep hill that was lightly trafficked. He had been braking a lot but at a certain point the brakes proved inadequate, and he was past the speed where he could downshift effectively. As the speedometer moved past 120 kilometers (75 miles) per hour, he told his turnman to retreat to the bunk compartment, where he might be slightly safer in the collision that now seemed likely. But Obadiah, hands glued to the wheel, miraculously made it around every turn and dodged every obstacle until, four miles later, the road flattened out.

"Some drivers can get scared, they panic! I do not. I was not scared. God gave me the responsibility and he will protect me."

Passing through rolling hills that afternoon, we saw giant tea plantations. We slowed for hamlets where a dozen people by the side of the road were all selling the same produce—carrots, in one place, scallions in another. Countless times we were waved to a stop by small-town policemen; Obadiah would slow to a crawl but seldom actually stopped, occasionally passing a 50-shilling note or a cigarette through the window to the officials, many of whom he seemed to at least recognize. I showed him pictures of my family and he told me of his: his younger brother, a teacher, had died just two months ago at age thirty-two, he said, "maybe cancer." His mother had died two years earlier, at home near Kisumu. This was a lot of sad news. He himself carried one photo in his wallet— that of his new daughter, Catherine, who was six months old.

"And we will see her tonight!" he said with a smile.

"We will?" I had expected another night in the truck.

"Yes! In Malaba. She lives on the border." He saw my quizzical look and laughed. "With her mother. My wife, Beatrice!* I have taken another wife!"

"Oh!" I said. "You have?" I knew that his first wife, and his two chil-

*Beatrice and Catherine are pseudonyms.

dren by her, lived in Mombasa. The next photo showed Beatrice together with her daughter.

"Much younger!" I observed.

Obadiah laughed again. "We were married two years ago. I asked her parents, and then I asked my other wife. All of them said it was all right. She is twenty-five.

"At first, Beatrice lived with my first wife, in Mombasa. But they did not get along. So she has moved here, so I can still see her often."

Malaba, on the border with Uganda, was part of his regular route, and border crossing usually involved at least an overnight stay, so the set-up was good: he could stay at home, and he and this part of his family could see each other.

Sixteen hours after leaving Mtito Andei, we arrived in Malaba, a small town with dirt streets and few buildings over one story tall. I was indescribably happy to climb down from the truck, and Obadiah seemed almost as pleased to be home. Dusk had fallen; a small, bright-green-painted mosque was broadcasting its call to prayer. We had pulled over next to an unfinished mini-mall that had a big dirt lot in front. Obadiah told me to bring along my bag as we left the rig.

We walked around to the back of the unfinished building, through tall grass and past a brick wall that separated it from the mosque. Obadiah climbed two steps up to a heavy metal door, and banged. We heard a bolt slide open, and were greeted by Beatrice and little Catherine. Beatrice was pretty; she had a warm smile and straightened, chin-length hair, and wore black jeans and a crisp pink blouse. She was gracious and welcoming, but Catherine seemed flabbergasted. I don't think she had ever met anyone who looked remotely like me. I set out to make her first impression a good one: I happened to be carrying a little rubber ball, and I bounced it to her on the kitchen floor. She sent it right back to me. Her initial concern, however, made me appreciate the apartment's remote location. Keeping a low profile would make life easier for me.

The apartment had three small rooms and no plumbing; outside there was an outhouse, and a tap where Beatrice filled jerry cans of water. But there was gas for a stove inside, and she quickly stood over it to make me and her husband a dinner of *ugali* (a starchy dish of ground meal) and chicken. We ate without utensils, as is common in Kenya, and by tradition with our right hands, though the family wasn't Muslim. Somehow,

Among the perks of Obadiah's seniority were a regular route (Mombasa to Kampala) and the means to support a second family. At their home in Busia, Obadiah holds Catherine, his daughter by his wife Beatrice.

while taking care of Catherine, Beatrice also heated two small tubs of water and carried them to another outbuilding, laying beside each tub a small bar of soap and a pair of flip-flops so that Obadiah and I could bathe. As dinner got under way, various people stopped by to say hello (and get a look at me), including Beatrice's mother, her sister, her niece (age six), and her friend Risper, who worked in a hotel not far away and wore a stiff, poufy dress. I was shown what Beatrice called the "guest bed," which had a mosquito net with some big holes in it—but some net is better than no net, and I looked forward to a night's sleep.

Unfortunately, it was not to be. I am not sure why, but part of the reason must have been the loud clock hanging on the wall just above my head. Black plastic, with gold plastic trim and hands, it ticked loudly and played a few bars of a famous popular tune at exactly fifteen minutes past the hour, every hour, all night long—"Auld Lang Syne," "Santa Lucia," the Largo theme from Dvořák's *New World* Symphony, "Für Elise," "Simple Gifts" (" 'Tis the gift to be simple, 'tis the gift to be free . . ."). As it happens, I had been plagued by the exact same model at a thatched-roof settlement where we'd stopped for the night on the river in Peru. It was made in China, of course, factory to the world; clearly, it had cross-cultural appeal. In my fatigue-fueled delirium I imagined a scene where Obadiah and Beatrice, all dressed up, were receiving the clock, in an elaborate ceremony, as a wedding present. But in the morning Obadiah said that no, he had admired it in Nairobi and bought it for Beatrice himself.

Even if Beatrice slept well, she couldn't have slept much more than I did: by the time I got up, around seven a.m., she had already washed Obadiah's clothes and mine, and fired up a charcoal brazier for our tea water. She cooked me eggs with bread and jam. As I ate, cute little Lisa, age six, Beatrice's niece, got up the courage to touch my blond arm hairs. Obadiah, out with the truck when I woke up, returned and Beatrice served him, too. She then showed me her small clothing shop, in the part of the building that faced the road. You could get to its back room through a little door in their apartment. Beatrice's mother was in there, rolling up a sleeping pad on the floor, and from the clothing and other effects nearby I realized that I had probably displaced the granny and Lisa, the niece, the night before. Yes, Beatrice said, it was true, but Grandma liked sleeping with the girl, no matter where it was.

Today, Obadiah explained, we would take the truck across the international bridge into Uganda—but clearing Customs there would likely take another twenty-four hours, so I could leave my things in the apartment as we'd be back there that night. That was good news: I was happy to have an easy day ahead. Little did I know . . .

Obadiah and I had this in common: on the road in East Africa, we both attracted the attention of people wanting money. I attracted it because of my white skin and presumed wealth; he attracted it because of the expensive vehicle he was in charge of. The driver of such a machine, they correctly assumed, even if he was not paid a high salary, could be presumed to have some cash on him, if only for incidentals incurred on a long trip.

Beggars require no pretext to ask for money: their destitution usually speaks for itself. But policemen usually do. The officers at the beginning of Braulio's trip down into the Amazon had only to point at the many passengers riding illegally atop his fuel truck. In Kenya, a truck driver could be legitimately fined if he had a crack in his windshield or mirror, a burned-out running light, or worn tire treads. The way it usually worked was that the policeman identified the flaw, declared the official penalty, and then did the offender a favor by accepting a couple of bills in lieu of the fine. If he couldn't find a flaw in the truck or its paperwork, then his negotiating ability was much diminished. Obadiah knew this well, and tried to begin every trip with his truck in the most unassailable condition possible. Except in extraordinary circumstances, as far as I could tell, the company did not reimburse drivers for bribes.

In front of Beatrice's clothing store, Obadiah hailed two *boda-bodas*, or bicycle taxis. Each had a small upholstered cushion behind the driver's seat, and pegs sticking out from the hubs for your feet. (Female passengers, whether wearing skirts or not, sat sideways on the back, just as they had upon *mototaxis* in Puerto Maldonado.) The name came from "border-border": south of here, in the Kenyan and Uganda border towns that are both named Busia, the immigration posts are separated by more than half a mile, and the taxi drivers solicit customers by calling "Border-border?"

The bikes took us to a Customs parking lot on the Kenya side of a small international bridge. Obadiah had already been there that morning and commissioned some local boys to wash the truck; at least four of them were sitting in the cab with the radio cranked up high. He paid them and they scattered. Obadiah invited me to drive across the bridge with him to the Customs yard on the Uganda side; from there we would walk back. But I was concerned: I had only a single-entry visa into Uganda. Wouldn't that mean I had to wait on the other side? He said no, the border zone was special—but I could check with the Uganda authorities just in case. I climbed up.

I was sleepy, and as Obadiah inched his big rig into the queue of trucks heading for the bridge, I slumped in my seat and drifted off. I was half awoken some time later by a man shouting, and then the truck jerking to a stop, right before the bridge. I sat up and looked out with alarm as my door swung open. An angry-looking policeman with a rifle in his hand gestured at me from the ground.

"Please alight! Alight now, please!" I looked around for my knapsack.

"Let me see your identification!" I handed him my passport, and he asked me what I was doing in the truck.

"Traveling, with the company's permission," I replied.

"It is against the law for this truck to carry a passenger," he declared hotly. "You will be arrested!"

At this point, Obadiah climbed down, too, and jumped into the fray. I could not understand what he was saying, but as the policeman's agitation mounted I sensed he was making things worse. Seeking to defuse matters, I interrupted: "Look, it's okay, it's not important that I ride in the truck today. I am happy to get out and cross on foot."

"It is too late!" said the policeman. "You have already broken the law!" At this Obadiah literally started screaming at the man. All traffic across the border had ceased; scores of people had stopped to watch. Deciding that Obadiah's passion might be a hindrance to resolving this, I told him to let me talk to the policeman alone. It took a lot of persuading, but after finding a *boda-boda* driver to take me home, Obadiah got back in the truck and drove it across the bridge.

Unfortunately, I had played right into the policeman's hands. "Now we will take you to the station," he announced, pointing to a building up the hill, still holding on to my passport. I repeated that I had the company's permission, that I had done nothing wrong, but that I would be happy to desist if that would make him happy.

He stepped very close to me and said in a low voice, hand on the rifle, "Let me see some dollars."

I had been wondering whether this moment would come. Under the circumstances, I thought acquiescing might not be a bad idea. I didn't have dollars, though; the only bills I had were 500-shilling notes, each worth about $7.50. I handed him one and immediately saw I had overpaid. There was no dickering, no quibbling: he simply grunted, handed back my passport, and walked away. I climbed on the *boda-boda* and, deeply relieved, rode home to Beatrice.

But the drama was only beginning. Obadiah, arriving home, asked me how much I had paid the man. I told him 500 shillings, not adding that I felt pretty good about getting out of the situation for less than ten bucks. But Obadiah went ballistic. "This man has *no right* to take your money! This man is very bad, very greedy. He has *no right!*" I agreed but was not upset; these things happened, in my experience, and as a traveler there wasn't much you could do about them.

This was not Obadiah's interpretation. His foreign guest had been ripped off, half a mile from his own home! In broad daylight! It was an outrage! He was livid, and getting madder and madder. Things were supposed to be different in Kenya now, he said. Didn't I agree we should file a complaint? At lunchtime he said, "I feel very heavy." And soon after that he said I had to come with him, President Kibaki had declared that corruption must cease; we couldn't let this stand!

Oh, boy.

Our first stop was the local Transami rep—the company maintained small offices in border towns like this, mainly to deal with Customs snafus. The man, who said he had witnessed the incident, was also in favor of complaining. He provided us with a signed statement on letterhead that said I had been authorized by the head office to ride in Obadiah's truck. The three of us then walked to the office of the chief of police. They had me wait outside. I wondered why I was so much more nervous than they were. I heard a lot of raised voices behind the closed door, but couldn't tell what they were saying.

Finally Obadiah and the rep came out. "Now he will go get the policeman," he told me. "We must wait."

"But how's it looking? What did the chief say?" I asked. Obadiah said it was too soon to tell.

The policeman arrived, and disappeared into the office for about ten minutes. Then Obadiah was ushered in to speak to the both of them; that took another ten minutes. The Transami rep, hanging out with me in an open hallway outside, where it was hot and muggy, predicted that we were going to win. Finally, I was invited inside and met the chief.

He was in a big chair at a big desk. Obadiah sat to one side of it and the policeman to the other. The chief asked me to tell him what happened, and I did. The chief appeared to mull matters over for a moment, then gestured at me and Obadiah.

"You have both broken the law. You by bribing a policeman and you by giving this man a ride." He looked at the wall behind me. "Do you understand?"

Suddenly I was as indignant as Obadiah had been. "Are you saying that when an armed policeman takes your passport, angrily says he's placing you under arrest, and demands that you produce some money, you should not do it? Because that's exactly what happened. This was not a bribe, it was extortion."

"Well," said the chief to Obadiah—he seemed unable to speak directly to me—"I see that he is a very clever and scheming man. Be that as it may, he now has two choices. Either the policeman returns this money and we settle it right here, right now. Or we wait until the court is in session Monday and settle it there."

I leaned over and conferred with Obadiah. Given that I had now been accused, I was willing to go to court if he wanted to. But it seemed life would be easier if I just accepted the money back. Obadiah said that was fine.

The policeman had my bill folded up in his shirt pocket. He handed it back to me. We all stood up and shook hands. The matter was finished—at least for us.

"That man will lose his job," Obadiah said as we left the police station, and the Transami man concurred. "He will lose it tomorrow."

"But the chief defended him!" I observed.

"The chief knows what happened," said Obadiah. "That policeman is a very bad man. He involved a *mzungu* and he involved Transami, and now he will be *out!*" And indeed, Obadiah later confirmed, the policeman was never seen working in town again.

That night we celebrated by going to a local bar, the Wangina—named, per custom, after the owner's mother. It was a couple of blocks off the main drag, down a dark dirt street. The heat of the day had dissipated in a great booming thunderstorm that knocked out the power that afternoon; in the wake of it, the air felt cool and clean.

The Wangina had a generator going, and used it to power a stereo (loud!), a television, and two dim bulbs that hung from a crossbeam under the corrugated metal roof. Three young locals played at a pool table. Handpainted on the wall was the injunction: *No Politics, No Dancing.*

"Will you take beer?" asked Obadiah. I nodded. He had already passed some money to Beatrice's sister. I had thought she was part of our entourage, but in fact she worked here: she took the money to a sort of cage across the room and passed it through a window to the owner, who sat inside it with the liquor. This cage, as it turned out, was the bar; apparently it was necessary to protect the owner from theft, of either liquor or cash. One didn't expect the crime threat in a small town to be so high, but clearly it was: the aluminum pot that Obadiah had given me the night before, in case I needed to pee during the night, wasn't just a convenience—they didn't want to unbolt the apartment door at night, no matter what.

Soon, he and I and Beatrice and Beatrice's friend Risper, wearing another poufy-sleeved dress, were drinking at a long table. There were other groups nearby, with most of the drinks apparently bought by two truckers whom Obadiah pointed out to me. Generally speaking, they were the guys in town with money.

Obadiah loosened up, and I noticed Beatrice rubbing her finger over his swollen knuckle. When I'd asked him about it before, he'd told me he had hurt the hand in a loading accident. But now he admitted that he'd gotten it from punching somebody the week before in a Mombasa bar. The victim, it came out with a little coaxing, was another Transami driver. The man had bought a beer for a woman without asking her, and felt greatly disrespected when she handed it to another guy. Somehow Obadiah had gotten caught up in protecting the woman from the driver's aggression; it had taken the blow to make him stop.

As he was finishing this story, the bar turned off its generator—the power was back on—and simultaneously there was a break in the music. For a moment we could hear both the call to prayer from the mosque next to Beatrice's apartment and the dialogue from the movie on the television, which now caught my eye: Charlie Sheen was playing a Navy SEAL whose mission appeared to involve blowing away large numbers of Arab insurgents. The juxtaposition was a bit unreal.

I chatted with Risper, who managed the front desk at a nice hotel near Busia, Kenya. "Obadiah told me you were interested in AIDS," she said. "Most people in Kenya do not wish to speak of it, but I think we should. In Uganda they have suffered the most, and come to grips with it. But in Kenya we deny." I asked Risper if she thought there was more safe sex now, more people using condoms. "Maybe some," she said, "but still not too many. Not enough. The problem is that if the man does not want it, the woman cannot insist. Like that girl!" She pointed to a young woman, maybe sixteen, in a red top, sitting by herself and with an expectant look on her face. Tonight she would sleep with a trucker "or with anyone who will pay her 500 bob [US$7.50] in the morning," Risper said. Or even for less: after a drink, a young and inexperienced girl might do it "for two or three reds" (100-shilling notes, meaning US$3 or $4.50). It was even possible that she'd forget to discuss price ahead of time, or else be too submissive and just wait and see what she was given. Discussing a condom, much less negotiating the use of one, was next to inconceivable for a girl like that, said Risper.

During my first journey with Obadiah, there had been lots of involvement with prostitutes. None of the truckers' wives were around, and their trip was many weeks long. Most of the places where we met women weren't brothels per se; they were just regular roadside lodgings. Most of the customers at these small hotels were men, and most of the women who worked at them, serving drinks or food, were understood to be available for sex. They didn't wear tight skirts or low-cut dresses or high heels, as hookers might in the West. Rather it was simply their presence in the bars or lobbies that signaled the men that they could be approached for paid sex.

Many of them approached me in a friendly way—if the truckers had money, their *mzungu* friend must be loaded!—but Obadiah and the others always got me out of it by explaining that I was obsessed with AIDS and didn't want to have sex. I might have put it differently and said that, in addition to being monogamously involved, I was *reasonably concerned* about AIDS, but the effect was the same.

Our brief overnight stays and my need to depend on the truckers as translators—due to the limited English of the rural women and my limited Swahili—had made it hard to press them about their work and their lives. But a few days after this second voyage with Obadiah, I contacted health educators who worked with prostitutes in Mombasa, as well as an advocacy group for HIV-positive women (including many prostitutes) in Nairobi, and had long conversations.

The women in Nairobi were particularly well-spoken and engaging. I bought lunch for seven of them at the headquarters of a group they belonged to, the Kenya Network of Women with HIV/AIDS (KENWA). They were better educated and better informed than many of their rural counterparts. The group's literature explained that they were offered vocational training and "seed money so they can sell sundries to become financially independent." Many of them had children, and KENWA tried to help with school fees, too. The group also offered medical care, including antiretroviral drugs, and helped feed some of the thousands of the city's AIDS orphans.

Among the more forthright of the seven women were Constance, Mary, and Jane. Constance was very pretty and wore an eye-catching black-and-white striped top, which was of a piece with her idea that "these men are attracted by sight—so you have to look good." The other women were neither unattractive nor glamorous. Mary was buxom and heavy; Jane was slender. All of them worked bars, they explained, and there was nothing secretive about it. "We boost their business," explained Mary.

Sometimes the bar had a back room they could take clients to, "or if the man wants to take you for a long time he will take you to a different place, or his hotel room," said Jane. On a good night, they might have sex five times, at 300 shillings (US$4.50) a pop. Oral sex was not common ("That costs more here," explained Jane), but all of them said they would do it if the price was right.

They flirted with me, saying *wazungu* (the plural of *mzungu*) made fine customers and they liked them very much. When they asked how much a prostitute cost in New York and I guessed that prices might start around $100, several laughed and asked if I would take them there immediately. Constance said that hooking could be better than being married, because you had more choice over the men you were with, and a husband might not give you enough to live on, might let you go hungry. "Here you are your own boss." But Jane made it sound almost like forced labor: "We go because there is nothing else we can do in life. And you don't need capital to get started! The only asset I need is what I have"—and she gestured to her body. Mary added that it was very, very difficult to go into another line of work after commercial sex, because you would have to work a month to make as much money as you might make in a few nights as a prostitute.

Occasionally the work was pleasurable. "Sometimes the man is sweet, and if you hadn't asked for money, you might forget," said Mary. Some of the men were funny, some would buy them drinks. But it sounded as though, more commonly, it was not. Men could be drunk, could be boors, could be rough. Some stank: "There are people you smell, and you can smell them the next day—seriously, you do not want to meet that man again," said Mary. Jane added, "Even after you get out of the shower, you can smell him!" And of course the downside could be much steeper. "Sometimes men are cruel, and they beat us." Every woman there had had a bad experience, including rape. Since it was a cash business, they were often robbed. And worst, of course, was that you could get various diseases, including AIDS.

I told them I appreciated their candor, and hoped to stay in touch—Mary and Constance had e-mail addresses. I told them I was making a donation to the group, as it seemed very worthwhile. I started to put away my notebook and get ready to leave.

"But what do you think?" Constance asked abruptly. None of the women, I noticed, were standing up. I sat back down.

"What do I think about what?" I asked.

"About our situation."

"Well, I think working to support a group like this is good, and paying close attention to your medicine and health is the right—"

"No!" said Constance. "We mean, about our *situation . . .*"

I was so thick. I thought I'd just been interviewing them about the work they used to do. "You mean," I said, "you're still hooking now?"

She nodded.

"All of you?"

They all nodded. I took a deep breath. "And you can't tell the men, or you would have no work. And your children would go hungry." Again they nodded. "But you can tell them to wear condoms—"

"Yes, but not all of them will," said Jane.

We sat and there was silence.

"I guess it means you should do other work."

"In Kenya," said Mary, "if you have no husband, and you have no degree, then there is little hope for you. All the jobs now are demanding HIV tests, especially the hotels."

"There must be some that don't . . . ," I said, not really knowing.

"What would you do, then?" asked Constance.

I was totally unprepared. "I like to think I would stop this work," I said. Could they be blamed for killing men if the men wouldn't wear condoms? What if the women didn't mention condoms, for fear of losing a sale? "I think you have to stop," I said. "But I'm not a hundred percent sure." And still I am not. This was so easy for me to say, and they knew it. They knew that I didn't know. Despite my education and advantages, I didn't know.

The road was usually a very male realm, so I was pleased to learn the next morning that Beatrice would be accompanying Obadiah and me to Kampala, the capital of Uganda. She did this periodically to restock her clothing shop, she explained—Kampala had a large clothing district and the prices were good. She would leave baby Catherine with her grandmother. We would have to make it a quick round-trip because Beatrice was breastfeeding and would become very uncomfortable if she was away from Catherine too long.

It was a Sunday. Finished with breakfast, bathing Catherine, and other duties, Beatrice went alone to the Church of the Apostle. She would join us shortly. Obadiah and I took *boda-bodas* to the bridge and then walked across. Many strangers waved at us. Because of our confrontation with the policeman, we were now celebrities. We hung around with other drivers at the Transami office on the Uganda side until our truck cleared Customs, just before lunch.

Women weren't allowed in the fenced-in Customs yard—an anti-prostitution measure—but Obadiah had arranged a rendezvous point with Beatrice just outside. I stepped out of the truck and helped her aboard. Obadiah immediately got into the spirit of it. "Yes, madame!" he cried. "Make yourself comfortable. Feel free!" (I loved his usage of this phrase, the literalness of it—not *Do as you wish,* but *Feel liberated!*)

The road to Kampala was good, though deeply grooved like so many others with the tracks of heavy westbound trucks. Kenyans described Uganda as green and beautiful and hilly, all of which it seemed to be. They spoke admiringly of Ugandans' cleanliness and knack for organization. It reminded me, funnily enough, of how Victorian explorers to East Africa saw Uganda as an exception to the "blank, amorphous barbarism" of surrounding parts, "an orchid in a field of poison ivy." There had been plenty of barbarity since pre-colonial and colonial times, of course, from the crazed genocidal reign of Idi Amin to the more recent terror of the Lord's Resistance Army. But Uganda, devastated by AIDS, had a good reputation for the measures it had taken to curtail the epidemic, and some essence of good organization had endured the hardships.

I'd brought a pair of sunglasses as a present for Obadiah, and as it was our first sunny day, I presented my gift. "Oh! It makes the atmosphere so very cool!" he said. We passed a giant cement plant in Tororo, and cotton fields with picturesque groupings of traditional houses nearby. They were round and made entirely of straw, which was why the local word for them, *kasisira,* Obadiah told me, translated to "no-smoking houses"!

Not long after, we began to get regular glimpses of East Africa's principal railroad line, which connected Kampala with the coast. In fact, our route had largely paralleled that of the railroad the whole way from Mombasa: the Uganda Railway (or "lunatic line," as some in Britain had dubbed it at its inception) was the region's first great infrastructure project, built in the last years of the nineteenth century—long before any highway. British hopes of making money from it took a back seat to strategic concerns: pieces of Africa were being claimed by European superpowers at the time, and Britain was eager to establish dominion around Lake Victoria, the source of the Nile, before anyone else did. Both the Germans (to the south, in Tanzania) and the French (in northern Africa) were actively interested and heading in that direction.

The railroad, which once carried British troops and even a disassembled ferryboat bound for Lake Victoria, succeeded in helping Britain cement her colonial claims. We drove through the town of Jinja, where the White Nile began its journey north from Lake Victoria, once an important stop on the train. But now the increasingly decrepit railroad mattered little. Three times a week, passengers could ride between Mombasa and Nairobi (a city which got its start, incidentally, as a depot on the new rail line). There was less frequent, and more dangerous, passenger service from Nairobi to Kisumu, and slow, sporadic freight service at different points inside Uganda and Kenya. But mainly the railroad served as a reminder of the colonial era, a time when white men ran everything, lions routinely ate people, and train tracks transformed landscapes and economies more effectively than pavement did.

Obadiah's Renault ground its way up a mountain into a pretty area called the Mabira Forest. Near the summit was a big clearing—a pull-off spot for cars and trucks—ringed with thatched-roof huts, each with a smoking grill in front. Our truck was quickly swarmed by vendors in blue smocks, each with a white number on his back, holding up skewers of beef and chicken as well as chapati breads, sodas, and roasted bananas. This was fast food, Uganda-style. We bought a lot and were soon on our way, the cab full of good smells. Between bites, Obadiah told me about a Transami driver who had been so hungry when he arrived at the food stop, he climbed out without setting the brake. The truck rolled backwards off the road and "Oh, you should have seen Mike. That man was a very bogus driver."

We arrived at the edge of Kampala late in the afternoon, the downtown skyscrapers just visible in the distance. Transami had a fortified compound that contained a smallish repair yard and then a mammoth yard with rows and rows of shipping containers stacked six and seven high. We parked the truck in their shadow, left via guarded gates, and proceeded on foot to one of those essentials of human existence that the city planners had barely left room for: a makeshift outdoor restaurant. Situated under a strip of what appeared to be the only trees for blocks, hard up against the company wall and looking totally impromptu, the place had a row of picnic tables and open cooking fires.

We were joined there by a Transami driver, Mbuvi, whom I had met that morning while waiting at the office at the border. He wore a red-striped button-down shirt, and I complimented him that it still looked every bit as crisp as it had ten hours ago. "Yes, well, I did not stop at the skewers restaurant is the reason why," he quipped.

"What are you suggesting?" I asked in mock offense, pointing to a spot on my own shirt where something had dripped.

Mbuvi was an interesting man. I'd met others like him in developing countries, overeducated for the sort of work they were doing—a former college professor who'd worked briefly at the mahogany camp in Peru was another example. Mbuvi had taught for ten years, he said, at a Christian technical college, before leaving it for this job "because I needed the money." He liked to rib Obadiah, and told me that Obadiah's tribe, the Luo, who had migrated many years before from lands north of Kenya, never got past Lake Victoria "because they like fish so much." After he heard Obadiah tell me what to do if I was ever pulled over by a policeman for speeding ("You must simply tell him, rubbish!"), Mbuvi said "That's why the Luo are not good politicians. They like to fight too much!"

He accompanied us as we walked a mile or so to a residential area and paid for rooms at City Harold's Guest House. Our quarters were hot but clean, and City Harold had an outdoor bar in front that was cool and comfortable. Mbuvi didn't drink—I was getting the impression that he was quite religious—but came out to sit with me and Obadiah and Beatrice. That morning, I'd heard him discussing Transami's AIDS training workshops with other drivers. (In the old days, as I mentioned, the disease was more often referred to as UKIMWI, the Swahili acronym—I'd listen for it in their conversations—but now everybody just said AIDS. Truckers also had a slang term for it: "slow puncture.") Obadiah mentioned a woman in Malaba who he thought must have AIDS by now because she had slept with "at least ten" company employees: "drivers, turnmen, everybody." Beatrice said she knew her. Then they discussed a Ugandan-made AIDS drug that, according to them both, helped you put weight back on but then suddenly you died. Obadiah proudly mentioned how Beatrice, pregnant with Catherine, had tested negative for HIV— and stated that a baby who "breasted" from an infected mother would live only five or six months. Beatrice said she was glad that Transami tested its drivers once a year—something I hadn't known. I was struck by this conversation, because I hadn't mentioned AIDS in a couple of days; on my earlier visit, it seemed I was the only one who ever brought the subject up. Now the people I was with talked about it frequently.

Beatrice finished her second beer and went to the room. Obadiah, Mbuvi, and I stayed outside a while longer. I asked Obadiah when the annual company AIDS test had begun. He didn't really answer, so I asked more directly. "Oh, I went in a little later," he responded vaguely. Mbuvi joined the inquisition. Again Obadiah dodged. "You wouldn't answer like that if it was just the two of us talking," Mbuvi snapped at him, with startling directness.

Mbuvi now took it upon himself to set the record straight: Transami did not have any annual AIDS test. The inescapable conclusion was that Obadiah wanted Beatrice to think he had been tested, when in fact he had not. A couple of weeks later, Mike would clarify matters further for me. Only prospective employees were tested, he said, and employees who required hospitalization. There was none of the right to privacy that American patients expected: drivers were not typically told they were being tested, and were notified of the results only if they asked.

I let the matter drop; I wasn't there to keep Obadiah honest, or to make him face up to deceptions. Lord knows, everybody has them. A woman in a tight dress walked by and we all watched her. Mbuvi finished his soda. "It's very hard to be a strong Christian in the world of transport," he said.

Obadiah's morning would involve trying to get the two loaded containers off his truck and two new, presumably empty ones back on for the return trip to the coast. The evening before, we had identified the trailers he had to load up: they were near ground level in separate tall towers of containers. Since two of the three mega-forklifts that moved these containers around the yard were broken, and other drivers were in line before Obadiah, it was going to be a long wait. I elected to go shopping with Beatrice.

We caught one of the little *matatu* minivan buses to downtown Kampala, which was clean and well kept, its tall modern buildings complemented by trees, shrubbery, and grass. From there we took another van to the famous Owino market, which had more than five thousand stores and stalls and was as crowded and busy as garment districts everywhere.

She went to a number of shops that she knew well. She wasn't buying in quantity: just items she needed to restock, and some special orders. She bought leather belts, men's and women's underwear, two men's shirts, a handbag, three blouses, and a girl's dress. Beatrice didn't appear to be getting a wholesale price; her profit would be the small markup you found in any small town. I acted as her porter, which enabled her to buy more. The main buying done, she checked out a couple of other places just for fun but didn't want to dawdle, in case Obadiah succeeded in loading up quickly. It started to rain and so, maybe two hours after we arrived, we were back at a crowded *matatu* lot.

We had just missed one departing minivan; the next to our destination was empty and would leave once it was full. Beatrice and I took shelter inside, our laps stacked with bags of clothes, and I asked her how she was feeling. A bit uncomfortable, she replied, but thought she'd be fine if we made it home that evening. I told her about my wife's experiences returning to work as a nursing mother; what seemed to interest her most was not the breast-pumping-in-the-restroom mechanics of this but the idea that a person as rich as I appeared to be had a wife who had to work. "We make more money than you do here, but life's a lot more expensive," I said, oversimplifying.

She turned the subject to Obadiah, their marriage, and how much happier she was living in Malaba than living in Mombasa, with his other wife. And she worried out loud about his life on the road, and possible infidelity. In particular, she said, she worried when he was gone a long time, as he had been a couple of years before, when Transami had lent him out to a Ugandan Coca-Cola bottling plant that needed extra trucks for a couple of months of product promotion. Obadiah had mentioned this experience to me, and though I said nothing, I tended to think her fears were not without foundation.

"But after that we stopped there once," she said. "I looked around to see if any women [prostitutes] asked about Obadiah, and I didn't find any." And on such slender shreds of evidence rested a willingness to love and to carry on. I liked Obadiah a lot, but I felt very sympathetic to Beatrice.

In 1993, three weeks into our earlier trip, our convoy of four Transami trucks had made it from Mombasa to Kigali, Rwanda. The densely populated country was a frightening place at the time: the apparent epicenter of the AIDS epidemic (approximately one-third of all adults were infected), it was also at the beginning of a bloody civil war. Our trucks awaited unloading in a fortified government truck yard called MAGERWA (Magasins Généraux du Rwanda) in the Gikondo district of the hilly capital, where during the day we watched funeral processions march by and at night we sought distraction in a beer garden and brothel known as the Snake.

Though Kigali was dangerous, life in the secure yard was a bit boring, especially for the turnboys. We sat there waiting for Transami's local affiliate to supply Bradford with the paperwork he needed for Customs, and then we waited for the Customs clerks to okay the unloading of our truck, and for the crane operators to actually do it. The drivers and I could leave now and then but the turnboys were stuck. Though we were in a secure yard, so were a lot of other trucks and employees, and things could get stolen. Obadiah's pants, for example, were swiped one day as they hung on a chain-link fence—a big loss. The turnboys could only get up to the Snake on rotation—if one of them covered another's truck, for example.

So I spent more time with the drivers and with Cromwel, the sharp young mechanic. And it was Cromwel I was with one evening when, leaving MAGERWA up the steep, rutted road that led to the Snake, we were approached by two Hutu soldiers. They were dressed in fatigues, with jackboots and berets. One bore his rifle properly, with the barrel behind his shoulder, but the shorter one had his reversed, so that the barrel pointed up into the nose of anyone he spoke to. They appeared to be sixteen or seventeen years old, and both, we soon realized, were drunk. (Soldiers were young there, I knew, because so many older men had died.) They were unable to speak any but a local language, Kinyarwanda, but that did not prevent them from communicating that they wanted my passport and wanted us to go with them to some place we'd never heard of.

We stalled and negotiated and I said my passport was up at the Snake. This was the beginning of a several-hour-long saga that ended when two tall blond men from the U.S. Embassy, whom I called from the fortified apartment of the manager of the Snake as things deteriorated, grabbed me by either arm and, brushing past the Rwandan militia, headed through the beer garden toward an SUV they had left running at the gate. I caught an unexpected glimpse of Obadiah and suddenly remembered my knapsack, which was in my room at the Snake. I handed him my room key and asked him to take charge of my stuff until we could reconnect. And then I was gone.

So preoccupied was I with my own problems that I never considered what having the key would mean to Obadiah, who'd been basically imprisoned in MAGERWA for about a week. He stayed the night in the room, of course. And he wasn't alone. The big surprise, however, came a week or ten days later, after I'd rejoined the convoy on its belated way out of town. We were in Bujumbura, capital of Burundi, when Obadiah, having noted the wealth of medicines I carried for emergencies (the kit filled about half my knapsack), asked about antibiotics; a "friend," he explained, needed some after a night in a certain hotel in Kigali.

I must have gasped as the pieces came together in my mind. "You didn't use a condom?"

"You know, the beer . . . ," he began.

"But you said—" I began. What I was going to say was that *he,* of all the drivers and turnboys, was the one who understood about infection by HIV, who understood how you had to use a condom every time you were taking a chance, and *particularly with a prostitute, for God's sake!*

"I know, I know," said Obadiah sheepishly. I gave him what antibiotics I had, and his infection, as far as one could be certain, soon went away.

From then on, I had worried about him, and wondered about him. Very few of us were utterly consistent and self-controlled when it came to sex. But more was going on here: though Obadiah was better educated than most, and understood science, science remained to him one theory among many. Even Cromwel, on that earlier trip, had told me that sex with a virgin could take away your AIDS, and he was no yokel. When I'd gone over with them the rudiments of the epidemiology of AIDS, they all nodded respectfully but I could see my words getting filed in the mental drawer labeled "Possible Explanations."

I understood that I lived in a culture that believed in the power of self-determination, where people could eat organic food in hopes of staving off cancer, where they could exercise and stop smoking to fight off heart disease, where many had routine physicals and sought the attention of a doctor when they got sick. But here it was different. Here you didn't have as much power over your health. I remembered how in Bujumbura I'd been bitten by mosquitos numerous times, despite having taken the prudent measures to avoid it—long-sleeved shirts at dusk, insect repellent on exposed skin. All drivers had long experience of malaria. Trying to take their point of view, I'd thought how one unlucky mosquito bite could perhaps be likened to one unlucky fuck: you'd probably already had it, and what was the incremental risk of just one more? I wondered if what had been called Africa's fatalism wasn't just a reasonable response to the fact that there was only so much you could do.

As the years went by and I checked in on Obadiah, I was continually elated to hear he was fine. Dr. Frank Plummer, a Canadian immunologist who worked for years in Kenya with Job Bwayo, told me they thought maybe one in twenty people had a natural immunity to AIDS: "It appears there is some genetic involvement that allows them to process HIV in the correct way." Who knew if Obadiah was blessed, just lucky, or immune? On he drove.

Back in the Transami yard in Kampala, Obadiah was under pressure. Beatrice was back, her breasts were bursting, and one of the containers Obadiah was waiting for was still at the bottom of a stack of five. I watched as he hitched a ride on the gargantuan forklift and disappeared around the corner. Mbuvi, the driver, watched with me.

"It is sad when you have to bribe people in your own company, isn't it?" he asked.

"What do you mean—he's going to *pay* that driver to do his containers?"

"Oh, yes—I expect he will," said Mbuvi.

Twenty minutes later, when the truck was finally ready, Beatrice and I joined Obadiah in the cab. He looked not at all put out to have had to pay the forklift operator. "It is how you do business in East Africa, Mr. Teddi!" he said happily.

By late afternoon we were back at the Kenyan border. It was not Malaba, unfortunately, but Busia: Obadiah had been routed that way so that we could pick up additional cargo in Kisumu, Kenya.

This time there were no snags at the crossing. Not far into Kenya, Obadiah pulled over at a taxi stand; it was time to say goodbye to Beatrice. He climbed out of the cab and walked around to help her down. In the meantime, she had picked out a purse from our shopping expedition as a gift for my wife, and as thanks to me for helping her. I promised to send copies of the pictures I'd taken during my visit. She gently shook my hand, and then Obadiah said, "Come, madame! It is time to send you home!"

There are so many ways to be a couple. I watched through the window of the cab as Obadiah walked Beatrice to the taxis and *matatus*, where he put down her bags, took out his wallet, and gave her some money. They stood close enough to speak quietly amidst the surrounding hubbub. My wife and I would have kissed, but theirs was a different intimacy.

As we continued on to Kisumu, a city on the far eastern shore of Lake Victoria that was home to many from the Luo tribe, Obadiah told me that his father (who had five wives) had been a *matatu* driver here and that he himself had attended primary school in town. *Matatu* drivers, he said, were more reckless than truck drivers because their earnings depended heavily on their ability to move quickly along a route.

Obadiah swerved to hit a snake, and saw me flinch. He explained: "You know, Teddi, you must hit a snake. You must run him over. If you do not, it will have the power to fly after you—up to fifty meters!"

"You believe that?"

"Oh, yes. It is true." His father, he said, was the first one to explain it to him, but many other drivers had confirmed it. "In fact," he remembered, "Mbuvi!" Recently the other driver had nicked, but not squashed, a big snake; moments later he saw it flying alongside him, out the window— "very frightening!"

We ate a fine dinner of grilled meats—beef, goat, chicken—at a large open-air restaurant near the Transami yard in Kisumu, where we were joined by Mr. Collins, who headed the local office. I took a room upstairs from the restaurant, while Obadiah resisted entreaties from an assistant of Mr. Collins to rent a room elsewhere and "fill it with girls." "I am very tired tonight," he told me, and would sleep in the truck.

I asked Obadiah about a driver back in the yard in Kampala who looked as though he'd been beaten—he and Mbuvi had been talking to the man.

"Yes. He was beaten by a burglar," Obadiah said. They had broken into his house in Kampala and stolen not just the silver and jewelry but, in African style, almost everything else, too, including furniture, and then beaten him up for good measure.

"Once they broke into my house in Mombasa while we slept," he recalled. "I keep a *panga* [machete] for that. I used it on them," and the burglars retreated.

I thought of a college friend I had visited in Nairobi years before who worked for an NGO. In addition to having a twenty-four-hour guard, or *askari,* at the gate of her small, walled-in compound, her house had barred windows upstairs and a "rape gate" on the staircase, so that she would not be surprised while sleeping. The landscapes we were rolling through looked bucolic, but whether in country or city, it seemed violence was lurking everywhere.

The next morning we passed back into the Great Rift Valley, which was filled with haze. This geological feature rends the earth all the way from northern Syria down to Mozambique. It is 3,700 miles long and has been slowly filling with silt for millennia, which is one reason so many important fossils of early humans and pre-human ancestors have been found there—notably the australopithecine skeleton called Lucy (between 2.9 and 3.9 million years old), and two other hominid ancestors—apes from which humans, gorillas, and chimpanzees diverged—that are 10 million years old.

The highway we were on, by contrast, had not been paved until the 1970s. In the years before that, writes journalist Richard Preston, who lived briefly in Kenya as a boy,

> it was a gravel road engraved with washboard bumps and broken by occasional pitlike ruts that could crack the frame of a Land Rover. As

you drove along it, you would see in the distance a plume of dust growing larger, coming toward you: an automobile. You would move to the
shoulder and slow down, and as the car approached, you would place
both hands upon the windshield to keep it from shattering if a pebble
thrown up by the passing car hit the glass. The car would thunder past,
leaving you blinded in yellow fog.

Fifty years before that, the route from the coast to Lake Victoria and
around the north side to central Africa would hardly have been dis-
cernible at all.

Now, as I had seen, there is constant traffic. Preston, in his book *The
Hot Zone*, goes so far as to suggest:

> If the [AIDS] virus had been noticed earlier, it might have been named
> Kinshasa Highway, in honor of the fact that it passed along the Kin-
> shasa Highway during its emergence from the African forest. . . . The
> paving of the Kinshasa Highway [which links Congo and central Africa
> to Kampala and East Africa] affected every person on earth, and turned
> out to be one of the most important events of the twentieth century. It
> has already cost at least ten million lives, with the likelihood that the
> ultimate number of human casualties will vastly exceed the deaths in
> the Second World War. In effect, I had witnessed a crucial event in the
> emergence of AIDS, the transformation of a thread of dirt into a ribbon
> of tar.

Of course, assuming that HIV did come from central Africa, the Kin-
shasa Highway wasn't the only way for it to get out. There are other roads
(such as the one I took on my 1993 trip, to the south of Lake Victoria),
and there are boats, and planes. And yet the main idea is right: if not for
the links to the outside, the virus might have stayed put. This is a cost of
global connectivity: the same trucks that carry medicine in may carry all
manner of germs out. It's not intentional, of course, and truckers only
begin the process; the rest of us complete it when we kiss and make love
and nurse and bleed or, sometimes, when we simply breathe the air.

The next day we passed back through Nairobi and found ourselves in a
traffic jam the likes of which I'd never seen. It wasn't that the holdup was
extremely long: we were at a standstill only for about an hour. But after
half an hour or so, drivers started getting restless. It was a two-lane high-

way, with partially paved shoulders. As the delay extended, trucks and others filled the shoulders. Then, seeking further movement, some in SUVs started driving down the scrub/savannah beyond the breakdown lane. I think the semi trucks would have done so as well, but the ground was muddy in places, and, Obadiah confirmed, big trucks risked getting stuck. Finally, to my surprise, the pressure of the wait led various vehicles to head over to the lane for oncoming traffic, which at the moment was empty.

"But as soon as the accident is cleared, they're going to get in the way of oncoming cars," I pointed out, as though Obadiah did not appreciate this. He shrugged. And, though it went against his nature, he basically stayed put. Eventually, and slowly, the jam cleared—much more slowly, certainly, than if everyone had just stayed put. And more slowly than if the crash that caused the pile-up—a large truck had tried to overtake a bus, then struck it when he ran out of room—hadn't been so bloody and spectacular. There were many injured.

Our last night on the road was spent in a small settlement called Emali. And our last day took us through a zone of national parks. We saw families of monkeys crossing the road (though we'd seen that outside of parks, as well), and a small herd of zebras. A westbound Transami trucker whom Obadiah, in his role as senior driver, stopped to help gave us a heads-up that there was a big obstacle ahead: somebody had hit an elephant.

Ten minutes later, we arrived at the dead elephant—or what was left of it. Though there were no dwellings in sight, twenty or thirty people were gathered around the carcass, most of which, by now, had been hacked away by their knives for food.

"How do you hit an elephant?" I asked Obadiah. The country was wide open; a driver would see a fast-approaching elephant without much trouble. And how could you hit an elephant and drive away? Just hitting a deer could total a car; if a vehicle hit an elephant hard enough to kill it, wouldn't that vehicle still be here? But there was no sign of any vehicle, just a huge pool of blood and bloody bones and a tableau of torn skin and flesh.

"Do you think those people killed the elephant, just for the meat?" I asked. "Maybe shot it? And did it here, so they could blame it on a truck and not get in trouble?"

"It is possible," said Obadiah somberly.

That afternoon we saw a corpse covered by a blanket at the side of the road, near a stretch populated by vendors selling scallions to passing motorists, and we both theorized about what might have happened. Obadiah confirmed to me what I had heard other drivers say in Africa: that if you ever killed someone while driving, even if it was clearly their fault, you never stopped; the risk of getting lynched by people nearby was too great. Rather, you drove on to the next town and reported it to the police there. Nobody would fault you for this; everyone, he said, understood.

In my various travels, it was always the idea of a random death that I most feared—being in the wrong place at the wrong time. Roads offered plenty of opportunities for that to happen, for sober people to get hit by drunks, for animals to step into the road, for accidents involving innocents. I did everything I could to minimize the chances of death—wore a seat belt, avoided cars or drivers that looked unsafe. But there was a limit to how much you could prevent. On our earlier trip, Obadiah had commented, "the road is very unfair, very harsh." That was it, exactly.

When we arrived in Mombasa, Obadiah stopped briefly at his house, where I got to meet his first wife and two of their three children, a teenage girl and boy. This wife was heavy and unglamorous, and the apartment was small; picturing Beatrice getting on here was difficult. Our trip ended as before, where it had begun, in the Transami yard. I would see Obadiah again in coming days, as I followed up with Mike; hung out with Suleiman, the dispatcher; and sought out other people in Mombasa.

But my first trip to Kenya had begun in Nairobi, with Job Bwayo, the medical doctor and immunologist, and it is with Job Bwayo that this journey should end. Since working on the study that had brought me to Kenya in the first place, Bwayo had become the country's leading HIV researcher, internationally known in the effort to find an AIDS vaccine. In subsequent work, he had tried to find out why a group of sixty Kenyan prostitutes he had discovered never caught the disease, despite presumably having had a great many exposures to it. As he told England's *Observer* newspaper in 2001, "They didn't have the virus or the antibodies. So they must have been getting rid of the virus so quickly that it couldn't get established. We took the HIV virus and white blood cells from the prostitutes, put them in a test-tube and—bang!—they reacted. The cells killed the virus." With funding from the International AIDS Vaccine Initiative, Bwayo had assembled a team of Kenyan scientists to work with scientists from Oxford University on using the sex worker research to develop an AIDS vaccine.

He was traveling outside Kenya when I returned in 2003. But in 2007, I tried to get in touch by phone and hear the latest on his work. That's when I learned that Job Bwayo had been murdered.

It happened around six p.m. on February 4, 2007, a Sunday. Bwayo, fifty-eight, had driven his wife and two other women, a friend from Australia and an American missionary from Oregon, to visit an ostrich farm. As they were returning to Nairobi they came upon what they assumed to be a police roadblock. In fact, three young men with AK-47 rifles who are thought to have just committed a robbery were engaged in a carjacking. Already they had stopped a car carrying a disabled man and his son; after putting the son in the trunk, they had shot and killed the father and then gotten the car stuck in a ditch. At this point another car appeared, carrying four people; it, too, was made to stop and the occupants forced to get out. When one of them had trouble with her seat belt, the young men had shot her in the head and killed her.

According to *The East African Standard*, "It was at that time that Prof. Bwayo ran into what was now a roadside siege. The thugs opened fire, killing him instantly before pulling him out of the car." They shot his wife in the mouth and the American companion in the face, gravely wounding both.

A colleague told London's *Guardian* newspaper that Bwayo had a way of describing his work to fellow researchers: "We know that in the search for an AIDS vaccine, many different vaccines will need to be tested. Vaccine development is a marathon, not a sprint—and as we all know, Kenyans are very good at marathons."

DOUBLE-EDGED ROADS

NAPOLÉON BONAPARTE IS KNOWN as the greatest road builder of modern Europe. Roads were key to his imperial designs; famously, in order to move his Grande Armée and its artillery over the Alps and into position to dominate Italy, he widened a Roman route through the Gondo Gorge and over the Simplon Pass in Switzerland between 1800 and 1805. His design specification: that it be possible to pull cannons over the pass. Five hundred lives were lost in building the nineteen miles of road, which included twenty-two bridges and seven tunnels.

His nephew, Louis Napoléon—elected the first president of France's Second Republic in 1848, before restoring the monarchy and becoming Emperor Napoléon III in 1852—focused more on home. The industrial revolution was taking hold in France; buoyed by a popular mandate to restore and remake his chaotic nation, Napoléon III undertook a program of massive urban renewal. The ramshackle, medieval quarters of Paris were symbols not only of poverty and disease but of insurrection. Among his early projects was construction of the grand boulevards of Paris. Though the Champs-Élysées had begun to take shape nearly two centuries before, Napoléon III (through his prefect, Baron Georges-Eugène Haussmann) expanded the concept, tearing down twisting crowded districts dating from the Middle Ages and remaking the fractious city by endowing it with, in Haussmann's words, "spaces, air, light, verdure and flowers, in a word, with all that dispenses health." While that sounds lovely, another agenda of the project was military: famous for their beauty, these streets "were dictated in purpose and geometry by the potential requirements of a defending army and the need to permit the free movement of troops into areas of Paris that had previously been sources of rebellion." In fact, early in his rule, Napoléon III halted street work in certain districts because the brick-shaped paving stones were being regularly repurposed as components of roadblocks and barriers. In the mind of the emperor, the plan "would slash the belly of this mother of insurrections."

But streets and roads, which require so much labor and money to build, often outlive our intentions for them. Napoléon's grip on power slipped before he could send those cannons over the Simplon Pass; it's now a tourist route over the Alps, famous for spectacular scenery. Another of his military routes through the Alps, the Grande Corniche, is a chiseled ledge that overlooks the Côte d'Azur in southern France, a celebrated touring drive and setting for numerous automobile ads.

And the same capacious, military-scaled roads that allowed Napoléon III to consolidate his rule provided the avenues of entry for the tanks and trucks of the Third Reich, which rolled into Paris on June 14, 1940, beginning an occupation of four years.

"Double-edged sword" seems the right phrase to describe this military importance of roads. On the one hand an expression of national pride and economic vitality, on the other roads are an invader's best friend, providing access to the centers of wealth and power. Hernán Cortés arrived on the Gulf Coast of Mexico in 1519, aiming to claim new lands for the king of Spain, thereby earning himself wealth and prestige. He and his men described their invasion as a mission to settle and convert the heathen to Christianity. They landed on the outskirts of the Aztec empire, in a precinct of one of its subject tribes, and followed the ever-widening roads toward Tenochtitlán, the center of Aztec power.

It must have been a heady experience, invading a "new world" and making it your own—or even, as Napoléon I and the Grande Armée had done, invading the "old world" nations of Europe, longtime rivals and ancient cultures, and adding them to one's empire.

And, for the other side, there was the terror of being invaded. Consider the fear of the Amerindians, who knew nothing of the Spaniards' giant wooden ships, their gunpowder, their finely forged swords, their horses, and their mastiffs; consider their villages in the Spaniards' path, subject to pillaging at best, at worst to infection with smallpox, torture, and murder.

Such horror, a leitmotif of the progress represented by roads, recurs throughout history: in the American South, where Native Americans forcibly removed from their lands in the 1830s walked west on the deadly "Trail of Tears"; in Warsaw many times over the past two hundred years; in Paris and Bataan during World War II; and in Indochina, where supplies flowed south on the Ho Chi Minh Trail and the unarmed fled their villages—such as the girl Kim Phúc, famously photographed running naked on a paved road with terrorized others, screaming with fright, burning with napalm. On roads, the triumph of invaders shadowed by the miseries of the vanquished; roads and flight.

South African novelist J. M. Coetzee's character Michael K, a dispossessed gardener, tries to walk across South Africa to return his mother's ashes to her place of birth. But as an individual on foot he is harried, subject to search by any marauding soldier, while trying desperately not to be noticed.

Of course, soldiers, too, can be afraid. One classic depiction is that of Lieutenant Giovanni Drogo, assigned to a remote border fortification in Dino Buzzati's classic *The Tartar Steppe*. Over months and then years Drogo sees but fails to report signs of a road being constructed in the wastelands beyond the fort, presumably by the enemy for purposes of invasion; his impulse to do so is thwarted by denials both personal and institutional. Over fifteen years, the enemy prepares on the distant steppe. When finally they lay siege, Drogo lies febrile and helpless, undone.

In 2003, the United States spent $190 million to rebuild a ravaged road across Afghanistan. The three-hundred-mile stretch of Highway 1, connecting Kabul to Kandahar, could theoretically now be driven in six hours instead of thirty. The day it was dedicated in Kabul, President George W. Bush in Washington issued a statement saying the highway would "promote political unity between Afghanistan's provinces, facilitate commerce by making it easier to bring products to market, and provide the Afghan people with greater access to health care and educational opportunities."

But despite this road's potential and the might of the country that built it, roads are vulnerable to disruption. To borrow a metaphor from the ecologists, they are all edge.

The Taliban had killed four Afghans working on the road three months before the dedication; eventually nearly a thousand guards had to be brought in for the road to be finished. Some Afghan officials who attended the opening ceremony said they had been flown to Kabul, according to *The New York Times*, "avoiding the road out of concern for their safety."

Not five years later, conditions along the road had vastly deteriorated. A convoy of fifty trucks carrying food and fuel for American bases was ambushed and set afire, seven of its drivers were beheaded. Two days after that, three American soldiers and their Afghan interpreter were killed along the road; the body of one of the soldiers, a National Guardsman from New York, was dragged off and cut into so many pieces that a patrol coming upon the scene initially thought it was two bodies. "The road," wrote the *Times* in a follow-up, "has become the site of extreme carnage."

Many prisoners from Afghanistan were incarcerated at the American naval base at Guantánamo Bay, Cuba. The super-secure prison there, Camp Delta, is slowly being phased out as I write; I visited it in 2002 for *The New York Times Magazine.* To get to Camp Delta from the main part of the base, one had to drive along one of the strangest stretches of road I have ever seen: a short section of pavement, maybe two hundred feet long, made into a piece of curly Christmas ribbon candy by a series of bright orange traffic barriers. It was like San Francisco's Lombard Street writ small and flat, and watched over by soldiers in machine-gun nests. My military minders wouldn't tell me anything about it, but I presumed it was that way to ensure that no vehicle could approach the fences of Camp Delta with enough speed to break through—and that there'd be plenty of time to blast to smithereens any vehicle that approached without permission.

A lesson: it's much easier to impede traffic than it is to speed it up, to make a roadway dangerous than to make it safe.

The largest, most fully developed highway system in the world belongs to the United States. President Dwight Eisenhower's Clay Committee sold it to Congress in 1955 as a national defense system for the movement of military vehicles and the evacuation of civilians. The same Congresses that authorized spending bills for the National System of Interstate and Defense Highways, as it was officially named, knew that all those excellent freeways would simultaneously serve to consolidate the country and help its economy grow. The military motivation was real—as it was in

Zanskar, so close to the site of military tensions on the Pakistan-India-China borders. But only occasionally does one see a military vehicle on an American highway.

That is not the case in other nations. Long convoys of military trucks are a commonplace in Ladakh: if you're driving somewhere you pray you won't get stuck behind one, because passing fifty trucks is such a daunting prospect, particularly on narrow, winding mountain roads. I have frequently shared roads with military vehicles, in Peru, in China, and, as you will see, in the West Bank. It's common in much of the world. Usually it's not too scary.

That changes in places where roads have come to be dominated by the military. In our time, that includes Iraq, Afghanistan, and the West Bank. Though photography in Iraq has been controlled by the U.S. military, one sort of image has become almost iconic: that of the burned-out military vehicle by the side of the road. It's as stark a signifier of modern warfare as you can get without having people—dead or alive—in the photo. It's the civilian road become a civilian no-man's-land, a route taken over by the military. It's the road as battleground, a place where moving vehicles can be shot by other vehicles, hit by missiles launched from aircraft overhead, or blown up by remote-controlled mines, or IEDs (improvised explosive devices). The main difference between still and video depictions of these scenes is whether clouds of black smoke in the background are billowing or not.

How similar some of these scenes are to dystopian movies filmed twenty years ago in Australia. The *Mad Max* series posited a post-apocalyptic world consisting mainly of junk-strewn desert highways traversed by baroque motorcycles and muscle cars, piloted by tanned and whiskered men carrying big guns. Gasoline was like gold. The road was a Hobbesian state of nature with elements of twentieth-century military and automotive technology.

Cormac McCarthy's harrowing novel *The Road* takes the dystopic premise of those films and subtracts sunshine and mirth and cars that still run. And it adds starvation, depravity, plenty of corpses, and the terror felt by a dying parent and an orphan-to-be. In *The Road*, highways become the setting for everything that still happens in the world, which means the wanderings of forlorn survivors of nuclear winter, people trying to scratch out a survival from the wreckage of houses, boats, and cars in a new dark age. Some of the pavement is scorched and buckled; some is covered with slush and ice; none of it, the protagonists find, is easy to traverse with a loaded grocery cart full of one's worldly belongings. The road is the largest remaining artifact of the pre-apocalyptic world, the source of all food and all danger, the only place to be.

FOUR

A WAR YOU CAN COMMUTE TO

AS A TEENAGER, Fares Azar expected that one day he would run the family business, a bus line connecting Ramallah to Jerusalem, fifteen miles south. But over the past few years things have changed. Now there is no direct service between the two towns. Instead, there are vans and group taxis from Ramallah to Qalandia, a heavily fortified checkpoint run by the Israeli army. Then, on the other side of Qalandia, there is another set of vans and taxis into East Jerusalem.

So Fares doesn't know exactly what to do. He attended college in Utah and ran a restaurant in Provo for a while with his brother. (A friend of a friend of mine knew him from there.) But he missed home and came back. Luckily, his family still has money: Fares drives around Ramallah in a speedy BMW, eats out most nights, parties when he can. He's a Palestinian Christian, and most comfortable around other Christians—and there aren't that many Christians in Ramallah. One day he picked me up in the late morning and took me to a Christian-owned coffeehouse, parking nearby in an abandoned lot between two buildings—his father's former bus yard. When we met I thought he was just laconic but now I could see he was depressed. He slept late, drank too much, and, though only twenty-nine years old, obsessed about the past. He ordered a coffee and I pulled out the map given me by a car rental agency in Tel Aviv; I wanted to ask him about roads. But Fares grabbed it and flipped it over, immediately scanning the room to see who might have noticed: the map had some big Hebrew lettering and a drawing of the Israeli flag. "They'll think . . . ," he started. He didn't need to finish.

As it turned out, he was a bad one to ask about roads in the West Bank: he stays home, loath to travel because of the humiliations it entails, even with a U.S. passport. "The Israelis don't respect a U.S. passport if it's in the hands of a Palestinian," he explained. "It doesn't make any

difference." Fares, with his U.S. passport, could in theory get a visa to cross into Israel, but he would risk losing his Palestinian residency permit if he did. The only practical way to get out of the West Bank—as he had done a few months earlier with a bunch of buddies going to a beach resort in Egypt—is to make the arduous overland trip east to Jordan, and fly from there. The thought of going through Jerusalem, the nearest big city, and negotiating Qalandia, subjecting himself to inspection by soldiers, to the detested security precautions that ruined the future, makes him vaguely sick.

I wanted to know: How could a mere checkpoint change a road, change a life? In the modern world we're used to waiting, and I wanted to see why this checkpoint was so potent. I'd been stopped by the police before; so what? You wait a while, you show your documents, you're on your way. Why was this different?

Fares wouldn't go with me. But he walked me to a street where I could catch a van of the sort that replaced his family's buses. We'd see each other tomorrow, have a another drink . . .

At first I was nervous to climb into a Palestinian taxi, walk around a Palestinian city—wouldn't people here suspect that I was an American? And wouldn't they be against Americans, as the principal donors of foreign aid to Israel? But nobody was unkind. When I needed to ask a question, people around me would find somebody who spoke English and could help. The man next to me in the van, an unemployed librarian, explained that I wouldn't need to know where to get out—Qalandia was the end of the line.

It was only a five- or ten-minute drive to the south side of Ramallah, along busy commercial streets with low concrete buildings and a few palm trees, until we came to the end of both businesses and trees. The road turned to dirt and was channeled by concrete barriers. An Israeli guard tower—cylindrical cement with blank walls and tiny windows, the tallest structure I'd seen in Ramallah—loomed over the area ahead. The taxi swerved into a dirt lot, where passengers paid and got out. As I fell into step with the dozens of people heading past the guard tower, past concrete road dividers spray-painted with graffiti ("Israel Out"), past the cameras mounted atop poles, toward a low structure ahead with a corrugated roof, a red light next to the single lane for cars, and cyclone fencing and loops of razor wire on the sides, Fares's reluctance to leave the town made more sense: this was starting to feel like prison.

The checkpoint queue was structured like a funnel: wide enough where it began for maybe thirty people to stand side by side, at the end of an open-air shed with a corrugated tin roof, but narrowing maybe thirty yards farther on, where everyone was pushing toward two tall turnstiles. That afternoon in the fall of 2004 it took forty minutes to reach the front. It was an exercise in gradual compression: I went from having some choice of movement (I headed for the left turnstile) to having none at all, as my footsteps were foreshortened by the people in front of me, my arms were pinioned by the presence of people beside me, and my shoulders were bumped by the people behind.

Checkpoint queues create a sense of instant community: a shared suffering, a shared imprisonment. And conversation provided relief. The man at my right, it turned out, was a doctor. He was returning home to East Jerusalem from work at a clinic in Ramallah, as he did every day. Israel's strategy is "to make it so bad we will leave," he said. They forget "we have nowhere else to go."

Because this was my first time through, I expressed some concern about the squeeze to which we were increasingly subjected. He warned me not to drop anything—an ID, for example—because it would be impossible now to stoop down and pick it up. He looked tired as he told me that it had been even worse before the Israelis put up the metal roof and created some shade.

I shuffled forward, resigned to no longer having much choice about things. If the crowd panicked, we would all be in trouble. Just a month earlier, I knew, bombers en route from Jenin to Haifa had exploded a device at this very checkpoint, killing two Palestinians and wounding six Israeli policemen. And only the day before, a Palestinian woman had blown herself up in the Jerusalem neighborhood of French Hill, just a few miles from Qalandia, killing two Israeli policemen.

The doctor and I were separated a few minutes later when the funnel moved us toward separate turnstiles. These were full height, like those in some less-trafficked New York City subway stations, and next to mine the pressure from behind had grown so great that the decision about when to step into it seemed practically beyond my control; I started leaning backwards to keep from walking into the ends of the turning bars and getting pinned. To my relief, a muscular man approaching the turnstile at the same time used his bulk, like a dike against the ocean, to create a small discretionary pocket of space for me. A minute later I

stepped through the turnstile of my own accord and said, *"Shukran"*—
thanks.

It would have been a relief to be on the other side, approaching the
end of the shed, except that this was where the guns were. About ten
Israeli soldiers were visible that day, all of them young and dressed for
combat, M4 assault rifles slung over their shoulders. Things moved faster
now. A young female soldier examined the contents of my shoulder bag.
Ten steps beyond her another soldier, protected by a wall of concrete
blocks, a thick plastic window, and goggles, motioned me forward. I
handed him my passport and journalist's ID. He studied them, pausing
(as Israeli officials tend to) at a visa I had gotten years before for a travel
magazine trip to Saudi Arabia. Then he handed them back wordlessly
and turned to the person behind me. Apparently I was through. Walking
out into the open air beyond, into the bustling taxi lot, I felt as though I'd
been paroled.

During the centuries of European expansion and colonization, roads
were built to consolidate empire and develop economies. (The plan for
the *chaddar* road in Zanskar has a similar goal, which now might be
called nation-building.) Recently, colonization is rarer, or subtler; when
armies are not at home, they may be *occupying* an unfriendly land, aiming
not to annex the territory outright but rather to chase out enemies and
install a friendly regime. Switzerland, as part of its effort to avoid occupation by the Nazis, booby-trapped the many bridges a traveler must
cross to traverse the mountainous nation by road. But the nations surrounding Switzerland had no such defense; their roads provided both an
entry for Axis tanks and an escape route for the thousands and thousands
of people who fled before them.

Occupations may be the characteristic military action of our time.
Scores have taken place in the past hundred years. While most occupations involve disputes between neighbors, air travel has made possible
not only American participation in the Vietnam War but far-flung occupations such as the present-day operations of the United States in
Afghanistan and Iraq. No matter how their armies got there, however,
occupying powers face a similar set of challenges. Their militaries need to
dominate by controlling movements of goods and of people, and these
travel on roads. At the same time, soldiers on roads are vulnerable in ways

they are not inside their bases. In this era of occupations, roads have shaped up as a principal battleground.

Israel manages its occupation of the West Bank—which is home to 1.3 million Palestinians and 400,000 Israeli settlers and is roughly the size of Delaware—to a large degree by restricting the travel of Palestinians. The most famous symbol of this restriction is the "security fence" still taking shape alongside and east of the Green Line, which marks the

In much of the West Bank, separate roads carry Israelis and Palestinians. This modern, elevated portion of the 60 Road carries settler traffic between Jerusalem and Bethlehem (over the horizon). The narrow, curving road beneath is for the Palestinian village of Beit Jala, out of view on the left. A series of concrete panels on the highway's left side, near the top, serves to protect Israeli vehicles from projectiles.

de facto border of pre-1967 Israel. Although the fence has become controversial for impinging on Palestinian territory and cutting off some Palestinian farmers from their land, it has succeeded in greatly reducing the number of suicide bombings inside Israel proper. But more meaningful than the security fence to daily life in the West Bank is Israel's dominion over Palestinian roads. The Oslo Accords, in 1993, and Oslo II, in 1995, granted Palestinians the right to govern their own cities, but gave Israel control over the main roads in the territories. One result is that Palestine may be said to resemble an archipelago of cities and villages cut off from each other. The checkpoints enforcing Israeli control of the roads, once few and temporary, have become numerous and often permanent. Although their number varies according to the security situation, about seventy checkpoints dotted the West Bank at the time of my visit. There are nearly as many five years later.

Each checkpoint has a different character. Most permit both vehicles and pedestrians to pass, but some allow only pedestrians. Some close at dusk and open at dawn, permitting no passage at night. Others are closed to vehicles at night but allow pedestrians through. Some allow anything to pass once the soldiers have left for the night. And some change the rules from day to day.

In addition to permanent checkpoints like Qalandia—which typically feature traffic dividers and concrete blocks behind which the soldiers stand, and sometimes roofs for shade and tanks of drinking water—there are "flying checkpoints," which exist for only hours at a time and may be run by as few as two or three soldiers or border policemen, often acting on intelligence tips.

Israeli officials say that like almost everything else Israel does in the West Bank, checkpoints are for security: they enable the Israeli army to interdict weapons and bombers. The army hopes to find some of these through random searches; others may be captured through the powerful Israeli intelligence agency, Shin Bet, which provides daily updates on who and what to look for. But soldiers at checkpoints spend most of their time examining the identity documents issued by Israel and by the Palestinian Authority to every Palestinian age sixteen and up. If a man's residence is in Nablus but he's headed for Bethlehem, the soldiers may turn him back. Or they may not. The arbitrariness of checkpoint rule enforcement makes life miserable for Palestinians. For them checkpoints have become not just bureaucratic irritants but symbols of Israeli arrogance.

Whether at crossings of the security fence or at strategic points inside the territories, checkpoints provide the human face of the occupation: this is as close as some Israelis and Palestinians will ever come. The face is seldom friendly: grim-lipped soldiers meet put-upon civilians, investigate their documents, and decide (often according to mood, Palestinians say) whether they may cross over to the other side. Sometimes the soldiers make Palestinians wait for hours in holding areas. For the soldiers, checkpoint life is often grindingly dull, stress-inducing, and alienating. For the Palestinians, it is monumentally frustrating, humiliating, and anger-provoking.

Checkpoints can also be brutal. During my visit, the Israeli military convicted the commander of the Hawara checkpoint, just south of Nablus, of beating numerous Palestinians and smashing the windows of ten Palestinian taxis. One of the army's own cameramen had videotaped the commander in the act of bashing a Palestinian man in the face with his fist while the man's toddler held on to his shirttails; the camera's audio then picked up the sounds of the man being punched or kicked in the stomach inside a hut where the commander had dragged him. One of the cruelest indignities to which they are subjected, Palestinians say, is the capricious and sometimes hours-long detention of ambulances carrying Palestinian patients; according to the Palestinian Human Rights Monitoring Group, at least seventy-one Palestinians have died because they were delayed unnecessarily at checkpoints.

According to the Israeli military, a total of fifty-six Israeli soldiers and border police officers have been killed at checkpoints and roadblocks since the Second Intifada began, in September 2000. In 2003 two were shot dead south of Jerusalem by a Palestinian man carrying a rifle rolled up in a prayer rug. In December 2004 members of Hamas and Fatah tunneled several hundred yards to place more than a ton of explosives beneath a checkpoint in Rafah, near the Egyptian border with Gaza. The attack killed five soldiers. And in December 2005 a Palestinian passing through the Qalandia checkpoint, right where I had walked, fatally stabbed a soldier in the neck.

Omer (the Israel Defense Forces let me talk to him on the condition that I not use his last name, or the last names of any of his soldiers) is a wiry, affable, red-haired man of twenty-six who commands a company of the elite 202 Paratrooper Battalion. His company consisted of about a hundred young army conscripts, and in the fall of 2004 they occupied a base camp atop a hill between Ramallah and Nablus, where I stayed for almost two weeks. The base is located just off a major highway known as the 60 Road.

The 60 Road runs north–south through the entire West Bank and is the main connection between the cities of Jenin, Nablus, Ramallah, Jerusalem, Bethlehem, and Hebron. In ancient times the route extended all the way north to Damascus and as far south as Beersheva. The problem with the 60 Road, Omer told me, is that it has become a thruway for terrorists. The security fence has yet to be completed in Jerusalem and many areas in the south—one reason, according to the military, that on August 31, 2004, ten days before my arrival in Israel, suicide bombers from Hebron were able to kill sixteen people in two separate attacks on buses in Beersheva. More recently other bombers have increasingly used the 60 Road to travel south from the politically turbulent cities of the north. So in addition to Hawara and the other permanent checkpoints along the road, the Israeli army deploys units like Omer's to patrol it. "A suicide bomber traveling from Nablus to Jerusalem will have to go right past us—and we'll try to stop him," Omer told me. His company sets up flying checkpoints, conducts surveillance missions, and makes nighttime arrests in nearby Arab villages, usually acting on tips from the Shin Bet.

Omer has already served nearly eight years in the army. He still carries shrapnel in his leg from fighting against Hezbollah in Lebanon in the late 1990s, yet he is nostalgic for those days, because in that job he was engaged in actual combat, which to him is real soldier's work. "The Hezbollah warrior was like me, dressed up like me—he had a gun," Omer told me one afternoon in his command trailer. "When one of our guys fell, it was like, hey, they were shooting, we were shooting. It was an army for us. It was sexier. And there was no question in terms of the conflict. There was Hezbollah, a clearly terrorist organization. But here the mission is trickier to explain to the soldiers—what you've achieved in terms of terrorism, how you buy time, buy intelligence, and at the end you will catch them."

He continued the comparison. In the West Bank "the collateral damage is unbelievably higher," he said. "In Lebanon the villages were either with you or against you—they'd fight alongside you, or else shoot back. Here the collateral damage in moral terms is unbelievably problematic, and that's a serious problem in the long term."

Innocent civilians, in other words, are inevitably damaged by the army's work in the territories. "Searching a house, looking for a gun, taking in nineteen- to twenty-one-year-old kids and telling them it's okay to turn the house upside down to find one gun. It's bad for the guy's four children in there—that's obvious. But what's not plain until the fifteenth time is that it's bad for you."

The United States invaded Iraq about eighteen months before my conversation with Omer. At the time, it was not clear that American soldiers would still be there years later. Nor did we know that among the duties of American soldiers in places like Tikrit, Mosul, and Baghdad there would be a lot of what Israeli soldiers had long been doing in the occupied territories: canvassing hostile neighborhoods, arresting people and pressuring them for intelligence, invading homes, worrying constantly about being killed. Except, of course, that the situation in Iraq was more combustible and lethal by several orders of magnitude. (In Iraq, roadsides are the most dangerous place for a soldier. Around 70 percent of U.S. combat deaths in Iraq have been caused by roadside IEDs.) When Omer referred to how occupation duty could mess a soldier up, it took me several months to begin to understand that this was what it was going to be like for American troops.

Israeli soldiers are posted to checkpoints for anywhere from two to six months; three months is typical. Before its current assignment, on the 60 Road between Ramallah and Nablus, Omer's company had spent a little more than three months at Hawara. Most of the Hawara posting, he freely admitted, had been exhausting and dispiriting. In rotating shifts the soldiers spent eight hours on duty, eight hours off, with few breaks. Every day five thousand Palestinians—a mass of humanity with whom it was difficult to communicate—passed through Hawara. Many of them were inclined to ignore, or even argue with, the soldiers' orders. Against this backdrop Omer's soldiers had to be ever on the lookout for the person in the crowd who might be wired to blow them up.

Fortunately for company morale, two incidents toward the end of their posting showed that hard work could pay dividends. In the first a female soldier, looking in the large gym bag of a ten-year-old boy, discovered a

*This paratrooper's T-shirt shows army rifles facing
down a suicide bomber outside Nablus (notice
the bomber's explosive vest). "They promised me
72 virgins in heaven," reads the shirt, "but instead
I got the soldiers of August 03 at the checkpoint."*

cell phone with wires attached, and beneath it a bomb. When ques-
tioned, the boy seemed to know nothing about the bomb. Apparently a
man near the checkpoint just a few minutes earlier had offered him a few
shekels to carry the bag through, presumably to move the bomb a little
closer to Israel. But Omer said that soldiers also were taught to worry
about the "default threat": the chance that the bomber, once discovered,
would set off the bomb when it was close to soldiers. (The life of the boy,
in that case, would be sacrificed to the cause.)

The second incident came nine days later. A soldier of Omer's named
Doron, nineteen years old and from the city of Rishon Lezion, just south
of Tel Aviv, had been in charge of a checkpoint line that morning. He
told me what happened: "It was maybe two p.m., and the Shin Bet called
me and said, 'There's a bomber in your line!' And I said, 'What do they
look like?' They said, 'Maybe a girl, maybe a boy, maybe fourteen, maybe

sixteen.'" The Shin Bet monitors cell phone transmissions in the area around the checkpoint, and had overheard the bomber making a call. Doron immediately closed down the checkpoint and ordered everyone waiting in line to stand back and then to approach the soldiers one at a time for a thorough pat-down. "Then a kid—we said, 'Remove the jacket,' and he didn't want to; he was shaking," Doron recalled. "But then he did, and we could see something under his jersey. So we said, 'Lift your shirt.'"

Meanwhile, Israeli military officials had called an Associated Press stringer in Nablus and arranged for a television camera to tape the incident—they wanted to be able to show the world the dangers faced by soldiers in the Palestinian territories. The first frames of the video show the boy lifting his shirt to expose a vest wired with explosives. Soldiers' guns are trained on him and he has been moved away from other people. Next, a small remote-controlled robot rolls up and delivers the boy a pair of scissors. He uses them to cut off the vest. Then he steps away from it and is arrested. Soldiers explode the bomb.

Omer said that once the boy was sitting down, reclothed, and eating yogurt in a debriefing room, he told intelligence officers that the militants had assured him that soldiers would inevitably kill him if he were caught—that they were, after all, Israeli, and all Israelis were devils. He seemed shocked to be speaking to human beings. Omer also told me that he believes the phenomenon of children carrying bombs and women "suiciding" with them is one his side unwittingly created, because kids fifteen and under don't need IDs to get through a checkpoint, and women's paperwork sometimes isn't checked.

Afterward, as a souvenir of the episode, Omer's soldiers had a T-shirt made with a likeness of the boy and a caption that read, "They promised me 72 virgins in heaven, but instead I got the soldiers of August 03 at the checkpoint."

After doing their time at the Hawara checkpoint, Omer and his company spent a few high-adrenaline months in Nablus, a city roiling with politics and rebellion. The Israelis considered it to be a major source of terrorism. Their experiences were both terrible and, to hear Omer tell it, thrilling. Under cover of night they would slip into town—sometimes in an armored vehicle, sometimes on foot, occasionally disguised—to arrest suspects. They drove through the impoverished Balata refugee camp, on the southeast edge of Nablus, attempting to draw fire from insurgents in order to discover their hideouts. They demolished the dwellings of Palestinians who, according to intelligence reports, had engaged in attacks against Israel. In one incident a Palestinian boy threw a stone that broke Omer's nose. In another Omer's second-in-command was ambushed, and Omer himself, coming from behind an ambulance that had been called to the scene, walked right into a boy who was holding a lighted Molotov cocktail. Omer shot him reflexively fourteen or fifteen times "in the legs"—"but he died."

Omer and some of his soldiers also recall having to drive into Nablus, in broad daylight on a number of occasions, to rescue buddies whose vehicles had become trapped or disabled. During some of these missions residents on rooftops assaulted the vehicles with an assortment of heavy objects, ranging from cinder blocks to an oven. I asked one of Omer's drivers, a dark-humored man named Adam, which parts of Nablus were the most dangerous. Which were the bad spots? "All of Nablus is a bad spot," he muttered.

One day Omer drove me up the hill overlooking the Hawara checkpoint, past an Israeli-only road leading to Bracha, a Jewish settlement of 400 to 450 people (checkpoint soldiers have barracks there, too), and, a little higher up, through an ancient town of Samaritans. (Famous for helping strangers, as in the New Testament's parable of the Good Samaritan, the group practices what they claim is the true religion of the Israelites, one different in various ways from Judaism. Samaritans are now Israeli citizens.) The hill, which is called Mount Gerizim, is mentioned in the Old Testament; Abraham, having just received the promise from God "I will make of thee a great nation," had brought his tribe to set up camp in the oak grove between Gerizim and Mount Ebal, a hill to the north. Out of that camp grew the biblical city of Shechem, which today is Nablus, home to 300,000 Palestinians. It's an affront to many of them, and illustrative of the problems facing this region, that Israeli road signs refer to their city not as Nablus but as Shechem.

My mental image of Nablus, based on the descriptions of soldiers I talked to, was of a large, foul-smelling slum. So I was surprised to see gleaming white buildings, many of them tall and invitingly perched on either side of a valley. At least from a distance, Nablus was beautiful. But to Omer the view was less glorious. He pointed out one landmark after another where bad things had happened to him and his company. As we made our descent, he pointed out a building that the soldiers called the Disco: it was a Palestinian party hall that the paratroopers had taken over during the tensions of 2002 in order to provide the settlers with additional protection. One night, as the soldiers slept, two Palestinian militants attacked, killing a sergeant and a lieutenant before they themselves were killed. Losing those two soldiers seemed to be Omer's most painful experience, and yet I could see that some part of him really wanted me to know what had happened in Nablus. It had been his idea to come here. Weeks later, when I met up again with Omer and told him I had gone back to Nablus alone, he seemed amazed—and also a bit envious.

Israeli civilians are forbidden by military order to enter Palestinian towns; indeed, it would be dangerous for most of them to do so. But I'd been told it wouldn't necessarily be dangerous for me, as a non-Israeli and a non-Jew. It felt very strange to cross sides, but I was spending a few days on one side and then a few days on the other. I wanted to understand the checkpoints around Nablus from a Palestinian point of view. One way to do this, I thought, would be in the company of a Palestinian commuter, and I found one in the person of Abdul-Latif M. Khaled.

Abdul-Latif, a hydrologist, is a tall, well-dressed man in his late thirties who was educated in the Netherlands. He lives not in Nablus but in Jayyus, a village about twenty miles to the west, a literal stone's throw from Israel. His daily commute had once been an easy thirty minutes, he told me. Now between home and office loomed two permanent checkpoints and as many as five flying checkpoints, and the trip often took more than two hours each way. I met Abdul-Latif in his office in Nablus and attended his presentation at a nearby hotel to officials from more than two dozen local villages on the subject of water conservation. At day's end, we boarded a shared "service taxi"—an aging yellow Mercedes station wagon typical of the semi-public transportation available in the West Bank—for the journey to his house in Jayyus.

As the two of us settled into the taxi, he chatted with the other passengers about the evening checkpoint situation, trying to assess what lay ahead. It was the Palestinian version of a radio traffic report. There was no alternate route, but at least he would know what to expect.

After passing through a flying checkpoint inside Nablus, we disembarked from the taxi at Beit Iba, a dusty neighborhood on the city's northwestern edge, and walked to a terminal-style checkpoint similar to the

ones at Qalandia and Hawara. With roughly 250 people massed in front
of us, Abdul-Latif predicted that it would take us about half an hour to get
through, assuming all went well. When I sighed, he told me just to be glad
we weren't there on a Thursday afternoon, when the students at nearby
An-Najah National University headed home for the weekend. Their
numbers, he said, usually swelled the queue to several hundred.

After fifteen or twenty minutes the tides and currents of the crowd
separated us, and I found myself pushed up against a man in a checked
shirt—or, rather, pushed up against his satellite dish. Apparently he
planned to hand-carry the waist-high dish through the queue. This
seemed absurd at first, but it soon occurred to me that he probably had
no other choice, and so I did what I could to help. Others did too. Before
long the crowd had deposited me at the turnstile just ahead of him.

As I waited in a short line to reach the soldier who would examine my
papers, I heard a clanking and saw that the satellite dish was stuck in the
turnstile. Undeterred, the man in the checked shirt managed to dislodge
the dish and started sliding it through a set of vertical bars next to the
turnstile. When the job was almost finished, I reached over to help steady
the satellite dish against the bars on my side.

Big mistake. The soldier in whose queue I was waiting stood up and
shouted at me, demanding that I come directly to the front. His English
wasn't good, but he made it clear that I had broken the rules and that
he was not happy about it. I was very apologetic; it was my first time
through this checkpoint, I said, and I hadn't realized I was doing anything wrong. When he took my passport and Israeli press pass, I thought
I was going to be okay. But he pointed to the back of the sea of humanity
in which I had recently been adrift and declared, "End of line!" Startled
by this punishment, I tried to stall, promising it wouldn't happen again.
Abdul-Latif, who was in front of the next soldier over, began to argue on
my behalf. For his troubles he was sent away to the holding pen, a small
area of hard benches behind a clump of bushes, which was filled with
eight or nine other men who, for whatever reason, had run afoul of the
authorities. Still I dug in my heels. "End of line!" screamed the soldier.

As I started to turn back, a silent alarm seemed to go off among the
soldiers: something had gone wrong toward the back of the line. My tor-
mentor and five other soldiers picked up their M4s and ran outside the
shed, quickly disappearing into the crowd. The checkpoint was now officially closed.

Twenty minutes later the soldiers returned and slowly resumed their duties. No explanation was offered, and the crowd was so big that I couldn't see what had caused the ruckus. The soldiers were uniformly young and dull-eyed, their burnout showing through and through. I approached my soldier again, and he began to reexamine my passport with an air of studied indifference. Abdul-Latif could see me from the pen and started shouting at the soldiers. They ignored him.

The soldier called over his commander, who asked me questions for fifteen minutes or so before deciding to let me pass. Abdul-Latif, however, had to stay. I walked past the soldiers and took up a position at the far end of the terminal to wait for him. The indignity of the regimen was hard to watch, but somehow it was especially unsettling to see a person of Abdul-Latif's stature treated disrespectfully: it was like a slam at Palestinian social structure. Several times he pointed at me; I feared that for championing my cause, he might get himself beaten up.

But after about twenty minutes the soldiers decided to let him go. Abdul-Latif was red in the face when he told me that his detention would have continued had he not been able to point at me and tell the soldiers about the bad publicity they were creating for themselves. When I blamed myself for his problems, he brushed it off. Before they would release him, he said, he had been forced to say, "I am *namrood.*" He asked if I knew what that meant, and I said it sounded like "nimrod"—"idiot"? "troublemaker"? Yes, he said, though in Arabic it was more like "naughty."

In the parking area beyond the checkpoint we ran into the mayor of Jayyus, who offered us a ride in his pickup truck. As we climbed in, Abdul-Latif said, "Sometimes they keep you in that pen until past closing time, until all the taxis have left." He pointed to a clump of bushes next to the lot. "Once I had to sleep there, next to those."

There was only one more checkpoint to navigate on the way home, but the relatively clear road didn't improve Abdul-Latif's mood. We came to an intersection where, he said, the week before, soldiers at a flying checkpoint had collected everyone's IDs, kept them for more than an hour, and then dropped them in a pile on the road. This prompted a mad scramble that had only amused the soldiers. Without an ID no Palestinian over the age of fifteen can go anywhere.

Nearing Jayyus, we passed a giant mound, more than fifty feet high, of what looked like construction debris and other refuse. I'd seen nothing similar in my travels around the West Bank and asked Abdul-Latif about it. He'd almost stopped noticing it, he said: it was actually a garbage dump used by settlers. The citizens of Jayyus had protested for years about the seizure of the land and the use to which it had been put; he himself had become involved in tests of polluted groundwater near it. But what finally got it closed, he said, in May 2003, were complaints about the stench from Al Fai Menashe, a different settlement from the one that created it.

Abdul-Latif's mood improved as we passed under one of those metal archways from the forties or fifties, a sort of "Welcome to X" construction at the entrance to town that was, surprisingly, still standing. Other than that, Jayyus had much in common with other West Bank villages: dirt roads, a centuries-old street plan with few right angles, few buildings over two stories tall, shops without windows that open completely onto the street and close with big gates, a chicken here and a goat there, and political graffiti spray-painted on most walls. Abdul-Latif, lugging his briefcase, spoke about the commute with other men on their way home from work as we walked, i.e., about checkpoints and where and for how long they had been stopped. We passed an old woman dressed in black, baking flatbread in a low brick oven.

Abdul-Latif's driveway had been recently paved and his two-story house recently built. His three young children, playing outside, ran up to hug him as he approached. Inside he introduced me to his wife, and showed me where I would sleep; getting back to Nablus at this time of day was out of the question. He had the trappings of a happy life. But though pleased to be home and shaking off the day and its frustrations, Abdul-Latif was not happy. After a drink of water he showed me his office in the town hall and then walked me a few yards out to a hillside to show me something else.

In the foreground were olive trees—orchards of this traditional crop surround many villages in this part of the world. Many are good-sized and laden with hundreds and hundreds of gray-green olives, their branches bent by the weight. It was nearing harvest time; in fact, one family was already picking. They had surrounded one tree and were picking it together, a cloth at their feet to catch any olives that fell. There was a basket nearby with some covered plates of food—this was also going to be a picnic. Abdul-Latif said many of his best memories were about family olive-picking.

"The harvest is like a festival. My memory is full of these days—I did it maybe twenty years," he said. His family would build a small wood fire nearby to heat water for tea. "I still remember the look on my father's face when he saw how the olives were every year. Because that decided how we would live—schools and food and everything."

But thinking of olives lately involved a lot of pain. First there was the price, depressed by the loss of Israel as a market since the intifada, the cost of exporting olives from an ever-more-isolated Palestine, and the decreased buying power of Palestinians in a depressed economy.

And then there was the loss of trees. And that's what the view spoke to. The olive orchards spread down the hillside and across a burnished plain, toward Israel and the Mediterranean Sea. I could see hundreds of trees, maybe thousands. But at the foot of the slope the sea of trees was rent by a road across the red earth, and a fence.

This was part of the "separation barrier," constructed by Israel to stop bombers and also—since it was mainly built east of the 1968 Green Line—to augment its territory and shrink that of the Palestinians. In cities like Jerusalem, it was a high blank wall, but out here in the country it was like this: a fence with razor wire and sensors and then, running alongside it to the west, a smooth new dirt road with a deep ditch on the uphill side to thwart anyone who might try to breach the line with, say, a big truck. What looked like a road shoulder, Abdul-Latif explained, was a soft-dirt zone where soldiers could look for footprints.

There had been harbingers of the fence construction. Surveyors had placed markers and tape, and spray-painted stones. Soldiers came and showed the mayor where it was going to be, indicating the olive trees that would be destroyed to make room for it. "Some of those trees were six hundred years old," he told me. "Some old men, they had been tending those trees for sixty years. They came and were crying."

The land on the other side had not been officially made part of Israel, he said—though the water rights effectively had. A limited number of Palestinians with traditional ties to the land were still allowed to go to their trees, though now it was difficult: there were only a couple of gates across the road, and the hours of passage were strictly limited. As the sun was about to set we saw an Israeli jeep with two soldiers approach one of the gates, near which some villagers had congregated. Within minutes, two carts drawn by donkeys and laden with olives had also appeared. Slowly they all passed through. Then the soldiers drove away.

The 202 Paratrooper company's base sat perched on a rounded hilltop, part of a bevy of rounded hilltops arrayed like beads on a string, some fifty miles southeast of Jayyus, and just off the 60 Road. This was also a contested area. On the sides of some hills were Palestinian villages, and on the tops of other hills were Israeli settlements, illegal under international law. It was easier to tell the villages from the settlements at night, when you could see that their lights were irregularly spaced and of varying brightness and color, with one prominent green light marking the mosque, whereas the lights in the settlements were regularly spaced and consistent in brightness and hue. This was because the settlements had been built subdivision-style, with many identical units.

The settlers had for years felt most unsafe not in their houses but out on the roads. Part of the 60 Road had been dubbed the "Highway of Death" four years earlier, according to Marc Prowisor, the security chief for the Shilo settlement, which I could see clearly from Omer's trailer. Many settlers had been shot at on the 60 Road and at least twenty-two had been killed. When a family of four from Shilo was attacked on the road (the parents were killed; the babies somehow survived), the settlers demanded protection from the Israeli army, and got it. Owing to the diligence of soldiers like the ones from 202 Paratrooper, Prowisor said, the road was much safer now.

I asked Omer how his unit had managed to reduce the number of attacks on the 60 Road. A combination of measures, he said: checkpoints, intelligence, raids on homes, and making the soldiers' presence known in various ways—by simply driving through villages, or by making use of the talents of his sniper squad. When I asked what, exactly, the snipers might do, he told me this story.

A month or two before, just after his company had moved into its base (which is known as the 773 Outpost, because it sits 773 meters above sea level), reports came in that stones were being hurled at night from a nearby hill at settlers' cars traveling on the 60 Road. Omer sent a squad of camouflaged snipers out to investigate, and one night, using special optics, they caught a twenty-year-old Palestinian man from the village of Sinjil in the act. They shot him just below the knee with a high-powered rifle. Oddly enough, Omer was standing by with a military doctor, and five minutes after being shot the man was being treated by the same army that had just maimed him. An Israeli ambulance took him to a hospital in Jerusalem, where the government paid for his treatment. Part of the man's leg had to be amputated, but the point was that he was alive, and could serve as a living warning. "Every day now his village will remember what happened," Omer said.

I asked Omer whether it had been necessary to shoot the man at all. Couldn't the soldiers simply have arrested him, or given him a stern warning? Omer found my questions puzzling. From his point of view, he had acted with restraint, because "legally we could have shot him—to kill." The man's actions posed a lethal hazard to those riding on the 60 Road; people could have been killed. In fact, as Omer reminded me, in March 2002, not far from where we were standing, a Palestinian sniper had opened fire on a 60 Road checkpoint known as British Police (after those who built it), killing seven Israeli soldiers and three civilians with an ancient rifle. The sniper had never been caught. British Police, which was near a stand of tall pines, was now abandoned, but the incident, like so many others in this part of the world, was far from forgotten.

At dusk one evening I went out with Omer and two of his men on a patrol of two Arab villages near the base, Sinjil and Jiljilya. Omer drove the Storm, a special armored jeep with bulletproof windows and flatproof tires. The narrow road on which we were driving, much of it dirt, wound its way up a hill and past the simple whitewashed houses of Sinjil, the first village, where a soldier pointed out to me a wall on which a map of Israel and the West Bank had been painted—the whole of it filled in with the green, black, and white stripes of the Palestinian flag. For the soldiers this was unmistakable evidence of the Palestinians' refusal to accept Israel's right to exist, and a clear sign that we were in enemy territory.

None of the soldiers had told me what to expect, so the flying rock took me totally by surprise. With a bang it bounced off the roof of the Storm and skittered across the hood, making me jump. We had left Sinjil, traveled maybe two miles across an arid, vacant hillside, and were just coming into Jiljilya. I looked through the Storm's thick windows to see where the rock had come from, but nobody was in sight. On either side of the road, however, were the remains of a makeshift barricade that had been constructed by locals; once it had spanned the road, but now it was a ruin of rocks, boxes, chairs, and a television. "I think we won't go all the way in tonight," Omer said, turning the car around at the other end of the village.

Only later did I learn that Omer considered it unsafe to proceed with only one truck. That was the next evening, after I had asked whether we might go back and drive in farther. Though he couldn't come himself, Omer okayed the trip, sending me out in the Storm with Adam, an experienced driver, and Rooey, a radioman. We were followed by other soldiers in a Humvee driven by a young woman who, like about a quarter of Omer's troops, was an immigrant from Russia. Speaking Hebrew, the soldiers chatted to one another and to the base on their radios.

The chatter stopped when the first stone struck the Storm with a bang—once again we were passing the scattered remnants of the barricade in Jiljilya. I jumped, but Adam drove on, smiling ruefully. "Even for us the first one is always a little scary," he said. "The first one?" I said.

Then two more stones hit the Storm, while others flew by, barely missing us. This time I saw where they were coming from: a bunch of kids behind a wall. But the soldiers ignored them, and we drove on to a third village, Abwein.

In Abwein, five minutes later, I heard a loud, shrill whistling for the first time—the signal Palestinians use to communicate that army vehicles are on the way. Another round of stones rained down on us, but our two-vehicle motorcade kept moving, neither speeding up nor slowing down, and Adam's face was expressionless.

"Why are we here, exactly?" I asked him.

"Just to show them we are here," he said. In other words, I thought to myself, intimidation.

Soon we reached the end of the road—the army had placed a big earthen mound across it. Such strategically placed road closures (as opposed to checkpoints) are common all over the West Bank; the army uses them to restrict access to roads favored by settlers, and to increase its control over Palestinian districts like this one. We started turning around, which took a long time on the narrow street, especially for the Humvee. "You mean we have to go back the way we came?" I asked. Adam thought this question was funny.

Numerous rocks pelted the Storm over the next few minutes, and again as we neared the tumbledown barricade in Jiljilya. There was no exit from the road we were on, and the rock throwers knew we'd have to retrace our route. "Is that all they've got?" Adam muttered as we rolled slowly through the hail of stones. That was when a Coke bottle filled with engine oil smashed against the windshield and I discovered, from the patches of dark oil on my arm and pants, that the Storm's seals weren't perfectly tight. I looked back to see what the Humvee would attract and saw a Molotov cocktail explode right in front of it, drawing a straight line of flame diagonally across the road between us.

Both vehicles stopped. Adam turned on the windshield wipers of the Storm and cursed when they managed only to smear the oil. "I wish they'd hit us with the cocktail instead," he said. The Humvee began to turn around, heading back in the direction we'd just come.

"What are they going to do?" I asked Adam.

"If they can catch them, they can shoot them in the lower legs," replied Rooey, the radioman, from the back seat. From the military's perspective, throwing a Molotov cocktail is aggression of a higher order than throwing stones. Shooting to hit the lower legs is standard practice if the provocation is violent but not likely to be lethal. (There is an Israeli children's game, like dodgeball, in which the object is to hit your opponent below the knee.) The Humvee disappeared for ten minutes as it rumbled

Omer's armored jeep, known as a Storm, back at the base after a bottle filled with motor oil shattered against my door

around the back streets of Jiljilya, but then returned in our rearview mirrors; it had failed to catch the throwers.

Back at the base Omer let his concern show more than usual. "The bottles and the rocks are normal, but the Molotov cocktails—that hasn't happened before on that road," he told me. "It says something very serious about them, about how ready they are to attack us. Molotov cocktails really can make a car explode."

"But aren't the armored vehicles immune?" I asked.

"Well, in theory," he replied.

A day later Omer invited me to come along as he and a handful of soldiers set up a middle-of-the-night flying checkpoint along the deserted stretch of road between Sinjil and Jiljilya. It was about two a.m., very dark and very quiet. A few steps from the checkpoint we could look west to the Mediterranean and see the bright lights of Tel Aviv. The scale here was so small.

There were almost no cars to be seen. But even when there's "a very low probability of actual contact with terrorist activity," Omer said, "checking a road in a random manner causes uncertainty, making it practically impossible to say when and where you can sneak out of a village without being checked." He continued, "Working in various times and places lowers the level of threat faced by our forces." When the first car finally approached the checkpoint, Omer's soldiers turned powerful spotlights on it at the last minute and appeared to scare the driver almost to death. The driver told the soldiers that he was a pharmacist returning from a late-night restocking of his shop, and he was very accommodating of their requests to search his trunk, his back seat, and under his hood. Another hour and only two cars later we headed back to the base.

My waiter in the restaurant in East Jerusalem—the Arab side—was a young man named Sameh who looked like either a weak and skinny Lance Armstrong or else country singer Lyle Lovett with much less hair. Sameh, about thirty, saw me talking to the restaurant's owner—we had a mutual acquaintance—and soon was telling me he was from Nablus. Oh, I was planning another trip to Nablus, I told him, recalling my recent visit with Abdul-Latif. He said I should look him up and so I did.

I bought him dinner at the rooftop restaurant of my hotel, the nicest in town. Only two floors of the multi-story hotel appeared to be in use;

the rest were all dark. Sameh came over about seven p.m. We sat at a table next to two middle-aged women who ordered a water pipe; it gurgled softly as we ordered, reminding me of the guttural sounds of spoken Arabic. The night was mild and it should have been a lovely scene up there on the roof garden, but this was Nablus: across the valley we heard occasional gunshots, and could see the flashing lights atop emergency vehicles. Sameh said most of the lights belonged to IDF checkpoints—he would have to pass two of them to get back home that evening. He pointed to a spot in the distance where he lived with his mother, a widow whom he supported with his earnings. Waiting tables at a restaurant like this, he said, the best in Nablus, you might earn 1,200 or 1,500 shekels (US\$350–\$440) in a good month (or \$200 in a more ordinary one); but in Jerusalem, you could earn twice as much, plus tips. That's why he worked there, even though he was illegal.

"I don't understand," I interrupted. "Why are you illegal? East Jerusalem is the Palestinian part of Jerusalem, right?"

Yes, he explained, except that Israel had assigned West Bankers a different status from Palestinians in East Jerusalem. Most were not allowed to work in East Jerusalem.

"So how hard is it for you to get there and back?" I asked. Sameh commuted every couple of weeks.

"Sometimes not bad—just a few hours. But sometimes very, very hard." Soldiers would sometimes stop him at particular checkpoints, make him wait for hours, and then turn him back. Occasionally he was tempted to try and walk around, as on the evening when, on his way home but finding the Hawara checkpoint closed, he hiked up Mount Gerizim. The soldiers who caught him beat him up, he said, and held a pistol to his head.

I told him about the Mexicans who sneak into the United States, seeking better-paying work, but noted the different quality of that migration—it involved an international border and raised questions about national sovereignty. Here migration looked different: the soldiers weren't keeping West Bankers out of Israel, they were merely keeping Palestinians from moving around too much. It reminded me of the way officers run a prison like Sing Sing: by dividing it up into discrete pieces, and forbidding or restricting movement between them. The twin goals of such a policy, I believe, are punishment (not giving prisoners too much freedom) and self-preservation (inmates who can move around can mass and organize, while inmates who are immobilized cannot). Self-preservation is particularly relevant where you are outnumbered: the only way you can run a prison where inmates outnumber guards fifteen or twenty to one is with plenty of locks, gates, and fences.

I asked Sameh if I could go with him when he returned to Jerusalem the next day. At first he laughed, but then he saw I was serious. "We might get dirty, and you might have to wait a long time," he said. I told him I didn't mind. He used my cell phone to call a friend, who would accompany me by taxi to Sameh's mother's house. We would leave from there around eight a.m.

The house was about two hundred yards from the Beit Iba checkpoint, where Abdul-Latif had been so humiliated—but we'd be backtracking and heading south, so I wouldn't have to go through again. Sameh's mother, in a dusty black dress, took one look at me and disappeared behind a piece of fabric that hung over the doorway to the kitchen. Sameh went back there a few minutes later and brought back tea—the first and last time I was served tea by a man in Palestine. There was a large photograph of his deceased father on the wall, and one of his nephew, who was in an Israeli jail. He had done two years of a four-and-a-half-year sentence. Sameh ignored my question about the nature of the crime, but told me the nephew had liver and hearing problems and had recently lost an eye: "They wouldn't take him to the hospital, after he got punched. They are trying to kill him slowly." On the table was a Bible—why did I keep assuming all Palestinians were Muslim?—and a thin black looseleaf notebook. Sameh opened it to two typewritten pages in plastic sleeves. These pages, in English, were translations of two adjoining pages, in Arabic. Sameh had written those originally, and an American journalist he had met two years before—indeed, he said he had dated her—had translated them and put them on the Web. They were an essay titled "Palestine in the Storm."

> Israel's occupation has created an unprecedented storm upon Palestinians. The worst storms are checkpoints, placed between each city, village, and road. . . . Every city and village has become a prison and a closed military area for anyone who wants to enter or exit these places. . . . If they try to return home, to work, to a hospital for treatment, there is

always someone waiting on the edge of every city and village. . . . They
humiliate and beat and kill.

He hadn't gotten married, he told me, because he was not yet well
enough off. But he had been fixing up his room in preparation for the
day. We climbed up an outside staircase and he showed me: it was lovely,
with a domed stucco ceiling, and white and blue floor tiles in geometric
patterns. He had done the masonry work himself, he said.

The cab was waiting and we got in. We passed through three checkpoints on our way back to the south side of Nablus, two of them temporary, set up next to army tanks. None delayed us more than fifteen
minutes. On the southern edge of Nablus was Balata, the refugee camp
that Omer had told me about raiding. Sure enough, idling on the road
alongside the camp was an IDF Storm, the same model as Omer's. Tank
tracks corrugated the debris-strewn pavement nearby. *How did all these
rocks find their way onto the road here?* I thought to myself. The answer
arrived seconds later when our driver swerved to avoid a group of children who approached the Storm and heaved stones at it.

Ahead loomed Hawara, the large terminal checkpoint where Omer's
troops had intercepted the bombs. I paid the taxi driver and Sameh and I
got in line, which was about forty-five minutes long. As we inched
toward the front, he showed me his ID card, a special one called a mag-
nesium card, he said, that could be read by a machine and showed he was
in the good graces of the army, didn't cause any trouble. Even so, he
admitted, he was pulled out of the line about four times out of five here,
because technically he wasn't permitted to travel in this direction.

We stood. We shuffled. Sameh reported what others around him were
saying—that, with the assassination of a leader of Hamas in Gaza the
day before, the soldiers were skittish today, worried about retaliation.

I made it through after a mere five-minute conversation with a soldier
behind a Plexiglas window. Sameh, I could see, got shunted off to an
open holding pen, where he sat along with a dozen other men about his
age. There was no place, really, for me to wait. I perched for the better
part of an hour on a concrete traffic divider until I got too hot in the sun,
and went to buy a soda near the cart of a vendor who had an umbrella.

As I drank, a white van pulled up and a number of Israeli women
climbed out, clipboards in hand, cameras around their necks. These were
not settler women, in the characteristic long skirts and head wraps, and it

took me a moment to figure out what they were. Then I saw the logo on the van door: Machsom Watch. *Machsom* means checkpoint, and this was the watchdog group of women, most of them from Jerusalem, who went to observe their country's soldiers in action at checkpoints, and try, by their presence, to prevent abuses. It was an impressive initiative, but the addition of middle-class women with concerned expressions and clipboards to the harsh tableau of the checkpoint made it all seem extra surreal.

I sat and sat and sat. I stood and walked around and sat again and wondered how many security personnel were watching me and waiting to see what I was doing there. I had been at this checkpoint with Omer just a few days before; that made me feel a little less alienated, but just a little. Then I noticed a soldier I had shared a few words with, an immigrant to Israel from India. He was bright-eyed, one of the few soldiers who did not look tired, and I went up and reintroduced myself. We chatted and I made an appeal for Sameh: I knew him a little and he seemed like a good guy, I said. Was there any chance his case might be expedited?

Fifteen minutes later, Sameh was free, and we were looking for one of the stalwart Mercedes station wagon group taxis, which lend the West Bank an air of tattered elegance. "What did you tell them?" he asked me.

"I just said I thought you were okay."

Our cab headed south, but within minutes our driver got a signal from another driver coming from that direction, and turned around: there was a two-hour delay ahead at the Tapuah Junction checkpoint, Sameh explained, so we'd detour. He continued, in a sort of triumphal tone that I heard several times among West Bank Palestinians: "If the next checkpoint is closed, we'll find a way around that, too. The Israelis want us to stop, but we'll keep going!" So we set off on a good but long and winding road to the east. The driver said the fare would rise from 13 to 17 shekels per passenger (roughly US$3.25 to $4.25), but nobody complained.

We passed through many villages, and on and off paved roads. We turned left on 505 and right on 458. Shortly, we were stopped by special police in a blue jeep. One of them made an attempt at humor: seeing how hot it was in the crowded cab, waiting in the sun, he said to me, "Tell the driver to turn on the AC." As he knew, there was none in the old car. So perhaps he was more cruel than funny. Later, when he returned my ID, he said, "Have fun in Qalandia."

Our plan, however, was to bypass Qalandia. It functioned as an international border; without the right ID, Sameh would never get past there. So, just before, we changed to a minivan cab and headed to Anata, a suburb on the northeast side of East Jerusalem. Though he wasn't allowed to be there, no wall or fence—yet—prevented a West Banker from entering the city on this side.

The cab continued south. To our right, we could see cranes lifting into place large slabs of concrete that were new sections of The Wall. When complete, it would separate East Jerusalem from West Jerusalem, continuing the same work accomplished by the fence near Jayyus. Armed guards supervised the constructions, and I asked Sameh why—were the builders of the wall subject to attack? "Not the workers, really, but the project—their equipment, their machines. No, the workers—the workers are Palestinian."

"You're kidding."

"No, of course they are Palestinian. We do all the work. We even build the settlements!" He pointed to a billboard across the highway, announcing a future Israeli settlement in the way an American builder might advertise a new subdivision: the sign pictured a wide street, lawns, pretty new houses. I was struck by the parallel with American prison history: the first cell block at Sing Sing, where I worked, was built entirely by inmate labor, prisoners brought down from New York's second prison, Auburn, to build Sing Sing, its third. The building in which, of course, they would be locked up.

We passed a Bedouin encampment on the left; centuries of human-kind seemed to compress here. We passed the Sharfat refugee camp on the right and then we got out. Walking quickly, I followed Sameh across a street on the right and onto another that led up a hill. Sameh, carrying his two heavy plastic shopping bags, threaded his way between houses. We reached the top and I followed him down the other side. There, as we came down the dirt hillside to a boulevard-like street, we saw a large group of men crouching behind a cinderblock wall, occasionally peering out onto the street. From behind, especially given the arid climate, it looked for all the world like a scene of Mexicans slipping through a U.S. border town.

"Who are they afraid of?" I asked.

"Police!" said Sameh. "It's East Jerusalem, but they look for West Bankers, especially near the big roads." He pointed to a man across the street with a walkie-talkie. "A cop?" I asked. Sameh shook his head. "Arab

Israeli. He's helping those guys with a ride." We waited behind a wall fifty feet or so behind the men in question. In a few minutes a van pulled into the parking lot of the strip-mall store at street level; on a signal, the men all rose and jogged down the hill into the van. It drove away and the man with the walkie-talkie disappeared.

"So who's coming for us?" I joked. Sameh asked to use my cell phone to try a driver he knew, but the man didn't answer. A Jerusalem taxi driver caught carrying a West Banker was liable for a 15,000-shekel fine and three months in jail, he said. Still, he thought, we'd be able to get a ride. "Okay, then. Ready?" he asked.

"Here's goes nothin'!" I said.

We walked down to the street and stood there, waiting to hail somebody, watching another group of illegals closer to the larger intersection a short distance away. It was a fraught fifteen-minute wait until a driver stopped for us—he must have known, but he stopped, anyway. We passed under the highway to French Hill.

I had told Sameh, more than once, that I wanted to go all the way to where he lived in East Jerusalem. But to my surprise, the driver pulled up in front of the Palestinian-owned hotel where Sameh worked and where we'd met. "No, no, no," I said to Sameh, "I'm going to where you *live*." He was clearly reluctant. My journey wasn't about me, I said, it was about him, and it wouldn't be complete until I saw him get home. He thought about this briefly and then gave the driver new directions.

We arrived at a multi-story office/hotel building that looked mostly closed; like my hotel in Nablus, parts were undergoing renovation or simply were not used. Sameh paid the driver and we walked into the empty but air-conditioned lobby.

Sameh chatted in Arabic with a couple of other West Bankers sitting on a couch, probably explaining me to them. Then he smiled and said, "So now you have seen it. My home in Jerusalem." He reached out to shake my hand goodbye.

I took him aside. "Sameh, this is a lobby. You don't live here. Where is your room?" This time he looked as if he was expecting the question I had just asked. For some reason he consulted with the men he'd been chatting to. Then he said to follow him.

Instead of taking an elevator, we climbed a staircase to about the sixth floor. The stairwell was barely lit, and opened onto a hallway that was completely dark, though there were people around, other residents. Light poured into the corridor as different men peered out of their rooms and greeted Sameh, staring at me. He opened the door to his own room. It had two unmade single beds and he sat down on one of them. "Here," he said, gesturing at the space, defeated. There wasn't much to it—only some clothing in small piles, a couple of books, a flashlight, and maybe fifty empty liter bottles of water. He explained: The floor had no water.

"And no electricity?" I ventured.

"Well, there is, but we don't want to use it." Then he confessed the whole story: the workers lodged here illegally. The Palestinian owners knew they were here, but outsiders couldn't, so no lights could shine through the windows at night. One aspect of the occupation is strict Israeli control over new construction; building permits are extremely hard for Palestinians to obtain. According to the Israeli human rights group B'Tselem, the government's apparent goal is to prevent Palestinians from expanding or even refurbishing space they own in Jerusalem. This use of the building wasn't, well, kosher. "But it's very inexpensive," he said.

I asked Sameh about his chances of getting a better ID card, one that would let him work in East Jerusalem legally. "It's very difficult," he said. "You have to help the army." What did he mean by that?

Sameh in his secret room in East Jerusalem, after we traveled from his mother's house in Nablus.

"You ask them and they say, 'Well, what can you do for us?' And they mean, *Who can you tell us about that is planning an attack? Who can you tell us about that is smuggling contraband? Who do you know in Hamas?* That is how you get your card."

I had not known—and yet it was very familiar. I taught Sameh two words in English he didn't know: "snitch" and "rat." It was how things run in a prison, how we did it at Sing Sing: you want some help, you give some help. In other words, you give somebody up. And then, God help you.

At a lecture I gave at a college in rural Pennsylvania, students in the audience asked what I was working on. A book about roads, I said. Which ones? they asked. A road in Peru, I said, a road in the Himalayas, one in the West Bank. . . . A student's hand shot up. "Why the West Bank?" he asked. "To understand how roads work in a military occupation," I replied. At a reception afterward the student who had asked about the West Bank came up and we chatted. His name was Ahmed al-Khatib. "I live in Hebron," he told me. "My family is there, though my father studied in the United States. You should go talk to them when you're there."

I liked Ahmed. He was far from the Mediterranean, practically the only Palestinian in freezing rural Pennsylvania, because the college had given him a lot of financial aid. His goal was a Ph.D. in biology (his father's Ph.D. was in chemistry). He seemed politically moderate, and had done a lot with Seeds of Peace, an organization that involved Israeli and Palestinian teens in joint activities in the hope of fostering trickle-up peace and understanding.

So I did seek out his family. Ahmed, the oldest of four brothers, first put me in touch with the second brother, Khaldoon, an intense, skinny, handsome, hyper, and somewhat haunted young man who was a third-year psychology major at Birzeit University in Ramallah. He had also worked as a freelance graphic artist, and had worked on network servers for a company that did internet support. Khaldoon gave me a fast walking tour of Ramallah that was very much road-related. Outside the city's former police station (it had been blown up by Israeli missiles after Israeli spies were taken into custody and killed), he showed me the tracks in the pavement left by Israeli tanks. A couple of blocks away at Al Manara, the central square—where four statues of lions, each representing an old Ramallah clan, were arrayed around a stone lighthouse—he showed me the wrought-iron fencing that he said was destroyed every time Israeli military vehicles rolled in.

We took a service taxi the short distance between Ramallah and the university, a stretch of road often blocked by checkpoints when tensions were high, said Khaldoon. (In fact, a checkpoint that had been in place for almost three years had been removed the previous December.) At night soldiers at the Surda roadblock, as the checkpoint was known, would close the road with barriers, preventing the passage of vehicles but not pedestrians. Khaldoon lived near Birzeit and around midnight would head home from his computer job in Ramallah along this same stretch of road. "There would be no soldiers I could see. But everybody knew that Israelis were out there, looking around with nightscopes." The passage was terrifying and thrilling. Khaldoon said it always reminded him of the night he was home in Hebron, walking downtown, when a red dot from a rifle's nightscope fixed on his chest. An IDF sniper, he was certain. "I would feel so sure it was going to happen here that I would move—like this." Khaldoon showed me the ducking, weaving walk he developed, suddenly dropping his head and moving his body sideways, hopefully thwarting any soldier who had him in his sights, left-right, left-right.

Birzeit University, founded in 1924 but largely built in the 1970s, had the outward appearance of a well-funded American community college: numerous multi-story buildings faced with the same tawny stone. Of course, it was anything but. Like all Palestinian universities and many schools, it had been closed for five years during the First Intifada, 1987–1992, by order of the Israeli military. Even now it was closed sporadically. As our taxi pulled into the entrance drive, Khaldoon pointed to a spot on the main road. "When they want to close it, they park one of their trucks here," he said of the military. "Sooner or later, somebody will throw a rock at it. They'll respond with tear gas. And that will be it"—meaning that the tear gas would result in even more rocks, providing the army with an excuse to close down the school.

We walked through the cafeteria and a building where psychology was taught, then browsed the many outdoor tables set up in a plaza by student organizations, most of them political and Islamist. "*Kha-li-doon!*" cried one of my guide's friends in greeting. There were many posters of *shahidi,* Muslim martyrs to the occupation—young people of college age. These were especially prominent around the building that belonged to the engineering school, and I asked Khaldoon about it. "One of the most recent martyrs was an engineering student," he explained. "Everybody here knew him." I asked him about the various student tables. "Many of them are student government," Khaldoon said. "It is controlled by Hamas, here and at every university."

"Do you support Hamas?" I asked him.

"Mostly," he said.

"Do you support the martyrs?" I asked.

"Well, I would never *be* a martyr," he replied, "but some of them I admire. Have you heard of the one known as the Engineer?" I said I had not.

"Yahya Ayyash," he explained. "He was very cool. He studied here at Birzeit—engineering. But the nickname came from his work with bombs. He would sneak into Israeli towns disguised as a Jew. Then he himself was assassinated by a booby-trapped cell phone in 1996. It blew up his head." Now I knew who Khaldoon was talking about. Ayyash had masterminded bombings that killed many, many Israelis in the days right after the Oslo Accords.

We left the university for a neighborhood not far away where Khaldoon shared a small house with his next-youngest brother, Tarak, and another student. The house was plain and barely furnished except for some large abstract oil paintings by Tarak. They had a puppy, which had pooped on the floor and nobody had cleaned it up; this upset Khaldoon. A partially disassembled computer was playing music in Khaldoon's bedroom. There were weeds behind the house. After the two brothers stopped arguing about the state of the house, I spoke for a while with Tarak. I would stay only for the night, I confirmed; then I'd accompany Khaldoon to Hebron. As we talked I looked more carefully at the clear vial that hung from a chain around Tarak's neck: Had something moved inside it?

He smiled and lifted it from his neck to give me a closer look. Inside it were two very small scorpions. Tarak had put them in the vial face-to-face, and periodically they attacked each other. "One day one of them will kill the other," he observed matter-of-factly.

———

"You should ask people, on roads, how do they feel?" Khaldoon said to me. "I feel terrible. What if the roads are closed? What if I get caught in a cross fire?"

We were heading south from Ramallah on the 60 Road, which skirted the east side of Jerusalem, then Bethlehem, and then arrived at Hebron, the second-largest city (not including Jerusalem) in the West Bank. It was Friday, and our destination was his parents' house, where we would spend the weekend.

As our service taxi passed near the now abandoned British Police checkpoint on the 60 Road, Khaldoon pointed it out as a landmark, just as Omer had. For him, however, the checkpoint had a different name, Ayoon al-Haramia (Eyes of the Thieves), and the massacre of the Israelis by the mystery gunman was not a tragedy but a triumph. "Even on the Palestinian side we still don't know how he did it," Khaldoon said, beaming. "It's like Spiderman!"

Traveling on the 60 Road with Khaldoon made it seem like another land entirely. As we rumbled on in a succession of service taxis, switching whenever a checkpoint or a barrier required it, he kept asserting that none of the checkpoints was impregnable. Show me a checkpoint, he

Khaldoon near an end of the Israeli "separation barrier," which was still under construction north of Jerusalem

would say, and I'll show you a way around it. The Qalandia checkpoint, between Ramallah and Jerusalem, was Exhibit No. 1: if you were willing to make a big detour and to pay about eight times the normal taxi fare, you could avoid it completely. South of Eyes of the Thieves we did just that, switching taxis at a junction called Arram and ending up in the taxi lot south of Qalandia. Our circuitous and costly route demonstrated why most Palestinians prefer to subject themselves to the checkpoint.

But in other places, Khaldoon told me, evasion was riskier. You could get around a checkpoint by taking a dirt back road or a remote footpath, but the army wasn't stupid: knowing the net had holes, they sent out patrols to catch the fish who slipped through. It was like the stories Sameh had told me. Service taxis are regularly fined or confiscated when caught detouring around a checkpoint. Khaldoon nevertheless sounded defiant. "They close a road, we find a hundred roads!" he proclaimed. "We will make more roads! Anywhere!"

I was starting to believe him when our service taxi stopped at Al-Quds University, in East Jerusalem. Across the street a panoramic view of the city had been replaced by a long section of Israel's new security fence—a blank, imposing structure that ran along the edge of the school's dusty playing fields. The original plan had called for the wall to cross the fields, rendering them useless, but it was revised after U.S. national security adviser Condoleezza Rice intervened. At that moment only one panel remained to be installed before the stretch of wall was complete. "You're not going to make a road around that," I commented. Khaldoon gave me an unhappy look and said nothing more on the subject for the rest of the trip.

Soldiers waved our taxi through the checkpoint outside Bethlehem known as the Container (a shipping container placed there by the army had for years been its signature feature). Checkpoint vigilance varied a lot from day to day, Khaldoon explained. A little further along, the road ended with a series of earthen barriers at a place called Al Khadr. We had to leave our cab, walk fifty yards or so over the mounds and past vendors of food and clothing, then climb into a new taxi. (Every barrier seems to produce this: a market and a taxi stand.) Khaldoon said the barrier was only about a year old. I was confused: Would the army install a barrier solely to inconvenience people? But Khaldoon explained that we were about to get back on the 60 Road, here used mainly by settlers, and the army tried to limit Palestinian traffic on it as much as possible. The closest thing in the American experience, I thought, was being near an inter-state highway that you couldn't get on because there was no entrance ramp nearby.

The 60 Road, only two lanes wide, had many small slabs of concrete erected along the shoulder where it overlooked Palestinian villages near Etzion—"to keep the people from shooting settlers," Khaldoon said.

Outside Hebron, Khaldoon used a cell phone to alert his father, Awni al-Khatib, that he would have to pick us up downtown. His dad called right back to say that traffic was so stacked up at the checkpoint near their house that it would be hours before he'd be able to get there. An alternative rendezvous point was picked. As we approached the city, the taxi dropped me and Khaldoon by the side of the road. We climbed a five-foot-high earthen barrier (another of the hundreds built by the army to keep Palestinian vehicles off main highways like the 60 Road) and hiked a quarter-mile or so down a back street to meet Khaldoon's father.

Awni, an engaging, outgoing man in his early fifties, welcomed us into his Volkswagen Polo, where we also met his youngest son, Muhammad. We drove about ten minutes to an intersection that was in total gridlock with long lines of cars and trucks.

"Uh-oh," I said.

But Khaldoon had a different reaction. "No, no—we're home!" he exclaimed. He clambered out of the VW, threaded his way across the road through the bumper-to-bumper traffic, and opened what turned out to be the gate to the family's driveway. After about five minutes the drivers nearby were able to make enough space for the VW to squeeze through, and we pulled through the gate and into a parking area. "You see what we have to put up with," Awni said, as Khaldoon closed the gate. I didn't at first, but then Khaldoon explained: those cars and trucks were all queued up for the local checkpoint, a hundred yards down the road. "When they set up the checkpoint, they don't put in enough sol-diers," Khaldoon observed. "People have to wait a long time."

Awni is a scientist with a doctorate in inorganic chemistry from the University of Florida at Gainesville. He received his bachelor's and mas-ter's degrees from Utah State University and was a Fulbright visiting scholar at the University of Oklahoma. He and his wife have four sons and a daughter. They all lived in an apartment block for years after they moved to Hebron, where Awni helped establish a science program at the university. (He proudly told me that the program had grown from thirty-

six students at its inception to one thousand today.) His promotion to
vice president of Hebron University had enabled them to build this gracious house, perched on a hillside on the edge of town, with a balcony,
flower gardens, and views of an olive orchard across the valley.

But then the problems had started. First was the news that the road
that the house fronted, which its driveway opened onto, was being con-
verted to a settler passage, the 35 Road toward Gaza. Like most settler
roads, there was no actual prohibition on Palestinian-plated cars; it was
simply that, as Awni explained, "There is no longer any place in Hebron
I can get to on that road." It was a limited-access highway, in other
words, and the only places it led to were Israeli settlements. The driveway
was now weed-strewn and useless.

I then understood that we had come in the back door; Awni smiled as
he watched me figure it out. With no road access to the front, he had had
to figure out a way to park his car in back. The house sat on a slope, its
flat roof roughly the same elevation as the back road we had come in on.
His front driveway thwarted, Awni had come up with an ingenious solution: he had built a concrete bridge to span the gap between his roof and
the back gate, which was located on the road we had entered by. We
walked around the house so he could show me the engineering involved,
and then took a seat with Khaldoon on a shaded patio outside the living
room. Latifa, Awni's wife, who was a schoolteacher, served us hot tea
with a smile but didn't stay to join the conversation.

The settler road had very little traffic, so at least the front of the house
was quiet. But the odd thing was the succession of men, single or in pairs,
who scrambled furtively past the garden every few minutes, prompting
wild barking from the family's German shepherd. Occasionally they
would nod our way, but mostly they did not; their goal was invisibility.
"They're getting around the checkpoint," explained Khaldoon. He was
referring not to the settler road in front of the house (which the evaders
also had to cross, after winding through the olive orchard across the way)
but to the occasional checkpoint that clogged up the local road in back—
the same one that had made Awni pick us up outside of town. As long as
the evaders didn't get caught, they'd save a lot of time.

Khaldoon and I watched television, and then Latifa and Majdoleen,
Khaldoon's sister, served dinner to Awni, Khaldoon, Muhammad, and
me. I had hoped the women would join us at the table so that I could get
to know them but that was not the custom; after serving us, they returned

The Khatib residence in Hebron. When the front driveway (out of the frame on the right) was rendered useless by the conversion of the road in front to a settler highway, the family built a bridge (left) to another street behind the house, allowing them to park on the roof.

to the kitchen. When we were finished Awni asked if I would like to meet a friend of his who was a journalist and I said certainly, so he invited over Khalid Suleiman, and we again retired to the patio for tea.

The visit got off to a good start. "I'm a Sooner!" said Suleiman by way of greeting: he, too, had attended the University of Oklahoma, where he met Awni. And he sported a baseball cap. But quickly it became clear that Khalid might not be an alumnus the university would be eager to claim. His master's thesis in journalism, he told me, was an examination of anti-Arab racism in Leon Uris's novel *The Haj*. I told him that I had known Uris but never read the book, and could practically see his lip curl.

The United States, he said, had a huge bias against Arabs. This was evident in books like *The Haj* (I later read the book and saw he had a point) and Margaret Truman's biography of her father, *Harry S. Truman*—"See for yourself, it's on page 169," Khalid said. (I later read the book and could see no bias at all.)

"How is it that you remember the actual page number?" I asked him.

"Because so many people like you ask me about it," he replied.

People like me? I wondered. He barely knew me.

The Israelis admitted their own racism, he continued, quoting Moshe Zimmerman, the head of German studies at Hebrew University in Jerusalem, who once called the children of Hebron's extremist settlers "Hitler Youth." (Zimmerman said he had made the comment after listening to a "radio interview with the children of settlers from Hebron on the first anniversary of the murder of twenty-nine people in a mosque by Baruch Goldstein. The kids said: 'Goldstein is our hero.' . . . These children are trained like the Hitler Jugend to think ideologically without criticism. They are led to believe in racist views of themselves as the master race superior to the Arabs.")

"But you can't claim that people with extreme views represent a culture," I said. "Uris didn't speak for the American mainstream on the subject of Arabs—and that was a minor novel of his. Zimmerman is seen as an extreme leftist in Israel."

Suleiman brushed those comments aside. My country was Israel's puppet, he said. We had a bit of a discussion about that idea. With any suggestion of disagreement on my part, Suleiman grew more heated; he wanted to vent, and wasn't interested in real discussion. Not everything he said was absurd ("When will we see the house of an Israeli bulldozed for his having killed a Palestinian?"). But as I pressed him on his views we finally arrived at his bottom line: Khalid declared that he was in favor of an Islamic caliphate—strict Muslim rule of the world. Contrary to the beliefs of some in the West, he said, the Middle East would be a lot safer and more stable if many nations had nuclear weapons, instead of just one (Israel). Then, at least, there would be mutually assured destruction.

With that he seemed to take a breath. Latifa appeared and poured us all more tea.

I was wondering how a person embracing this ideology could possibly function as a journalist. It was difficult at the moment, Khalid replied; his permission to travel had been revoked by Israel after he had filed a story in Egypt for al-Jazeera that evidently provoked someone in Israeli intelligence.

"So how do you do your work?" I asked. He said from home, but I knew that would be impossible for most journalists and could see that, more than many, he was a prisoner. With that his anger became more recognizable: he was like many I had met who were incarcerated at Sing Sing, radicals who fulminated, who pontificated.

Awni had been conspicuously silent during most of this. I sensed he mainly wanted to expose me to his friend's views. Still, I was glad when he finally stepped in, preaching moderation. "I do not want to see Muhammad cornered by the hatred," he said. That's why he had his youngest son taking Hebrew lessons: because coexistence was inevitable.

"I do not follow the hatred path. I think it is wrong on both sides," he said. He didn't like suicide bombings, in part "because it suggests a people cannibalizing itself."

Looking into the future, Awni said he didn't think that Israel could afford endless conflict. "They depend on Jewish immigrants, and immigrants aren't going to want to move there if it stays this bad."

I enjoyed talking to Awni, but trying to speak with Khalid had been an exhausting and upsetting end to a long day. I took one of the twin beds in Khaldoon's room, and when the lights were out I replayed in my mind the conversation with Suleiman. It reminded me of nothing so much as an encounter I'd had in a Tel Aviv laundromat two weeks before. I had left Omer's base for the weekend and was staying in a hotel. But my jeans were stained by the oil that had splashed through the window of the Storm the evening I drove through the Arab villages with Omer's men. A friendly older woman at the laundromat hailed from Detroit, and she offered me advice for getting the stains out. "How did you get them?" she asked.

Her husband, a retiree, also from Detroit, sitting in a nearby plastic chair, overheard my answer. "Arabs are animals," he growled. "You're not even safe from them in the U.S. anymore." The comment had infuriated me and soon the husband and I were in a loud argument. The wife tried hard to separate us. "Some people will never see eye to eye" was her take on our dispute, and that night in Hebron it resonated with me: extremism was all around me here, a wall all its own, impermeable to discussion.

Khaldoon and I watched television news in the morning, after which he observed that, given the several Palestinians killed by the IDF in Gaza the night before, it might be a good idea if we were to leave Hebron before the midday mosque services let out. And there were a few things he wanted to show me first: his friend's clothing shop; the Ibrahimi Mosque where the crazed settler Goldstein had murdered all those worshipers (and wounded about 125 others) in 1994; and the old town center, now a hostile enclave of settler extremists protected by the army. As we ate a breakfast that included *labne* (cream cheese made from yogurt) spread on pita, Khaldoon observed that the checkpoint was up again: a trickle of people were stepping gingerly through olive groves down the hill across the way, preparing to dash up the hill by the house—skirting the checkpoint, in other words. We would have to pass through that checkpoint to get into town, so we left early to allow extra time.

The line of cars and trucks was already long. We walked alongside the vehicles to the underpass, where two soldiers stood before a crowd of maybe forty Palestinian pedestrians. A third stood guard up on the hill, by the 35 Road; I knew three to be the checkpoint minimum. Only one soldier, a red-haired young man who looked to be about twenty years old, was examining documents.

People were allowed to approach the soldier one at a time. Being American, I discovered, did not speed things up. After more than half an hour, when I finally got the nod, the soldier examined my documents and then stepped close enough to whisper in my ear that it was dangerous in town. "If I were you, I would climb up there," he confided, pointing to the settler road up the embankment, "and hitchhike out of here."

"But I'm with a friend," I responded, and gestured at Khaldoon. "A family friend." I thought that might sound a bit more persuasive. But the soldier only looked puzzled. He called up Khaldoon. "Okay, family friend," he said finally. He returned our documents. We were clear.

It was Rosh Hashanah, the Jewish New Year, and Omer invited me to the holiday dinner at the family home of his longtime girlfriend, Orit. Orit was a student of veterinary medicine, and her parents lived in a townhouse in Netanya, about twenty minutes north of Tel Aviv and maybe two hours from the paratrooper base north of Ramallah. Work in the West Bank, Omer had told me, was "a war you can commute to."

I'd never been to Netanya, but I knew its recent notoriety: in the spring of 2002, a suicide bomber had blown himself up at a seder in the city's Park Hotel, killing 29 people and injuring 140. The event, which has come to be known as the Park Hotel Massacre or the Netanya Passover Massacre, was the climax of a bloody month that saw 130 Israelis killed in suicide and other attacks. Days later, the IDF responded with a major offensive called Operation Defensive Shield, invading most of the Pales-

tinian cities of the West Bank and focusing particular wrath on Jenin, site
of a refugee camp from which they believed many of the attacks originated. Palestinian casualties at the camp—fifty-two, according to the
IDF—have led Palestinians to refer to it as a massacre. Suicide bombings
inside Israel have dwindled since then (in 2007 there was only one, and
the same in 2008), due largely to the construction of the "security fence"
and the ongoing efforts of army units like Omer's.

I'd had some trouble reading the highway signs at night, and so was the
last to arrive at dinner. In addition to Omer and Orit and her parents, her
two older brothers were there with their wives; one couple had an infant
daughter, the other a toddler son. Both brothers (and one of the wives), as
it turned out, had spent four years in the army but clearly felt that was
enough: they had moved on to careers in other fields. Omer, I now saw,
was seen as something of an oddity, a smart young person with many
other options who remained in the military because, well, he liked it.

As the group passed around the brisket, the capon, and the kugel and
asked about my work, it became clear how interested they were in letting
Omer know it was time to get out. Omer had already told me about the
trouble his soldiers often had with their West Bank service: their families
didn't want to hear about it. Even if families approved of their country's
conduct in "the territories," also known in Israel as Judea and Samaria,
they didn't necessarily want to know the details, because much of it was
frankly unpleasant. But somehow I had imagined that Omer, the wise
and senior leader who observed all this, was somehow immune to such
pressure.

Not at all. Orit's family appeared to be left-leaning, and therefore that
much more disapproving. Her father said, more than once, that work
in the territories was morally insupportable. "To work a week there—
impossible," he said. "To work a month—impossible. To work a year
there—impossible!"

Most Israelis, a sister-in-law added, were "against the West Bank policy." I hadn't known that and asked her why, in that case, had they elected
a prime minister like Ariel Sharon? She told me she wasn't sure, that it
was complicated.

"Will you finish soon?" ventured Orit's mom.

"Yes, I'm applying for programs in graduate school," Omer confirmed.
He had already told me this, but had added that he would probably
return to the military once he was finished.

Omer and Orit and I took the parents' boxer for a walk when the main meal was finished but before dessert. Orit, Omer had already told me, was firmly against his working in the territories, on political grounds. Though they had lived together nine years and planned to get married, she had never once visited his posts in the West Bank. "Did he tell you about the time he was attacked in Nablus?" Orit asked me as we walked.

I said he had—the kid who'd come around the ambulance with the Molotov cocktails whom Omer had shot. I knew it had been horrific for him, killing a boy, but hadn't known it was also a crisis for Orit. "It made me hate the Arabs," she disclosed. "That they make a boy do that."

Omer returned to something he had told me earlier, the example of a nighttime home invasion. I knew these bothered him, but I also knew he had to do it all the time, and the searches often bore fruit: to the army, finding a weapon justified the horror. And yet a horror it was: "When soldiers invade a family's home and terrify the boy sitting on the bed in order to find a weapon, I think we've probably just created another terrorist," he said, echoing an earlier comment. (A few days later, al-Jazeera posted a manifesto purportedly from Osama bin Laden lambasting the United States with these words: "Your allies in Palestine . . . terrorize the women and children, and kill and capture the men as they lie sleeping with their families on the mattresses, [and] you may recall that for every action, there is a reaction.") And yet, from Omer's point of view, it was crucial work that had to be done.

Whatever his shortcomings as a potential son-in-law, I thought that Orit's family would have a hard time finding a better soldier.

Omer kept referring to "the old 60" and "the new 60," and one day I asked what he meant. The old 60, he explained, had connected all the major Palestinian cities of the West Bank. But with the growth of Israeli settlements in the territory, and with Israeli settlers encountering trouble when they traveled through Palestinian cities, bypass roads had been created. The peak of this construction was in the late 1990s. Bypasses now constitute the main 60 Road, which skirts not only the cities but many of the villages as well.

One morning, intelligence reports indicated that bombers out of Nablus would be heading to points south, and Omer decided to set up a flying checkpoint on the new 60 Road where it intersected the old 60, just below the company's base. After all, a smart bomber might decide to avoid the main routes, with their permanent checkpoints, in favor of a longer journey on back roads.

Four soldiers went out at midmorning with a Humvee driver to set up the flying checkpoint, and I went along to observe. In charge of the operation was one of Omer's most trusted platoon leaders, a twenty-one-year-old named Ori, who unloaded from the Humvee two ammo boxes containing the *pakal machsom*, the checkpoint kit, which included reflectors, a warning sign on a tripod, and two lengths of "dragon's teeth"—collapsible spikes that extend about six feet across the road, to make sure cars stop where they are supposed to.

I had talked to Ori at length the evening before, at a picnic table on the base. Short, handsome, and conscientious, he had served two years in the army after an eight-month stint in the navy. Like many of his buddies, he was still trying to make the adjustment from his active life as a soldier patrolling Nablus to a relatively more passive one manning checkpoints. "In Nablus you feel like a warrior," he told me. "You arrest people, you bring them to justice, and all of that. But here you don't see the fruit of the work. The challenge is the people and their problems and all the pressure they put on you, and your soldiers looking at you and trying to see how you do it. And you need to deal with the threats, which at a checkpoint are very large. The threat could be in a lady's bag, or in the engine behind an air cleaner, or behind the nearest hill, or a grenade could be thrown at you from fifty meters." As Ori spoke, I thought of his platoon's symbol: a clown juggling grenades.

The low points of his military service, Ori told me, had been the three months he spent working the Hawara checkpoint, and a recent dangerous assignment in Gaza. He had been sent to Gaza the day after a rocket-propelled grenade killed five Israeli soldiers traveling in armored personnel carriers. Ori's challenge, in the middle of taking fire from snipers, was to try to retrieve small body parts of the slain soldiers, so that their relatives would have something to bury.

But today he was back at a checkpoint, battling the heat and the boredom of examining each and every document handed to him from a slow-moving line of cars. As the line began to stretch back over a hill and out of sight, much like the scene in Hebron as I had waited with Khaldoon, Ori, exposed on the blacktop, summoned one vehicle at a time to move ahead of the rest, and then spoke to the driver in the Arabic phrases he had learned during his boot-camp training. The first, of course, which every soldier knew, was Stop!, or *Wakkif!* But Ori knew many more.

Wain raieh? (Where are you going?)

Jai min wain? (Coming from where?)

Lahalak fi al-saiara? (Alone in the car?)

Laish raieh? Shu al-shughul? (Why are you going? On what business?)

Itfee al-saiara! (Turn off the car!) This order is often ignored at first.

Itla min al-saiara! (Get out of the car!)

Iftah al-sanduq! (Open the trunk!)

Irfa qameesak! (Lift up your shirt!)

All morning long I watched Ori and his colleagues do their work. I watched them stop an ambulance and make everyone get out, including an old man in back who was apparently on his way to a hospital and looked pretty close to death. Later, in their defense, Ori and other soldiers pointed out that ambulances had been used on more than one occasion to carry explosives.

I watched them allow cars with yellow-and-black Israeli license plates, as opposed to white-and-green Palestinian ones, to skip the queue and pass through the checkpoint by using the oncoming-traffic lane. Most made eye contact with Ori before proceeding, but some just zoomed by.

I watched them make a pregnant woman wait more than twenty minutes in the broiling sun while a soldier ran her ID through a computer back at the base.

I watched them order several Palestinians to pile out of a service taxi, leaving inside an incapacitated man whose foot was wrapped with gauze through which blood had oozed. Wary of a trap, Ori then made the man, despite his evident pain, get out of the taxi and hop over to him with his documents. After getting the all clear the man was carried back to the taxi by the other passengers.

I watched an old woman climb out of the car she was riding in and hobble up the road, saying that her husband could pick her up once he got through the checkpoint, but she was not going to wait a minute more. "Go ahead and shoot me!" she told Ori as she walked by.

Standing there in the sun (I'd been issued a helmet and a bulletproof vest as well), I recalled Khaldoon's remark that he "hated" traveling on roads. And then I thought of my son's soccer team back in the USA. There were many players from other countries, including a wonderful Israeli kid, Eden, whose father was a general posted to the U.S. for purposes of military fund-raising. Soon after the American invasion of Iraq, when the inadequate armor of our vehicles was becoming clear, he had told me that Israel had quietly loaned the U.S. "many" armored vehicles as a stopgap, the IDF being well seasoned in the challenges of occupation. Iraq, of course, with its bloody internecine power struggles and the profusion of IEDs that took such a high toll of coalition soldiers, was a much more dangerous place to be than the Palestinian territories. But the war-without-end of an occupation, and the centrality of roads to the effort, were two things they had very much in common.

After about three hours Omer arrived and decided that although no bomber or contraband had been interdicted, the checkpoint had served its purpose. Back at the base Ori and the other soldiers seemed glad to take off their heavy combat gear and eat lunch. Ori told me that he would have liked to be a soldier in the time of the Haganah—the Israel Defense Forces' precursor—or of an early elite strike force like the Palmach. Such fighters, he said, recruited themselves, lived in a group, and worked together for one purpose. "Now it seems so complicated—you don't know who's right and who's wrong, and if we've done the right thing every time."

Surely this sentiment is shared by thousands of soldiers—Israeli, Russian, American—at the dawn of the twenty-first century, when it appears that the hardest thing is not taking control of a territory (the West Bank, Chechnya, Iraq) but attempting to run it once you are there. The battlefield is no longer a highly militarized beachhead, plain, or jungle but a road, a checkpoint; and the challenge is picking out the enemy—a teenager in a long coat; a woman with a baby carriage—from the large mass of civilians who are noncombatants, without creating additional enemies in the process. The great risk, as you contend against the unseen, is that you may come to demonize even those who are not part of the resistance. That's what the job does. No wonder Ori felt nostalgic for the old days.

And no wonder Omer, in command of a base surrounded by historical enemies, didn't seem at all fearful of traditional defeat. His side clearly enjoyed overwhelming military superiority. But Omer did worry a lot about his men's state of mind. I knew this in part because, for a few days, I shared his bunk room in the radio trailer on the paratrooper base. The room was small—three cots—and messy: uniforms and underclothes were piled here and there, bullets were scattered around the floor. Omer didn't spend much time in there; his days started early and usually ended late. He wanted to be near the radio in case there was urgent news. More than once I woke up in the morning to find him asleep in his uniform, even his boots still on. One night, after I'd been asleep about four hours, he and his lieutenant, Eyal, arrived back after a particularly difficult arrest in a Palestinian village. I'd gone along on other nights but this time, at the last minute (around one a.m.), the Shin Bet radioed I couldn't go. Too sensitive, Omer guessed. And so I'd missed it, but from the other operations I had an idea of what had transpired: the village, dark and silent, the soldiers quietly taking up positions all around the house in question, and finally Omer and his top guys bursting inside to look for the person or the weapon. It was scary, but when it was over it was sad.

By the time Omer returned it was almost dawn. Eyal flopped down on the third bunk and fell asleep almost instantly. In the low light beginning to show through the window, Omer sat on his bed and unlaced his boots. Yes, he told me, they had got the bad guy. "But it was hard." He didn't need to mention a girl's shaking, a mother's sobbing, a father's veiled fury. I knew his concern was always for his soldiers, and they loved him for it. "The real daily fight," he had told me more than once, worried about the toll on his soldiers, "is fighting for a soul."

SPEED UP!

A BLOCKED ROAD is a thwarted intention.

A good road—smooth, straight, free of roadblocks—allows us to go fast. Speed, in fact, is not only the advantage of a good road but one of its great pleasures.

In the pre-Hispanic Americas, speed was a fast runner. Spaniards introduced the horse, which, according to early chroniclers, the Aztec saw as an intelligent being, even a god. Larger and faster than any other creature they knew, a horse with a soldier on its back formed a huge, intimidating fighting machine.

With time, Native Americans came to understand, breed, and ride horses with a skill commensurate with that of the cowboys and soldiers they battled. Around the world, in Mongolia and Scandinavia, in Australia and Argentina, pastoral people used horses for transportation and, yes, for the pleasures of racing.

Earlier, though, other civilizations had taken it to the next level. Four-wheeled chariots appeared in Mesopotamia between 3000 and 2500 B.C., pulled by oxen or donkeys. As their use spread to India, China, and Europe, they became more nimble with the use of spoked wheels, and by 2000 B.C., they were pulled by horses, two, three, or four of them—a potent innovation for battle. They could go faster than a single horse ridden by a soldier in full armor, and they allowed soldiers better access to weaponry. As we know from sources including the movies, Greeks and Romans put them to use in races and other pageantry.

The Greeks, in addition, found a place for chariots in their mythology. Phaeton, challenged by his friends to prove that Helios, the sun god, was his real father, asked to drive his chariot (the sun) for a day. Helios tried to talk him out of it, but to no avail. Phaeton, reins in hand, quickly lost control: the chariot came too close to earth, setting rivers and oceans to boil; "whole cities burn, / And peopled kingdoms into ashes turn." Libya became a desert and the Moors' skin blackened.

Finally Zeus, god of the sky, intervened, striking the runaway chariot with a bolt of lightning. Phaeton, perhaps history's first teenage driver, plunged to earth with his hair on fire and perished.*

Horses pulled carts and wagons of various kinds for centuries, but not until the eighteenth century did a combination of better roads and better cart technology result in vehicles that brought wheeled speed to large numbers of people. The French were leaders in this development, with the horse-drawn *cabriolet*, a lightweight, two-wheeled, open-air cart for two; sturdier *coupés;* and the *turgotine*, a narrow stagecoach. The convenience, excitement, and utility of these innovations resulted in a boom: the number of vehicles in Paris went from 320 in 1658 to 20,000 by 1765. "Everyone has become a driver," wrote the Chevalier d'H. in 1819. "It's the fashion of the day."

England, too, was transformed. Over seventy-five years the number of carriages shot up from 18,000 in 1775 to 106,000 in 1840. Roughly corresponding to the French conveyances were the English curricle (two wheels, one axle), phaeton (four large wheels, minimal body), and mail coach. Like the French vehicles, and like the fallen god, and indeed like the modern sports car, all were known as fast and dangerous, thrilling to drive but a peril to pedestrians. With vehicles "came efforts to widen and straighten out streets, regulate traffic, differentiate sidewalks from roadways . . . efforts that had the effect also of encouraging a further acceleration of motion."

A significant enabler of speed, of course, was McAdam's better pavement. In combination, smooth pavement and horses pulling lightweight carriages brought the pleasures of speed to a larger number of people than ever before. As angry as pedestrians were with the newfound perils of the street, drivers and passengers became ecstatic with motion. The hero of Nikolai Gogol's *Dead Souls* (1842) exulted in his travels from town to town in a *britzka* drawn by three horses:

---

* Two millennia later, Jim Stark, the seventeen-year-old played by James Dean in the movie *Rebel Without a Cause* (1955), raced another teenager down a highway toward a cliff to see who would be the first to chicken out. The other kid meant to stop but couldn't, and a boy in his vehicle again dropped to his death.

Selifan perked up and, slapping the dapple-gray on the back a few times, which made him break into a trot, and brandishing his whip over them all, added in a thin, singsong voice: "Never fear!" The horses got moving and pulled the light britzka along like a bit of fluff. . . . Chichikov just smiled, jouncing slightly on his leather cushion, for he loved fast driving. And what Russian does not love fast driving? How can his soul, which yearns to get into a whirl, to carouse, to say sometimes: "Devil take it all!"—how can his soul not love it? Not love it when something ecstatically wondrous is felt in it? It seems an unknown force has taken you on its wing, and you are flying, and everything is flying: milestones go flying by, merchants come flying at you on the boxes of their *kibitkas* [small horse-drawn wagons], the forest on both sides is flying by with its dark ranks of firs and pines, with axes chopping and crows cawing, the whole road is flying off no one knows where into the vanishing distance, and there is something terrible in this quick flashing, in which the vanishing object has no time to fix itself—only the sky overhead, and the light clouds, and the moon trying to break through, they alone seem motionless.

Meanwhile, travel in England was being transformed by a system of fast government mail coaches. Pulled by four horses, they could carry four passengers inside, but mail delivery took priority. Danger courted the coaches: a post office guard stood outside in the back, on the lookout for highwaymen. And they were prone to accidents, the driver's seat being the riskiest. An additional passenger was allowed to sit with the driver. An Oxford student who was fond of doing so, Thomas De Quincey, famously recalled his experiences in his essay "The English Mail Coach":

> The vital experience of the glad animal sensibilities made doubts impossible on the question of our speed; we heard our speed, we saw it, we felt it as a thrilling; and this speed was not the product of blind insensate agencies, that had no sympathy to give, but was incarnated in the fiery eyeballs of the noblest amongst brutes, in his dilated nostril, spasmodic muscles, and thunder-beating hoofs.

These sensations of speed, De Quincey wrote, had a large role "in developing the anarchies of my subsequent dreams," by which he appears to refer to the experiences behind his book *The Confessions of an English Opium-Eater.* The idea of velocity as a sensation-heightening narcotic is not new.

The mail coach system had stopped by 1846, largely replaced by railroads. Looking back, De Quincey doubted whether this was progress: not only do you not *feel* the velocity of a train, he complained, but the visceral connection between passenger and horse was gone, replaced by "the pot-wallopings of the boiler." Jeffrey T. Schnapp, a Stanford professor who spent years as a competitive motorcycle racer, adds that the mail coach was invigorating because it was irregular, an experience of speed that defied tedium because it always contains "the promise/threat of accident."

Commercial airliners likely would have bored De Quincey. Perhaps even space travel would: as the fastest human beings to date, astronauts orbit the earth at 17,500 miles per hour while looking perfectly relaxed. (The more potent symbols of speed in the twentieth century are the faces of test pilots like Chuck Yeager, who were photographed in the late 1940s breaking the sound barrier while g-forces grotesquely wrinkled and pulled back their cheeks, exposing their teeth.)

But the future was not devoid of promise. With the rise of horses and carriages, argues Schnapp, individuality became "identified with administration of one's own speed" as never before. This trend only continued with the rise of the automobile, and its domination of roads around the globe.

At a writers' conference in Aspen, I had the pleasure of teaching a workshop that included Janet Guthrie, the first woman to drive in the Indianapolis 500. She was working on a memoir, since published; here is the ninth paragraph, describing a moment from the Indy of 1977:

> The Lightning had long since become an extension of myself. I was melted into it, centrifugal force smearing me like putty against the torso support and headrest as the side loads rose in the turns. My nerve endings extended out to the contact patches where the tires gripped the pavement, like the fingertips and toes of a rock climber.

Guthrie's racetrack experiences remain extreme, the province of a few talented drivers. But from the free falls of sky divers and bungee jumpers to the theme park roller coasters so beloved of teenagers, people are finding ways to go faster and faster.

There remains, however, something singular about the accelerator, about controlling it yourself. I suppose this is one reason that traffic so thwarts driving pleasure: it effectively caps acceleration, and subtracts most of the skill from driving. Similarly, repetition—of driving the same route again and again, in the same car, even if it's a Corvette—kills the thrill. The road must be open, and winding, and you can't be headed to work.

I grew up a passenger in a Rambler station wagon, and then an Oldsmobile. My first experience of incarceration was being buckled into the back seat of that Oldsmobile as my father drove the family across the seemingly endless American West on a summer vacation.

But then, in addition to a station wagon, we got a second car: my father, like so many other dads, wanted something more. He bought a blue Porsche 912. The excitement he felt for it was infectious. At thirteen, I loved riding in that car with him, seated so close to the ground, accelerating so quickly when the light turned green, touching the wooden shift knob and smelling the leather interior. There were two vent windows in the rear; I'll never forget my dad repeating what the seller, Glen Somebody, had told him: that leaving them ajar "creates a nice cross-breeze." It was like gospel. As was the wisdom that the noisy, air-cooled rear engine *liked* running at high RPMs—that's what the tachometer was for, to make sure the Porsche got the sports car equivalent of *exercise*.

Dad had a client up in Cheyenne, Wyoming, about an hour an a half from Denver if you ignored the speed limit. Which I must conclude Dad did, and who could blame him? One night he returned home from Wyoming after dark. I was the first one outside in the morning, and the first to notice the pelt of an entire rabbit dangling from Dad's car, partly embedded in the grille. *Damn,* I thought.

In high school the car I drove was the current station wagon, a Pontiac Catalina. But the spring of my senior year, a girl from Florida I'd met while teaching skiing on weekends wrote me to say she'd be up in Aspen for a week with her family. It corresponded with my spring break. I asked my parents if there was any chance I could borrow the car and go up there for a couple of days.

I got a "no, sorry"—my mom needed the wagon for various errands. But then, the day before break, Dad took me aside. Would I like to take the Porsche to Aspen? he asked. Was he kidding?

He handed me the keys with a bit of trepidation, murmured something about downshifting on hills to save the brakes—but it was all just ceremony. The main thing was *he had handed me the keys*. It was the closest thing I'd ever have to a teenage rite of passage.

The trip to Aspen took four hours that time of year. I'd never driven so far from home by myself. But I knew how to go. An after-school job kept me from leaving until dinnertime. By the time I reached the mountains, it was dark. The national speed limit at the time was fifty-five, but even going faster I could seldom put the Porsche into fifth gear, had to stick with fourth, the engine growling satisfyingly as I climbed hills in the passing lane.

Then I came to Glenwood Canyon. The interstate highway ended there (later it would go through, in a magnificent feat of engineering that cost hundreds of millions of dollars and involved lots of dramatically elevated roadway). At the time, the mid-1970s, the road turned into a curvy two-lane highway that ran alongside the Colorado River. High rock walls rose on either side of the narrow canyon, softened by willows at road's edge and the occasional waterfall.

I drove as fast as I possibly could, pushing around corners as the engine roared. It was late March; there was no snow and the road surface was clear. I had the windows open and the heater on. My heart beat fast because of the chance I could crash. The Blaupunkt radio played a song I loved. There was a girl from Florida at the end of the road. All was motion, moment, potential, thrill.

FIVE

CAPITALIST ROADERS

ZHU JIHONG CANNOT WAIT to get started on his holiday road trip. At six a.m. on Saturday, the first day of the October National Day week (one of three annual Golden Weeks in China, intended to promote internal tourism and ensure that workers take some time off), Zhu has parked his brand-new Hyundai Tucson SUV, with its limited-edition package of extras like walnut trim and chrome step-bar, in front of my hotel in downtown Beijing. He is half an hour early, but he is in a hurry. He cannot believe I'm not ready.

Li Lu, my interpreter, has found me in the hotel restaurant. She was rousted even earlier than I, at her apartment a couple of miles away, and calculates that Zhu, to make it into Beijing from his home on the city's outskirts, must have gotten up at four. She adds that she's a bit concerned: she helped me book a spot on this car trip and had assumed that the driver whose car we shared would be a person of, well, culture. But Zhu, she says, is "not educated."

"What do you mean?" I ask as we leave the hotel's revolving glass doors and come upon Zhu.

Zhu is nicely dressed, in the dark slacks, leather loafers, and knit shirt of many Chinese businessmen. Cigarette in one hand, hair recently cut and wavy on top, Zhu, in his forties, has a somewhat dashing, youthful air. Before Li Lu and I are out the revolving door, he is at the back of the Hyundai, making room for my knapsack and pointing me in the direction of the leather passenger seat. He stops to shake my hand only after I pause and offer mine. Li Lu is our intermediary and tries to effect the introduction I'm after, but Zhu is not one for formalities; he gives a tiny nod, then circles the car, hawks noisily and spits by his door, climbs in, and turns the key. Li Lu, from the back seat, gives me a look that says, *See? What did I tell you?*

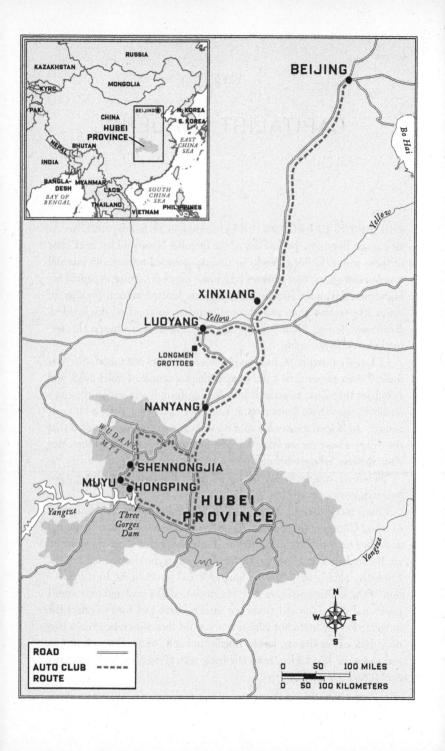

But as the car fills with smoke from his cigarette and the CB radio battles for supremacy with operatic Red Army tunes on the CD player, I don't much mind Zhu's manners (which, Li Lu explains, reflect the factory owner's peasant background) because we're off on an adventure and Zhu's excitement is infectious. Our trip is a seven-day excursion from Beijing to Hubei province in central China, including stops at the Three Gorges Dam and a mountainous forest preserve called Shennongjia, home to a fabled race of giant hairy ape-men. And though the trendy enterprise we are part of is known as a "self-driving tour," we are not going alone: a dozen carfuls of other people have signed on with the tour, organized by the Beijing Target Auto Club, one of the for-profit driving clubs that are sprouting all over China.

Zhu is ready for a long day at the wheel—our destination, Nanyang, is more than 500 miles away—but it's going to be even longer than he thinks. Our rendezvous with the other cars at the Zhuozhou rest stop, normally an hour away, will be delayed four hours, as thick fog closes the expressway. Heavy rain will fall, and our early start will count for little by midday as the highways swell with holiday traffic. There will be wrecks, like the fatal one-car rollover we'll pass on a bridge around midnight, an upside-down Beijing-plated Mitsubishi. The hotel's dinner will be waiting for us at one a.m., and we'll all be happy to see our rooms. But right now Zhu is pouring himself tea from a thermos and telling Li Lu how rich he is and how lucky we are to be in his car.

"He says he is an excellent driver and we will go very fast," she reports wearily.

I had never been to China before 2005. I was born in Okinawa, Japan, where my father was stationed as a navy pilot, but I'd never been back. Instead, as I mentioned, I grew up in Denver, which has a relatively brief history as a settled place—125 years or so—compared to China's many centuries of civilization. The foreignness of East Asia, to me, had as much to do with its antiquity as with any strangeness of language or custom.

And yet, since Deng Xiaopeng's economic openings of the 1990s, something had been growing in China that did seem familiar to me, and that was a culture of cars. Zhou Enlai's "Four Modernizations" picked up speed under Deng, and by the early years of the twenty-first century,

Deng's "socialism with Chinese characteristics" was taking hold and turning the country into a huge economic powerhouse. "Socialism does not mean shared poverty," Deng said, and millions of Chinese mobilized to see what it might mean instead.

On its way to becoming the world's factory, China began to manufacture its own cars, trucks, and buses—over a hundred distinct brands of them by 2007, as well as foreign makes developed in joint partnerships with Volkswagen, General Motors, and Hyundai, among others. It was only a matter of time until lots of people had the money to buy a car; the desire to drive one, I would learn, had already been around a good long while.

I'd heard about the driving clubs springing up in big cities in China. They organized group trips for members of the new driving class, and I wanted to sign on. A friend's mother was just back from a more conventional tour of China, and put me in touch with the guide she'd had in Xi'an, in western China. We started to instant message. It was too bad I hadn't asked her a couple months earlier, the guide said; she and her boyfriend were just back from a driving trip, and I would have been welcome to join them. Short of that, she was able to recommend a well-known club in Beijing. They had a trip leaving in a few weeks, they said, and while most members came with friends or family, a few were solo and would welcome a passenger.

All I lacked was a translator. Often serendipity enters into these matters, and it did this time: a Little League dad with whom I chatted during my son's games turned out to have worked in Beijing and knew just the person. Her name was Li Lu, he said; he'd met her when she came to teach English to some of his bank's Chinese employees. Right now she was teaching in one of the city's most famous language schools. He would call her for me.

And so it was that Li Lu (Lucy Li, to me) greeted me the moment I stepped off the jetway at Beijing's airport (the boyfriend of a former student of hers was a security supervisor at the airport, and got her into the secured zone). She was about thirty, petite and effervescent. Her hennaed hair had bangs and, I later realized, long extensions. She wore an orange skirt and high white leather boots that had sneaker laces and soles. Her contact zipped us through Customs and I followed Lucy outside and into a black car whose driver was waiting for us.

We sat in the back and Lucy asked if I was surprised by the large size of the car. It was a Red Flag, she explained, a Chinese-made car that until recently had been used exclusively by high officials. The car was about the size of a Honda Accord, but boxier; I confessed that my car at home was about the same size.

It was drizzling rain and the midafternoon traffic was very slow. As we creeped onto a roundabout, Lucy said that we were entering the 6th Ring Road, which took me by surprise; my recent-edition guidebook referred to only five of these major arteries that encircle the city, three of which had been built in the past ten years. Probably by the time this book comes out, there will be a seventh.

We ate an early dinner at a neighborhood restaurant near her school and my hotel, the fancy Jade Hotel, where Lucy knew the manager. At the restaurant, two moms were eating at different tables, each with one child, while the children did homework. "Their fathers often get home very late," Lucy explained. She was divorced, she told me, with no kids. "Shame?" she asked. Divorce in China is not common, and there is still stigma in it. "No shame with me," I said, explaining that my own parents had divorced, that it was common in the States.

She loved to eat and we ordered a lot more than we could finish; she took the rest home to the room she shared with a teacher on the campus of Beijing Normal University. She was taking some days off to help me out—not to make money, though I would pay her for her trouble, but because the car trip sounded interesting. Her friends, she said, were surprised by the news that she'd be hitting the road with me and the driving club. "I'm just a Beijing girl, a taxi girl!"—not a sporting, auto-club type. But she was game. "Everything is changing now in China!" she explained to me, needlessly, more than once. You had to be ready for the next new thing.

The figures behind China's car boom are stunning. The country's highway miles at the end of 2007 totaled at least 33,000, more than triple what existed in 2001, and second now only to the United States. There were about 6 million passenger cars on the road in 2000 and over 24 million in 2008. Car sales were up 54 percent in the first three months of 2006, compared with the same period a year before; every day, 1,000 new cars and 500 used ones are sold in Beijing. The astronomical growth of China's car-manufacturing industry will hit home for Americans and Europeans as inexpensive Chinese automobiles start showing up for sale here over the next few years.

But of course the story is not only about construction and production; car culture is taking root in China, and in many ways it looks like ours. City drivers, stuck in ever-growing jams, listen to traffic radio. They buy auto magazines with titles like *The King of Cars, AutoStyle, China Auto Pictorial, Friends of Cars, Whaam* ("The Car—The Street—The Travel—The Racing"). Two dozen titles now compete for space in kiosks. The McDonald's Corporation expects half of its new outlets in China to be drive-throughs. Whole areas of major cities, like the Asian Games Village Automobile Exchange zone in Beijing, have been given over to car lots and showrooms.

In other ways, though, the Chinese are still figuring cars out and doing things their way. Take the phrase used to describe our expedition, "self-driving trip." It is called self-driving to contrast it with the more customary idea of driving in China: that someone else drives you. Until recently, everyone important enough to own a car was also important enough to have his or her own driver. Traditions grew up around this, like the chauffeur joining his boss at the table for meals while on duty—something still commonly seen.

But those practices are growing fusty. What are new and explosively popular are car clubs. Some are organized around the idea of travel, like the Beijing Target Auto Club, and others around the idea of . . . well, simply fun. The Beijing VW Polo Club, for example, has an active Web site and hundreds of youthful members. (The Polo is a small VW model popular in Europe and Latin America—and was the car driven by Dr. Awni al-Khatib in the West Bank. It is now manufactured in China as well.) Club members meet regularly to learn about maintenance, deliver toys to orphans, and take weekend pleasure drives reminiscent of America in the 1930s and 1940s. To celebrate the forthcoming 2008 Beijing Olympics, four dozen members turned up in a giant parking lot to form the Olympic logo with their compact, candy-colored cars, each circle a different hue. Single members have found mates in the club, and at least one of their weddings featured an all-Polo procession through the streets of Beijing.

In the West, cars can still excite, but the family car soon becomes part of the furniture. In China, however, it's nothing of the sort. Li Anding, author of two books on the car in China and the country's leading automotive journalist, told me why a few weeks later at a dinner with some of his industry pals in Beijing. "The desire for cars here is as strong as in America, but here the desire was repressed for half a century," he began. All private cars were confiscated shortly after the Communists came to power in 1949, supposedly because they were symbols of the capitalist lifestyle. Having a car became the exclusive privilege of Communist Party officials.

Li Anding's colleague Li Tiezheng explained that "people my age loved Russian movies. They gave us the idea we should all own a car, and we all wondered why we couldn't." Li Tiezheng bought his first car, a Polish-made Fiat, when private ownership was finally permitted in the mid-1990s. But the stigma against ownership was still huge: "The pressure was so great, I couldn't tell anyone. I lied that I had borrowed it."

That didn't last long. By 2000, enough regulations had been removed, and enough people were making money, that car ownership became a reality for many Chinese for the first time. Li Anding, born in 1949, said he was still astonished at the change: "When I started writing about cars, I never expected to see private cars in China in my generation, much less some of the world's fanciest cars, being driven every day."

As the men around the table listened to Li's history and added to it, there was a palpable sense of pride. This wasn't simply progress on the level of a convenience—analogous, say, to your neighborhood moving from dial-up to high-speed internet. To them it meant China was finally entering the world stage and participating fully in human progress. It had the additional meaning of something long denied that could finally be acquired, like a wrong being rectified. Over and over again, the group described car ownership with a term I would never have thought to use:

"Once China opened up and Chinese people could see the other side of the world and know how people lived there, you could no longer limit the right to buy cars."

"This right is something that has been ours all along."

"Driving is our right."

When Li Lu noticed the sign for the Zhuozhou Service Area of the Jing-shi Expressway, Zhu Jihong was on one of his favorite subjects: destinations. He had done self-driving to Mongolia and Manchuria, he said, to Xinjiang and to Xi'an and the Silk Road. He made a round trip to

Tibet—fantastic!—and was considering one to Hong Kong. The main problem with our current itinerary, in his opinion, was that it was too short: "A week isn't long enough to really feel like you've been away." His wife was less and less interested in these odysseys, preferring, lately, to stay home and mind the hotel and restaurant he had bought near his hometown outside Beijing. His teenage son, the victim of untold days and weeks of bouncing around in the back seat, told me he was no longer interested in driving at all—he just wanted to play soccer.

Li Lu interrupted Zhu and made sure he noticed that this was where we were to pull off and finally meet the group. Though it was early afternoon now and Zhu had been driving for hours, he barely looked tired. I peeked at the odometer of his two-month-old Hyundai as he slowed; it showed 7,700 kilometers, or nearly 4,800 miles. That was an annual rate of nearly 30,000 miles, most of them from pleasure driving.

Though the first time most members of the trip had seen one another was in this parking lot, they had been talking for hours. In recent days each driver had stopped by the Beijing Target Auto Club office to pick up a CB radio and rooftop antenna. The rendezvous was on one side of the lot, and in the middle of the group was a vehicle with the biggest antenna of all, a thickly bumpered, sticker-plastered, red-flagged Korean-made four-by-four belonging to the president of the Target Club, Zhao Xiangjie.

Zhao and his truck were decked out for safari: he was wearing a khaki utility vest with many zippers, busily greeting new arrivals. Across the lot, a self-driving group from Guangzhou was similarly mustered, easy to spot by the big stickers with numbers on everyone's side doors and rear windows. And this, it turned out, was Zhao's next duty, to adorn each vehicle in our group with its numbers. Zhu accepted his with great ceremony, cleaning his doors first to ensure good adhesion, making sure the number decals were straight and even. If one theme here was safari, another was road rally, with the decals suggesting that everyone was part of a speedy team.

Though most Chinese car clubs are organized around the idea of trips, they come in many flavors. Some clubs are run by dealers (like a Honda dealership in Guangzhou), and others (like the VW Polo Club in Beijing) are nonprofit and organized around a particular model. At least one is the offshoot of an outdoor-recreational-gear manufacturer. Many are just for four-wheel-drive vehicles and aim to go to the back of beyond. Travel agencies sponsor some; others are run for and by motorcyclists.

Maybe half of the vehicles in our group were SUVs. The rest were passenger cars—not the cheaper Chinese models that make up the majority of vehicles on the road, the Fotons, Geelys, Cherys, and JACs, but rather foreign brands like Toyota, Volkswagen, Mitsubishi, and Citroën, most of them manufactured in China in joint ventures with Chinese companies (some state-owned or -controlled), an arrangement the government hoped would encourage the growth of a domestic car industry. One of the foreign cars caught my eye: a flashy white Volvo S80, driven by a man who was also a distinctive dresser. With his white leather loafers, tight jeans, white belt with a big silver buckle, and white shirt ("Verdace," read the logo), Fan Li, a television producer, cut an intriguing figure. He was accompanied on this trip by his pretty twenty-four-year-old daughter, Fan Longyin, who was recently back from film school in France. Longyin was quickly becoming friends with Jia Lin, a single woman in her thirties. Jia was a reporter for the *Beijing Youth Daily* but was traveling for pleasure, not work. She wore a tan leather jacket with a winged glossy-lip logo on the back that said "Flying Kiss." Like me, Jia had come without a car, but it looked as if she would start riding with the Fans.

And then there was the attractive young family in the white Volkswagen Passat, the Chens: Xiaohong (who uses the name Peter with English speakers), a personable information technology executive; his wife, Yin Aiqin, an electric power consultant; and their four-year-old daughter, Yen Yi Yi, who, I would soon learn, was already taking voice lessons at home from a member of the Beijing Opera.

More nerdy but genial were the bespectacled Wangs in their Citroën Xsara: she ran part of the back office of Air China; he worked for an international freight firm. They, too, had an unattached passenger who shared the driving and expenses. He was the urbane Zhou Yan, a partner in China's third-largest law firm.

Rounding out our group of thirty-odd people were the businessmen. Organized by a cement-plant owner, Li Xingjie, these ten or eleven men from the same Beijing suburb, Fangshan, rode in SUVs and tended to stick to themselves. Some of them owned coal-processing plants, which meant they were rich.

Soon all eleven cars were bedecked with numbers and the club logo.

*Zhu and members of the Beijing Target Auto Club pause to sightsee on a
new highway bridge over the Yellow River near Zhengzhou.*

Pit stops and snack purchases were completed. The service area looked a
bit like one on an American toll road, though there was no landscaping,
the simple restaurant was not a fast-food franchise, and the convenience
store was not as elaborately stocked as one in the States. An attendant at
the state-run Sinopec gas station filled the tank of Zhu's Hyundai, and
I paid in cash, gas and tolls being my contribution to expenses. (Sinopec stations only recently began accepting credit cards.) The gas was
unleaded and a few cents cheaper than in the United States, due to government subsidies. Everyone piled back into their cars, and we hit the
road. We would reconvene for dinner.

Zhu's mention of the Silk Road had gotten me thinking about ancient
travel. Travel agencies hawked Silk Route tours to Xi'an and Lanzhou,
Dunhuang, Urumqi, Turpan, and Kashgar, towns, now cities, that the
network of trails between China and the Mediterranean had indeed
passed through. But long gone were the pashas with their tolls, the
traders and bandits and monks, epic sojourners like Marco Polo, the carriers of bubonic plague (which hit China in the 1330s and then made its
way west, killing up to half of all Europeans in the Black Death of the
1340s), and the secrecy surrounding China's luxury export, silk, prized by

the West since Roman times. With the decline of the Mongol Empire later in the fourteenth century, the Silk Road had withered away. The search for a replacement ocean route to the Orient motivated a generation of European explorers in the fifteenth and sixteenth centuries, Columbus among them.

But weren't we the modern version of a caravan heading through the desert, this rest stop our oasis? Centuries before, I suppose, we'd all have been mounting our camels or ponies just now, having watered or fed them, and setting forth at roughly the same time, for both companionship and safety. We'd reconvene at another way station to rest or sleep or eat. We'd be charged tolls along the way by authorities who controlled passage. We'd get to know our fellow travelers in the ways travelers do: seeing them react to the new and the unexpected, watching how they handled difficulty, learning how they felt about sharing and about strangers—all of this was exactly the same.

China's first modern expressway, the Guangzhou–Shenzhen Superhighway, was built in the early 1990s by the Hong Kong tycoon Gordon Y. S. Wu. Wu studied civil engineering at Princeton in the mid-1950s, when construction was beginning on the U.S. Interstate Highway System. At the same time, the New Jersey Turnpike was being widened from four lanes to many lanes, and Wu has said it inspired him. (His powerful firm, Hopewell Holdings, is named after a town near Princeton.) Though Wu ran short of money and the ambitious project had to be rescued by the Chinese government, the toll road model of highway development caught on.

Wu's Guangzhou–Shenzhen Superhighway was the beginning of an infrastructure binge that seems to be only picking up steam: the government recently announced a target of 53,000 freeway miles by 2035. (The U.S. Interstate Highway System, begun in 1956, presently comprises about 46,000 miles of roads.) Some new roads, especially in the less-developed western parts of the nation, are as empty as South Dakota's: China is encouraging road construction ahead of industrial development and population settlement, assuming those will follow.

The goal, of course, is not simply to replicate the boom of coastal areas, where the majority of the country's population now lives. China's larger aim is to consolidate the nation. Its version of Manifest Destiny—

the "great development of the West" or "Go West" policy begun in January 2000—envisions far-western territories, like Tibet and the fuel-rich Xinjiang province (the name translates as "New Frontier"), fully integrated, ethnically and economically, with the rest of the country. It seems quite likely that local indigenous cultures stand to lose along the way. What the United States gained (and lost) with the Pony Express, covered wagons, and steam trains, China may achieve with roads and automobiles.

If highways in China's west are awaiting traffic, easterners have the opposite concern. As we headed south from Shijiazhuang toward Zhengzhou, the roads were packed with vacationers and truck traffic and Zhu jostled for position with all the other people who were late getting where they were going. His style of driving helped me understand better why China, with 2.6 percent of the world's vehicles, had 21 percent of its road fatalities in 2002, the most recent year for which figures were available at this writing.

Of course, there must be many reasons. The large number of new drivers is one; few of today's Chinese drivers grew up driving, and road-safety awareness seems low. Many roads are probably dangerous—though not, I would venture to say, the beautiful new expressway we were on. It was like an American interstate, only sleeker: the guardrails were angular and attractive, not fat and ugly, and in the divider strip there was typically a well-pruned hedge, high enough to protect drivers from the glare of beams from opposing traffic at night. Beyond the guardrails, grassy embankments sloped down to buffer areas carefully planted with a single species of tree, often poplar. The road surface was perfectly smooth, transitions even, signage sparse but clear. Periodically we saw orange-suited workers hand-pruning the center hedge or sweeping the wide shoulder with old handmade brooms. There was never a maintenance truck nearby; wherever the sweepers came from, they apparently walked.

It was the sweepers I worried about. Officially, there were two lanes of travel in each direction. But each side also had a shoulder, and on this expressway the shoulder was exactly as wide as the travel lanes. Thus Zhu and others used the shoulder as the passing lane, despite signs asserting that it was forbidden. Occasionally, of course, a sweeper would loom, or a disabled vehicle, and Zhu would slam on the brakes and veer into the truck lane. Once past the obstacle, he would floor it and swerve back out, brake once again, swerve, honk—it was almost like being in a video game, except that video games end or you can walk away. We, on the other hand, had a long way to go, and Zhu's passion for risking all in order to move one or two car-lengths ahead showed no signs of abating.

People traveling abroad worry about their plane going down and they worry about disease. More than one had asked me, before I came to China, if I wasn't concerned about the recent SARS epidemic. I was a little bit, I confessed, but mainly I was worried about car travel. I knew that China's highways were the deadliest in the world, and I knew that they were especially dangerous over these National Days holidays (more than six thousand people would die during this one). And I knew one more statistic, which, as I lurched from one side of my seat to the other, I wanted to share with our driver.

"Li Lu, does Mr. Zhu know that the leading cause of death for Chinese men up to age forty-five—for guys like him—is road accidents?" I asked her. She translated. Zhu looked at me and laughed. "I think he didn't understand," she said.

"I don't want to be rude," I said to her, "but I really would like to live to the end of this trip." We consulted, and soon Li Lu announced from the back seat that we both really wished he would slow down a bit. Zhu looked at me sidelong and then, if anything, speeded up.

The next morning Zhu was tired, finally, and asked if I wanted to drive. I hesitated for a moment. I had researched the issue and was fairly certain that foreign tourists were forbidden to drive between cities in China. Most Chinese seem never to have considered the possibility of foreigners behind the wheel. But Zhao, early on, had asked whether I would be willing to help with the driving, and I had said sure. Far be it from me to shirk this responsibility. So I climbed into the driver's seat.

This day's driving was different from the previous day's. As we moved farther from the coast and its expressways, we spent more time on national highways, which generally are two-lane and pass through a lot of towns. Everyone in the club stuck pretty close together, and there was a lot of chatting over the radio. Zhao began by apologizing for the previous day's overlong drive. Even if there hadn't been a highway closure due to fog, and slowness due to rain and holiday congestion, it was too long a drive for the first day, and he was sorry. But he was also upbeat and sounded excited about getting to Three Gorges Dam that afternoon. He

I take the wheel of Zhu's Hyundai Tucson.

moderated the CB chat that followed, prompting each car's occupants to take turns introducing themselves. Some told a joke, some sang a song. Fan, in the white Volvo, put on an Elvis Presley CD and held his mike to the speaker, broadcasting "Love Me Tender" in honor of me, Elvis's countryman. Not long after, another man recounted how he once got a ticket for urinating at the side of the road—a fairly common practice here. Soon after, as we passed through a village, a clamor rose for a pit stop.

The men had little trouble finding places to relieve themselves near the edge of town, but the women were in more of a bind. China's car culture—not to mention consumer culture—had not yet reached the countryside, and there was no restaurant nearby, no fast-food joint, no gas station/convenience store. Chen Yin Aiqin, her daughter at her side, knocked tentatively on the door of a farmhouse and was soon welcomed inside and ushered to the latrine out back. Afterward, before their car pulled away, she dashed back to the farmer's door with a small box of chocolate from Beijing.

The lack of infrastructure for touring drivers is one reason that these organized self-driving tours are so popular. Besides having planned in advance (through arrangements with local travel agents) where we would stop to eat and sleep every day, Zhao had an expert mechanic, Dai, in his four-by-four: repair garages were few and far between, and one of the Beijingers' main fears was breaking down out in the sticks, with nobody familiar nearby to help.

The national roads, while more interesting to drive than the expressways, were also more nerve-racking. There were considerable numbers of people on bicycles, on foot, and on small tractors; there were crossroads; and there were countless tollbooths. The tolls were often modest—10 yuan (US $1.40) for a car—but sometimes a tollbooth would come only five or ten miles after the last, and after a while it added up. Over our CB radio, the grumbling grew: according to law there had to be at least 20 kilometers (12.4 miles) separating provincial tollbooths, so some of these were clearly illegal. "We should go to the newspapers with this!" complained one driver. I was impressed to hear that people thought that might work.

Perhaps least expected by me, there were many places where I had to swerve toward the middle of the road because farmers had appropriated a strip of pavement along the edge for drying their grain, usually corn. Sometimes the grain was laid out on blue tarps; other times the drying zone was outlined by rocks or boards; more than once, traffic slowed because of it. I had heard of Chinese farmers sometimes laying their wheat across the road so that passing vehicles would thresh it for them. But there was something aggressive about this appropriation of the highway.

The suggestion of rural hostility toward traffic put me in mind of the famous "BMW Case," which had received a lot of media attention two years before. A rich woman in a BMW, probably traveling on a people-filled road like this, was bumped by a farmer transporting his onion cart to market. Enraged, she hit him with the car and then revved it up and drove into the crowd. The peasant's wife was killed, but despite widespread outrage, the woman received only a suspended sentence.

BMWs seemed to be a sort of class-divide lightning rod. Recently, the number of kidnappings for ransom has shot up in China: the government reported 3,863 abductions in 2004, higher than the 3,000 a year reported on average in Colombia, the previous world leader. "In one case," according to *The Chicago Tribune*, "police searching the apartment of kidnappers in Guangdong Province found a list of all BMW owners in the city that appeared to have come from state vehicle registration rolls."

To needle Zhu a bit, I asked him, if he was so rich, why didn't he have a BMW?

"Bad value," he said, explaining that unlike the foreign cars made in China under co-ventures and sold at a reasonable price, BMWs were imported, with huge taxes added on. Tariffs and taxes add about 50 percent to the price of imported cars, making them high-status items. If you wanted to be really ostentatious, you did what rich coal-mine owners (and others) from Shaanxi province increasingly did and came into the city to buy a Hummer, which cost more than $200,000. But Zhu thought that was ridiculous. The Volkswagen Passat he bought for his wife to drive was made in China—"like my Hyundai," Zhu said proudly, putting his cigarette in his mouth so he could pat the dashboard. "Made in Beijing."

Not long after lunch, we started seeing signs for the Three Gorges Dam and accessed the site through tunnels along an expensively built mountainside road. Security was tight, with numerous guard posts, cameras, and warning signs, and I was happy to swap seats with Zhu after we pulled into a roadside waiting area—just before an official came by to collect every driver's license. A guide boarded our leader's car and, over the radio, began a running commentary for all the cars in the group. Between her remarks, I asked Zhu what he thought of my driving.

"He says you are a good driver, but he has some advice," Li Lu reported. "He says to improve, you must be more brave!"

Three Gorges Dam, one of the largest construction projects in history, seemed a fitting first attraction for our trip, evoking superlatives in this land of superlatives. It had cost an estimated $75 billion so far; it will ultimately require that more than a million people be relocated; it will generate more hydroelectric power than any dam ever has; it spans the Yangtze, the third-longest river in the world; and it presents a huge military target.

Like so much in China, the scale is almost too large to fathom. The thirty-odd people in our group parked and then boarded buses that took us up to a visitor center above the dam. We peeked at a model dam

Zhao, our group leader, and interpreter Li Lu at the Three Gorges Dam

indoors and then, like scores of others, scrambled around the viewpoint, taking lots of pictures. Fan turned out to have a serious interest in photography: his daughter posed, posed, and posed again as her father assumed an exaggerated wide stance with his heavy Nikon digital camera.

Others focused on the astonishing dam, proudly making sure I got a good look. From our vantage, we could see directly across the top of the massive structure. Cranes were still in place because construction was ongoing. To our right was the new lake, which began filling in 2003 and will be full in 2012. We could barely see across it. To our left, below the dam, was a view of the river as perhaps it had looked before, except for the spray from five or six discharge ports high on the dam's face. These shot huge jets of water high into the air, where it diffused and arced into mist. The spray was backlit by afternoon sun, to spectacular effect. I joined my tripmates in taking in the sight, a larger work of humankind than I'd ever seen. In childhood I was taught little about the Chinese apart from their Communism and their numbers. Now I was seeing something altogether different: here were Zhu and Zhao, the Chens and the Wangs, Li Lu and Fan Li, proud witnesses to this monumental construction and the change it implied who were themselves, as driving

Chinese, touring Chinese, Chinese out to see the world, harbingers of a change larger than any of us could fathom.

Zhu was back at the wheel the next day as we drove from the Three Gorges area to Hongping, a town deep in Hubei province and the jumping-off point for visits to Shennongjia, the forest reserve where everyone hoped to see a yeti.

His Hyundai had a six-CD changer in the dash, and among the titles in it was *The Relax Music of Automobiles,* which turned out to be instrumental versions of the love songs of Deng Lijun, the Taiwanese pop singer of the 1970s. What Zhu really loved, however, was the old-time music on *The Red Sun: A Collection of Military Songs, Volume II.* He played the CD again and again. The soaring, triumphalist music evoked bygone days, and I expressed surprise that a modern businessman like him loved the old socialist music. Zhu responded that it was the music he grew up with. He had worked on a farm, he said. His grandfather had been rich, but the Communists took it all away.

"Don't you dislike Mao for that?" I asked. He looked at me full on when Li Lu translated the question and then, at 60 miles per hour, turned sideways in his seat to show me the pin on his left lapel. It was a dime-size brass relief bust of the Great Helmsman himself. Steering with his knees, he put his chin to his chest, unpinned it, and handed it to me as a gift.

"Many people still admire Mao very much," Li Lu said. "They know he made mistakes, but they also think he did much good. He got rid of the Kuomintang. He brought China together. He is still a very big hero, like a god to some."

Fan, the television producer, I had noticed, was also in the worshipful camp. He had the leader's portrait, in Lucite, affixed to the top of the dashboard of his Volvo so that he could not see anything through the windshield without Mao appearing in his peripheral vision. After I asked about that and complimented him on the DVD screens built into the back of the front seats (for rear-seat passengers), Fan invited me into the Volvo for the better part of a morning's drive. Longyin, his daughter, took a seat in the back, along with Jia Lin, the reporter, and offered some background on her father. "My parents both suffered a lot in the Cultural Revolution," she began. Fan interrupted impatiently.

"Oh!" Longyin said. "My father is saying: 'There is no such thing as a perfect person. Everybody makes mistakes. Mao saved many people, but to do it he had to sacrifice his son, his wife, his whole family—everything. Now he's gone, but I want to go back to that time, when people shared everything.'"

But do you really want to share everything? I asked Fan. Wouldn't sharing equally mean that a privileged few wouldn't be able to own new Volvos?

"I think now is a necessary period," Fan said, as his daughter translated. "We have to advance."

"Capitalism is something we've been waiting to try for a long time," Longyin said. She added, "Personally, I hate the whole Mao thing. I think it's weird. I don't miss the sound of those old days at all." She did miss France, however, and her French boyfriend. She said she hoped to play a part in the growth of the Chinese film industry, perhaps by becoming an actors' agent. And some time in the next two or three months, she hoped to get a driver's license.

I was pleased to get to Hongping. The mountain hamlet was shrouded in mist, and the air was cool. Steep hillsides covered with deciduous trees rose on either side, and a creek ran through town, both reminiscent of Vermont. We arrived at our hotel early in the afternoon, a nice change. It had three stars, and was clean and basic. But it did not have a restaurant, an elevator, or easy parking, so soon we were checking out. "Beijingers are very picky," Li Lu told me. They didn't like the hotel, and so Zhao had to find another. The new place he selected seemed only incrementally better to me, but others were satisfied by the change. At dinner, Zhao was back to apologizing profusely for his poor judgment. But the matter seemed quickly forgotten, dinnertime having become one of the trip's great attractions.

This night we ate upstairs in a rustic wooden building, each room big enough for only one of the round tables favored by Chinese, where everyone uses chopsticks to share dishes placed on a lazy Susan in the middle. At my table sat Li Lu; Zhou, the urbane lawyer; the Chens and their daughter; single Ms. Jia Lin; and Dai, the club's mechanic. Dai quickly produced a flask of strong spirits that made its way around the table—the men drank, the women did not—while we waited for our waitress to bring beers. Drinking here was something that men tended to do while women watched; Li Lu advised me not to get caught up in it ("Some of these men are very good at drinking!"), advice that I tried but usually failed to follow. As the trip went on and people got to know each other, the drinking often advanced to contests such as the counting game, where each person around the table would count (one, two, three) except that you had to skip any multiple of seven (seven, fourteen), or a number with a seven in it (seventeen, twenty-seven). If you messed up you had to take a drink.

On this night, however, Chen gallantly toasted all the women on the trip. The tall and elegant Zhou, already a bit red in the cheeks, followed this by toasting only Chen's wife, to raucous laughter.

The high spirits continued after dinner. Vendors were still on the sidewalk when all of us rolled out of the restaurant, and Fan made us—and even them—laugh with his uncanny shrill imitation of an older woman who had been hawking a melon. Zhou and others had heard there was a "cultural promotion," a show featuring local ethnic talent, on the edge of town and proposed we attend en masse. Zhu demurred, asserting that a strip club would be more fun, if only one could be found. We walked there without him, arriving early and securing a row of seats in the front.

Though Zhou spoke almost no English, I very much enjoyed his company. He was witty and sophisticated and, after a drink, warm and outgoing; every time he opened his mouth, it seemed, he made Li Lu break into laughter. The show, with lots of singing and dancing, was fun even though we had to give up our good seats at the front when a large group of local Communist Party officials arrived at the last minute.

The absent Zhu had his good side as well. He bubbled with energy and always seemed to be in a good mood. He kept a hot thermos bottle of high-quality green tea in the front seat, and gladly shared it with me and Li Lu—as he did the contents of a large box of yellow Asian pears from his home district, stored in the back of the SUV. They were some of the best pears I'd ever had, crunchy like apples and mouthwateringly sweet.

Along with being Zhu's passenger, however, I was also his roommate, a difficult proposition. He smoked heavily, whether while sitting naked after a shower, braying into the phone at his wife, or watching TV in bed, his head propped up by pillows. Often I knew he was awake in the morning by the click of his lighter and the smoke wafting over my bed. He snored raucously. He didn't believe in lifting the toilet seat. And always he fell asleep with the television on. This wasn't such a bad thing: usually I just reached over to the night table and clicked it off with the remote.

But that night in Hongping, there was a snag. When I came back from the cultural show, Zhu was lying in bed on top of his sheets, watching a famous black-and-white movie from 1956, *Railroad Guerrilla*, about Chinese peasant fighters throwing off the yoke of their Japanese imperialist occupiers. The guerrillas were just entering the imperial administrator's quarters when I came out of the bathroom: an extended storm of hacking machetes ensued, the Japanese falling left and right. Zhu murmured appreciatively and soon drifted off. I watched Japanese get cut down until I couldn't believe any could be left alive on the planet and then, over Zhu's rising snores, looked for the remote. It was nowhere to be found. The television itself had no on-off button, and its plug was hidden behind a heavy dresser; I needed to find the remote itself. Finally I spotted it, poking out from underneath Zhu's butt. I turned him over and extracted it, switched off the TV, put in my earplugs, and went to sleep.

The next morning, Li Lu sympathized with my desire to switch roommates. Zhou had said he would happily share with me. But she declared it was an impossibility: Zhu would lose face if I abandoned

Zhu asleep (notice television remote under his elbow, smoking paraphernalia on night table)

him. "And there is nothing worse for a man like him than losing face," she said.

The next day we hiked through the misty, craggy hills of Shennongjia. The area, known as "the Roof of Central China," is a UNESCO biosphere reserve of 272 square miles, with six peaks measuring up to 10,190 feet above sea level. Among our group, it was equally famous as the home of China's Bigfoot. This creature, in the local lore, lumbered through the mists with a big-bosomed mate; an artist's rendition of the hairy couple appeared in the corner of a billboard advertising the reserve. But though the trails were beautiful and mysterious and we could imagine an apeman happy there, none were spotted.

The police were directing traffic at the park entrance, and as we left, one officer noticed me in Zhu's passenger seat and waved us over. Foreigners are not permitted to travel in the direction we were headed, he declared, pointing to a sign. Zhu pulled over and summoned Zhao on the radio. Our entire group stopped, and major discussion ensued, which resulted, some twenty minutes later, in the policeman consenting to my passage. Zhao could be very persuasive.

"What was that all about?" I asked Li Lu.

"There are army bases in the mountains ahead," she said. "It is thought there are missiles there, to protect the Three Gorges Dam. You can't see them from the road, but the army is afraid of spies."

"But times are changing, right?" I asked. She looked uncertain, and I wasn't sure the answer was yes.

We drove for more than an hour, stopping for lunch in another little mountain town, Muyu. Halfway through the meal, a policeman looked in the room where we were eating. *Uh-oh*, I thought. As we left, a different policeman spotted me and uttered something grave. Zhao was summoned again. Other policemen arrived. My passport was requested, a phone call was made. Word came down: I had to go back. The old China was still around.

Zhao took me aside reassuringly and pressed a roll of yuan bills into my hand. Li Lu and I were to take a taxi back to Hongping, he said, while he figured out an alternate plan. We would call his cell phone from there.

The solution appeared arduous: either we would have to take a taxi, train, and another taxi, meeting up with the group the next night, or we could take one long and expensive taxi ride, meeting up with them the next afternoon, but missing the Wudang Mountains and their monasteries, which are famous for martial arts. As we waited for a driver, a call came in from the group up ahead: the cops in Muyu went home at dusk, they had heard. After dark, we should be able to blow through without any trouble. We consulted with some locals, and they concurred. And so it was decided.

We zoomed through Muyu without a hitch and, around midnight, passed as well through a couple of checkpoints staffed by sleepy soldiers; they raised the red-and-white-striped boom arms across the road with a wave at the driver. I entered my hotel room in Wudang around two a.m. Naked on his bed, Zhu was sawing loudly, the television was blaring, and the lights were all on. It was good to be back.

The next morning found us standing in line for gleaming cable cars to a cloud-shrouded monastery atop the Wudang Mountains. It was possible to hike, and I would have liked to, but nobody else was game. This area, a UNESCO World Heritage Site, was a traditional home to Chinese *wushu*, or kung fu; for centuries, Taoist monasteries had nurtured martial arts in conjunction with meditation, natural medicine, and agriculture. The view from the gondola reminded me of classical Chinese landscapes on rice paper scrolls: the peaks were high but rounded, covered with small trees and shrubs, dotted with small wooden houses wherever they weren't too steep. The monastery consisted of several gorgeous stone buildings with sloping, green-tiled roofs set off by red-painted walls; all were connected by stone paths and staircases. The steeper drops had chains across them to keep people from falling. For years it had been in vogue in China for young couples to buy a padlock and affix it to the chain, thereby pledging their bond to each other. The practice had stopped here, but hundreds or thousands of rusting padlocks remained.

On one patio, an entrepreneur had set up a large plaster lotus leaf, painted pink. For a few yuan, he would let you sit cross-legged under it and be photographed by your friends. The first taker in our group, of course, was Zhu, who I was glad to see had an appreciation of camp. He pulled his loafered feet under his legs, placed his hands together in front of him in prayer, and tried not to smile too broadly as we took his picture.

One small temple had a dark and narrow passage around its periphery. Li Lu explained to me that walking the passage, in conjunction with making a cash donation, could help certain wishes come true. It was too claustrophobic for me to attempt, but after conferring a moment with the attending monk, Jia Lin made a largish donation (100 yuan, more than $12) and disappeared into the passage. Li Lu explained to me that Jia really wanted to find a husband and hoped to effect that result. This was, in fact, the reason she came on this trip, which she imagined to be the kind of exciting adventure where you might meet a man. So far, however, things weren't panning out for her.

Prayer, then, was alive in China. What was less clear to me, after my brush with the police in the mountains, was how many in the urban, affluent world of self-driving tourers still believed in government authority.

My test question was speeding. National highways were typically posted with limits of 50 miles per hour, and up to 75 miles per hour on expressways. The orientation brochure that each driver had received from the Beijing Target Auto Club insisted that we adhere to those limits. ("This is only self-driving, not car racing!" the brochure read. "Speeding is not necessary.") Yet all the drivers, including Zhao, paid the rules no attention whatsoever, often driving 100 miles per hour or more. Police cars were seldom seen; when drivers spotted them, to my surprise, they totally ignored them. The cops rarely used radar, it turned out, and they almost never tried to pull you over.

What did concern Zhu and the others, though, were the speed cameras mounted unobtrusively on poles in the median. If you went too fast past a camera, it snapped your picture, and a ticket would arrive in the mail. Zhu knew the location of most of the cameras along his normal routes around Beijing, but whenever he headed farther afield, the tickets piled up, costing $70 or $80 a month.

His solution? Friends in the police department. They had given him a special red license plate that was affixed beneath his regular one. He believed this stopped a lot of the tickets in their tracks. But Zhu, like many others on the trip, was also intrigued by a device in the Nissan SUV of Li Xingjie, forty-two, the leader of the Fangshan businessmen's group. The short, bald man was widely envied among members of the tour for his radar detector, which was to detect not only radar but also cameras. I joined him one afternoon, and he proudly demonstrated that indeed was the case; the device also gave advance notice of tollbooths and service areas. Made in Taiwan, the detector cost Li $350 and, as it stated in English on its bottom, detected "all speed equipment on mainland!" He used to pay about $1,250 annually in fines, but now paid very little.

"But isn't this kind of seditious?" I asked via Li Lu. "Isn't this Taiwan helping to undermine the laws of the mainland?"

On the contrary, Li said, "This detector helps me obey the law. You have to obey laws. We have to obey the government!"

I wasn't sure whether he was sincere. As we blew by an aging police cruiser at more than 100 miles per hour (the cruiser, by my reckoning, was traveling closer to 50), I asked him to help me unravel more mysteries of Chinese highway law enforcement. "Why isn't anybody worried about those police? Why don't they chase anybody and give out tickets?"

That's just not how it's done here, Li said. Occasionally you were hit with an expressway fine when you stopped at the next tollbooth, but ordinarily, unless there had been an accident or some other irregularity, cops wouldn't chase you. Police cars were slow, but the mails were reliable.

Li portrayed himself as very straight: "Twenty years ago, I was driving a tractor—I was a model peasant! There were almost no cars in China. I didn't learn to drive until 1988. Under Deng Xiaoping, I got lucky because I was uneducated. Educated people think in traditional ways, but Deng said we should take chances." He did, and now he owns the Beijing Fangshan Banbidian Cement Factory, which he started when he was twenty-eight. Li was mild-mannered and unassuming, but when I later showed Li Lu his business card, she was in awe: "This cell phone prefix means he has had the phone a long time—since they were really expensive. He is very, very rich!"

I considered this as the group reconvened for the last time, just on the other side of a glitzy new toll plaza, its lines limned in neon that had been illuminated as the sun started down. All of the cars in our group, like the majority of cars you see in China, were recent models. Almost all the wealth of the drivers was first-generation. The digital cameras, the shiny wristwatches—where I come from all of it said nouveau riche. But the pejorative back home is the normative here: practically every wealthy person is nouveau riche, so the idea is meaningless.

The more instructive comparison, as we stood on this fancy bit of highway surrounded by rice fields and, here and there, people at work in them, was with the rural poor, the peasantry, the hundreds of millions of Chinese who do not yet (and, you imagine, will not in their lifetimes) share this prosperity. Many villages still are not connected to roads at all. When an expressway just south of here was completed last year, I was told sotto voce in Beijing, a series of demonstrations by peasants at a toll plaza delayed its opening. They were angry because the road had taken their land, and this, we are now seeing, is the story all over China: the government counted nearly 80,000 mass protests in 2005 alone. The country's economic growth is fantastic, the urban atmosphere heady, but the cost is growing inequality, that invidious distinction the Communists worked so hard to erase. The agricultural poor are called *nongmin*, Peter Hessler explains in *River Town:* "City dwellers . . . can recognize a peasant at a single glance, and often they are victims of prejudice and condescension. Even the word for soil—*tu*—can be applied to people as a derogatory adjective, meaning unrefined and uncouth." Spotting the *nongmin* in a Chinese city hardly takes a trained eye: they are the people, mostly men, in coarse clothing, burlap bags at their feet, standing around in public places looking utterly from another planet. China's problem, and it's hardly new, is these city *nongmin* represent hundreds of millions of others: they constitute about 75 percent of the population of China. Whether in a city taxi or here, on the highway, you can see them through the glass, almost standing still while people like Zhu and Li and Lucy and I zoom by.

Zhu, ex-*nongmin* himself, was not squandering any of the opportunities associated with his rise in status. By the time I arrived with my suitcase at our room in our four-star hotel in Luoyang, Zhu had already welcomed two sleek female "massage therapists" to our room. They were perched glamorously on the edge of my bed—legs crossed, lips glossed, high heels dangling—and beckoned me to join them. Zhu chortled with glee at my reticence, and I wondered which part of car travel he enjoyed most: the hours behind the wheel or the hours just after? Certainly, he seemed to take full advantage of all of them.

   Temporarily exiled from my room, I repaired to the hotel's "business center" to check my e-mail. The attendants had me fill out a chit—internet access cost 65 yuan, or about US$10 an hour—and logged me on to one of the four terminals. I was the only customer, so I was a bit surprised at how sluggish it was: downloading a single e-mail took two or three minutes. Finally I asked the attendant about it. Oh, she explained, it's probably because we're downloading movies, and she pointed to her monitor. "Only a few minutes left." From the progress bar on her screen, it looked as though it would be a lot longer than that.

"You know, I think I want my money back," I said. That would be easier than discussing her incompetence. She cheerfully handed back the chit.

I called Lucy on a house phone, and she said she'd meet me at the hotel bar. Most of the other customers appeared to be beautiful single massage therapists, and they eyed me like raw meat. This was the last night of our trip. I ordered a whiskey and thought about the real versus the virtual. The internet could show you a glass of whiskey, but it could not supply the smell or the taste. It could show you a naked woman but it couldn't rub your back. At the very least, I appreciated how Zhu wanted the real thing. He wanted rapid acceleration and curves in the road, that new car smell, and women you could touch.

Lucy arrived and ordered a soda. We talked about her ex-husband and the desires of men. She said that, even after all these days with the group, she still didn't really get the driving thing. But I thought that now I did: I told her how, like my sisters after me, I'd gotten my learner's permit on the very day I turned fifteen years and nine months old, and how I'd tried to get my parents to let me practice driving every single evening thereafter until I earned my license. Our learning car was the huge gold Pontiac Catalina station wagon with its V-8 engine, three rows of seats, and skylights. My dad had been pretty nervous with me behind the wheel, occasionally stamping the imaginary brake pedal on the floor in front of him when he thought I was slow to do so. But my mom had just mixed herself a bourbon-and-water, climbed in, and said, "Okay, you drive!" Unsurprisingly, I drove better with my mom.

Anyway, to me the license was freedom—a way to go places with friends, a private space outside of the house—as it still is to millions, including, now, grownups in China, like Zhu.

The end of the trip the next day was an anticlimax: everyone was heading back on the same expressway, and Beijing was less than a tank of gas away, so there was no further need to stick together. Chatter on the CB dropped off slowly until the radio was utterly quiet, and the group dimension of the trip was over.

Li Lu seemed pleased as Zhu's Hyundai eased into the perpetual traffic jam that is Beijing, chatting excitedly on the phone with her friends as we were slowly enveloped by the bad air of the city. Zhu, however, seemed a bit disappointed to be off the open road. When Lucy got off the phone, he told her he wanted to treat us to dinner at a favorite noodle restaurant near the city center. First, of course, we had to get there.

Creeping along on the highway, we talked about how the Beijing government was trying to control the huge new popularity of cars. One solution to the growing chaos of the streets has been to severely restrict motorcycle use in the city. Zhu thought that was better than Shanghai trying to cut down on car ownership by setting a high price (presently almost $5,000) on car registration. Trying to ease traffic and cut down on accidents, Shanghai had even banned bicycles from many main streets, news that surprised me. But as the outlines of buildings grew fuzzy with all the smog, I thought how one could make a public health argument for keeping cyclists out of all the exhaust.

That very same month, the journal *Nature* had reported that Beijing's air pollution was much worse than previously thought. Concentrations of nitrogen dioxide had increased 50 percent over the past ten years, and the buildup was accelerating. According to *The Wall Street Journal*, Beijing's sulfur dioxide levels in 2004 were more than double New York's, and airborne particulate levels more than six times as high. The World Bank says that of the twenty cities in the world with the dirtiest air, China has sixteen. Vehicle exhaust accounts for 79 percent of the air pollution. In 2005, China enacted its first comprehensive emissions law, but it was expected to have little effect on the transport sector's copious carbon dioxide emissions, which are predicted to be the highest in the world by 2030.

That distinction, meanwhile, belongs to the United States, and Chinese have a point when they say that those in developed countries who complain about China's pollution are like ex-smokers who walk into a room of people smoking and declare, "No smoking!" When you are the world's factory you necessarily make a bit of a mess, and most of it, after all, affects *you* more than anybody else.

One could also note, in China's defense, that the typical Chinese person's carbon footprint remains tiny. The average person in China travels about 1,000 kilometers (621 miles) per year, compared with 15,000 kilometers (9,320 miles) per year for Europeans and over 24,000 kilometers (14,913 miles) per year for Americans. In 2004 there were only 9 cars per

1,000 people in China, compared to 700 per 1,000 in the United States, "400 in Japan, 350–500 in Europe, and 150–200 in middle income countries like Mexico, Brazil and Korea." Per capita, the Chinese in 2006 stood where Americans were in 1915.

Of course, everything was changing rapidly. The rate of Chinese "motorization" was shooting up. We inched along in the end-of-holiday Beijing traffic, willingly immersing ourselves in a miasma of smog, one of those things you do that you know isn't good for you but you go right ahead and do because to do otherwise would mean rearranging your whole life. We did the same thing in Denver during the smog-filled 1970s, descending from the Rockies after a day of skiing, into the Great Plains at an angle that let us get a good look at the "brown cloud" from above before we cruised down into it like hamsters put back into a dirty cage.

At least there wasn't this traffic. If this was early in China's motorization, how would it look in 2010, 2015, or 2030, when the Chinese were projected to have as many cars as Americans? Was a state of full-time gridlock a theoretical possibility? Could you get to the point where nobody could move, and it was harder and harder to breathe? China had all the ingredients required to conduct the experiment and find out.

A policeman friend of Zhu's met us at the restaurant and even picked up the tab. (Zhu's rapport with the police department was quite impressive.) I asked him about street racing in the city, which I had heard was becoming a problem. Yes, he said, he had heard of it but had not seen it himself, yet. Zhu looked a bit too interested in the subject.

A few days later, Zhu entertained me and others at the restaurant-hotel he ran as a hobby on the outskirts of Beijing, in the shadow of a big dam. The food was surprisingly fine. Then Zhou the lawyer treated a group of us, including the Wangs of the Citroën, to a fabulous dinner on Houhai Lake. Clearly, nobody wanted the trip to end. ("Was it really that relaxing?" I had asked several of them, many times, after twelve-hour days at the wheel. All had sworn that it was. Several of them said they liked the fact that since you were with people you didn't know on an organized self-driving trip, you could really be yourself. In other words, you didn't have to watch your step as you would around people in higher positions.)

My longest reunion would be with Zhao, the driving club owner, who invited me to accompany him to a weekend summit of other club owners, the 2005 Auto Clubs and Fans CEO Forum, in Tianjin, a couple of hours from Beijing. Zhao lived in one of the spanking-new, car-friendly suburbs of the capital, and we rendezvoused at a local hotel. Zhao parked his big Korean SUV ("Galloper," it said on the dash) in the semi-circular drive in front of the hotel and came into the lobby to get me. By the time we returned to his car, a Volkswagen Santana had parked a couple of feet behind him. As he started to leave, Zhao somehow didn't notice the Santana and backed into it forcefully.

To my surprise, he did not get out to see if there was damage, but instead tried to drive away. Alas, his vehicle had a poor turning radius, and he had to back up again to extract his car from the space. While he was thus maneuvering, there came a loud *whack* on his window: the owner of the VW was standing outside, and he was furious. Zhao ignored him; he must have thought, *A couple more inches and I'm out of here!* As he shifted again, the guy pounded his door again—really hard this time.

Zhao was now the very picture of obsequious apology. He got out, and together the two examined the damage: a bent license plate and a scrape to the plastic bumper, Zhao all the while trying to place his hand lightly on the aggrieved man's shoulder, bowing, extending his business card, looking contrite. It took ten or fifteen minutes before the man cooled down enough for us to leave.

Zhao didn't want to talk about the incident as we drove; instead, he wanted to tell me about his agenda for the conference. Car clubs and in fact the entire automotive service industry needed more government involvement if they were to evolve in an optimal way, he said. This conference was for, among others, car club organizers, car industry executives, magazine editors, and television producers who felt the same way, and wanted to get the word out.

Our hotel was adjacent to a rebuilt stretch of the Great Wall. Some seventy people had paid roughly $100 each to attend the gathering, sponsored by *Auto Friends,* a government-affiliated magazine. There was an executive from Chery Automobile (which hoped to begin low-priced exports to the USA) and one from Fiat China. There was a representative of a motorcycle club. There was somebody from SinoLube, the government oil company. Perhaps most important, there were some high officials: the deputy secretaries general of the China Automobile Dealers

Association and the China Automotive Maintenance and Repair Trade Assocation (both quasi-governmental groups), and the manager of the office that leases all the retail space to car dealers around the Asian Games Village area, a major car-selling zone of Beijing.

Zhao, dressed in suit and tie, was clearly a player in this world. He had worked as a composer, filmmaker, and official celebration organizer; success in business, for much of his career, had consisted of knowing important government officials and getting them to steer work his way. His auto club offices are in the government-run Olympics Center. As he gave his talk to an attentive audience, it occurred to me that Zhao probably wouldn't mind being China's first undersecretary of car clubs.

I spoke too, at Zhao's behest, mostly about how families have fun driving in the United States. While driving clubs existed, I explained, you didn't actually need a club in order to take a trip; there were motels and restaurants along every main highway. In fact, you could even *fly* to another city, rent a car, and begin your trip there. Many hands went up at this idea. How would you know whom to rent from? I was asked. I explained about travel Web sites and nationwide car rental franchises. What if you broke down? I spoke a bit about groups like the Automobile Association of America. What about robbers? It was not a major worry on American roads, I said.

The speaker after me told the kind of story that illustrated why crime was on people's minds. He was the editor of *FBRoad,* a glossy car magazine, and he sported a white silk scarf around his neck. While on his way back from Tibet recently, he said, he had stopped for a meal in Chengdu and his jeep was stolen by two Tibetans. (There were knowing murmurs in the audience; Tibetans seemed to have a criminal reputation among Han Chinese.) He wondered whether to call his insurance company or the police. The police, he concluded. Then he called the leader of the Chengdu jeep club. He in turn summoned all of the club's members via radio, describing the stolen car and the presumed perpetrators. "They sent a few groups of young strong men with proper 'weapons' to stand guard at different highway junctions."

The car was located and stopped within a few minutes. The Tibetans abandoned it and fled. More than thirty jeeps soon converged on the spot where the stolen jeep had been intercepted. Then the leader and the editor went to the police to file a report. "You're more efficient than we are!" said the police. Local papers gave the incident front-page headlines.

In another story, he told of breaking down near Xinjiang and needing a part he didn't have. Parts were scarce on the frontier, but a phone call to an industry friend in Beijing led to an introduction to a parts distributor in Xinjiang, who soon supplied what the editor needed. The moral in both cases was that informal networks of car fans could produce quick results in times of need. If the government lent its support to drivers' needs, imagine how similar benefits might accrue to those who weren't similarly "plugged in."

It was a different take on government intervention than I was used to. My translator explained that having a government imprimatur could help a business in many ways. But I knew that not everyone felt the same about close involvement with the government.

In Beijing, I had interviewed another big player in this world, Chen Ming, who helped run what was apparently the biggest self-driving organization in China, the auto club arm of traffic radio FM 103.9. His forty or so employees occupied a floor and a half of a new office building near downtown. By contrast with Zhao, who—by Zhu's reckoning and others', might have lost money on the Hubei trip—Chen Ming had high volume and a rapidly growing business. Members paid $27 a year and received benefits that included group insurance rates, end-of-the-year gasoline rebates, "auto rescue" within Beijing's 5th Ring Road, and free rental cars if a repair took more than three days.

Linking an auto club to a traffic radio station seemed inspired. Chen got his start in the business as Zhao's protégé: he was assistant manager of Beijing Target Auto Club. Chen said he grew to believe that Zhao's approach, his eagerness to stay involved with the government, was outdated, and perhaps he's right.

I didn't mention Chen Ming to Zhao. Both might succeed, for all I know. Certainly Zhao is ambitious enough; what he wanted to do the following summer, he told me as we drove home from the summit, was lead a trip of one hundred Americans from Beijing to Lhasa. This route, as many had confirmed to me, is one of the world's most spectacular drives. What should he do, he asked, to realize this goal?

I ticked off the two obstacles that were obvious to me: (1) the impression among many Americans that China had invaded Tibet (most Chinese believe they had *liberated* it), and that they might therefore feel awkward going with a Chinese company, and (2) the question of who would drive the cars, if the Americans themselves weren't allowed to.

Zhao was undaunted. A simple education campaign could solve the first problem, he believed. Did I know the Tibetans used to practice slavery? As for the second problem, laws would eventually be reformed to allow foreigners to drive themselves, Zhao said, but until they were, he could easily provide every carful of Americans with a Chinese driver.

I didn't think this plan had legs, but once again, Zhao was undaunted. In order to develop contacts and learn more about Americans as a potential market, he told me at the end of our drive back to Beijing, he had organized for adventuresome Chinese a self-driving trip around the American West! They'd see San Francisco, the Grand Canyon, and Las Vegas before crossing the country to the East Coast. His group already had their visas, and he hoped I'd consider joining them to chronicle this maiden voyage of Chinese drivers to the United States.

I regretted having other commitments that would keep me away, I said. And I meant it. The rise of Chinese-as-tourists was a big story, but even more, it was an enjoyable story: Zhao's cohorts were likely to be successful middle-aged men, as thrilled as kids by their new adventure. If they were like Zhu, they were going to have a great time.

An ebullient atmosphere surrounds the automobile in China. You can see the excitement continuing, even growing, as more people buy cars. It is reminiscent of a fading romance in American life, this crush on the automobile, the thrill of car ownership, and to witness it is to feel both nostalgia and the excitement of the new at the same time. Lord only knows where it all could be headed—in terms of congestion and pollution, in terms of competition for increasingly scarce and expensive fuel, it is not hard to predict a slow-motion, multi-car pileup in China's future. But it felt unfair to raise those issues in the presence of Zhao and the rest. They were out to have fun, the kind we've already had. Who are we to say they can't?

GROWING BROADWAY

THE WORLD HAS ONLY A HANDFUL of really famous streets. The most famous is probably the Champs-Élysées. From there you might think of London's Downing and perhaps Oxford Streets, Barcelona's Ramblas, Tokyo's Ginza, Mexico City's Paseo de la Reforma, possibly Berlin's Ku-Damm (Kurfürstendamm), Jerusalem's King David Street, Nevsky Prospekt in St. Petersburg, and several in the American West: The Strip in Las Vegas; Sunset, Wilshire, and Hollywood Boulevards and Mulholland and Rodeo Drives in Los Angeles; and San Francisco's Embarcadero and Lombard Street. Possibly Boston's Memorial Drive or Commonwealth Avenue.

Oh, and the one near me: Broadway.

Broadway is famously in Manhattan, but it continues north through the Bronx and traverses Yonkers in Westchester County before finally getting a new name north of Tarrytown: Albany Post Road. Under that alias and others, including U.S. Highway 9, it continues up the Hudson River to Albany and from there nearly to the Canadian border—about 330 miles. For many years, though, the street at the southern tip of Manhattan that became Broadway was quite short. The story of Broadway's birth and growth links to my own New York story.

In 1625, settlers organized by the Dutch West India Company began building Fort Amsterdam at the southern tip of Manhattan. They were not the first people on the island: Wickquasgeck Indians, one of the Lenape (Delaware) tribes, had seasonal camps and trails that they used for hunting and, soon, for selling beaver pelts to the Dutch. The main thoroughfare of New Amsterdam—the future Broadway—was called Heere Straat, or High Street, and may have followed the route of an Indian path. It began at a wide clearing at the Dutch fort, tapering to a street still wider than present-day Broadway that extended several blocks north. It ended at the town's limit, which was a twelve-foot-high earth-and-wood fence fortified by palisades—sharpened pikes of wood—all the way across the lower island. This protective boundary was eventually the path of Wall Street. The Dutch were worried about aggression from the English, who had already settled Boston, Philadelphia, and Virginia, and from Native Americans. (In 1632, a different Lenape tribe wiped out a colony of thirty-two Dutch settlers in Delaware.) At Heere Straat there was a gate through the wall that allowed passage to the wilds farther north.

Among the founders of New Amsterdam were my great-great-great-great-great-great-great-great-grandfather, Wolphert Gerritsen Van Kouwenhoven; his wife, Aelte Jans; and their sons Gerret, Jacob, and Pieter. (Two other sons had died.) Wolphert worked as a farmer and Aelte as a fur trader. Heere Straat was tiny New Amsterdam's principal street, and one imagines they spent a lot of time on it.

When the British took over New Amsterdam in 1664, Heere Straat was renamed Broadway. The British tore down the stockade along Wall Street, leaving Broadway (and the former Dutch settlement) free to grow. By the mid–eighteenth century, hills on it just north of Maiden Lane had been flattened, shade trees planted along its sides, and Broadway reached the Commons (present-day City Hall Park). On July 9, 1776, following a public reading of the Declaration of Independence ordered by George Washington, who listened to it while seated upon his horse, "a mob spilled down Broadway to Bowling Green and pulled to earth the statue of George III." Washington was elected president in 1789 and moved into "the finest private building in town, the four-story McComb House" at 39 Broadway. Lower Broadway and the area west of it was the tony place to live. (To the east was the notorious slum Five Points.)

As New York grew, so did Broadway. By 1800, straight, lined with poplars, and paved with cobblestones, it reached Astor Place (in the present-day East Village, a block from my office), where it ended at a fence marking the southern boundary of a farm. An 1811 commission charged with rationalizing the growing city's streets into a grid recommended straightening Broadway so that it would conform with everything else—but it failed. By 1815, Broadway was two miles long and had veered northwest at 10th Street—so as not to destroy an influential farmer's cherished tree, according to legend. More likely, wrote journalist and historian David W. Dunlap, the bend was engineered to make "for a smoother and more direct junction with the angle of the Bloomingdale Road at 16th Street." The Bloomingdale Road, which didn't conform to the grid either, dated from 1703 and led to a country area that is now the Upper West Side. It was a natural extension of Broadway; the two routes would eventually become one. But not quite yet. By 1840, when Manhattan's population stood at 312,710, Broadway had reached 14th Street. "How this city marches northward!" exulted one citizen in his journal.

Better transportation helped to make that possible. Horses, carts, and horse-drawn carriages (like the *cabriolet*), both personal and for hire, predominated in the early 1800s. They were joined by stagecoaches that could carry four to six passengers—you could catch one heading downtown at Broadway and Houston. More "mass" were the omnibus coaches that began to appear around 1829: boatlike wagons with benches, drawn by two or four horses. The slaves who had helped build New York, starting with New Amsterdam, were still excluded—public transport was segregated. "When a black man hailed one of the new omnibuses going up Broadway, the driver warded him off with a whip, convulsing white bystanders with laughter."

For a century starting in the early 1700s, Broadway had been popular for promenading; "young men and women arose at five o'clock in the morning to stroll the thoroughfare," wrote historian Edward Robb Ellis. Charles Dickens, visiting in 1842, remarked on the "lively whirl of carriages" and well-dressed people shopping and window-shopping at Broadway's high-end stores—the stretch from Canal Street to Houston Street was especially booming. Wrote Dickens, "Shall we sit down in an upper floor of the Carlton House Hotel . . . and when we are tired of looking down upon the life below, sally forth arm-in-arm, and mingle with the stream?" In the late-afternoon promenade hour, *New York Tribune* reporter George Foster observed in 1849, the street became "a perfect Mississippi, with a double current up and down of bourgeois ladies and gentlemen" who were checking out the goods in the windows of upscale shops—and each other. This kind of commentary, the impressions and speculations of gentlemen sauntering the streets, had grown into an art form in Europe in the 1820s, and Americans could benefit. The *flâneur* (or "stroller") perspective, as elaborated by Baudelaire, promoted the idea of city-watching and made bewildering, stressful street life something to appreciate, even celebrate. Looking for material for his newspaper, *The New York Aurora*, in 1842, Walt Whitman donned top hat and frock coat and sauntered down Broadway every day. Observing from the sidewalk or from a mobbed omnibus, he extolled the "continued, ceaseless, devilish provoking, delicious, glorious jam!"

Of course one person's glorious jam is another's hell on earth. Dickens had noted (and made light of) the stray pigs that found the thoroughfare intriguing. The excrement of the various livestock that used Broadway, particularly horses (horse-drawn streetcars first appeared in 1832), was just one aspect of unpleasantness. A visiting Englishman (obviously no *flâneur*) complained about the "driving, jostling, and elbowing" on Broadway and Wall Street. "Add to this the crashing noises of rapid omnibuses, flying in all directions, and carts (for even they are driven as fast as coaches are with us), and we have a jumble of sights and sounds easy to understand but hard to describe. The most crowded parts of London can scarce be compared with it."

Shops and department stores began to be lit with gas at night, adding to the glamour of Broadway. Electric bulbs arrived in the late 1880s. Electrical light was soon used in advertising; the huge illuminated signs (one at Madison Square was fifty by eighty feet and used 15,000 bulbs) gave rise to the moniker "The Great White Way" for the stretch of Broadway between 23rd and 34th Streets.

Theaters, many of them featuring burlesque, used the lights to advantage, and extended the entertainment zone of Broadway up to 42nd Street, which at the time was still considered uptown. Beyond was "the country," though already it had many residents, some of them wealthy farmers with large estates. A stage line up woodsy Bloomingdale Road toward an area called Bloemendaal (after a town in Holland's tulip-growing region) had been running since 1819. As the city and "plebeian" commercial establishments grew, wrote *Putnam's* magazine in 1853, New York's wealthiest "fled by dignified degrees up Broadway." By then it was continuous with Bloomingdale Road, which was widened and straightened in the late 1860s, after which (following a period when it was called the Boulevard) it was renamed Broadway in 1899, and the two became one.

And still Broadway grew. In 1892, Columbia College began a move from the east side to the seventeen-acre estate of the former Bloomingdale Lunatic Asylum (which relocated to White Plains) between West 114th and 116th Streets. Despite concerns among some that the area was "about as remote and inaccessible as Mt. Kisco," Barnard College and Teachers College soon followed, and quickly the area felt more central. By 1901 the Interborough Rapid Transit (IRT) Company had begun tearing up Broadway along its entire length in order to build the country's first large-scale subway. In late 1904 the IRT began service, running between City Hall and 145th Street in Harlem. By 1908 the "Broadway line" had extended all the way to its current terminus in the Bronx, at West 242nd Street/Van Cortlandt Park, near where I live.

My first visit to New York City was for Thanksgiving dinner with a college friend my freshman year. I took the bus from Massachusetts down to the Port Authority terminal on Eighth Avenue. I looked as though I had just arrived from Colorado, which I nearly had: I carried a frame backpack and wore a down parka and heavy hiking boots. My classmate, Rob Vogel, and I walked along 42nd Street to Times Square to catch the Broadway subway to his parents' apartment uptown.

This was 1976, and Times Square was deep into its decline. I liked the aroma of roasted nuts from vendors' carts, but was a bit overwhelmed by everything else: the flashing signs, the guys selling drugs, the touts beckoning us into peep shows, the honking, the crowds.

A four-foot length of galvanized pipe crashed to the sidewalk just beside me as we approached the subway entrance off Broadway at 41st Street; it bounced and rolled off into the gutter. Rob and I looked up: Had it fallen off a scaffold? Had it been thrown? I thought to myself: *This is why my ancestors got the hell out of here.*

Fifteen years later, for reasons involving a girlfriend named Margot, my work as a writer, and perhaps a strain of counterphobia in my personality, I became a resident of Brooklyn. One cold weekend in January, my friend Seth came to town and, to get some fresh air, we decided to walk the length of Manhattan. Broadway seemed the logical route. On a sunny Sunday morning, we rode the subway to the financial district downtown. Its off-grid, short streets would have been more congenial to pedestrians 150 or 200 years earlier; on this frigid morning, the high-rise office buildings channeled the wind and blocked the sun. The most imposing of these, of course, were the Twin Towers of the World Trade Center. They stood a block west of Broadway between Liberty and Vesey streets, just about ten minutes into our fourteen-mile walk.

Around City Hall Park, the open space and trees provided a respite from all the giant buildings, as well as a good view of the Brooklyn Bridge. Up next was Chinatown, less crowded than usual given the weekend, then across Canal Street into SoHo, less crowded yet, going through a transition to the upscale, and also fun to walk through, with its cobblestone streets and cast-iron building facades.

There was a hint of Greenwich Village across Houston, but the next real attraction was Union Square Park, the only thing in the city that Broadway really has to bend to get around. We crossed the bottom corner of Madison Square Park at 23rd Street (okay, it bends a little bit there, too) and caught sight of the Empire State Building on our right as we entered the low 30s.

Times Square had come up a lot since that first visit of mine in 1976 but still gave me a headache, even on a Sunday. We bought hot dogs from a vendor at Columbus Circle and ate them while sitting on the granite steps of the monument to Columbus there; we were honoring a previous rendezvous we'd had one spring break, when we met at noon in Barcelona under the statue of Columbus at the end of the Ramblas. Where Barcelona offers a view of the sea from Columbus, however, New York offered a view of the ugly Coliseum exhibition center, a Robert Moses project that no longer exists.

From there, things got better. Broadway runs boulevard-style through the Upper West Side, with a planted center island. The sidewalks are wide. Margot, back when she lived in the East Village, explained to me that the Upper West Side was "suburban," a concept that it took me a while to grasp. She meant, I think, that it was newer, more oriented to families, and had among its big stores some of the franchise businesses found in malls.

We had a lunch of sweet potato pie at Wilson's soul food restaurant (now defunct), just north of 125th Street on Amsterdam. Then we walked back to Broadway. Nobody bothered us. Harlem (named after the Dutch city of Haarlem) had bottomed out a few years before and still had plenty of abandoned buildings. Street life, and people speaking Spanish, increased as we passed into the Dominican neighborhoods around Inwood and Dyckman (200th) Street (Dyckman had been a burgher in old New Amsterdam). We stopped at a diner for coffee, then made our last push: over the metal bridge (it can rise up when a ship needs to pass underneath) that carries both Broadway and the elevated subway over the Harlem River into the Bronx (named for Jonas Bronck, 1600–1643, a sea captain who became a farmer nearby).

We deserved a beer. On West 231st Street, just a few doors off Broadway, we walked into a neighborhood bar. It was late afternoon and full of regulars, all white, who nevertheless stared at us, maybe because of Seth's ponytail. There was a bar with stools, there were booths, there were beer steins hung on the walls. We drank our fill and then, sore of foot, climbed up metal stairs to the subway and zipped back downtown.

That bar is no longer there. I know because I pass by a couple of times a week while doing errands; I live about a mile away. I also ride my bike downtown a lot, using the Broadway Bridge to access the bicycle paths along the Hudson River in Manhattan. Sometimes when I'm riding across its metal mesh roadbed I think back to that walk with Seth. But a fresher memory is from the afternoon of September 11, 2001, when I drove to the bridge to pick up Margot, now my wife, who had made her way that far on foot and by taxi from her office in midtown after the attacks on the Twin Towers.

Just north, past the end of the subway, is one of the city's great parks, Van Cortlandt, once a vast grain plantation owned by the Dutchman Frederick Van Cortlandt (1699–1749). Broadway runs alongside it up to Yonkers, and I spend a fair amount of time cruising it in our car, looking for a place to park when I pick up the kids from soccer practice. Van Cortlandt is heavily used, not just by youth soccer teams but by cricketers from the West Indies, Irish curlers, baseball players (including a lot of police teams), joggers, cross-country runners, dog walkers, and enthusiasts of remote-controlled model race cars. Not many of them look Dutch. But I do, and feel at home there. It took Broadway a few generations to get this far, and me a couple more to return to the city where my father's family began.

SIX

DRIVE SOFT—
LIFE NO GET DUPLICATE

A HIGHWAY PASSED OVER ANOTHER HIGHWAY. Drivers could exit the top highway to get onto the one beneath; the ramp that made this possible curved 270 degrees as it sloped gently down. It was like one petal of a cloverleaf, and within it was a little circle of land. On the edge of that circle my ambulance sat, awaiting a call on the radio.

The slanted sunlight of afternoon streamed through the open rear doors. The crew had the right-side door of the big Mercedes van open as well, hoping for a little breeze. This was optimistic, both because the air was still and very hot and because this post was a busy one, and the crew might have to close up the doors and respond to an accident any second.

In the meantime, there was little rest for the nurses, Rasheedat Lawal and Florence Bada, because the presence of the ambulance attracted walk-up patients, and, even though we were inside an exit ramp, there were a lot of people around. People compete for seemingly every square inch of Lagos, Nigeria, and traffic circles are no exception. On the other side of a big dusty bush and the ambulance Port-a-Potty, which was kept padlocked, a bunch of men sold plants for landscaping. Most vendors, though, were mobile, because every congested road in Lagos doubles as a market, a selling opportunity for people hawking plastic spatulas, car telephone chargers, kola nuts, newspapers, phone cards, meat pies, and just about everything else. They competed for space with beggars, such as the legless boy who used a kind of skateboard to move himself up and down the ramp, slapping the ground with his hands.

Many of the vendors sold little plastic bags of water, and among their biggest customers were a detachment of policemen who were always hanging around the shoulder of the Apapa–Oworonshoki Expressway about twenty yards upstream of us. Two lanes of traffic exited there for Ikorodu Road beneath, through a channel of traffic cones; this was the

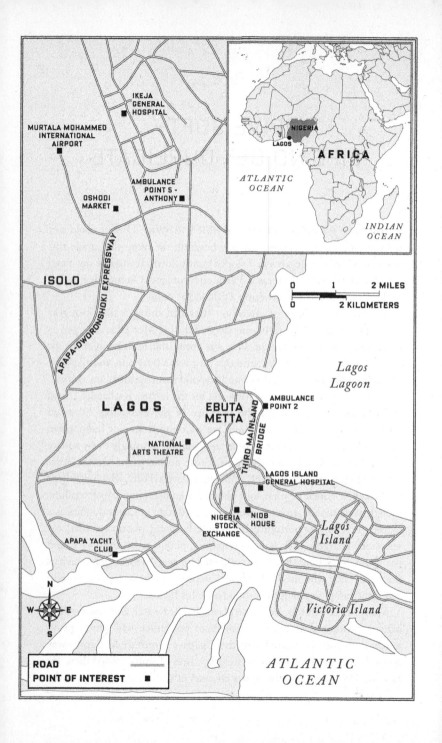

cops' fishing pond. While they waited for drivers to charge with infractions, they drank from the bags of water. Spent bags are everywhere, a part of the city's notorious trash problem.

Down the ramp, behind us and just visible, was a funky sculpture gallery squeezed between the roadway and a high wall that ran alongside it. The gallery's main feature was a stone-and-mortar elephant head with a gaping mouth, the whole thing five feet tall, that you ducked through to enter the "office." Beyond that stood a ten-foot-high plastic bottle of beer—an advertisement—and another group of policemen, from a different division of government. Underneath the bridge, in the dark and out of sight, lived a group of "area boys"—homeless gang members, which the single Nigeria travel guide I had found warned me "use physical intimidation to get what they want and simply stop people and demand money or property whilst threatening them with belts, whips, sticks or worse, guns." The roads were the area boys' hunting grounds as well, though I wouldn't really see how until later.

Everyone in the vicinity treated the ambulance as a sort of mobile health clinic. Florence and Rasheedat were generally happy to attend to cuts and bruises, dispense "analgesics" (aspirin), and offer quick (if tentative) diagnoses of the neighbors' many ailments. I watched as a woman brought in an old man, maybe her father, whose eye was swollen closed. Florence put on latex gloves, took the man's temperature, and looked closely at the eye with a flashlight. She told him to use warm compresses and have it examined by a doctor. Next came a teenager with a scrape on his arm. Rasheedat handled this one; she put on gloves and went looking for antiseptic wipes.

In the cab, meanwhile, the third member of the crew, Nurudeen Soyoye, monitored the radio. He was a young man, handsome and powerfully built. As "pilot," or driver, he made only about half what the nurses did, but, like most low-paid Lagosians I met, he seemed grateful to have steady work. He taught me how to listen to the calls. Generally they came from mainland ambulance headquarters at Base 1, Ikeja General Hospital, a few miles to the north. There was another dispatch center, Base 2, at the general hospital on Lagos Island, and seventeen ambulance waiting spots, or "points," around the city. We were at Point 5, also known as Anthony, a central location well-known for getting a lot of calls.

One came in just as the nurses were enjoying a lull, sitting on the part of the gurney that was out of the sun and treating themselves to bags of

The ambulance crew at the Anthony post alongside the Apapa–Oworonshoki
Expressway: nurses Florence Bada and Rasheedat Lawal and pilot Nurudeen Soyoye

water. "Let's go!" called Nurudeen through the little window that connected the cab to the rear. "Truck crash," he explained to me. The nurses
closed the doors and battened down the hatches. Everyone buckled in.
The engine roared to life; emergency lights and siren were activated. A
bit of adrenaline began to pump in me, but soon I wondered if that was
only because I was still new to this; as Nurudeen eased over the low curb
and into the traffic, the wailing siren seemed to make about as much difference as Zhu's had, back in Hubei province. Traffic was so heavy that
other cars could barely move out of the way if they wanted to, and most
didn't seem to want to. The road was packed, and we were in the same
sardine can as everyone else.

In cities, roads turn into streets. Roads that connect two towns often
become avenues or boulevards (sometimes named after the places they're
coming from or going to) when those towns grow up, principal corridors
in a network of streets; they intersect and get lined with businesses,
houses, apartment buildings. Even as the global road network grows,

with more throughways linking more places together, other roads are subsumed into urban street grids.

The rise of cities is a defining trend of our time: half of the world's people now live in metropolitan areas, and the proportion is growing. For millennia, cities, though centers of civilization and economic activity, attracted only a small percentage of the human population; as late as 1900, 86 percent of the world's population lived in rural areas, and 14 percent in cities. Though opinions vary about why cities are growing so fast, one important factor is, of course, advances in agricultural technology: fewer people are now needed to grow food, and so, globally, fewer people can make a living at it. From dying small towns of the American Midwest to rural villages almost everywhere else, young people can tell you: the action, the opportunity, the future are in the city.

The cities, of course, are hugely various, ranging from planned self-contained communities in Florida, to new suburbs in Edinburgh, to entire new megalopolises now rising in China, complete with megatowers. The majority of people, however, are living in cities that are growing in a way that governments can barely monitor or control, much less plan for. These are cities whose populations have jumped manyfold in the past half-century, places like Alexandria, Egypt; Jakarta, Indonesia; São Paulo, Brazil—and Lagos. They may not be as wealthy or advanced as celebrated world capitals like London, Paris, Moscow, Montreal, Sydney, and New York, but they are quickly becoming larger. The world's population of 6 billion will increase by 2 billion over the next thirty years (it is tentatively expected to peak around 10 billion), and almost all of that increase will be in cities in Asia, Africa, and Latin America. By virtue of their sheer size these megacities will be, in certain ways, the most important in the coming century.

I chose to end my travel in Lagos for a number of reasons. One was its extremity: of all those fast-growing cities, its growth has for years been projected to be the fastest. In 1950 Lagos had 288,000 people; as I write it is estimated to have 14 million; by 2015, predicts the Population Reference Bureau, it will be the third largest city in the world, with over 23 million souls. Another reason was how relatively little known Lagos was, and still is: when I polled a dozen of my best-traveled friends, I found that none had ever been to Africa's largest city. It has a daunting reputation for corruption, starting at the airport. It would be a very hard city to traverse with a backpack. And for a white-skinned Westerner to feel safe and comfortable there, he would need to spend much more money (on guides, safe hotels, private transport) than he would in, say, Amsterdam. "And what would you go there to see, exactly?" asked one culture-minded friend. She had a point. Lagos has few museums, not too many antiquities, only a handful of public spaces or buildings of note, and stunningly little natural beauty. It does, however, have a reputation for crime, and lots and lots of people.

But people are interesting. So is crime. Finally, I chose Lagos because, as a subject, it seems to inspire extreme reactions. Most typically, Lagos is Exhibit A for observers worrying about the population explosion and urban planning crises in the Third World. Western observers, perhaps rightly, seem to fear it, linking it to the possibility of apocalyptic disease or massive civil unrest. Nigeria, writes Jeffrey Tayler in *The Atlantic*, "is lurching toward disaster." Rapid urban growth, argues Mike Davis in *Harper's*, "has been a recipe for the inevitable mass production of slums. Much of the urban world, as a result, is rushing backward to the age of Dickens."

It could also be said that many of the people in the new urban world, driven by need but also by ambition, are fashioning inventive new ways to get by. Despite the congestion and chaos in Lagos, its pollution and absence of infrastructure (most neighborhoods lack running water, central sewage, and dependable electric power), many millions of people survive there. The hundreds and thousands who arrive each day evidently believe their prospects to be better there than in the places they left behind. Architect Rem Koolhaas has drawn criticism for focusing on the undeniable vitality of Lagos rather than on its equally undeniable pathology. While teaching at Harvard, he visited the city several years in a row. "Dangerous breakdowns of order and infrastructure in Nigeria are often transformed into productive urban forms," he and his students wrote. "Stalled traffic turns into an open-air market, defunct railroad bridges become pedestrian walkways." As part of the "improvisational urbanism" that is Lagos today, he notes that the city "has no streets; instead, it has curbs and gates, barriers and hustlers . . . even the Lagos superhighway has bus stops on it, mosques under it, markets in it, and buildingless factories throughout it."

Until recently, it had very little of this. Named by Portuguese slave traders after Lagos, Portugal, the port on the Algarve through which many slaves were brought to Europe, the settlement on Lagos Island had an active slave market for at least two hundred years. Three and one-half million slaves are estimated to have been taken from pre-colonial Nigeria, of a total of 15 million taken from all of West Africa. Britain shipped more slaves than any other country until 1807, when it declared the transatlantic slave trade illegal and set out to quash it. The tribal rulers of Lagos Island who profited from the trade were slow to conform to the new law, which Britain cited as a justification for annexing Lagos in 1861, making the city a British colony.

Southern Nigeria, including Lagos, was joined to the Muslim north in a loose affiliation in 1914. Oil was discovered in the Niger delta in 1959; it quickly supplanted palm oil as a major export. Nigeria gained its independence from Britain in 1960; by 1971, it was the world's seventh-largest oil producer. (As of this writing it is estimated to be the world's tenth-largest producer, after Venezuela.) The whole coast of West Africa, from Senegal to Gabon, is densely populated, but Nigeria has the most people of all: its population was estimated by the United Nations to be 141 million in 2005, and may reach 289 million by 2050.

Oil wealth started making a difference to Lagos in the 1970s, funding the construction of skyscrapers, the airport, some roads and bridges, the military, and large villas in places like Ikoyi (formerly an island adjacent to Lagos Island but now, due to landfill, a part of it) and neighboring Victoria Island. Some made its way to Abuja, the inland capital city built during the 1980s, and to Muslim precincts further north. But the main oil-producing part of the country, in the Niger delta area in the south, has scarcely benefited at all and remains impoverished; likewise, the blessings of oil have barely helped the common citizen, instead remaining in the hands of a small but often fabulously wealthy elite. According to the World Bank, 54 percent of Nigerians live on less than one dollar a day.

Lagos began to grow quickly beginning in the late nineteenth century with British administration and the connection to international markets. The British introduced the railway, electric lighting, and the telephone. As the largest city in the region, Lagos attracted a mix of returning expatriates, migrants from the various neighboring countries, many fleeing rural famine and drought, and refugees from the Biafran war (1967–70), in which a southeastern province, Biafra, attempted to secede from Nigeria. The continuing popularity of Lagos, and its ability to assimilate new arrivals, whether foreign-born or native, surprises not only foreigners but Nigerians themselves.

The growth of Third World megacities repeats patterns seen in nineteenth- and early-twentieth-century Europe and North America but also "confounds" these precedents, writes Mike Davis. It's the confounding parts that interest Koolhaas and others. Are these cities moving toward a robust, vibrant future, or into the apocalypse?

Either way, Lagos represents the future for perhaps the majority of people on the planet, a compelling example of what happens when the track through the wilderness comes to the center of society. I wanted to see what it was like.

I didn't know a soul in Lagos. But, years earlier, I had bought some life insurance from a Nigerian in the Bronx. Given the e-mail scams emanating from Nigeria, its reputation for chaos and crime, I knew that might lead friends to question my judgment. But the term life policy Agbonifo Akpata touted in a mass mailing happened to be exactly the one I had identified through an online broker, and I thought: *Why not give the commission to an immigrant? What, actually, could go wrong?*

So I had called Akpata and he had visited our house, where I'd signed papers and everything had turned out . . . perfectly. Now that I was Lagos-bound, I tracked him down. He'd left the insurance biz; of the hundreds or thousands of people he'd approached via postcards to my zip code, he said, I was the only one to actually buy a policy. He was now trying his hand at real estate brokerage and a bit of property management. But yes, he was from Lagos, and yes, he had friends and family there he would put me in touch with.

Agbonifo's second cousin, Biola, was married to Oritsejolomi "Bill" Okonedo, and Agbonifo soon enlisted him to meet me at the airport. He also mentioned a man who drove for his brother, an executive with the telephone company in Lagos. I was delighted and relieved, because the Lagos airport is an almost mythically awful place, notorious among travelers for shakedowns by officials, and also the only airport on earth about which the U.S. government had seen fit, at various times, to post signs in American airports alerting travelers that "the U.S. Secretary of Transportation has determined that Murtala Muhammed Airport, Lagos, Nigeria, does not maintain and carry out effective airport security measures." I read the phrase again on a special page of my plane ticket, and was reminded to pass my arrival information on to Agbonifo so that he could tell Bill. No sooner had I said "airport" on the phone than Agbonifo told me to make sure I arrived in the morning, so that I wouldn't have to drive into the city when it was dark: bandits prey on cars leaving the airport at night, he warned. But it was already too late—I was set to arrive around dinnertime. Should I change my ticket? I asked him. "Well, hmm. Maybe things are better now," he said, doubtfully.

As it happened, I was met at the airport by both Bill and the brother's driver—Agbonifo, wanting to make certain I was covered, had sent both. The driver took me to my guesthouse in a stately old Mercedes, with Bill following doggedly in his battered red Toyota Starlet sedan to make sure everything was okay. The journey went well until I was delivered to the guesthouse, a small, fortified compound operated by an agricultural NGO for scientists and others who had to spend a day or two in transit through Lagos. There the driver quoted his price for the services just rendered. Bill was outraged at the number—5,000 naira, or US$42—and argued long and heatedly on my behalf. The battle became quite intense, and the angrier Bill got, the more I liked him. Finally, the driver compromised: 3,500 naira ($30). When, a few days later, Bill invited me to move out of the guesthouse and into the apartment he shared with his wife, I happily agreed.

Bill and Biola's small two-bedroom setup was located in Isolo, a working-class suburb. The guesthouse, with its eight-foot cyclone fences topped with razor wire, barred windows, and watchmen at the gate, had felt like a fortress, but I was surprised that their apartment did too. It was on a short street of two-story, multi-family stucco and cinder-block houses that had creaky gates at both ends; security guards locked them after dark. The house also had a big front gate that was locked at night (once the Toyota Starlet was inside), gates on the doors that were always locked, and grilles on every window. It lacked the niceties of the guest house such as internet and air conditioning, but, on a barred-in, cagelike terrace, Bill and Biola had their own small gasoline-powered generator so they could watch television and use lights and a fan at night during the outages in electrical service. (The city's electrical grid is a shambles; NEPA, the National Electric Power Authority, is also said to stand for Never Expect Power Again. During my stay, electricity in Isolo was off about three-quarters of the time.) It was noisy with the generator on—

but then again, it was often noisy in Isolo, anyway. The apartment was small and often very hot; but the couple had given me the larger of their two modest bedrooms, and I felt grateful.

Bill was up and out early in the morning. He is a vigorous man in his fifties, a journalist who covers the cyberworld for a South African–owned business newspaper. Biola, in her forties, made him breakfast and then divided her time between tending to the house, taking a history course at a local college, making plans to start a catering business, and attending church functions. Like many Lagosians, she is an evangelical Christian. She belonged to Faith Tabernacle (which, I would see, is literally the biggest church in the world, capable of holding 50,000 people). She went out to buy fresh food every morning, since the refrigerator was seldom cold, and usually she would cook me an egg with toast for breakfast. And then I would leave for the day, an event that, I eventually realized, filled her with relief, for as dangerous as it was for me to walk alone on the street in a city where robbery was common, it was risky for them to lodge me: having a white-skinned tenant was tantamount to saying "We have a lot of money in here!" (It happened to be true: credit cards, travelers checks, and banking machines are essentially not used in Nigeria, so I had brought with me, and kept in my room, a couple of thousand dollars in cash.)

But I liked living with people. Even nice hotels are so lonely. Bill and "B," it seemed, were suspicious of most of their neighbors—they advised me not to speak to others on the street, including the people upstairs, whom they did not socialize with. But they were friends with the neighbors behind. A second two-story house occupied the space in which a backyard would otherwise be, and the ground-floor neighbor was a single mom with an inquisitive daughter about ten years old. Motorola, as she was named, loved to come in and see what I was doing. I was always glad to show her my things, and she enjoyed telling me what was new with her. Often it was her hair: the girls at her school coordinated the pattern of their braids, changing styles weekly; the day we met, the braids were tied with colorful thin wires and coiled into tiny spirals. "Bill," I asked, "is she named after the electronics company?" No, he said—but nobody else I asked had ever heard of a person with that name.

When I wasn't with an ambulance crew or out doing an interview or having a beer with Bill after work, there were a number of interesting Lagosians I could hang out with, mostly contacts I had drummed up before leaving on my trip: a doctor affiliated with the police department (brother of a friend of my own family doctor), a young woman at an advertising agency (sister of a former student of a friend of mine), a young stockbroker (brother of a friend of my wife's), and a European financier (friend of a friend of my father).

The truck driver and those in his path were lucky to be alive. The scene of the accident was a highway exit about a mile from our post. The semi-trailer rig had apparently taken the turn too fast; it had flipped and now was lying on its side, the tractor's windshield smashed. The ground across which it had slid had been a vegetable garden but now was flattened. The driver, shirtless and bleeding, sat on a stump, looking dazed. Florence and Rasheedat put on latex gloves, helped him into the ambulance, and cleaned him up. They told him he should come to the hospital for X-rays, but he said he did not want to.

He claimed his brakes had failed. I passed this information along to Nurudeen, our driver, who gave a rueful little laugh. "It's possible," he said. "But now it doesn't matter. He will lose his job."

The nurses gave him a shot for pain, and we drove back to our post,

A truck driver who rolled his semi rig (in the background) while exiting the expressway sits in the ambulance doorway as Florence checks his blood pressure.

past a road sign in pidgin that read, *Drive Soft—Life No Get Duplicate*. A mother came by with her daughter, who looked about six and had a fever, maybe malaria. She wore only flip-flops and underpants and looked very unhappy when Florence gave her a shot.

Quite a while passed with neither walk-ups nor calls from headquarters, but time at the post was far from boring. I joined Nurudeen up in the cab, and we watched the area boys working the traffic jam in front of us. The highway had three lanes of traffic in each direction, with a concrete divider between them. Northbound traffic was on the far side of the divider from us, and usually was slower than the southbound, perhaps because of the time of day, perhaps because it was on an uphill incline. Whatever the case, the area boys would perch on the divider or on the shoulder near us and then casually, almost gracefully, they would mount a big truck like lampreys and climb up to the driver's window. Some of the drivers were clearly startled and combative; more than once we saw the driver make a fist as he tried to rid his rig of this unwanted guest. Others had "cutlasses," said Nurudeen, by which he meant knives; when the area boys got stabbed in the course of their work, he said, the ambulance was the first to know.

"So what are they doing? Are they extorting money? Do they threaten the driver?"

"I don't think they usually threaten them. They just ask for money."

"And why would a driver give them money?"

"Well, many drivers have come from the country. They don't live here, and they've heard stories about the area boys. Then suddenly there is the boy, upon their truck! I don't think the boys would attack the drivers. But I think sometimes the drivers believe they will. And so sometimes they pay."

I watched the area boys for hours. Hopping aboard trucks wasn't the only way they worked the traffic. They were constantly on the lookout for anything that fell off a truck onto the roadway, and a surprising number of items did. We'd know something had when several area boys materialized at once, quickly weaving through traffic to converge at the same point. One would come away with the prize: a sack of flour, a carton containing goods, some pieces of wood. He would place it on his shoulders, wade back through the traffic in his flip-flops, and disappear under the bridge. It was money in the bank.

I'd already had an experience with area boys that left me wary. It was during evening rush hour. I was leaving Lagos Island via one of the three bridges that connect it to the mainland. I was part of a sea of yellow, the particular shade that the thousands of private vehicles that supply Lagos with public transportation are required to be painted. *Okadas,* or motor-bike taxis, which are as common as flies, can be any color at all. But taxi-cabs, the shared minivans called *danfos,* and the unwieldy, oversized truck-buses called *molues* all must be painted yellow and have two black lines all the way around them. The *danfos* and *molues,* in addition, must have their fixed routes painted on them. In many principal routes on the transportation grid, traffic at rush hour is more than 90 percent yellow, and all the more striking for the dingy, hazy landscape it passes through.

I was in a *danfo.* These rolling wrecks are typically stuffed with about a dozen people and have side doors that are either missing or permanently open. The driver's assistant, or tout, stands in the doorway, shouting the destination and collecting fares. He signals the driver when to stop or go by banging on the roof with his hand. Having already missed three *danfos* that were full, I'd spotted one that had room for me, just barely, on the edge of a wooden bench that looked out the door. I jammed myself inside.

The driver was soon in a traffic jam, or *go-slow,* and our lack of forward progress led him, abruptly and apparently on a hunch, to reverse down the shoulder and then turn and exit on an entrance ramp. It had the promise of enterprise and creative thinking, but two-thirds of the way down the curving ramp he saw something unpromising—more traffic? construction?—and abandoned his plan. He started doing a three-point turn to change direction again; we would go back the way we had come.

Meanwhile, in the gloom, we could make out a dozen or so area boys playing soccer on the ground inside the cloverleaf. As we halted our reverse, they halted their game. And as our driver stalled out halfway through his about-face, they became very interested in us. The reason was almost certainly me: a white guy perched on the edge of a wide-open doorway was like a fat peach on a low-hanging branch.

They started jogging toward us. The other passengers began yelling at the driver. The driver's tout, standing in the doorway, began banging on the roof to convey the urgency of the situation. To myself I thought, *I am fucked.* Then, with maybe five seconds to interception, the engine came to life in a cloud of acrid smoke and the *danfo* accelerated back up to the populated highway. The soccer players gave up the chase.

That had been about a week before. I wasn't exactly haunted by the memory but, as far as area boys were concerned, I did consider myself a kind of prey.

It was hot in the cab of the ambulance. I offered to buy cold sodas for the ambulance crew and they accepted. Rasheedat said there were cold ones for sale nearby and that she would go there with me. But as she headed toward shrubs and a path that I knew led under the bridge, I stopped in my tracks. "But that's where the area boys are!" I exclaimed, surprised that she'd even consider it. Rasheedat laughed.

"Oh, they're not so bad," she said. "Would you like to see? Come on, I'll show you." It took some convincing; Lagos had made me feel susceptible to attack even when I wasn't doing anything risky, and this looked like something risky. But surely a *nurse* would not lead me to harm . . .

I followed her down a dirt footpath. We passed through some bushes and then into the shade of the overpass. About a dozen young men, mostly teenagers, were sitting on the concrete skirt underneath the roadway, watching us. Rasheedat greeted a young woman who lived in a shack down there; its roof was the side door of a *danfo*. One of the two children at her feet was throwing crumbs to chickens in a makeshift pen. The chickens ate them and then took a drink from an oily puddle. There were no other women around. One of the young men came down from the bridge and asked the nurse a question in pidgin. She looked at me and said my name, "Mr. Ted." He didn't look at me but nodded at her and walked away to rejoin the others up under the roadway. With that, about half my fear disappeared.

"Most of them are okay," she said to me as we walked toward a nearby stall selling drinks. Next to it was a shack where, another day, we'd buy yamcake, *eko* (a corn-flour gruel), and *akara* (fried balls of ground bean mixed with onion) for lunch. "Some of them are bad. But mostly they have no parents and no place to live. I do not think they will hurt you."

The drinks stand consisted of pieces of corrugated metal that formed a kind of counter, and some nearby boxes where you could sit and drink. As we sipped, I saw two boys soaping themselves up with water from an open tank next to a car wash. I supposed car wash water was somewhat clean; the day before, at ambulance Point 1 to the north of here, I'd watched other kids sudsing themselves up in water that poured out of an effluent pipe at the edge of a big Pepsi-Cola plant.

Three of the area boys rose to their feet as we headed back, and my heart skipped a beat. But they weren't interested in me. They wanted to talk to Rasheedat and they did so, fervently and for several minutes, pointing several times to the roadway overhead. They looked as though they were complaining to her, trying to persuade her of something. It gave me a chance to size them up a bit. Earlier I'd learned how to tell an area boy from a regular kid. "They look like miscreants!" someone had explained, but that required a certain baseline knowledge. Partly, you could tell by where they were and whom they were with. Most looked as though they'd had tough lives. I saw an earring or two, facial tattoos and scars (some of the scars denoted tribal ritual, and therefore a country background), some missing teeth, and a lot of swagger. Two or three from the underpass appeared to be brothers. "If you see guys in clean clothes with even the slightest paunch," a friend told me, "they're not area boys."

Rasheedat offered them some words of assurance and we left for the ambulance. They were in a dispute with the policemen, she explained. The night before, an oil tanker had caught fire on the highway. The area boys had been instrumental in putting the fire out, and the grateful truck driver had said his boss would send a reward. But when the reward arrived, the boys said, the policemen had kept most of it, though they'd done very little. And that made the young men angry.

That afternoon, the dispute would spill over onto the highway. But first, to clarify: In Lagos, there are at least five different kinds of policemen concerned with roads and traffic, and each is known by its acronym. Three are federal, including the Mobile Police (MoPol) of the Nigerian Police Force (NPF); the Federal Roads Maintenance Agency (FERMA), and the Federal Road Safety Commission (FRSC). One, the Lagos State Traffic Management Authority (LASTMA), belongs to Lagos State, which is only slightly larger than the city of Lagos. In 2003, a quasi-governmental group called Kick Against Indiscipline joined the mix. Each has its distinctive uniform. The recurring turf battles between the different forces occasionally break out into street fights.

The contingent of police who hung out near our exit ramp wore maroon trousers and beige shirts: LASTMA men. One or two had motorcycles and one or two had cars, but most were simply on foot. They waved over motorists with whom they wanted a word, which generally was not difficult as most were only creeping along in traffic. My observation, and that of many others, was that most of the police spent the day involved in small acts of extortion. They would point out a minor infraction (changing lanes without signaling, say) or irregularity (cracked glass on the rear-view mirror), announce the driver's arrest, and settle for a small fine paid directly to them. In other words, like so many others in Lagos, they were hustlers.

So it did not come as a complete surprise that afternoon to see the group of area boys in hot argument with a group of policemen, on the side of the highway. Each group had two or three spokesmen who launched charges at a member of the other group, while the non-spokesmen massed behind. The area boys appeared to be incensed, but faced with this passion the police merely shouted back, occasionally raising a hand as though about to land a blow but never actually doing so.

It was an unlikely sight, the "miscreants" challenging the police, one group of hustlers to another. In the middle of it, I noticed that two of the area boys peeled off; opportunity must have beckoned on the highway. I marveled at the ease with which they crossed the center divider, almost like synchronized swimmers: left legs up, butts over, kick up right legs, glide between cars, all while wearing the thinnest flip-flops. I could see, finally, how the highway was the river of life to the area boys. They sheltered under it and subsisted on it, by begging, thieving, and running after dropped loads. In some places, I knew, they worked with *danfo* drivers, taking bribes ("dash") to let them stop in places they weren't supposed to stop.

The cops lived off the highway, too, but less enterprisingly. There was something rotten about the way they used their authority to prey on Everyman, or Everydriver. The area boys, lacking official authority (and guns and radios), appeared to leave Everyman alone—at least, during the day. Nurudeen said that at night, all bets were off: they'd attack even him.

Another call came in, this one from a private clinic: a patient was coughing up blood and needed to be transferred to Ikeja Hospital. On went the lights and siren, and about half an hour later we arrived at the small clinic. The man was old, gravely ill, and very large. Unfortunately, he was on the second story of a building with a narrow, winding staircase and no elevator. The ambulance crew and orderlies strapped him onto a board and then together we, along with the man's son, tipped and tilted the patient and board down the stairway. He lost so much blood in transit that it filled every container the nurses could find. They had to hose out the back of the ambulance once he was delivered to the emergency room.

The patient looked to be at death's door, but three days later, when I stopped by the intensive care unit, he had stabilized—an ambulance success story. I doubt the same could be said, however, for a woman we encountered the next morning. This time the call came not over the radio but from a pedestrian. We were headed from the base to our post at Anthony when a man tapped on the pilot's window and directed us to a business about three blocks away. Lights on, the ambulance sped to the scene, and paused.

On a patch of ground in front of a small clothing shop, in full sun, lay an unconscious woman. Flies swarmed about her. There was a gash on her leg. The ambulance rolled forward a few more feet and her face came into view. I thought she was dead. Florence put on her latex gloves, climbed out, and bent over her without touching. Then she came back in, closed the door, said a couple of words quietly to Nurudeen, the pilot, and we drove off.

"So she was dead?" I asked.

"No, she was alive."

"Then why are we leaving?"

"She is a derelict."

"Yes, but . . ."

"She does not require medical services, she requires rehabilitation."

"Okay, but right now—"

"No. You see, he is calling social services," she said, pointing at Nurudeen through the little window that separated the cab from the back of the ambulance. "They will come get her and take care of her, put her into a special home."

"She needs more than a special home! She's almost dead! She needs—"

"Mr. Ted, she is a derelict. We have very few ambulances in Lagos, and if we picked up derelicts it would be even less. Also, we do not pick up corpses, though everybody thinks we do."

I kept my peace, but guiltily. In my world, you did not walk away from somebody that sick. But I knew Lagos was different. And I knew the ambulance service was different from a Western one. For one thing, it had only been launched in 2001 and so was still in its infancy. Sikuade

Jagun, M.D., director of the service, had explained that having a small number of ambulances relative to the population was just one of his challenges. (Lagos State's twenty-one ambulances worked out to one for every 666,666 people. In a Western city, the ratio is typically one for every 18,000–20,000 people.)

A bigger challenge, ironically, was that the ambulances were underused. This was because, in the public imagination, ambulances were indeed for transporting corpses. This had been the principal function of various private ambulances for years, taking cadavers from hospital to mortuary, and from home to morgue. Still, many people I spoke with in Lagos remembered how commonly one would see corpses by the roadside during the 1970s and 1980s. But recently the government had started a service to pick up corpses exclusively, and without the use of red lights and sirens—a step meant to help the traffic situation, because every official and his sister apparently had the right to attach lights and siren to their vehicle. "We have seen even the hospitals using sirens, just to transport supplies. Everybody wants to get around the traffic." But of course, overuse of that equipment devalued its currency. That was the reason real ambulances like ours were so commonly ignored. To deal with the problem, Dr. Jagun had proposed fining ambulances using lights or sirens for non-emergencies.

Anyway, to change their image, the Lagos State Ambulance Service (LASAMBUS) now strictly *forbade* ambulances to carry a corpse. And they forbade them to treat "derelicts."

No matter what the restrictions, Lord knows there could probably never be enough ambulances for Lagos. Later in the day of the derelict episode, five minutes from base, we stumbled onto another accident, wholly by chance. An *okada*, one of the omnipresent motorbike taxis, had collided with a car. The way we noticed was that maybe sixty other *okada* drivers had stopped and surrounded the driver of the car. They were tossing him around by his shirt and looked as though they might lynch him. For his part, the *okada* driver was limping and appeared dazed, and the gas tank of his motorbike had a big dent in it. Florence waved him over to the ambulance and gave him a quick once-over and a shot of painkiller. He didn't want to go to the hospital. I suggested that we wave the Mercedes driver over, as well, to save him from mayhem. Florence looked as me as though I were daft: "They'd attack the ambulance if we did that!"

There was nothing we could do for him short of sending a squadron of police.

Nurudeen piloted the ambulance away, but again I felt bad: the Mercedes driver might have been completely innocent. *Okada* drivers were notorious for illegal and dangerous maneuvers, for driving drunk, for hitting pedestrians, and even for injuring their own passengers. The weekend before, stuck in traffic as I returned home from church with Biola and some of her friends, we had watched an *okada* driver zip down a pothole-strewn dirt median in the rain, his passenger clinging on behind him as though to a bucking bronco. As he skidded into one deep hole and then bumped out of it, the motion launched his passenger into the air. The man landed on the ground with a splash. Furious and dripping with mud, he energetically berated the driver. So commonly were *okada* drivers involved in crime that a law now forbade them to stop in front of a bank. At the same time, they were notorious for standing up for their fellow *okada* drivers, no questions asked.

I was looking for something uplifting, something beautiful, something in Lagos that was a pleasure. Eating "pick & kill" catfish at a neighborhood bar was the best thing I'd found so far—the fish were live when you ordered, then baked with hot sauce, and delicious. But I was thinking larger scale. Bill suggested I visit the National Museum near Tafawa Balewa Square. A "borrowing" from its collection of Benin bronze sculptures— by a former president, who gave the bust to Queen Elizabeth!—had recently been in the news. Bill was going to take me but got called to the office.

Instead, my local stockbroker friend gave me an after-hours tour of the Nigerian stock exchange. It was a stately looking room full of computer monitors and desks. But what was frankly more interesting was the disrepair of the 1970s high-rise in which it was located. Out of a bank of four elevators, only one worked. And the car did not stop even with the floors it serviced; at one floor, it stopped nearly a foot too low, so those who exited first turned and lent a hand to other riders who were less spry.

That building's troubles were nothing like those of the twenty-story NIDB House, just a couple of blocks away on Broad Street. In March 2006, following a fire, a portion of the top eight floors of the skyscraper had collapsed onto the ones below them, killing two people; twenty more were injured when the large water tank atop the building landed on the street. From a distance, it looked as though a small plane had struck the top of the building. More amazing, though, was that months later, the situation had not been rectified; the building was still unusable, the streets around it still closed off to pedestrians and other traffic. But this was simply more disaster, not what I was after.

A driver I hired, Hassan, took me by the National Arts Theatre, a large venue for plays, dances, and art shows that looked impressive (lawns surrounded it! open space!), if beset by mildew. But my hopes of going in were dashed when an apparently counterfeit policeman approached Hassan's old Mercedes in traffic nearby, slapped the windshield hard, and angrily ordered him over to the side of the road. Hassan pretended to comply but then, as traffic loosened, saw an opening and got the hell out of there.

Maybe public facilities were the wrong idea. Fair-skinned expats in Lagos, or *oyibos,* tend to stay close to their walled compounds in Ikoyi or on Victoria Island. Shell Oil's, among the largest and most prominent, is like a small, self-contained suburb. So were the true pleasures of Lagos mostly private? Dr. Jagun, the head of the ambulance service, took me in his BMW for drinks at the boat club in Apapa, an upscale quarter of the city. It had a large, secure yard with storage for fifty craft, most of them speedboats. It had a ramp for launching them, and it had a small clubhouse with windows overlooking the water. It was like an annex to an expat compound—the crowd at cocktail hour was European workers and us. The view across the narrow channel of water was all industry: rusty tanks and warehouses. The water itself looked murky and unwholesome. The landscape reminded me of the Bronx River, which I'd canoed with a conservation group out to revive the long-polluted inner-city passage. We'd passed through the formerly industrial South Bronx, with its abandoned factories and junkyards. But the water was no longer dirty, abandoned cars and tires had been removed, and, miracle of miracles, a beaver had recently been sighted, the first in a hundred years. The area was on its way back.

Not Lagos, however, at least not yet. A German at the bar told me that members regularly toured the lagoons around the city's islands, and up and down the coast beyond, but always in groups of several craft, the biggest danger being "things in the water," which he explained as meaning logs, trash, wires, and carcasses including human remains. "And sometimes they make your motor stop working."

My search for a legitimate tourist attraction in Lagos continued. I made dates to visit The Shrine nightclub, the temple to Afropop music run by legendary musician Fela Kuti and then by his son, Femi, but each fell through. I wanted to take a stroll on the beach off Victoria Island, but people nearby warned me away: I'd surely be robbed, they said.

But then Dr. Jagun assigned me to Point 2, the ambulance post located halfway across the Third Mainland Bridge, occupying a few square yards of a turnout. And there, beyond the shadow of a doubt, I realized that what I'd been looking for had been in front of me all along. It was the bridge itself.

At 7.3 miles, the Third Mainland Bridge, Africa's longest, connects the sprawling slums and settlements of the mainland to Lagos Island, home to the city's high-rises (and most of its remaining historical buildings, including a handful of colonial houses with deep verandas and "Brazilian houses" with Baroque styling brought home by returning slaves in the nineteenth century). The Carter and the Eko bridges connect Lagos

The Third Mainland Bridge and high-rises of Lagos Island,
as seen from the midbridge ambulance post

Island to the mainland, as well, but they are modest, even stolid, while the Third Mainland Bridge is grand. Completed in 1990, it is easily the most impressive public work in Lagos.

For one thing, it is beautiful to look at from a distance: long, low, silver, gracefully spanning Lagos Lagoon at about a hundred feet above the water's surface. For another, in a city that is utterly flat, it affords amazing views: of the lagoon, dotted with fishing boats and net traps; of the tall buildings of Lagos Island; of the ocean horizon (the South Atlantic); and, perhaps most memorably, of the horrific lumber mill zone. Ebute Metta, just a few hundred yards from the bridge, looked like the set for an ambitious dystopian movie. Smoke rose from smoldering mountains of sawdust and drifted across the bridge, obscuring views of wooden mills and shacks with rusting corrugated roofs, casting it all in the browning yellow of a sepia photograph, a tropical shantytown version of Manchester, England, in the early nineteenth century. Flames shot up as well, though it was hard to determine the source—you just saw flashes among the blackened timbers of docks and the sooty facades of market buildings and warehouses. The smoking sawdust piles gave a sense that the land itself was combustible, a level of hell risen to Earth's surface. Narrow channels of water seeped into (or out of) the district from the lagoon, and maybe that was behind the drama: here were earth, water, and fire juxtaposed. Rafts of logs from Nigeria's dwindling forests floated under the bridge and queued up wharfside to meet their fate, as convincing a depiction of the "end of nature" as anyone could devise.

I'd been on the bridge many times in taxis before the ambulance assignment. But back then I'd just enjoyed the chance to go fast. For most of its span the bridge is a long straightaway uninterrupted by cross streets, so traffic on it sometimes flows freely outside rush hours; the temptation to really step on it is irresistible.

But going really fast in Lagos seems in many ways more perilous than going really fast in other places. One problem is that a few other vehicles, such as donkey- or human-pulled carts, might be going really slowly. Another problem is that most of the vehicles in Lagos are in poor repair, with bad tires and worn suspensions, and dangerous when driven fast. So, despite the bridge being a place where one might imagine there are few accidents, in fact there are many. And thus the ambulance post.

I waited in the ambulance during the morning with Josephine and Lara, the nurses, and Ganiu, the pilot. All the doors were open, and there was a nice ocean breeze. Occasionally a work crew would pull into the turnout where we were stationed, or a police motorcycle. In the late morning an *okada* dropped off a freelance mechanic. He walked to a large storage bin and produced a bag of tools from a hiding spot underneath. Like us, he was waiting for trouble to happen.

Through the open back doors of the ambulance, I could look down on the water. The occasional rafts of logs with small boats attached, heading to the sawmill district, reminded me of the river in Peru: sometimes wood didn't need a road to get where it was going. But the more common craft were dugout-style traditional fishing boats, with single, ancient-looking trapezoidal sails. You would look at them, then look at this impressive, expensive bridge, and think: *The parts of this picture don't fit together.* It was like the beggar with no legs who rode on another man's back, and begged beside backed-up cars on the Lagos Island end of the bridge, or the girl with no hands who would tap on your window within sight of the high-rise district, ancient need juxtaposed with the veneer of civilization that oil money and international markets had provided. The existence of the new and gleaming was rendered less authentic, less convincing, by the persistent needs of the least fit, still unmet.

The bridge transferred its vibrations to us. It felt like a living thing. When a heavy truck rumbled by, we'd sense it; if a gust of wind came up, you could feel the sway. (Months later, engineers would cite excess movement as a symptom of poor maintenance, and closed parts of the bridge for repair.) After two hours an urgent call came in: a *danfo* van full of passengers had blown a front tire and "somersaulted" on the southbound side of the bridge. We were on the northbound, and would have to go all the way to the end and make a U-turn. Doors slammed shut, seat belts were fastened, and off we roared.

Fifteen minutes later, we arrived at the scene of the accident. But the victims had already been transported away. "Did another ambulance already come?" I asked, confused. "No, no," answered Cecilia, one of today's nurses. "They were probably taken to the hospital by Samaritans," by which she meant nice people. Since it was almost lunchtime, we continued on to Lagos Island.

I'd spent a fair amount of time there already—most of it on foot, since getting around the thronged commercial areas in a vehicle was practically impossible. Authorities had lost control of the streets, and everywhere you went, it seemed, there was a bazaar, the stalls and vendors having taken over the sidewalk, impinging on the street from both sides. Seldom was there room for more than a single vehicle, so the streets were one-way. And, even if you were in that vehicle, you crept along at a snail's pace while scores of people flowed around you.

It was area boys, I'd been told, who controlled the streets, if anyone did. Gangs allocated commercial stall space on the basis of fees, and certain kinds of drivers—I was never clear exactly which ones—had to pay, as well. I'd seen small groups of young men terrorizing taxi drivers, for example, trying to take their keys just like policemen did. And I'd seen someone making a delivery getting punched through the window of his small station wagon: if you didn't pay their "tax," that's what would happen.

I was still surprised, though, by what happened to us after Ganiu, the pilot, grabbed some bread at a shop and eased back into traffic. We were midway between the highway and the really congested zone, on a narrow street where two small cars might pass each other going opposite direc-tions, but not two large ones. Our ambulance was sizable, and when we came upon a passenger car heading in the opposite direction, I fully expected the other driver to pull over—if he'd put two wheels over the curb, which other cars did all the time, we could handily pass.

But he refused. The standoff escalated, first with honking, then with gesticulating, then with the driver of the car and his two passengers get-ting out and approaching the ambulance.

"Who wouldn't get out of the way of an ambulance?" I asked Josephine, the other nurse, who was watching with me.

"They are area boys," she explained.

That explained their brazenness. The area boys didn't care. These were not street soldiers: they had jewelry and nice shoes and fancy cell phones, and one was calling somebody. Ganiu didn't immediately back down, but I saw him gulp. And then, as area boys leaned on different parts of the ambulance, I saw him blink. Still swearing and gesticulating, he shifted into reverse, waited for cars behind him to give us a little space, and then eased the ambulance back over the curb. The gangsters glowered as they finally drove by.

For some time after, Ganiu didn't talk. Finally, he sighed and said sim-ply, "Oh. This city." It was three more days until he went to his village, he explained. He lived in the countryside two hours outside Lagos, working seven days in the city before returning home on the eighth for two days' rest. No, he said—he did not wish to move his family to Lagos. "I make 9,000 naira" a month (US$76), he explained. "I could not keep them here."

I had been to the countryside with people at the other end of the income scale. My internist in New York had a Nigerian-born colleague whose brother, Dr. Okaa, in Lagos, had close connections to the police. On the evening I arrived I gave him a call. He asked if I wanted to come along to a "burial" in the country the next day. I imagined he was something like a coroner, and thought, *Hmm, this could be interesting.* He told me to be at his house by eight a.m.

It was a gated two-story brick house, sprawling though sparsely furnished, in Ikoyi. Dr. Okaa's Mercedes sedan was soon joined in the circular driveway by those of his friends Terry and Josiah. Terry had trained as a pharmacist on Long Island but had returned home to more lucrative opportunities; inexplicably, he now ran a firm that designed offshore oil drilling platforms. Josiah was in real estate. All were dressed in Yoruba tribal finery. Dr. Okaa wore a lime-green *agbada*, or ceremonial tunic, with a cherry-red *fila* cap. The code words here were "rich" and "connected."

We made one stop before hitting the Lagos–Ibadan Expressway: police headquarters, where we picked up an armed guard. His name was Sergeant Bisong, and he sat in the front of Dr. Okaa's car wearing a bulletproof vest, his submachine gun across his lap.

We were stopped at seventeen police checkpoints on our two-hour journey to the burial. We did not have to pay our way out of any of them, and did not once have to get out of the car. This, I concluded, was what our guard was really for, more than to protect us from unofficial brigands. We were Friends of the Police.

The burial was that of an old man, a janitor by trade but chief of his village, who had recently died. His son, improbably, had recently ascended to the board of the Nigerian National Petroleum Corporation. To honor his father's memory, the son had paved the last mile or two of the previously dirt road to the village. He had assembled three massive party tents. He set up live remote closed-circuit television broadcasts under additional tents for the dignitaries who couldn't fit inside the local church, which was most of them. And me. As we waited for the service to begin, we browsed through a commemorative magazine produced for the occasion. Each page had a reproduction of a letter of condolence from somebody important—other oil company bigwigs, state governors, clergymen, and chiefs such as "His Majesty Kaegborekuzi I, the Dein of Agbor." And then we ate fish and chicken and drank beer and watched dancers for several hours—but not too late, because it was important to drive home while it was still light.

Daylight matters in Lagos, too, when it comes to safety. An acquaintance of mine whom I'll call Sven is the local representative of a multinational corporation. He also lives in a walled compound in Ikoyi. Peacocks wander his gardens; he has three cars and two drivers; and among his house staff is a chef talented in continental cuisine. Spending an evening at his place, after a night with no fan at Bill and Biola's, was more than a little refreshing.

But there was only so much you could do to insulate yourself from Lagos. To get back and forth from the airport, his lifeline to the outside world, Sven had to travel the same roads as anyone else. One of the worst spots was near the Oshodi Market on the Agege road, where it intersects with the Apapa–Oworonshoki Expressway—not far from the Anthony ambulance post. Oshodi was a notorious slowdown spot; the rise of the overpass somehow brought traffic to a near standstill there, seemingly no matter what time of day. It was prime territory for vendors, who wandered freely among the snail-paced vehicles. And also convenient for thieves, who used the occasion to take a good look through the windows of expensive cars. Sven had lost his laptop to armed robbery there; he wouldn't share the details, only swear that he would never again pass by the Oshodi Market after dark. If a flight he was taking left at ten p.m., he'd leave for the airport at three and spend the intervening hours in the airport's executive lounge.

At dusk the ambulances retreated to their bases. Ganiu and the nurses returned from the Third Mainland Bridge to the base at Lagos Island General Hospital. Typically the ambulances did not go out at night; it was too dangerous. If calls came in after dark, I was told, the dispatcher would decide whether the location was safe enough to make an exception.

So I waited, on a Saturday night, in the emergency room of Lagos

Island General Hospital. I started out in the Dispatch Room, where a young woman sat at a small desk upon which were a telephone and a Bible. Lagos had a new medical emergency call-in number: dial 1–2–3, I was told, and the phone would ring here. But, after a couple of hours passed without a single call, the woman retired to a couch and promptly fell asleep. I wandered out into the ER and met the attending physician, young Dr. Joseph Nugabod ("Call me Doc Boddy"), who let me tag along as he treated a drunk teenager who had been hit by a car and had a pretty bad head injury. Doc Boddy couldn't do an MRI or CAT scan, but he stitched up some cuts and otherwise cleaned the man up as best he could. An orderly kept him for observation.

If we were lucky, he said, we'd have a slow night. It was much better than the alternative. A month before, they'd been inundated with burn victims from an oil pipeline explosion on nearby Atlas Creek Island that killed two hundred people. (Poor people had been "bunkering," illegally tapping a pipeline for fuel, when a spark had ignited the oil.) Two years before, a munitions store had blown up in Isolo; Doc Boddy said over a thousand people had died in the panicked aftermath. Tonight would probably be more typical: *okada* accidents, and shootings of and by area boys.

"In fact, there is one here already. I will introduce you." Doc showed me into a room where a young man lay without a shirt. A bandage around his chest was partly soaked through with blood.

"This is Mr. Conover," said Doc Boddy to the patient. "Would you like to tell him about your accident?"

The man glared at Nugabod and we left the room. "He claims he walked into a sharp pole, you see," explained the doctor. "What I see, quite clearly, is the entrance and exit wounds of a bullet. And of course I had to report him to the police—we always do with a gunshot wound. If I did not, the police could accuse me of harboring knowledge of a crime, of being in cahoots with gangsters."

Dealing with gangsters and area boys was one of the more challenging aspects of Doc Boddy's work. Recently he'd treated a well-known mobster, who was called Stainless for the finish of his pistol. His presence, however, sparked several skirmishes between rival gangsters on the hospital grounds, and finally, to Doc Boddy's relief, he was transferred to Ikeja on the mainland, about ten miles away. A sign taped to the entrance of the ER announced in large type: *GUNS ARE NOT ALLOWED.*

A sign on the emergency room door at Lagos Island General Hospital

Something like 60 percent of admissions involved road accidents, the majority of them involving *okadas*. Two men came in around midnight, one a driver (who got the worst of it) and the other his passenger. Apparently, a car began backing up as the *okada* came up behind him. The driver of the *okada* then lost control and they collided. The driver was a big, muscular man, parked in the hallway on a gurney, with a badly cut-up arm (again, the gauze was soaking through with blood), abrasions to his neck and jaw and to his head behind the ear, and, said Doc Boddy, a blunt chest injury. His passenger, inside a room nearby, had a head injury. Both men would be X-rayed.

"I don't know whose fault this was. But some of the *okada* drivers start drinking in the morning. Nobody wears a helmet. Most have no training at all." It was also not a crime to drive drunk.

The next patient to come in, around three a.m., was also involved in an *okada* accident. A fifty-something woman had been crossing the street when a speeding *okada* hit her—and then sped on. Doc Boddy explained to me that her right tibia and fibula were both broken. She had a very large gash on her shin, and had lost a lot of blood. Hospital staff had already given her a pint of blood, and Doc Boddy said she might get up to three more. I made the mistake of watching as a nurse arrived to change the bandage: it was a terrible wound, and the woman was in a lot of pain.

"I don't think she'll survive," Doc Boddy said to me in a low voice as we left. "She's lost so much blood."

We got cups of tea, and I asked about the paucity of ambulance calls (the supposed ambulance dispatcher remained sound asleep on the couch). The phone had not rung all night, and this in a city of 14 million people! Doc Boddy explained that communications workers had been on strike for three days, and one of the casualties was the emergency call service—it wasn't working.

He continued to speak candidly. The bottom line, said Doc Boddy, was that few people would think to call an ambulance. "White men think to pick up the phone," he said. "The black man just brings the wounded in himself." But why, I asked, when the service was there—and free? Well, he said, it was so new that most people didn't know about it. Uncertainty over whether an ambulance would respond at night didn't help matters. In addition, most people didn't have extra minutes on their mobile phones—emergency calls weren't free. Many, in fact, didn't have phones at all.

In my mind, when I arrived in Nigeria, a delayed ambulance was one of life's catastrophes: medical help tragically forestalled, with needless death the possible result. But now the picture for me was changing. Ambulance service was an aspect of Western modernity that perhaps didn't fit this new kind of city. With enough money you could bring in an idea like that, just as you could build a skyscraper, but that didn't mean it would become an organic part of local life. Maybe non-mobile clinics made more sense. Lagos barely even had a fire department; I'd seen an abandoned firehouse off the freeway, and been told there were fewer than a dozen trucks for the entire city. These emergency services didn't function as coherent system. Rather, they were latent possibilities, ideas that were merely being tried.

In the ambulance parking lot at Ikeja, I'd seen a vehicle that was different from the others and seldom used. The ambulance was a gift from Cook County emergency services, in Chicago. "It's always broken," explained Moshood Kazeem, the administrator at Ikeja. "You see, it needs air conditioning, because in the back there are no windows that open. But it's expensive to fix, and we can't get the parts." The second-hand ambulance, a gesture of goodwill, had become something of an albatross to LASAMBUS. It was useless and a money sink, and it possibly made the Nigerians feel inept.

People typically arrived at Nigerian emergency rooms using other means of transportation. "Actually, it is usually a *danfo* or taxi," said Doc Boddy. Even without an ambulance, "people will find a way." He meant a path, a route, a means of arrival, a road.

One of the nurses at Point 5, observing the knot of policemen who hung around the ramp nearby, had commented: "As we say here, the fear of LASTMA is the beginning of wisdom." I wondered about the person at the top of the traffic police bureaucracy, wondered if there was a glimmer of method behind the madness. Could he be the most corrupt of all? I had the idea that interviewing Lagos's top cop would be tantamount to encountering Kurtz, way up the tropical river in Joseph Conrad's *Heart of Darkness*. And who wouldn't want to do that?

The "river" in this case was the Apapa-Oworonshoki Expressway, and the chief, Young Arebamen, was not hard to find. His office sits atop a four-story walk-up building just down the highway from Point 5. The corridors are on the building's exterior, out of the range of air conditioning, as is the reception area outside his office, where two uniformed officers sit at desks and another, wearing a gun, stands guard. A dozen citizens, men and women, had arrived before me. They sat on hard benches waiting for an audience with the chief.

A local reporter had given me the chief's cell phone number and I'd made an appointment with him directly, so I got to jump the line. Arebamen was a fit man in his late forties, wearing not a uniform but dark slacks and a light gray button-down shirt. He stood up from behind his desk and reached over it to shake my hand. He wanted me to see him in action before the questions began, so after ushering me to a black leather couch, he called in two citizens from the queue. The first was a gray-haired man, well-dressed and with a folder in his hand. He asked the chief to reduce the fine levied against his driver (25,000 naira, or US$212), which had to be paid before the car would be released; his driver had been caught going the wrong way down a one-way street.

The chief, speaking in English (perhaps for my benefit), reminded the man that his driver had committed a serious crime, and that the usual punishment—mandatory psychiatric evaluation that could last several days—had somehow been spared the driver. He was sorry, but there could be no further reduction in penalties.

Next up was a woman who had left her car on a bridge while she did some shopping. The car wasn't confiscated, but she had received a 10,000-naira (US$85) ticket.

The chief probed her circumstances and, seemingly impressed by her contrition, reduced the fine to 1,000 naira. He pointed toward the door, but the supplicant persisted, asking him to erase the fine altogether. At this Arebamen became strict and dismissive, pressing a button under his desk. A guard opened the door, she was shown out, and the theater was over. It was my turn.

Arebamen acknowledged that there was corruption. He blamed it on lack of training, a culture he'd had to inherit (he came from the Nigeria Police Force, where I later learned that he had a reputation for honesty), and low pay. A higher budget would increase professionalism. As a symbol of his want, he asked me to look around the office. "Do you see any screens with traffic conditions? Don't you think that would make sense, in a city of 14 million people?" I agreed but found myself riveted by a set of photos behind him.

Photographs of traffic officers injured by motorists paper the wall behind the desk of Young Arebamen, head of the LASTMA police in Lagos.

I don't know how I hadn't noticed: the glossy photos were practically a wallpaper, so many of them covering the wall behind his desk. Each one showed an officer who had been attacked. They had swollen eyes, split lips, bloody noses; all of them had been beaten by drivers. "It's a very dangerous job; there are many motorists who are not law-abiding."

I'd had a photo like that taken of me at Sing Sing after I was spit on and punched in the head by an inmate. But I didn't especially sympathize with these officers. I'd seen LASTMA men in action and knew that nine out of ten of them had probably provoked their attacks.

"You know that some of them deserved it," I said.

Arebamen sharply differed. "Nobody deserves this," he countered, gesturing angrily at his men. "There would be little order at all without them." If you looked at it that way, he was probably right.

I was thinking about that on the day of my final interview, with Ayobami Omiyale, the chief of another group of highway cops, the Lagos State Federal Road Safety Commission (FRSC). He had invited me to interview him at home, and I was being driven in a taxi to the Alakuko district, near the city's northwestern edge. Our conversation would focus largely on the mentality of Lagosian drivers, particularly what Omiyale called the Road Accident Immunity Delusion Syndrome, which was pretty self-explanatory, but would touch as well on fatalism and the idea of the road as harboring evil. Many Nigerians, said Omiyale, saw the hand of God in any accident involving themselves. The Yoruba concepts *aiyé* and *òtá* were part of this; *òtá* were one's personal or spiritual enemies and *aiyé*, as explained by Damola Osinulu and other scholars, was a spirit world that could work against the individual, and "against whose strategies, tactics must be deployed." It reminded me of Nigerian novelist Ben Okri's idea of the road as a creature with a malevolent, consumptive power of its own (in *The Famished Road*).

I particularly remembered this story of Omiyale's: Many drivers, he told me, carry a protective talisman. One driver in a fatal crash—the driver who lived—carried a shell on a string in his pocket. As he reached for his wallet, to show identification to Omiyale, he saw that the charm had broken and threw it away into the weeds.

"You see," the chief explained to me, "it was his good-luck charm. And because he was still alive, he gave credit to the charm. But obviously it had broken in the effort to save him, and had no power left."

This literal belief in charms was a bit different from my own, though perhaps not entirely—I had been carrying an umber-colored, charmingly twisted piece of a stick in my daypack on all these trips—something my wife had picked up on a hike and given to me, declaring offhandedly that it was good luck. Which I supposed it had been, and would be—until it wasn't anymore.

As was commonly the case, the electricity was out as my taxi took me to Omiyale's, and therefore so were the traffic lights. Each major intersection was thus an exercise in brinksmanship, in closely following any car that seemed to have momentum, because the idea of alternating was lost in the volume and lack of well-defined lanes. My driver had nerves of steel, and had passed through several chaotic junctions when we came to one that looked relatively uncrowded. It looked as though we'd be able to creep through without even stopping when the lights came back on and, seemingly within a space of two or three seconds, a policeman stepped into the traffic in front of us, blowing his whistle and pointing accusingly at my cab. He directed us to the side of the road where there were several others in uniform, told the driver to put the car in Park—and then reached in and took the keys! The driver prepared to get out to discuss the matter. On his way, he reached above the visor and pulled out a 1,000-naira ($8.50) note. That happened to equal the agreed-upon fare to the house of Omiyale.

"It wasn't your fault!" I said. "You couldn't have known the light would come on at that second. Don't pay him!"

The driver nodded and shrugged. "He's got the keys," he said.

It was all over but the arguing. The driver hemmed a bit, but I could see his heart wasn't really in it. The money landed in the policeman's palm. Soon the keys were back in the driver's.

A different kind of stress lay ahead. The road we were on became a highway, which meant only that it was divided, with maybe twenty feet of dirt separating the two directions. The vehicles in our direction slowed to a crawl. A vestigial median divider disappeared and, as traffic jammed up, cars going our direction, seeking incremental advantage, left the pavement and drove onto the median, filling it up. In other words, our side of the road literally expanded, becoming maybe six or seven vehicles wide. The median was slanted and rutted but soon we were on it, too, inching ahead, looking for an opening, however small. Spaces too tight for a car were soon occupied by motorcycles. These buzzed everywhere, many with customized narrow handlebars to let them squeeze through narrow spaces.

For a driver accustomed to obeying lane lines and feeling taken advantage of when somebody zoomed up the shoulder, the situation represented the complete breakdown of order. Here was Hobbes's state of nature, every man out for himself. Of course, it wasn't quite that extreme—a bit of enlightened self-interest kept most drivers from colliding with adjacent cars—but it was close. I noticed that the pressure became even more intense after a while because traffic slowed in the opposite direction, too, adding to the buildup on the median. As I sat in the back of the cab, I felt as though I was in the middle of a giant automotive mosh pit, helplessly part of an aggressive crowd.

Much of the time, other banged-up cars and trucks were so close that I couldn't have opened my door to escape even if I had decided to. But that was a hopeless idea. In another hour, actually, I would find myself in the spacious but strangely empty living room of Police Chief Omiyale, drinking tea brought in by his wife, peered at by young children who hovered in doorways, discussing the cosmology of Nigerian roads and the strange political process that had resulted in five competing police forces in Lagos. At the moment, however, I was trying not to look at the young vendor who had assumed a fixed position directly outside my window. Dangling from his outstretched arm was a string of dead rats. He bumped them against the window to get my attention. I knew what these meant now, but a couple of weeks ago I had not. "Oh my God," I remembered saying to Biola. "Who would buy dead rats?"

It had taken her a moment to understand what I was thinking. Once she did, she began laughing almost uncontrollably. "They're selling poison, rat poison," she explained between hoots of laughter. "Those dead rats just show it works. It's advertising."

After my interview with the chief, in the same taxi back to Bill's, we found ourselves in the same kind of jam. This time my way of coping, as the sides of trucks and buses replaced the view of shanties and billboards, was to imagine an aerial perspective of the mess, à la Google Earth. From above, I could see that the battle for the median strip was in a way a version of the volume control engineered in places like New York's Tappan Zee Bridge. On the Tappan Zee, custom vehicles known as "zipper machines" move a line of concrete dividers from one side of the roadway to the other depending on which direction has the heaviest traffic; similar systems are in place in Honolulu, Dallas, Philadelphia, San Francisco (though the dividers on the Golden Gate Bridge are plastic, not concrete), Ontario, and Auckland, New Zealand. In Lagos, you could argue, the same thing seems to happen, but without the intervention of traffic engineers. I know which one I prefer.

In my mind I kept rising, so that I could see for blocks and blocks. I could imagine the yellow of the buses and taxis standing out against the gloomy gray of almost everything else; the other specks of color I conjured up were the pinks, greens, oranges, and reds of women's traditional robes. I could visualize the evangelists' billboards ("Lord, let us tell Good from Evil so that we do not Die of the Unexpected," "Satan, Stop That Mess! A Prophetic Breakthrough Sermon"), beckoning men and women to lives of purpose and moral conduct. Evangelical Christianity and populist Islam were the fastest-growing religions here, and they were of a piece with the worldly grime and grit. They offered a path to higher ground, a spiritual elevation from the omnipresent squalor and constant threat of scam.

Higher yet, I could picture the boundaries of Lagos, those edges where creeping urban settlement met with field and forest. Roads connected the megacity to smaller ones, but this megacity was hardly alone: Lagos is "simply the biggest node in the shantytown corridor of 70 million people that stretches from Abidjan to Ibadan," as Mike Davis has observed.

At night, from space, you'd be able to see an amazing band of lights across the coast of West Africa. At least, if the power was on.

EPILOGUE

ONE OF THE GREAT CHALLENGES in writing a book about roads is to avoid the inadvertent use of road metaphors. So essential a part of the human endeavor are roads that road- and driving-related metaphors permeate our language. Who among us hasn't come to a fork in the road or been tempted by the road to ruin? Speed bumps, in the newspapers, are faced by everyone from Middle East peace negotiators to baseball teams making their way to the playoffs. Leaders who are asleep at the wheel routinely send our enterprises into a ditch. We spend so much time "on the way" in cars, ideally pedal-to-the-metal but more often stuck in a jam (what other non-human artifacts experience "congestion"?) or, the good Lord willing, *cruisin'*, that roads have become central to the way we think.

Your career puts you in either the fast lane or the slow. Some will choose the high road, others the low. Either way, there may be detours en route—you may find yourself on a rocky road, or a long and winding road, or you may hit a bump in the road. If that should happen, don't let it drive you around the bend. Hopefully someone will help pave the road to your recovery. If not, you'll fall by the wayside, running on empty, and it's all downhill from there. So get a grip (on the wheel, that is), and consider taking the road less traveled.

The road to x is paved with y. That idea is up my alley. Don't worry about the road ahead—it's a straight shot. There's a lot going on under the hood. Now that you're in the driver's seat, you're going to want to avoid that deer in the headlights. You'll also want to take a peek in the rear-view mirror. When you reach the crossroads, look both ways. If you keep going the way you're headed, you're going to drive it into the ground. It's a total dead end. But the straight shot, that one's paved with gold, so let's green-light it. Let's step on it!

Disagree? Then you can eat my dust, because this ain't no two-way street. It's my way or the highway!

And that, friends, is where the rubber meets the road.

Why are there so many road-related figures of speech? I guess because roads are the best metaphor we have for talking about life. The idea is a bit strange when you think about it: something that can be measured in miles likened to something that can be measured in days or years. But roads are all about passage, distance over time—*miles per hour*—and navigating a road involves choices.

With the most expansive metaphors, the road stands for an entire worldview. When we talk about "the road we're on now" or "if we keep going down this road," we're talking about a whole set of choices and understandings about life or policy. The Chinese character *tao* means "way," "path," or "route," and sometimes "doctrine" or "principle." The Japanese word *dō* (pronounced "doe") refers to a spiritual and physical "way"; *karate-dō* is the way (practice) of karate. In Spanish the words *rumbo* and *camino*, literally "path" and "way," both frequently connote life choices and mindset.

My friend Jay, with whom I've done a lot of driving, observed to me once that roads have a dual nature. On the one hand a road is a purposefully constructed, even intrusive element of the landscape; on the other hand it's self-effacing, just a means to an end. From a driver's point of view, "it's no place in particular, it's always receding," he observed—which reminded me of the Mac Davis lyric, "I thought happiness was Lubbock, Texas / in my rearview mirror."

"Unless you get stuck," Jay added. "Then you feel the doom of being nowhere, of being in a random somewhere not of your choosing."

And that's the foil to the whole road-as-means-of-self-discovery idea: a traveler can run out of psychic gas. While travel can be enlightening and eye-opening, we've probably all had moments when the movement came to seem just a waste of time—a spinning of wheels, if you will. The British writer Will Self, who walks places and then writes about it, decided to go by foot from John F. Kennedy Airport in Queens to Manhattan. He saved the $45 taxi fare but had this to say in Brooklyn:

Far from being elevated by Crown Heights, I can feel my mood dipping. Far from feeling the walk to New York as an achievement, I'm beginning to think this is just another slog away from commitment and engagement, and towards empty-headedness.

This idea, of course, is a heresy to the road-as-wisdom camp. It probably took an Englishman to write it.

In the American tradition, the road as setting for novel or movie resonates with our national passion for mobility, and our view of the road, articulated by Whitman, as a place where everybody meets everybody, where democracy happens. Leo Marx has commented that Mark Twain de-Europeanized the American novel "with one inspired stroke when he chose an illiterate fourteen-year-old boy, the son of the town drunk, as the narrator of his own road novel." Huckleberry Finn and Jim the escaped slave travel not on a road, of course, but down the Mississippi River. But it's still a road novel, not least in the way that their raft, just like the Beats' car in Kerouac's *On the Road*, is a distinctively male space that permits its occupants "to be together without the need to answer questions about why they want to be together." And, of course, to seek holiness and truth, much as Christopher McCandless, aka Alexander Supertramp, did in 1991 and 1992, as recounted in Jon Krakauer's book *Into the Wild*.

I was sorry not to be able to spend more time in the settlement of Samaritans, near Nablus, because the parable of the Good Samaritan, from the Gospel according to Luke, has long struck me as an essential story about the meaning of roads. A good Samaritan, as everybody knows, helps somebody he doesn't know. The parable unfolds as a lesson from Jesus to a lawyer who has asked, "What must I do to inherit eternal life?"

Jesus asks him what he thinks one needs to do.

"Love the Lord your God with all your heart and with all your soul and with all your strength and with all your mind; and, Love your neighbor as yourself," answers the lawyer. But one part of that is not entirely clear: "Who is my neighbor?" he asks Jesus.

Jesus explains by way of this story: "A man was going down from Jerusalem to Jericho, when he fell into the hands of robbers. They stripped him of his clothes, beat him and went away, leaving him half dead. A priest happened to be going down the same road, and when he saw the man, he passed by on the other side. So too, a Levite, when he came to the place and saw him, passed by on the other side. But a Samaritan, as he traveled, came where the man was; and when he saw him, he took pity on him. He went to him and bandaged his wounds, pouring on oil and wine. Then he put the man on his own donkey, took him to an inn and took care of him. The next day he took out two silver coins and gave them to the innkeeper. 'Look after him,' he said, 'and when I return, I will reimburse you for any extra expense you may have.' "

Jesus then instructs the lawyer, "Go and do likewise."

I'm not a Christian, actually, but I like this story because it touches on the moral implications of roads. To me it's like this: the world has many needy people. It also has fortunate people with various abilities to help. But who deserves help? Well, if you live in a small community, you help your neighbor. Fine, but what if there's a road—and via that road, outsiders arrive? Are they your neighbors? Or if you yourself use that road to travel to another place, and while traveling you encounter somebody who needs help: is that your neighbor? (There's a greater chance that you will meet this person on the road, because trouble happens on the road, and people needing help sometimes take to the road.) It's an essential question of morality: who is our neighbor? And therefore, whom do we help and whom do we not? And it is roads, obviously since biblical times and probably since long before, that complicate this question, by introducing us to strangers.

What else does a road test beyond one's conscience? Jay's idea is that the road lends itself to experiments of all kinds because it is liminal, an in-between place outside the immediate control or supervision of constituted authority, where things can happen that are not permitted elsewhere;* lawlessness is both danger and opportunity. A related notion is that of the "roadhouse," a honky-tonk outside of town where local restrictions do not apply and forbidden things are sometimes possible.

Last, roads have long provided a solution, in American life and elsewhere, to disappointments and the lack of local opportunity. You go somewhere else, you start again. Or you get started for the first time. As

*Unless, of course, there is highway patrol in the vicinity.

Bruce Springsteen sang in "Thunder Road": "It's a town full of losers / And I'm pulling out of here to win."

That ethos might be poised for reassessment in light of high oil prices, the concept of the carbon footprint, and the notion that, given the disappearance of the frontier and the recognition that there is limited space on earth for ever-growing numbers of people, we need to stay put and clean up after ourselves, not simply forever move on.

And yet, stasis is not an option. In the words of Ibn al-'Arabi, a twelfth-century philosopher from Spain, "The origin of existence is movement. Immobility can have no part in it, for if existence were immobile, it would return to its source, which is the Void. That is why the voyaging never stops, in this world or the hereafter."

ACKNOWLEDGMENTS

When I first conceived of this project, I had no idea how to fund it. Overseas research is costly. The answer came in three parts: Alfred A. Knopf, my publisher, which advanced me royalties; the John Simon Guggenheim Foundation, which granted me a research fellowship; and several magazines, which assigned me road-related stories and paid for associated travel. I would like to thank *National Geographic*, *The Atlantic*, *The New York Times Magazine*, and *Virginia Quarterly Review* for their interest, and these editors for their support: Robert Vare, Gerald Marzorati, Ted Genoways, and Margot Guralnick (who also happens to be my wife).

Back in the early 1990s, *The New Yorker* sent me to East Africa to write about truckers and the AIDS epidemic. Twelve years later, I revisited some of the same places with the same men for chapter 3 of this book. Thanks to Robert Gottlieb for his early belief in me.

I owe a large debt of gratitude to Kathy Robbins, my agent, as well as to David Halpern and everyone at the Robbins Office. But most of all, I'd like to thank Jonathan Segal of Knopf and my longtime friend Jay Leibold. Jon brought a series of ideas to the project that improved and deepened it in more ways than I can say. So did Jay, with whom I have been talking and thinking about writing (and a lot of other things) since we were fourteen. He is a generous and patient friend, an inspired and incisive editor, and the brother I never had. This one's for you, Bold.

For a variety of assistance and support, my thanks to Nicholas Dawidoff (general counsel), Sharon Olds (protective shrine), John Thorndike (keen eye), Michael Collier and everyone at Bread Loaf (sounding boards), Estelle Bond Guralnick (rural haven), Lane Anderson and the Hertog Fellows program at Columbia University (research), Rollo Romig and Shahnaz Habib (more research), Joey McGarvey and Susanna Sturgis at Knopf; and Sarah and Geoffrey Gund, Frances Beinecke and Paul Elston, and Elizabeth and David Beim, for helping to keep Dodgewood great.

I would also like to acknowledge:

Peru (and Brazil): Timothy Currie, Peter Porteous, Antonio Ponce, Braulio Quispe, Geraldine Coll, Avecita Chicchón, Amyas Naegele, Carlos Llerena, Mikko Pyhala, Peter Menderson, Chris Kirkby, Dick Smith, Irving Foster Brown, Ph.D., Alfredo García Altamirano, Gene Reitz, Douglas Daly, Ph.D, Christiane Ehringhaus, Ph.D., and Anton Seimon, Ph.D.

Zanskar: Seb Mankelow, for help above and beyond; Dorjey Gyalpo, Lobzang

Tashi, Sonam Stopgais, Brigadier M. A. Naik, Colonel Sabu-Joseph, David Dunbar, Peter Getzels, Venu Gopal, and everyone at the Oriental Guest House in Leh.

East Africa: Josephat Ogutu, Suleiman Abdallah, Job Bwayo, M.D., Ph.D., Ludo Lavreys, Kishor Mandaliya, M.D., Henry Pollack, M.D., Brad Wells, and Jody Guralnick. *And from my 1993 trip:* Harry Hanegraaf, Lawrence Richter, Chris Grundmann, Maggie Bangser, Raymond Bonner, and Osman Mohammed.

West Bank: Cullen Murphy, Fares Azar, the al-Khatib family, Michael Tarazi, Blu and Irving Greenberg, Bob Reiss, Tabitha Thompson and Tarek Mango, Tom Casciato, Bob Abeshouse, Ghazi Abuhakema, Brooke Kroeger and Alex Goren, Tom Stern, George Bisharat, and Haim Handwerker.

China: Richard Henry, Li Lu, Shang Yuan, Xiangjie Zhao, Zhu Jihong, Zhou Yan, Paul Tough, Susan Lawrence, Li Man, Cathi and Bette Hanauer, Jing Zhao, Amelia Newcomb, Asil Gezen, Graham Smith, Juhong Chen, Wang Yang, Robert Larson, Ling Huang, Guan Xiaofeng, Wang Hongsheng, Jake Hooker, and Donovan Webster.

Lagos: Biola and Oritsejolomi "Bill" Okonedo, Banks Akpata, Shey Tata, Tony Eprile, Buki Papillon, Lara Olajide, Jack W. C. Hagstrom, M.D., Sikuade Jagun, M.D., Moshood Kazeem, I. K. Mustapha, M.D., Kristen Mertz, M.D., Peter Nnaemeka, M.D., Vincent Okaa, M.D., Philip Heinegg, M.D., Laura Jones, Eric Anyah, Ogbonnaya Nwachuku, Pamela Chibogu Okechukwu (and her husband, Henry), Aino Ternstedt Oni-Okpaku, Blessing Njoku, Chris Adigwe, George Packer, and Paul Austin, M.D.

Also:

Peter Whiteley, Paolo Pellegrin, Breyten Breytenbach, William C. Chittick, Beth Conover, Ken Snyder, Rick Larson, Carl Howard, Teresa Keenan, Richard Cohen, Tim Dickinson, Jonathan Veitch, Carlton Bradford, Jack Noon, Craig Childs, and Mark Curby.

And at world headquarters, the center of my universe: thank you, Margot and Asa and Nell, more than I can express, for the long and loving leash.

NOTES

INTRODUCTION

5 SOLDIERS—ROADS WERE BUILT BY THE MILITARY: see Victor W. Von Hagen, *The Roads That Led to Rome*, pp. 34–35.

6 EVENLY CUT STONE BLOCKS: see M. G. Lay, *Ways of the World*, pp. 77–78. The only recent innovation is the addition of a waterproof layer of tar or asphalt over the stones.

8 LIKE SO MANY SONGS OF THE DAY: Hank Williams had recorded his own song "Ramblin' Man" in 1951. And though the Temptations' 1972 recording turned "Papa Was a Rollin' Stone" into a soul classic, the Undisputed Truth, another Motown act, had recorded it earlier that year.

9 "ILLUSTRATED THE BREADTH OF EMPIRE": see John Noble Wilford, *The Mapmakers*, p. 57.

9 AS I WRITE, INDIA: see "Mile by Mile, India Paves a Smoother Road to Its Future," by Amy Waldman, *New York Times*, December 4, 2005.

9 IN FACT, ALMOST 1.5 PERCENT: see "U.S. Constructed Area Approaches Size of Ohio," by Christopher D. Elvidge et al., in American Geophysical Union, *ESO Transactions* 85, no. 24 (June 15, 2004), p. 233. The ratio is between impermeable manmade surfaces and the non-water area of the coterminous United States.

One FOREST PRIMEVAL TO PARK AVENUE

14 HE WATCHED THE MAHOGANY AVAILABLE TO HIM: The greatest demand for genuine mahogany comes not from furniture makers, but from shops doing architectural millwork—moldings, paneling, etc.—and from manufacturers of musical instruments, especially guitars. Louis Irion, a Pennsylvania dealer who specializes in wood for the furniture trade, said that artisans particularly prize mahogany from Peru. It is darker and denser than other true mahogany, and its grain is "wilder" (more interesting and harder to predict) than the lighter mahogany favored by millwork shops.

27 "THE QUECHUAN GUIDES I'VE WORKED WITH": Hugh Thomsen, *The White Rock*, pp. 31, 34, 36.

29 A HIGHLY EXPLOSIVE BUS: A race against time in a truck filled with nitroglycerin, which is needed to extinguish oil derrick fires in an unnamed South American republic, is the premise of the French novel (1950) and film (1953) *The Wages of Fear.*

30 WE PULLED OVER AT OROPESA: "Oropesa" translates roughly as "gold is heavy"—perhaps the lament of someone who had to carry it.

30 TO THIS HERNANDO PIZARRO COLDLY REPLIED: William H. Prescott, *History of the Conquest of Peru,* vol. II, p. 79.

41 JUST WHAT WERE THE BAD EFFECTS?: see Marc Dourojeanni, "Impactos Socioambientales Probables de la Carretera Transoceánica (Río Branco–Puerto Maldonado–Ilo) y la Capacidad de Respuesta del Perú," p. 313 in *La Integración Regional Entre Bolivia, Brasil y Perú.*

42 A SCIENTIST FROM THE WOODS HOLE RESEARCH CENTER: Irving Foster Brown, Ph.D., personal communication, March 22, 2002.

48 "OCCASIONALLY, TO SEE HOW FAR HIS OBSESSION": Mario Vargas Llosa, *The Storyteller,* pp. 21–22.

49 EVER SINCE THE CONQUISTADORS: Aldo Leopold, "The River of the Mother of God," in Leopold, *The River of the Mother of God & Other Essays.*

ROAD OR NOT A ROAD?

66 SACBES: The plural of *sacbe* in Yucatecan Maya languages is *sacbeob;* I use *sacbes* for simplicity.

66 INSTEAD OF CURVING SLIGHTLY: Kathryn Gabriel, *Roads to Center Place,* p. 22.

67 EVIDENCE SUPPORTS THE IDEA: Richard E. W. Adams, *Prehistoric Mesoamerica* (Boston: Little Brown, 1977), p. 160.

67 THE LONGEST AND BEST-KNOWN: Anna Sofaer et al., "The Great North Road," pp. 365–76. See also http://www.solsticeproject.org/greanort.htm. In his 1999 book, *The Chaco Meridian: Centers of Political Power in the Ancient Southwest,* Stephen H. Lekson posits that the north–south orientation was so central to the ancient Pueblo Southwest that the three sequential centers of culture aligned themselves on the same cartographic line: "first, Chaco (900–1225) in northwest New Mexico; second, Aztec (III–1275) in the Mesa Verde region; and third, Paquime (1250–1450) in northern Chihuahua. A ruling elite emerged at Chaco and perpetuated itself by moving a ceremonial city along Chaco's meridian" (pp. 70–71). Later he speculates that this straight-line orientation goes even further–all the way south to present-day Culiacán on Mexico's Pacific coast. "Is it yet another coincidence that the capital of the northeastern frontier of Mesoamerica lies practically due south of Chaco, Aztec, Paquime?" (p. 187).

68 THE EARTHENWARE WAS NOT MADE LOCALLY: see http://www.nps.gov/history/museum/exhibits/chcu/chcu_alltext.htm.

68 THEIR TRADITIONS VARY: F. H. Ellis and L. Hammack, "The Inner Sanctum of Feather Cave, a Mogollon Sun and Earth Shrine Linking Mexico and the Southwest," in *American Antiquity* 33, no. I (1968), pp. 31, 33; and Edmund J.

Ladd, "Pueblo Use of High-Altitude Areas: Emphasis on the A'shiwi" in *High-Altitude Adaptations in the Southwest*, ed. Joseph C. Winter (Albuquerque: U.S. Forest Service, Southwest Region Report No. 2, 1983), pp. 168–76, both cited in Sofaer et al.

68 THE ROAD TO THE *SHIPAPU*, FREQUENTLY DESCRIBED AS "STRAIGHT" . . . "CROWDED WITH SPIRITS": Matilda C. Stevenson, "The Sia," in *Eleventh Annual Report of the Bureau of American Ethnology (1889–90)* (Washington, D.C.: Smithsonian Institution, 1894), pp. 41, 145, cited in Sofaer et al.

68 MANY PUEBLO COMMUNITIE REENACT CREATION: Phillip Tuwaletstiwa, personal communications, November 30, 2006, and November 22, 2008.

70 "IT'D BE BETTER JUST TO CALL THEM PATHWAYS": The Irish novelist Flann O'Brien played with the idea of alternative meanings for roads in *The Third Policeman* (written in 1939–40 but not published until 1967). The book's narrator admires a fictional historian, de Selby, and says, "Elsewhere de Selby makes the point that a good road will have character and a certain air of destiny, an indefinable intimation that it is going somewhere, be it east or west, and not coming back from there. If you go with such a road, he thinks, it will give you pleasant travelling, fine sights at every corner and a gentle ease of peregrination that will persuade you that you are walking forever on falling ground. But if you go east on a road that is on its way west, you will marvel at the unfailing bleakness of every prospect and the great number of sore-footed inclines that confront you to make you tired" (pp. 37–38).

70 "CHANNEL FOR THE LIFE'S BREATH": A. Ortiz, 1987, private communication, cited in Sofaer et al.

Two SLIPPING FROM SHANGRI-LA

71 AT ABOUT 11,500 FEET ABOVE SEA LEVEL: Henry Osmaston and Philip Denwood, eds., *Recent Research on Ladakh 4 & 5: Proceedings of the Fourth and Fifth International Colloquia on Ladakh, Bristol 1989 & London 1992* (London: SOAS Studies, 1995), p. 370.

74 THE ROAD CONNECTING ZANSKAR TO KARGIL: John Crook and Henry Osmaston, eds., *Himalayan Buddhist Villages*, p. 52.

88 CROWED ITS SUCCESSES IN LARGE SIGNS: Also notable were the road builders' small yellow public-service signs. "After whisky, driving risky," you would be reminded alongside some steep hairpin turn. "Better Mr. Late than late mister." Or "Safety on road, safe tea at home." I appreciated these particularly because of a family legacy (which perhaps inspired them): my mother's grandfather, Clinton Odell, and her uncles, Alan and Leonard Odell, had innovated the use of rhyming doggerel to sell a brushless shaving cream, Burma-Shave, starting in 1925. The small wooden signs were set up in a series alongside American rural roads: "The bearded lady / Tried a jar / Now she's famous / Movie star / Burma-Shave." Highway safety was a recurring theme: "He tried / To cross / As fast train neared / Death didn't draft him / He volunteered / Burma-Shave." And "Don't lose / Your head / To gain a minute / You need your head / Your brains are in it / Burma-Shave."

106 NOMADS . . . WITH WHOM THEY EXCHANGED GRAIN FOR SALT AND WOOL: see Janet Rizvi, *Trans-Himalayan Caravans*, pp. 120 ff.

106 GADDI SHEPHERDS . . . FROM WHOM THEY GOT WOOL: John S. Mankelow, private communication, June 19, 2004.

107 "SINCE LADAKH IS IN MANY WAYS A MODEL SOCIETY": Helena Norberg-Hodge, "Appropriate Technology and Co-operative Culture in Ladakh," in *Replenishing the Earth: The Right Livelihood Awards, 1986–1989*, ed. by Tom Woodhouse (Bideford, U.K.: Green Books, 1990).

110 THEIR ISOLATION AND LACK OF KNOWLEDGE: In his book *Cosmopolitanism*, Kwame Anthony Appiah, a native of Ghana and professor of philosophy at Princeton, bemoans the small-mindedness of many traditional communities and asserts, "People who complain about the homogeneity produced by globalization often fail to notice that globalization is, equally, a threat to homogeneity" and, therefore, a good thing (p. 101). The "ideal of contamination," he continues, "has no more eloquent exponent than Salman Rushdie, who has insisted that the novel that occasioned his fatwa 'celebrates hybridity, impurity, intermingling, the transformation that comes of new and unexpected combinations of human beings, cultures, ideas, politics, movies, songs. It rejoices in mongrelization and fears the absolutism of the Pure. Mélange, hotchpotch, a bit of this and a bit of that is how newness enters the world. It is the great possibility that mass migration gives the world, and I have tried to embrace it' " (p. 112).

111 TRADITION HAS IT THAT CHILING'S SMITHS: Janet Rizvi, *Ladakh*, p. 160.

ROAD ECOLOGY

114 THE FLORIDA PANTHER, DOWN TO FEWER THAN A HUNDRED INDIVIDUALS: "Florida panther deaths increase from collisions with vehicles," news release from Florida Fish and Wildlife Conservation Commission, June 29, 2007.

114 EDWARD O. WILSON'S RESEARCH: Robert H. MacArthur and Edward O. Wilson, *The Theory of Island Biogeography*.

114 OTHERS HAVE SINCE APPLIED: see David Quammen, *The Song of the Dodo*, pp. 443 ff.

114 EDGE ZONES CAN ALSO BE AFFECTED BY CHEMICAL RUNOFF: Richard T. T. Foreman et al., *Road Ecology: Science and Solutions*, p. 4. Roads also change patterns of water runoff and erosion, which affect the immediate landscape and may also impact the downstream flow of a watercourse.

114 TUNNELS FOR MIGRATING REPTILES: Ibid., pp. 17, 19.

115 "AS COLLABORATING TRANSPORTATION SPECIALISTS": Ibid., pp. xv–xvi.

Three THE ROAD IS VERY UNFAIR

127 KENYANS WERE TOLD BY THEIR GOVERNMENT: See "Death of Kenyan Vice President Leaves Hole in Country's Coalition Government," by Matthew Rosenberg, Associated Press Worldstream, August 24, 2003. Rosenberg cites a government source for kidney failure as cause of death.

127 UGANDA'S GOVERNMENT-OWNED *NEW VISION* NEWSPAPER: see "Kenya: Vice President Dead," *New Vision* (Kampala, Uganda), August 24, 2003.

127 NAIROBI'S *THE NATION* DID POINT OUT: "Lessons from Wamalwa's Death," by David Makali, *The Nation* (Nairobi, Kenya), September 9, 2003.

127 DEATH BY AIDS WAS STILL DEEPLY STIGMATIZED: Kenyans, of course, have no corner on denial of AIDS: the pocket notebook I used on this trip came with packaging that boasted the brand had been the favorite of Bruce Chatwin, a writer I much admire but one who denied his own AIDS up until his death from it, saying, among other things, that he was sick from the bite of a Chinese bat.

131 "LAST WEEK THE POLICE SHOT TWO ROBBERS HERE": Carjackings had been on the rise in Kenya ever since insurance companies, trying to combat car theft, required owners to install anti-theft transmission locks. The effectiveness of these locks had resulted in more thefts of cars with people in them.

133 MOST DRIVERS SPOKE SWAHILI: A concise and nuanced history of the language can be found in John E. G. Sutton, *A Thousand Years of East Africa* (Nairobi: British Institute in Eastern Africa, 1990), pp. 57–60.

136 TRUCKS CARRIED GOODS IN FROM THE COAST: Freight transport in Africa is famously inefficient. *The Economist* of October 16, 2008, citing an unnamed U.S. government study, said that it costs less to ship a ton of wheat from Chicago to Mombasa than it does from Mombasa to Kampala.

137 WE CAME TO THE LIP OF A HUGE ESCARPMENT: Parts of the road between Nairobi and the Great Rift Valley were paved by Italian prisoners of war during World War II. They had been captured by British colonial forces in Abyssinia and Italian Somaliland; they were held in camps in Nanyuki and Nyeri. See Christine Stephanie Nicholls, *Red Strangers*, p. 231.

150 VICTORIAN EXPLORERS TO EAST AFRICA: Charles Miller, *The Lunatic Express*, p. 116.

152 OBADIAH'S TRIBE, THE LUO: The father of Barack Obama was a Luo. A senior economist for the Kenya government, he died in a traffic accident in Nairobi in 1982.

159 "IT WAS A GRAVEL ROAD": Richard Preston, *The Hot Zone*, p. 383. The next long quotation ("If the [AIDS] virus had been noticed earlier . . . ribbon of tar") comes from the same page.

162 "THEY DIDN'T HAVE THE VIRUS OR THE ANTIBODIES": "Aids Vaccine Gives Africa Ray of Hope," *Observer*, February 18, 2001, news pages, p. 22.

163 "IT WAS AT THAT TIME THAT PROF. BWAYO": "Top Aids Researcher Killed in Another Violent Attack," *The East African Standard*, February 5, 2007.

163 "KENYANS ARE VERY GOOD AT MARATHONS": "Job Bwayo: Kenyan Scientist at the Cutting Edge of AIDS Research," *The Guardian*, February 23, 2007, obituaries, p. 45.

DOUBLE-EDGED ROADS

164 ROADS WERE KEY TO HIS IMPERIAL DESIGNS: see M. G. Lay, *Ways of the World*, p. 96.

164 THE CHAMPS-ÉLYSÉES HAD BEGUN TO TAKE SHAPE NEARLY TWO CEN-
TURIES BEFORE: see http://www.britannica.com/EBchecked/topic/105234
/Champs-Elysees.

164 "SPACES, AIR, LIGHT, VERDURE AND FLOWERS": See Lay, *Ways of the World*,
p. 97.

164 NAPOLÉON III HALTED STREET WORK: Henry Law and Daniel Kinnear
Clark, *The Construction of Roads and Streets* (London: Crosby, Lockwood & Co.,
1877), p. 321.

165 "WOULD SLASH THE BELLY": Lay, *Ways of the World*, p. 97. "Boulevard,"
according to the *Oxford English Dictionary*, "originally meant the horizontal part
of a rampart; hence the promenade laid out on a demolished fortification." It
apparently derives from a Teutonic word, as does the German *Bollwerk*, meaning bulwark, "a substantial defensive work of earth, or other material."

166 FORCIBLY REMOVED FROM THEIR LANDS: The tribes affected were the
Cherokee, Chickasaw, Choctaw, Muscogee (Creek), and Seminole, who had
been living in the Deep South; they were "removed" to present-day Oklahoma.

166 THE TALIBAN HAD KILLED FOUR AFGHANS WORKING ON THE ROAD:
"Link Between Afghanistan's North and South Is Restored," by Amy Waldman,
New York Times, December 17, 2003, Sec. A, p. 10.

167 CONDITIONS ALONG THE ROAD HAD VASTLY DETERIORATED: "Scars of a
Deadly Insurgency Line Afghanistan's Main Road," by Carlotta Gall, *New York
Times*, August 14, 2008, Sec. A, p. 1.

167 SOLD IT TO CONGRESS IN 1955: Lay, *Ways of the World*, p. 99.

Four A WAR YOU CAN COMMUTE TO

173 BOMBERS EN ROUTE FROM JENIN TO HAIFA: "Bomb That Exploded at
W. Bank Checkpoint Was Meant for Haifa," by Amos Harel, *Ha'aretz*, August 15, 2004.

173 A PALESTINIAN WOMAN HAD BLOWN HERSELF UP: "Female Suicide
Bomber Kills Two Policemen in Jerusalem, Injures 30," *Ha'aretz*, September 23,
2004.

176 ABOUT SEVENTY CHECKPOINTS: "Forbidden Roads: Israel's Discriminatory
Road Regime in the West Bank," B'Tselem Information Sheet, August 2004,
p. 10. The same figure is used by an IDF spokesman cited in "IDF: 29 Palestinian Civilians Killed in W. Bank in 2004," by Amos Harel, *Ha'aretz*, August 12,
2004.

177 THE ISRAELI MILITARY CONVICTED THE COMMANDER: "IDF: 29 Palestinian Civilians Killed in W. Bank in 2004," by Amos Harel, *Ha'aretz*, August 12,
2004.

177 ACCORDING TO THE PALESTINIAN HUMAN RIGHTS MONITORING GROUP:
"Checkpoints Take Toll on Palestinians, Israeli Army," by Molly Moore, *Washington Post*, November 29, 2004, p. A1.

177 IN 2003 TWO WERE SHOT DEAD: Ibid.

177 MEMBERS OF HAMAS AND FATAH TUNNELED: "5 Soldiers Killed in Rafah
Tunnel Attack," by Amos Harel, *Ha'aretz*, December 13, 2004.

178 SUICIDE BOMBERS FROM HEBRON: "16 Die in Be'er Sheva Bombings," *Ha'aretz*, September 1, 2004.

179 AROUND 70 PERCENT OF U.S. COMBAT DEATHS: "IED Casualties in Iraq Drop Sharply," by William H. McMichael, *Army Times*, September 28, 2008. Online at http://www.armytimes.com/news/2008/09/military_ied_statistics _iraq_091708w/.

179 EVERY DAY FIVE THOUSAND PALESTINIANS: "Checkpoints Take Toll on Palestinians, Israeli Army," by Molly Moore, *Washington Post*, November 29, 2004, p. A1. Omer said the number was between 5,000 and 6,000.

181 THEY PROMISED ME 72 VIRGINS IN HEAVEN: "The soldiers of August 03" refers to the group of Omer's troops who enlisted on that date. The army encourages soldiers to self-identify by enlistment date as a morale booster.

183 A BUILDING THAT THE SOLDIERS CALLED THE DISCO: Per Omer, in e-mail communication, March 25, 2005.

188 MANY SETTLERS HAD BEEN SHOT: From a list of incidents with casualties along the 60 Road from September 2000 to September 2004, supplied to me by the IDF press office.

189 A PALESTINIAN SNIPER HAD OPENED FIRE: From an announcement by the IDF press office, March 3, 2002.

205 AWNI IS A SCIENTIST: In 2010, Awni Khatib became president of Hebron University.

208 "RADIO INTERVIEW WITH THE CHILDREN": See "Climate of Hate Still Seethes on Israel's Right," by Patrick Coburn, *The Independent* (U.K.), November 26, 1995. Online at http://www.independent.co.uk/news/world/climate-of-hate-still-seethes-on-israels-right-1583739.html.

210 DAYS LATER, THE IDF RESPONDED: *War Without End: Israelis, Palestinians, and the Struggle for a Promised Land*, by Anton La Guardia (New York: Macmillan, 2003), pp. 348, 355.

211 SUICIDE BOMBINGS INSIDE ISRAEL HAVE DWINDLED: "Shin Bet: Number of Terror Attacks on Israel Swelled in 2008," by Jonathan Lis, *Ha'aretz*, January 4, 2009. However, as the article reports, the number of Israelis killed inside Israel rose from thirteen in 2007 to thirty-six, eight of them victims of the shooting at the Mercaz Harav Yeshiva on March 6. Others were killed by rockets launched from Gaza.

212 AL-JAZEERA POSTED A MANIFESTO: "Transcript: Translation of Bin Laden's Videotaped Message," *Washington Post*, November 1, 2004. Online at http://www.washingtonpost.com/ac2/wp-dyn/A16990-2004Nov1.html.

SPEED UP!

218 "WHOLE CITIES BURN, / AND PEOPLED KINGDOMS INTO ASHES TURN": Ovid, *Metamorphoses*, Book II, translated into English verse under the direction of Sir Samuel Garth by John Dryden, Alexander Pope, Joseph Addison, William Congreve, and others, 1713. Online at http://ancienthistory.about.com/library/bl/bl_text_ovid_meta_2.htm.

218 THE FRENCH WERE LEADERS IN THIS DEVELOPMENT: Wrote historian Fer-

nand Braudel, the French "thought them dangerous, demoniacal . . . They went at an insane speed. Accidents were numerous, and no one compensated the victims. Furthermore, only a narrow central carriageway was paved on main routes. Two carriages could not pass at the same time without a wheel plunging into the mud at the side of the road." *Civilization and Capitalism, 15th–18th Century*, vol. I: *The Structures of Everyday Life: The Limits of the Possible* (London: Collins, 1981), pp. 424–25.

218 AND THE *TURGOTINE, A NARROW STAGECOACH*: Of the turgotine a contemporary wrote, its "body is narrow and seats get so crowded that everybody asks his neighbor for his leg or arm back when it comes to getting down . . . If by ill chance a traveller with a big stomach or wide shoulders appears . . . one has to groan or desert." L. S. Mercier, *Tableau de Paris*, vol. V (1781–1788), p. 331.

218 THE NUMBER OF VEHICLES IN PARIS: Christophe Studeny, *L'Invention de la vitesse. France, XVIIe–XXe siècle* (Paris: Gallimard, 1995), p. 67, cited by Jeffrey T. Schnapp, "Crash (Speed as Engine of Individuation)," *Modernism/Modernity* 6, no. 1 (1999), p. 14.

218 "EVERYONE HAS BECOME A DRIVER": *De l'aurigie, ou Méthode pour choisir, dresser et conduire les chevaux de carosse, de cabriolet et de chaise; suivie d'un nobiliare équestre, où Notice sur les races précieuses de Chevaux Étrangers, leur éxterieur, qualités, tempérament, régime, et sur les diverses soins qu'ils reçoivent* (Paris: Dondey-Dupré, 1819), p. 272, cited in Schnapp, "Crash," p. 15.

218 THE NUMBER OF CARRIAGES SHOT UP FROM 18,000 IN 1775 TO 106,000 IN 1840: Gordon S. Cantle, *A Collection of Essays on Horse-Drawn Carriages and Carriage Parts, Carriage Museum of America* (York, U.K.: Image Print, 1993), p. 38, cited in Schnapp, "Crash," p. 15.

218 "CAME EFFORTS TO WIDEN AND STRAIGHTEN OUT STREETS": Schnapp, "Crash," p. 15.

219 "SELIFAN PERKED UP": Nikolai Gogol, *Dead Souls*, pp. 283–84.

219 "THE VITAL EXPERIENCE": Thomas De Quincey, "The English Mail Coach and Other Writings," in *The Works of Thomas De Quincey*, vol. 4 (Edinburgh: A. and C. Black, 1863), p. 302.

219 "IN DEVELOPING THE ANARCHIES": Ibid., p. 287.

220 "POT-WALLOPINGS OF THE BOILER": Ibid., p. 303. Jeffrey Schnapp explains that "the forward-most seat, shared with the coachman, was considered the most dangerous of all" (p. 24). He cites a contemporary account: "I need scarcely to remind travellers that the most dangerous place about a coach is the box, inasmuch as, should she upset, they are less likely to avoid some part of her falling on them. The hinder seat, or gammon board is the most secure in the event of an upset . . ." In Charles James Apperley, *My Horses and Other Essays*, ed. E. D. Cumming (Edinburgh and London: William Blackwood and Sons, 1928), p. 183. Schnapp is the author of *Quickening*, an "anthropology of speed" forthcoming from Yale University Press.

220 "THE PROMISE/THREAT OF ACCIDENT": Schnapp, "Crash," p. 26. For more on technological advance and its connection to accidents and disasters, see Paul Virilio, *The Original Accident* (Cambridge, U.K., and Malden, Mass.: Polity, 2007).

220 "IDENTIFIED WITH ADMINISTRATION": Schnapp, "Crash," p. 13. This began earlier, he suggests, with the arrival of horse-drawn carriages of all kinds.

220 "THE LIGHTNING HAD LONG SINCE": Janet Guthrie, *Janet Guthrie: A Life at Full Throttle* (Toronto: Sport Classic Books, 2005), p. 4.

Five CAPITALIST ROADERS

234 CHINA, WITH 2.6 PERCENT OF THE WORLD'S VEHICLES: See *World Report on Road Traffic Injury Prevention*, ed. Margie Peden (Geneva: World Health Organization, 2004). Also at http://whqlibdoc.who.int/publications/2004/9241562609 .pdf.

237 COUNTLESS TOLLBOOTHS: According to the *China Daily* of February 28, 2008, "Some 16 provinces and municipalities, including Liaoning and Hubei provinces, have built 158 illegal toll stations on 100 highways under their jurisdiction and had collected a total 14.9 billion yuan ($2.1 billion) in passage fees by the end of 2005, the National Audit Office said yesterday on its website." Online at http://www.chinadaily.com.cn/cndy/2008–02/28/content_6490949.htm.

237 A RICH WOMAN IN A BMW: "China Clamps Down on Online Justice," by Tom Luard, BBC News Online, January 19, 2004. Online at http://news.bbc.co.uk/2/hi/asia-pacific/3409995.stm.

237 THE NUMBER OF KIDNAPPINGS FOR RANSOM HAS SHOT UP: "Kidnapping Industry Is Booming in China," by Evan Osnos, *Chicago Tribune*, January 22, 2006, p. 4.

249 UNSURPRISINGLY, I DROVE BETTER WITH MY MOM: My father was not being unreasonably cautious. Two weeks after I turned sixteen and got my license, on a family ski trip I piloted the Catalina down an icy road from our condo toward town. A jeep suddenly appeared in front of me as I rounded a bend, I touched the power brake, the Pontiac skidded, and we crashed; it was totally my fault. Fortunately, nobody was hurt. But the Pontiac was nearly totaled and the jeep, which was being driven by the girlfriend of the Aspen district attorney, was badly damaged.

250 BEIJING'S SULFUR DIOXIDE LEVELS IN 2004: "As China's Auto Market Booms, Leaders Clash over Heavy Toll," by Gordon Fairclough and Shai Oster, *Wall Street Journal*, June 13, 2006.

250 OF THE TWENTY CITIES IN THE WORLD WITH THE DIRTIEST AIR: Shahid Yusuf, Ton Saich, et al., *China Urbanizes: Consequences, Strategies, and Policies* (Washington, D.C.: World Bank Publications, 2008), p. 11.

250 79 PERCENT OF THE AIR POLLUTION: "In Land of Bicycle, Car Boom Brings Freedom of Open Road," by Amelia Newcomb, *Christian Science Monitor*, August 3, 2005.

250 IN 2004 THERE WERE ONLY 9 CARS PER 1,000 PEOPLE: "China Motorization Trends," by Lee Schipper, Ph.D., and Wei-Shiuen Ng, in "Growing in the Greenhouse: Protecting the Climate by Putting Development First," World Resources Institute, December 2005.

252 A REPRESENTATIVE OF A MOTORCYCLE CLUB: Some of their members rode

sidecar motorcycles, which I'd seen on Beijing ring roads. An old East German model is still manufactured in China.

GROWING BROADWAY

256 THEY WERE NOT THE FIRST PEOPLE: Edwin Burrows and Mike Wallace, *Gotham*, pp. 5–7. "Wickquasgeck," in this book, is spelled "Wiechquaesgeck." Dunlap has it as "Weckquaesgeek."

257 THE PATH OF WALL STREET: Russell Shorto, *The Island at the Center of the World*, pp. 254, 255.

257 AMONG THE FOUNDERS OF NEW AMSTERDAM: The name Van Kouwenhoven morphed over the years in the American fashion. Wolphert's son Jacob spelled his name Van Couwenhoven. A couple of generations later descendants were spelling it Covenhoven, then Covenor, and by the early nineteenth century, Conover.

257 "A MOB SPILLED DOWN BROADWAY": Edward Robb Ellis, *The Epic of New York City*, p. 161.

257 "THE FINEST PRIVATE BUILDING IN TOWN": Ibid., p. 188.

257 IT ENDED AT A FENCE: Ibid., p. 194.

257 MORE LIKELY, WROTE JOURNALIST AND HISTORIAN DAVID W. DUNLAP: David W. Dunlap, *On Broadway*, p. 91.

258 BROADWAY HAD REACHED 14TH STREET: Ellis, *Epic*, p. 251.

258 "HOW THIS CITY MARCHES NORTHWARD!": George Templeton Strong, quoted in Ellis, *Epic*, p. 258.

258 THE SLAVES WHO HAD HELPED BUILD NEW YORK: Burrows and Wallace, *Gotham*, p. 547.

258 "YOUNG MEN AND WOMEN AROSE": Ellis, *Epic*, p. 117.

258 CHARLES DICKENS, VISITING IN 1842: This passage can be found in Kenneth T. Jackson and David S. Dunbar, eds., *Empire City: New York Through the Centuries* (New York: Columbia University Press, 2002), p. 187.

258 "A PERFECT MISSISSIPPI": cited in Burrows and Wallace, *Gotham*, p. 720.

259 WALT WHITMAN DONNED TOP HAT AND FROCK COAT: *Walt Whitman of the New York Aurora, Editor at Twenty-two*, ed. Joseph Jay Rubin and Charles H. Brown (State College, Pa.: Bald Eagle Press, 1950), pp. 4–5.

259 OBSERVING FROM THE SIDEWALK: Burrows and Wallace, *Gotham*, p. 706.

259 A VISITING ENGLISHMAN: quoted in Ellis, *Epic*, pp. 258–59.

259 SHOPS AND DEPARTMENT STORES BEGAN TO BE LIT WITH GAS: Burrows and Wallace, *Gotham*, p. 1066.

259 A STAGE LINE UP WOODSY BLOOMINGDALE ROAD: Peter Salwen, *Upper West Side Story*, p. 9.

259 "FLED BY DIGNIFIED DEGREES": *Putnam's Magazine* of 1853, quoted in *New York Times*, November 12, 1911, p. xxi.

259 BY THEN IT WAS CONTINUOUS: Salwen, *Upper West Side Story*, pp. 59, 69, 124.

259 IN 1892, COLUMBIA COLLEGE BEGAN A MOVE: Dunlap, *On Broadway*, pp. 263–70.

260 "ABOUT AS REMOTE AND INACCESSIBLE AS MT. KISCO": Frederick Paul Keppel, *Columbia* (New York: Oxford University Press, 1914), p. 79, cited in Dunlap, *On Broadway*, p. 263.

260 BY 1901 THE INTERBOROUGH RAPID TRANSIT (IRT) COMPANY: http://www.nycsubway.org/faq/briefhist.html.

260 BY 1908 THE "BROADWAY LINE" HAD EXTENDED ALL THE WAY: From northernmost Manhattan, the IRT runs not underground but on elevated tracks over Broadway, as it does around 125th Street.

261 THE UGLY COLISEUM EXHIBITION CENTER: The New York Coliseum was demolished in 2000 and replaced by the Time Warner Center, an office and commercial complex.

Six DRIVE SOFT—LIFE NO GET DUPLICATE

263 IT WAS LIKE ONE PETAL OF A CLOVERLEAF: This style of exit is known to civil engineers as a jughandle.

265 THE SINGLE NIGERIA TRAVEL GUIDE I HAD FOUND: Lizzie Williams, *Nigeria: The Bradt Travel Guide*, p. 124.

267 FOR MILLENNIA, CITIES . . . ATTRACTED ONLY A SMALL PERCENTAGE OF THE HUMAN POPULATION: From "Cities of the Future: Today's 'Mega-cities' Are Overcrowded and Environmentally Stressed," by Divya Abhat, Shauna Dineen, Tamsyn Jones, Jim Motavalli, Rebecca Sanborn, and Kate Slomkowski, *E/The Environmental Magazine*, vol. 16, no. 5 (September–October 2005). Online at http://www.emagazine.com/view/?2849.

267 AS LATE AS 1900, 86 PERCENT OF THE WORLD'S POPULATION: "Managing Planet Earth: Experts Scaling Back Their Estimates of World Population Growth," *New York Times*, August 20, 2002, p. F8.

267 THE WORLD'S POPULATION OF 6 BILLION: Ibid.

267 IN 1950 LAGOS HAD 288,000 PEOPLE: Abhat et al., "Cities of the Future," online at http://www.emagazine.com/view/?28450.

268 "IS LURCHING TOWARD DISASTER": Jeffrey Tayler, "Worse Than Iraq?," *The Atlantic*, April 1, 2006.

268 "HAS BEEN A RECIPE": Mike Davis, "Planet of Slums," *Harper's*, June 2004, pp. 17–18.

268 "DANGEROUS BREAKDOWNS OF ORDER AND INFRASTRUCTURE": Boeri et al., *Mutations*, p. 686. Also see Abhat et al., "Cities of the Future," online at http://www.emagazine.com/view/?2850.

268 NAMED BY PORTUGUESE SLAVE TRADERS AFTER LAGOS, PORTUGAL: For a particularly harrowing eyewitness account of slaves being unloaded in Lagos, Portugal, see Peter Edward Russel *Prince Henry "the Navigator": A Life* (New Haven, Conn.: Yale University Press, 2000), pp. 241–44.

269 THREE AND ONE-HALF MILLION SLAVES: *Encyclopaedia Britannica*, "Slavery," retrieved May 12, 2009, from Encyclopædia Britannica Online: http://search.eb.com/eb/article-24160.

269 NIGERIA HAS THE MOST PEOPLE OF ALL: "World Population Prospects: The

2008 Revision Population Database," United Nations Population Division, http://www.un.org/esa/population/publications/wpp2008/wpp2008_highlights .pdf, p. 41.

269 ACCORDING TO THE WORLD BANK: See World Bank's Nigeria Country Brief, http://go.worldbank.org/FIIOT240K0.

270 THE GROWTH OF THIRD WORLD MEGACITIES REPEATS PATTERNS: Davis, "Planet of Slums," pp. 17–18.

272 CAPABLE OF HOLDING 50,000 PEOPLE: Lamin O. Sanneh and Joel A. Carpenter, *The Changing Face of Christianity: Africa, the West, and the World* (New York: Oxford University Press, 2005), p. 11.

276 ONE OF THE YOUNG MEN: English is the official language of Nigeria, taught in schools and used in formal communication. Pidgin is commonly used in informal exchanges between members of different tribes. The tribal languages most commonly heard in Lagos are Yoruba, Ibo, and Hausa.

277 FEDERAL ROAD SAFETY COMMISSION: The FRSC was founded, surprisingly enough, by Nigerian playwright Wole Soyinka, the Nobel Prize winner, when he was a professor at the University of Ife. Among his areas of oversight was the security of public roads; a special police were needed, he argued, to stop robberies of students. Over the years, that corps grew until it had a presence nationwide.

280 IN A WESTERN CITY, THE RATIO IS TYPICALLY: Personal communication with Timothy Kiehl of TRKKLLC Consulting, of Bethesda, Maryland, and with Mike Smith, director of emergency medical services for Durham County, North Carolina. Many places have fewer ambulances per capita; others have many more. British Columbia and Vancouver, for example, had 462 ambulances around the time of my visit to Lagos, serving a population of 4,113,487, or a 1:8,904 ratio.

281 A "BORROWING" FROM ITS COLLECTION: The Benin bronze head had been taken in 1973, but only recently had the missing item been discovered . . . among the collection at Buckingham Palace. As it turned out, General Yakubu Gowon had secretly removed it from the museum and presented it as a gift to the queen in 1973. Palace curators had assumed it was a replica until a query by an arts journalist in 2002 revealed that the bronze head was 400 years old. See "President 'Liberated' Bronze for Queen from Museum," by Nigel Reynolds, *The Telegraph*, September 16, 2002. Online at http://www.telegraph.co.uk/news/uknews/1407331/President-liberated-bronze-for-Queen-from-museum.html.

288 ONE OF THE WORST SPOTS WAS NEAR THE OSHODI MARKET: See Boeri et al., *Mutations*, p. 693, on the character of Oshodi.

289 POOR PEOPLE HAD BEEN "BUNKERING": Another oil pipeline explosion the day after Christmas would kill 500 Lagosians.

294 THE YORUBA CONCEPTS *AIYÉ* AND *ÒTÁ*: Akintunde Oyetade, "The Enemy in the Belief System," in *Understanding Yoruba Life and Culture*, ed. Nike Lawal et al. (Trenton, N.J.: Africa World Press, 2004). Cited in Damola Osinulu, "Painters, Blacks and Wordsmiths: Building Molues in Lagos," *African Arts* 41, no. 3 (Autumn 2008), pp. 44–53.

294 "AGAINST WHOSE STRATEGIES, TACTICS MUST BE DEPLOYED": Osinulu, "Painters, Blacksmiths and Wordsmiths," p. 52.

294 *THE FAMISHED ROAD*: The title comes from a poem of Wole Soyinka, "Death in the Dawn" (1967), collected in *Idanre and Other Poems* (New York: Hill & Wang, 1987), p. 11: "May you never walk / When the roads waits, famished." Among the best African fiction I have read concerning roads is Bessie Head's short story "The Wind and a Boy," in which a boy in a village is killed by a truck while riding his bicycle. See Head's *The Collector of Treasures, and Other Botswana Village Tales* (London: Heinemann, 1992), pp. 69–75. Also see Joyce Cary's *Mister Johnson*.

297 "THE BIGGEST NODE IN THE SHANTYTOWN CORRIDOR": Davis, "Planet of Slums," p. 18.

EPILOGUE

299 THE WORDS *RUMBO* AND *CAMINO*: *Sendero* in Spanish means footpath. Thus *Sendero Luminoso* (Shining Path), the Maoist revolutionary movement in Peru.

300 "FAR FROM BEING ELEVATED BY CROWN HEIGHTS": Will Self, *Psychogeography*, p. 57.

300 LEO MARX HAS COMMENTED: Leo Marx, professor at MIT, letter to *The New Yorker*, October 22, 2007.

300 A DISTINCTIVELY MALE SPACE: Louis Menand, "A Critic at Large: Drive, He Wrote," *The New Yorker*, October 1, 2007. The notion of cars as "male space" also explains the transgressive appeal of the movie *Thelma and Louise*, about a road trip by two feisty women.

300 THE PARABLE OF THE GOOD SAMARITAN: The quotations in this section are from *Today's New International Version of the Bible*. I chose it from various translations of the parable because of its clarity. Online at http://www.ibsstl.org/bible/verse/index.php?q=Luke%2010.

302 "THE ORIGIN OF EXISTENCE IS MOVEMENT": Ibn al-'Arabī, *Le Dévoilement des Effets du Voyage* (Kitāb al-isfār 'an natā'ij al-asfār), edited and translated by Denis Gril (Combas, France: Éditions de l'éclat, 1994), p. 4.

BIBLIOGRAPHY

Appiah, Kwame Anthony. *Cosmopolitanism: Ethics in a World of Strangers*. New York: W. W. Norton and Company, 2006.

Boeri, Stefano, et al. *Mutations*. Barcelona: ACTAR, 2001.

Braudel, Fernand. *The Wheels of Commerce* (Part II of *Civilisation matérielle, économie et capitalisme*). Translated by Siân Reynolds. New York: Harper & Row, 1982.

Brown, Kurt, ed. *Drive, They Said: Poems About Americans and Their Cars*. Minneapolis: Milkweed Editions, 1994.

Burrows, Edwin G., and Mike Wallace. *Gotham: A History of New York City to 1898*. New York: Oxford University Press, 1999.

Buzzati, Dino. *The Tartar Steppe*. Translated by Stuart C. Hood. Boston: David R. Godine, 1995.

Caro, Robert A. *The Power Broker: Robert Moses and the Fall of New York*. New York: Alfred A. Knopf, 1974.

Crook, John, and Henry Osmaston, eds. *Himalayan Buddhist Villages: Environment, Resources, Society and Religious Life in Zangskar, Ladakh*. New Delhi: Motilal Banarsidass Publishers, 1994.

Davis, Mike. *Planet of Slums*. New York: Verso, 2007.

Dunlap, David W. *On Broadway: A Journey Uptown over Time*. New York: Rizzoli, 1990.

Ellis, Edward Robb. *The Epic of New York City*. New York: Coward McCann, 1966.

Föllmi, Olivier. *Le Fleuve Gelé*. Paris: Éditions de La Martinière, 1996.

Foreman, Richard T. T., et al. *Road Ecology: Science and Solutions*. Washington, D.C.: Island Press, 2002.

Gabriel, Kathryn. *Roads to Center Place: A Cultural Atlas of Chaco Canyon and the Anasazi*. Boulder, Colo.: Johnson Books, 1991.

Gogol, Nikolai. *Dead Souls*. Translated by Richard Pevear and Larissa Volokhonsky. New York: Alfred A. Knopf, 2004.

Grossman, David. *The Yellow Wind*. Translated by Haim Watzman. New York: Picador, 2002.

Hessler, Peter. *River Town: Two Years on the Yangtze*. New York: HarperCollins, 2001.

Hilton, James. *Lost Horizon*. New York: William Morrow and Co., 1933.

Homberger, Eric. *The Historical Atlas of New York City*. New York: Henry Holt, 1994.

Hyslop, John. *The Inka Roads System*. New York: Academic Press, 1984.

Jackson, J. B. *The Necessity for Ruins and Other Topics*. Amherst: University of Massachusetts Press, 1980.

Kerouac, Jack, and Douglas Brinkley, eds. *Jack Kerouac: Road Novels, 1957–1960 (On the Road, The Dharma Bums, The Subterraneans, Tristessa, Lonesome Traveler, Journal Selections)*. New York: Library of America, 2007.

Law, H., and D. K. Clark. *The Construction of Roads and Streets*. London: Crosby Lockwood and Sons, 1907.

Lay, M. G. *Ways of the World: A History of the World's Roads and of the Vehicles That Used Them*. New Brunswick, N.J.: Rutgers University Press, 1992.

Lekson, Stephen H. *The Chaco Meridian: Centers of Political Power in the Ancient Southwest*. Lanham, Md.: AltaMira Press, 1999.

Leopold, Aldo. *The River of the Mother of God & Other Essays*. Edited by J. Baird Callicott and Susan L. Flader. Madison: University of Wisconsin Press, 1992.

MacArthur, Robert H., and Edward O. Wilson. *The Theory of Island Biogeography*. Princeton, N.J.: Princeton University Press, 1967.

Matthiessen, Peter. *The Snow Leopard*. New York: Viking Press, 1978.

McCarthy, Cormac. *The Road*. New York: Alfred A. Knopf, 2006.

McNeill, William H. *Plagues and Peoples*. Garden City, N.Y.: Anchor Press, 1976.

Miller, Charles. *The Lunatic Express: An Entertainment in Imperialism*. New York: Macmillan, 1971.

Némirovsky, Irène. *Suite Française*. Translated by Sandra Smith. New York: Alfred A. Knopf, 2006.

Nicholls, Christine Stephanie. *Red Strangers: The White Tribe of Kenya*. London: Timewell Press, 2005.

Noon, Jack. *The History of Sutton, New Hampshire*, Volume 2. Sutton, N.H.: Sutton Historical Society, 2007.

Norberg-Hodge, Helena. *Ancient Futures: Learning from Ladakh*. San Francisco: Sierra Club Books, 1992.

O'Brien, Flann. *The Third Policeman*. Champaign, Ill.: Dalkey Archive Press, 1999.

Prescott, William H. *The Conquest of Peru: With a Preliminary View of the Civilization of the Incas, in Two Vollumes*. London: Routledge, Warne, and Routledge, 1862.

Preston, Richard. *The Hot Zone*. New York: Random House, 1994.

Quammen, David. *The Song of the Dodo: Island Biogeography in an Age of Extinction*. New York: Scribner, 1997.

Rizvi, Janet. *Ladakh: Crossroads of High Asia*, 2nd ed. New Delhi: Oxford University Press, 1996.

———. *Trans-Himalayan Caravans: Merchant Princes and Peasant Traders in Ladakh*. New Delhi: Oxford University Press, 1999.

Salwen, Peter. *Upper West Side Story: A History and Guide*. New York: Abbeville Press, 1989.

Schnapp, Jeffrey T. *Speed Limits*. Milan: Skira, 2009.

Self, Will. *Psychogeography: Disentangling the Modern Conundrum of Psyche and Place*. New York: Bloomsbury, 2007.

Shaw, Justine M. *White Roads of the Yucatán: Changing Social Landscapes of the Yucatec Maya*. Tucson: University of Arizona Press, 2008.

Shorto, Russell. *The Island at the Center of the World: The Epic Story of Dutch Manhattan & the Forgotten Colony That Shaped America*. New York: Doubleday, 2004.

Sofaer, Anna, Michael P. Marshall, and Rolf M. Sinclair. "The Great North Road: A Cosmographic Expression of the Chaco Culture of New Mexico," pp. 365–76 in

Anthony F. Aveni, ed., *World Archaeoastronomy*. Cambridge: Cambridge University Press, 1989.

Stilgoe, John R. *Outside Lies Magic: Regaining History and Awareness in Everyday Places*. New York: Walker and Company, 1999.

Tejuoso, Olakunle, et al. *Lagos: A City at Work*. Lagos: Glendora Books, 2005.

Thomsen, Hugh. *The White Rock: An Exploration of the Inca Heartland*. Woodstock, N.Y.: Overlook Press, 2004.

Vanderbilt, Tom. *Traffic: Why We Drive the Way We Do (And What It Says About Us)*. New York: Alfred A. Knopf, 2008.

Vargas Llosa, Mario. *The Storyteller*. Translated by Helen Lane. New York: Picador, 2001.

Von Hagen, Victor W. *Highway of the Sun*. Boston: Little, Brown, 1955.

———. *The Roads That Led to Rome*, Cleveland and New York: World Publishing Company, 1967.

———. *The Royal Road of the Inca*. London: Gordon & Cremonesi, 1976.

Wagner, Allen, and Rosario Santa Gadea Duarte, eds. *La integración regional entre Bolivia, Brasil y Perú*. Lima: CEPEI, 2002.

Wilford, John Noble. *The Mapmakers*. Rev. ed. New York: Vintage, 2001.

Williams, Lizzie. *Nigeria: The Bradt Travel Guide*. Guilford, Conn.: Bradt Travel Guides, 2005.

INDEX

Page numbers in *italics* refer to illustrations.

ALSO BY TED CONOVER

COYOTES

A Journey Through the Secret World of America's Illegal Aliens

In this classic tale of life among the illegal migrants of the U.S.-Mexican border, Ted Conover immerses himself in a world few Americans ever see and fewer still come to know. He cuts life-threatening deals with tough guys trafficking in human sweat, gets himself smuggled across the border, works on citrus ranches, experiences the world of undocumented workers in industrial L.A., and travels deep into Mexico to understand the poverty that begins the whole cycle. By turns harrowing and hilarious, *Coyotes* is an intimate journey with those who brave hardship and danger to seek a better life north of the border.

Adventure/Current Affairs/978-0-394-75518-2

NEWJACK

Guarding Sing Sing

When Ted Conover's request to shadow a recruit at the New York State Corrections Academy was denied, he decided to apply for a job as a prison officer himself. The result is an unprecedented work of eyewitness journalism: the account of Conover's year-long passage into storied Sing Sing prison as a rookie guard, or "newjack." As he struggles to become a good officer, Conover angers inmates, dodges blows, and attempts, in the face of overwhelming odds, to balance decency with toughness. Through his insights into the harsh culture of prison, the grueling and demeaning working conditions of the officers, and the unexpected ways the job encroaches on Conover's family life, we begin to see how our burgeoning prison system brutalizes everyone connected with it.

Current Affairs/978-0-375-72662-0

ROLLING NOWHERE

Riding the Rails with America's Hoboes

Hopping a freight in the St. Louis rail yards, Ted Conover embarks on his dream trip, traveling with "the knights of the road." Conover immerses himself in the peculiar culture of the hobo, equipped with rummage-store clothing, a bedroll, and his notebooks. The people he meets along the way are, by turns, resourceful and desperate, generous and mistrusting, independent and communal, philosophical and profoundly cynical—a segment of humanity outside society, yet very much like the rest of us.

Travel/Adventure/978-0-375-72786-3

WHITEOUT

Lost in Aspen

Irreverent, poignant, and revealing, *Whiteout* is a meditation on wealth and the vainglorious quest for paradise in Aspen, Colorado. Even as Ted Conover tells of how he crashed Don Johnson's Christmas party, or what it was like to sit in on the taping of John Denver's holiday video, he is turning the lens of his craft upon himself and is documenting his own seduction by the Aspen mystique. The result is journalism with the laser moral focus of enduring satire.

Travel/Adventure/978-0-679-74178-7

VINTAGE BOOKS
Available at your local bookstore, or visit
www.randomhouse.com